Reinventing Human Resource Management: Challenges and New Directions

Edited by
Ronald J. Burke and
Cary L. Cooper

Routledge
Taylor & Francis Group

LONDON AND NEW YORK

First published 2005
by Routledge
2 Park Square, Milton Park, Abingdon, Oxon OX14 4RN

Simultaneously published in the USA and Canada
by Routledge
270 Madison Ave, New York, NY 10016

Routledge is an imprint of the Taylor & Francis Group

Typeset in Perpetua and Bell Gothic by
Florence Production Ltd, Stoodleigh, Devon
Printed and bound in Great Britain by
TJ International Ltd, Padstow, Cornwall

British Library Cataloguing in Publication Data
A catalogue record for this book is available from the British Library

Library of Congress Cataloging in Publication Data
A catalog record for this book has been requested

ISBN 0–415–31962–5 (hbk)
ISBN 0–415–31963–3 (pbk)

Contents

Illustrations

FIGURES

TABLES

Contributors

Mark D. Agars, California State University, San Bernardino
Ronald J. Burke, York University
David Carnegie, UBS, New York City
Wayne F. Cascio, University of Colorado-Denver
Cary L. Cooper, Lancaster University
Elizabeth F. Craig, Boston University
Robert L. Dipboye, Rice University
Colette A. Frayne, Seattle University
Jay Galbraith, University of Southern California
Douglas T. Hall, Boston University
William M. James, Northeastern University
Ralph Katz, Northeastern University
Mary P. Kosarzycki, University of Central Florida
Janet L. Kottke, California State University, San Bernardino
Cynthia A. Lengnick-Hall, University of Texas at San Antonio
Mark L. Lengnick-Hall, University of Texas at San Antonio
David Lepak, Rutgers University
Shad Morris, Cornell University
Lisa H. Nishii, Cornell University
Eduardo Salas, University of Central Florida
Marc J. Schabracq, University of Amsterdam
Benjamin Schneider, University of Maryland and Personnel Research Associates
Scott A. Snell, Cornell University
Scott I. Tannenbaum, State University of New York—Albany

Acknowledgments

I would like first to thank my friend and colleague, Cary Cooper. This volume is our fourth collaboration and there are more in the works. The seeds for this effort were sown at the 2001 meetings of the Academy of Management in Washington, DC. Catriona King was an early supporter. We have also found a way to bridge the distance between Toronto and Lancaster. The Schulich School of Business provided resources to make the journey easier. I am grateful to our international contributors for sharing their latest thinking on ways to unleash the talents of people in organizations. We do know how to make organizations both more satisfying for those who work in them and more effective. The staff at Routledge has proven to be helpful and professional at every turn.

Finally, I am grateful to Susan. I have always been intrigued by the question of how far people would go for a second chance. She demonstrates daily that the answer is very far. I admire her courage and am richer for it.

Ronald J. Burke

I would like to acknowledge the support given to me throughout my career by Professor Sir Roland Smith (recently deceased) and Sir Terry Leahy—both good friends and colleagues.

Cary L. Cooper

Part I

New directions in Human Resource Management

Chapter 1

The human resources revolution
Why putting people first matters[1]

Ronald J. Burke and Cary L. Cooper

The world of work and organization has become increasingly demanding and turbulent (Burke and Cooper, 2004). Ulrich (1997) lists eight major challenges currently facing organizations. These are: globalization, responsiveness to customers, increasing revenue and decreasing costs, building organizational capability, change and transformation, implementing technology, attracting and developing human capital, and ensuring fundamental and long-lasting change. Thus, levels of competition among organizations have increased. Most organizations today can copy technology, manufacturing processes, products, and strategy. However, human resource management (HRM) practices and organization are difficult to copy, thereby representing a unique competitive advantage (Pfeffer, 1994, 1998). To be successful in the future, organizations will have to build organizational capability. HR professionals and HRM practices will be required to create value by increasing organizational competitiveness (Ferris *et al.*, 1999).

Traditional views on competitive advantage have emphasized such barriers to entry as economies of scale, patent protection, access to capital, and regulated competition. More recent views have highlighted a different source of competitive advantage, a firm's human resources and human capital (Huselid *et al.*, 1997). New demands facing organizations as a result of heightened competition, globalization, and technological advances have put a premium on creativity and innovation, speed and flexibility, as well as efficiency. The critical firm assets do not appear on a balance sheet but reside, instead, in people and management systems (Ichniowski *et al.*, 1996). The role of firm strategy, human resources, and HRM in firm performance is being rethought. Rather than seeing the HR function as a cost, an HRM system that supports a firm's strategy should be seen, instead, as an investment, a strategic lever for the organization in creating value.

The 1990s witnessed a growth in research interest in examining the link between HRM strategies and practices and a firm's financial performance (Becker and Gerhart, 1996). Studies have shown a strong positive relationship between the two, and this relationship has been observed in studies of one firm, one industry, and multiple industries (Becker and Huselid, 1998). Becker and Huselid have shown in three separate national surveys (over 2,400 firms) an economically and significant impact on several measures of firm performance. They observed a link between changes in the sophistication of a firm's HR architecture

3

fast changing
fast-mgrs-

and dollar change in market value per employee, suggesting three stages of HRM practices on firm performance.

How do we create organizations that add value to investors, customers, and employees? Organizational capability is the key and both HR professionals and line managers need to work together to achieve this. Pfeffer (1998) articulates the reasons why a people-based strategy pays dividends. High-performance management practices (selective hiring, extensive training, sharing of information, etc.) lead to performance results (innovation, productivity) while being hard to copy; in the long run, profitability is maintained.

HRM practices influence employee skills through the acquisition and development of human capital (Wright *et al.*, 1994). Effective recruitment and selection practices can provide the firm with highly qualified applicants. Training and development opportunities contribute to increasing human capital. HRM practices can also influence levels of motivation through the use of performance appraisals, pay-for-performance incentives, and internal promotions systems based on merit (Brown *et al.*, 2003). HRM practices can also influence the design of work so that highly motivated and skilled employees can use what they know in performing their jobs (Wright and Boswell, 2002).

The past decade has produced research evidence supporting the critical role human resource management plays in the success of an organization. This evidence has been generated in a variety of different types of organizations including manufacturing, professional services, and health care (see Liker, 2003). *Case studies?*

The human resources function has, for a number of reasons, been typically viewed by executives as peripheral to the successful performance of their organizations. Human resource management, as a course in most MBA programs, is often not seen as useful as offerings in finance, marketing, or information technology. Yet, managers with full-time work experiences report that their major challenges involve people.

REINVENTING HRM

The human resources field is, itself, in a time of ferment and self-reflection. For example, the Human Resources Division within the US Academy of Management had a pre-conference workshop at the 2002 Annual Meeting in Denver (August 9) titled "HR Education: Is it dead or just sleeping?" This example reflects efforts to reposition human resources in a more relevant way.

Ulrich (1997) depicts the role of the HR department in a new light. HR professionals must create policies and practices that make employees more competitive. They need to have both HR theory and practice in their tool box. HR initiatives must have a measurable impact on business results. These efforts should increase intellectual capital and add value. Managers need to implement these best practices. HR professionals need to position HRM as a competitive advantage that adds business value.

Line managers need to understand that HRM practices build up organizational capabilities which, in turn, become a critical source of competitive advantage. In addition, managers need to invest time and resources in expanding organizational capability.

Lengnick-Hall and Lengnick-Hall (2003) advocate that HRM focus on the role of human capital steward. This would include deciding on the investments in human capital, developing flexible individuals and organizations able to respond to changing demands and use human capital effectively to reach organizational goals.

For too long, organizations have increasingly become short-term, bottom-line focused with more attention paid to cost cutting than training and development. The trade-off between profits and people is, in fact, an unnecessary opposition. The most successful companies balance an interest in people and productivity (Cameron *et al.*, 2003; Waterman, 1987; Katzenbach, 2000). This collection endorses this balance: healthy people and healthy organizations go together.

It is also important to consider the contemporary context. Organizations, facing increased needs for innovation, speed, and productivity are demanding more of their employees— both their hearts and minds. In turn, the most highly educated workforce the world has ever seen is demanding more of their organizational employers. They want challenge, influence, recognition, development, and ownership.

IS HRM ANOTHER FAD?

It is easy to view much of the HRM writing on new approaches to managing people and organizations as faddish. Ulrich (1997, p. 63) lists the characteristics of HRM practices likely to be "cute, popular and faddish HR trends."

1 It is simple and claims to solve complex problems.
2 It claims to apply to and help everyone.
3 It is not anchored or related to any known and generally accepted theory.
4 Proponents hesitate to present it in academic settings or write about it in refereed journals.
5 Proponents cannot tell you exactly how it works.
6 It is a "track" topic at 75 percent of the conferences you attend.
7 Its proponents claim that it has changed their lives and that it can change yours too.
8 Its greatest proponents are those with the least experience in the field.
   a Proponents claim that the only way to really understand it is to try it personally.
   b It cannot be explained or demonstrated.
9 It is just too good to be true.

While amusing, these statements ring all too true. For too long, HRM practices have been adopted as "quick fixes" and implemented in a rushed and superficial manner (Whitney and Tesone, 2001). When expected immediate benefits were not evident, organizations jumped to the next "one-minute" solution (Micklethwait and Wooldridge, 1997).

Pfeffer argues (1994) that HRM practices that are likely to be successful are *not* faddish, hard to understand, or hard to understand why they work, or contingent on a firm's particular organizational strategy. But to be effective, these HRM practices must be interrelated and internally consistent.

Although we are beginning to understand more about effective HRM practices, significant challenges remain in the application of this knowledge. It takes significant time to achieve a competitive advantage through the workforce. Organizations doing well may feel

5

no need to change; organizations doing poorly may face immediate pressures making it, too, unlikely to change. Managers may not use the knowledge they have about effective HRM (Pfeffer and Sutton, 2000). There also may not be enough communication of best-practice knowledge. In addition, managers may know something that researchers do not. Finally, some HRM practices may be risky and often fail.

However, Pfeffer estimates that only about one-eighth of efforts to change management and organizational approaches will introduce HRM practices that lead to organizational success. Of those who read about these concepts, one half won't believe the evidence, one half (of the other half) will attempt a quick fix, and only one half of those undergoing substantial change will persist in their efforts.

WHY DON'T WE USE HRM BEST PRACTICES?

Considerable research has shown that organizations do not use current or innovative HR best practices (Johns, 1993; Rynes et al., 2001). In fact, very few HR practitioners even read the research literature (Terpstra and Rozell, 1997, 1998). HR research has become increasingly technical, making it more difficult to keep up with the literature. It may also be that HR practitioners do not see the HR research as being relevant or useful in meeting their needs (Adams, 2003; Ford et al., 2003).

Rynes et al. (2002) surveyed HR managers to determine whether their beliefs about HR best practices were consistent with the latest research findings. It was assumed that HR professionals were the ones responsible for spreading information about effective HRM to their organizations and helping line managers develop HRM strategies to achieve business objectives. They concluded that HR practitioners lacked knowledge about best practices supported by research evidence.

Rynes et al. (2003) conducted a study of business recruiters' espoused preferences for students with both technical skill and behavioral skill. Students tend to believe that recruiters favor technical skill. Although recruiters indicated a preference for students that combined both, they gave the same employability rating to students who only took functional/technical course work. There is considerable evidence that business students are skeptical about the value of courses in HRM and Organizational Behavior (OB) (Rynes and Quinn, 1999).

Yancey et al. (2003) believe that HR practitioners and HR researchers move in different circles (i.e., belong to different professional associations, read different publications, attend different conferences). They surveyed 45 industrial-organizational psychologists, examining where they published, what conferences they attended, and what they knew about the HR practitioner community. Their findings indicated that industrial-organizational psychologists shared their research ideas with each other rather than with HR practitioners.

What can be done about this state of affairs? Rynes and her colleagues (2003) believe the first step is to see this crisis in HRM/OB legitimacy as a systemic, not a local, problem. Other suggestions include: more clearly defining the HRM/OB knowledge base, forming alliances with other teaching disciplines having greater legitimacy, doing better research on the teaching of HRM/OB, being more critical of negative practices and proposing even more positive organizational futures (see Cameron et al., 2003, for examples).

THE GAP BETWEEN RESEARCH AND PRACTICE

Case studies and research projects conducted over the past two decades have shed considerable light on the characteristics of successful and satisfying work places. We know what needs to be done to satisfy both human and business needs (Katzenbach, 2000). If you accept these statements to be true, why are so few organizations implementing best practices?

Some of the reasons for the gap between research and practice lie with the researchers themselves (Mohrman *et al.*, 2001; Dossahoy and Berger, 2002). They spend most of their time communicating with other researchers and little time conversing with practitioners (Blanton, 2000; Boehm, 1980). Much of the scholarship of the research community is not read by most practitioners or even most academic researchers.

One must also look at the teaching programs of most MBA courses. Many of the professors in schools of business are, themselves, researchers, or the consumers of research findings. Few business schools teach OB or HRM in ways that illustrate the usefulness of this knowledge to increase organizational health and performance. Traditional OB texts review countless motivation theories and leadership theories which, if entertainingly presented, can be interesting to students, but the link between these concepts and bringing about peak performance is thin at best. Few business schools address the implementation of concepts, models, and research findings.

One might expect that line managers would not be aware of the current thinking on unleashing potential of staff but that HR specialists would. The evidence does not bear this out. Most HR specialists do not read the more research-oriented HRM journals. Rynes *et al.* (2002) report that fewer than one percent of their sample usually read the academic literature while 75 percent reported that they never do so. Yet, Terpstra and Rozell (1993) found that firms whose HR managers read and used the academic literature had higher financial performance than those that did not.

Latham and Latham (2003) write that the gap between researchers and practitioners creates "two solitudes." Managers are either unaware or unconvinced of the value of HRM research findings. They offer eight ways to break down the two solitudes:

1 Set mutually interdependent goals. Researchers and practitioners have to be on the same team.
2 Act like an insider.
3 Identify a champion who is an influential member of the other solitude.
4 Build an alliance of a researcher with an HR manager. Learn to speak the language of the other solitude.
5 Write in practitioner outlets.
6 Support the education of both solitudes by the other.
7 Fund collaborative research projects by business organizations. This would provide a common focus to the project.
8 Build networks of researchers and HR managers who, through contact and communication, will expedite knowledge transfer.

COUNTRY DIFFERENCES AND INTERNATIONAL PERSPECTIVES

Although we have included material by authors from four countries in this collection, there is a North American bias in both content and orientation. Other writers (e.g., Brewster, 1994; Brewster and Hegewisch, 1994; Roe and van den Berg, 2003) have addressed HRM issues in Europe. Some HRM concerns were seen as similar in both North America and Europe while others were different. In addition, HRM policies and practices differ across European countries themselves (Brewster and Larsen, 1992). Not surprisingly, countries that are geographically and culturally closer to each other have similar HRM practices (Dany and Torchy, 1994; Ryan *et al.*, 1999). Labor unions are much stronger in Europe than in North America. Central governments also play a larger role in dictating HRM policies to industrial sectors in Europe than in North America. Europe has generally had a higher rate of unemployment than is the case in North America.

European organizations have adopted similar strategies, as did North American organizations, to compete in the global economy. These have included strategic alliances, use of outsourcing, flattening the hierarchy, downsizing and restructuring, varied employment relationships, and an emphasis on a greater market orientation and flexibility.

These transformations have raised the importance of HRM efforts as organizations attempt to increase productivity and performance while reducing labor costs and, although these efforts may be similar to those observed in North America, the broader economic social and cultural environment must be considered to better understand particular HRM practices in various countries.

Although some have noted a growing convergence in HRM policies and practices in Europe, the entrance of countries from Central and Eastern Europe, which had different soviet-based labor relations systems, into the European Union, adds new dimensions to the European HRM picture.

THIS COLLECTION

This collection reviews the most current thinking and evidence on HRM practices associated with high levels of current organizational performance and likely to be responsive to the new challenges facing organizations over the next two decades. Hence the title—*Reinventing Human Resource Management*. Human resources will need to mobilize in new ways to meet the demand of this period of time. These practices are shown to be a key part of the managerial jobs, not merely the domain of the human resource department. Building on a comprehensive framework incorporating HRM practices, strategies and organizational needs, traditional HRM functions are addressed in a new way.

What human resource management practices characterize effective organizations? What emerging human resource challenges face organizations in their search for managerial talent? How do peak performing organizations develop and nurture talent? Why are human resource management practices becoming more critical for success in the new world of work (Cooper and Burke, 2002)?

Readers of this collection will gain a better appreciation not only of why reinventing HR is vital to continued organizational success, but how this has been done in a variety of organizations in Europe and North America. The rhetoric that "people are our most important asset" has, in fact, been realized in organizations that have made HRM a central aspect of managerial accountability.

Much of the current HRM writing is aimed at the HR professional. Our approach, while still relevant for this audience, positions HRM activities as a central feature of the managerial job, having demonstrated value to organizational success. Our approach is, therefore, similar or compatible with Pfeffer's work (1994, 1998).

This volume also directly addresses the concern that HRM has not received its due. What can be done about this and why is it critical to continued organizational performance and innovation? It also provides concrete research evidence as well as company best practice, showing the tangible benefits from reinventing human resources—the strategic positioning of people, as the key element in sustaining peak performance.

We have assembled contributions from a number of different countries as new human resource initiatives are occurring throughout the industrialized world. This is vital since different countries have produced research and writing reflecting examples of best practice in various areas or sectors of organizational functioning.

This collection is divided into four parts. Part I makes the case that effective HRM matters and describes potential roles for the HR function in the new world of work. In this first chapter, Ronald Burke and Cary Cooper have offered a wide-ranging review of the challenges facing organizations today, why HRM practices contribute to organizational effectiveness, the reasons many companies do not adopt effective HRM practices, and suggestions for organizational culture change. They conclude with a summary of each chapter that follows.

Ronald Burke then sets the stage for the chapters that follow in making the case that human resources represent a critical, perhaps the most critical, competitive advantage. Challenges facing contemporary organizations are first identified, suggesting that it is now more difficult than ever for organizations to be successful. New approaches to achieving peak performance are needed as a result. Some empirical evidence showing that the use of effective HRM practices increases firm performance is then offered. When employees are managed effectively, they work both smarter and harder. Jeffrey Pfeffer's list of effective HRM practices is reviewed along with the contributions of key writers such as Edward Lawler, John Katzenbach, Jim Collins, and Jerry Porras. Unfortunately, many organizations do not emphasize HRM and reasons for this are considered. The chapter concludes with some thoughts on implementing effective HRM practices.

Mark Lengnick-Hall and Cynthia Lengnick-Hall examine the HR function in the new knowledge economy. They see the HR function at a crossroads. HR will play a secondary role (automated, outsourced) if HR professionals continue to see themselves as deliverers of services. HR can play a significant role, however, if it transforms both how it is organized and its purpose. HR needs to be a key factor in the creation of competitive advantage. Competitive advantage results when knowledge is developed and used to build individual and organizational resources and capabilities that allow the organization to provide superior value to customers. People are the essential ingredient in these processes. They suggest four roles for HRM in the new economy: human capital steward, relationship builder, knowledge management facilitator, and rapid deployment specialist.

Part II considers new challenges for HRM as both an academic discipline and an area of practice. Shad Morris, Scott Snell and David Lepak offer an architectural approach to strategic human resources management. They first develop an architectural framework for managing human resources and show how this framework relates to different employment relationships within an organization. They then consider how human capital can be recombined through two specific HR architectures: cooperative and entrepreneurial. HRM practices are then identified that support the flow of knowledge within organizations which contributes to a sustainable competitive advantage.

Colette Frayne identifies three ways that international HRM has been characterized and developed in research and, in a preliminary way, in practice. The first involves a comparison of HRM practices across countries; the second considers the internalization of business functional areas across countries, and the third examines the intersection of the HR function with business strategy and stages of internationalization of the firm. She then describes a university course she developed that incorporates these three themes. This unique course has the same title as her chapter. She concludes with a summary of the implications this line of research has for the firm and for HR professionals and their development.

Robert Dipboye then addresses the gap between HRM practice and academic HRM. While the gap is wide, Dipboye believes there are legitimate reasons for it. HR practitioners are unfamiliar with the academic HRM literature or adopt academic HRM concepts but implement them poorly. He considers three reasons for the gap: failure of academics to communicate their research and theory to practitioners, failure to research topics of importance to practitioners, and deficiencies in the education of practitioners. Dipboye also believes that the gap serves important organizational purposes. These include: helping organizations deal with fast changing and unpredictable environments (keep unstructured, loose, flexible); helping organizations work in other cultures, to conform or imitate important organizations or constituencies; to gain competitive advantage by using HRM practices that are unique or not easily copied; and maintaining the organizational culture. In addition, individual HR practitioners face different demands in their jobs than do academics (assigned tasks, a short time frame), face different roles (selling their HR services), can easily modify "soft HR practices," and HRM practitioners have their own needs and values (for variety, satisfaction, fairness, power, and influence). Dipboye concludes with three suggestions for bridging the gap between HRM theory and research, and practice. First, HRM theory and research needs to embrace a multilevel perspective; HRM practices found to be ineffective at one level may be effective at another. Second, HRM research and theory must live with the paradoxes and conflicts inherent in organizational life. Third, there is a need for compromise between the rigors of science and the intuition of practice.

Part III focuses on the role of HRM practices on the development and utilization of talent as well as on the long-term well-being of employees. Elizabeth Craig and Douglas Hall advocate a new model of organizational career development (OCD) in which career development work is spread throughout the organization. In an increasingly competitive economy, driven by knowledge work and dependent on the talents and knowledge of the workforce, career development becomes strategically more important. OCD not only builds talent and skills but also increases employee commitment. They view the career as learning stages—an ongoing acquisition of new skills. To be successful, OCD systems need to build self-awareness and adaptability in employees. They identify developmental experiences, developmental relationships, meaningful feedback, and a culture of development as key OCD levers. They also believe that OCD is best done by the line organization with a supporting role played by the HR function. Organizations will need to learn how to best diffuse their learnings in operationalizing their OCD systems and to capture and develop the strategy, systems, and structures necessary for OCD to work effectively.

Eduardo Salas, Mary Kosarzycki, Scott Tannenbaum, and David Carnegie note the increasing use of teams by organizations to achieve their objectives. For teams to work effectively, they must receive organizational support. The HR function and HRM practices have evolved to meet this new challenge; teams cannot flourish without supportive HRM practices. They illustrate these best practices in a number of areas: recruiting and hiring, training, compensation, performance management, leadership, organizational culture, and communication. They also stress the alignment of these practices to gain maximum value.

Mark Agars and Janet Kottke focus on HRM innovations in diversity management. Diversity management requires initiatives across HRM responsibilities and areas of organizational functioning. They identify a range of HRM practices central to managing diversity: recruiting, structural support, accountability, training, measurement of results, and large-scale system change. They conclude their chapter with recommendations for more tightly integrating diversity management and HRM practice with theory.

Wayne Cascio focuses on the role of HRM in organizational downsizing. He defines organizational or employment downsizing as an intentional proactive management strategy. Downsizing has been undertaken in all developed countries, but unfortunately the anticipated benefits do not always materialize. Some firms have become more productive and successful following downsizing. Cascio contrasts several myths about downsizing with facts, using many company illustrations. Distinguishing two approaches to downsizing—employees as costs to be cut and employees as assets to be developed—he raises nine issues to be considered before any organization undertakes this transition.

Marc Schabracq reviews the ways in which HRM can enhance employee well-being and health. Organizational initiatives to address employee well-being and health concerns will become more important strategic factors in global competition. The HRM perspective places human capital—healthy and effective employees—as the main assets of the organization. Building heavily on the Dutch experience, Schabracq describes potentially useful HRM interventions. These include the role of executive leadership in articulating the underlying philosophy and values, training, selection, staff utilization and development, and work design. He envisions a significant role for HRM specialists or co-managers in these efforts.

Part IV examines the contribution of HRM practices to organizational effectiveness. Lisa Nishii and Benjamin Schneider discuss the HRM implications of both increased internationalization and domestic diversity for service firms. They first review the role of HRM in the delivery of quality service with a particular emphasis on identifying contingencies that specify the nature of the relationship between HRM practices and desired outcomes. They then proceed to examine the ways in which internationalization influences the relationship of HRM practices to these outcomes. Best practices identified in the West may not be effective in other cultures. Thus, some HRM practices need to be adapted to local cultural norms

11

and expectations. This notion is then applied to increased diversity in local markets as well. Whether one likes it or not, HRM has boundary conditions.

Jay Galbraith illustrates the role of organization design in the creation of organizations that act with speed, flexibility, and integration. Using specific company models and examples, he shows how internal consistency and external alignment of strategy, structure, and HRM practices can provide solutions to customers. He identifies specific roles, mechanisms, and HRM practices (e.g., selection and attraction, training, reward systems) critical for success.

Finally, Ralph Katz and William James examine the role of HRM practices in organizational innovation. This is a tall order requiring HRM practices to function effectively in the present while supporting innovation in the future. HRM practices are seen by the innovating community as doing a good job of managing the present but not supporting innovative RandD efforts. What would be helpful here are HRM practices that impact motivation (e.g., work redesign, reward systems, utilization and development, clear goals and accountability, and feedback).

IMPLICATIONS

We may be on the threshold of a renaissance in the application of HRM knowledge and best practices. Organizations may have no choice given the critical importance of dealing with the increased level of global competition and pace of change. In addition, a lot of threads are coming together (TQM, re-engineering, learning, core competences) to give higher priority to HRM. Consider the following conclusions which we believe to be valid:

1 Human capital has become the key to competitive advantage.
2 The traditional relationship between people and organizations has been shattered; a new relationship is needed.
3 We now know a lot about individual competence and development and organizational effectiveness.
4 We now know a lot more about changing organizations to deliver "best practices."
5 There is an urgent need to create peak performing organizations and we know how to do that.

To the extent that organizations can unleash the hidden value in their people, they will increase their chances of success, particularly as knowledge and intellectual capital become more important. Some companies have achieved high levels of performance over a long period of time. Why are these companies successful? The accumulating research evidence has identified powerful reasons that are applicable to almost all organizations (O'Reilly and Pfeffer, 2000). Employee commitment and motivation come from involvement and from the ways that people are treated. Organizations have found that giving people a stake and a say in what they do is important in building high levels of commitment. It is possible to use the ideas, thoughts, and wisdom of the people who do the work every day to help the organization become more productive and efficient. This requires leaders of organizations to have the courage to put people first if they are to successfully meet these challenges.

NOTE

1 Preparation of this Introduction was supported in part by the Schulich School of Business, York University and Lancaster University.

REFERENCES

Adams, A.M. (2003) Mitigating risks, visible hands, inevitable disasters, and soft variables: Management research that matters to managers. *Academy of Management Executive*, 17, 46–61.

Becker, B.E. and Gerhart, B. (1996) The impact of human resource management on organizational performance: Progress and prospects. *Academy of Management Journal*, 39, 779–801.

Becker, B.E. and Huselid, M.A. (1998) High performance work systems and firm performance: A synthesis of research and managerial practice. *Research in Personnel and Human Resource Management*, 16, 53–101.

Blanton, J.S. (2000) Why consultants don't apply psychological research. *Consulting Psychology Journal: Practice and Research*, 52, 235–247.

Boehm, V.R. (1980) Research in the "real-world": A conceptual model. *Personnel Psychology*, 33, 495–504.

Brewster, C. (1994) European HRM: Reflection of, or challenge to, the American concept. In P.S. Kirkbride (ed.) *Human Resource Management*. London: Routledge, pp. 56–89.

Brewster, C. and Hegewisch, A. (1994) *Policy and Proactive in European Human Resource Management: The Price Waterhouse Cranfield Survey*. London: Routledge.

Brewster, C. and Larsen, H.H. (1992) Human resource management in Europe: Evidence from ten countries. *International Journal of Human Resource Management*, 3, 409–434.

Brown, M.P., Sturman, M.C., and Simmering, M.J. (2003) Compensation policy and organizational performance: The efficiency, operational and financial implications of pay levels and pay structure. *Academy of Management Journal*, 46, 752–762.

Burke, R.J. and Cooper, C.L. (2004) *Leading in Turbulent Times*. Oxford: Blackwell Publishers Inc.

Cameron, K., Dutton, J., and Quinn, R.P. (2003) *Positive Organizational Scholarship*. San Francisco, CA: Berrett Koehler.

Cooper, C.L. and Burke, R.J. (2002) *The New World of Work*. Oxford: Blackwell Publishers Inc.

Dany, F. and Torchy, V. (1994) Recruitment and selection in Europe: Policies, practices and methods. In C. Brewster and A. Hegewisch (eds) *Policy and Practice in European Human Resource Management: The Price Waterhouse Cranfield Survey*. London: Routledge, pp. 68–88.

Dossahoy, N.S. and Berger, P.D. (2002) Business school research: Bridging the gap between producers and consumers. *Omega*, 30, 301–314.

Ferris, G.R., Hochwarter, W.A., Buckley, M.R., Harrell-Cook, G., and Frink, D.S. (1999) Human resources management: Some new directions. *Journal of Management*, 25, 385–415.

Ford, E.W., Duncan, W.J., Bedeian, A.G., Ginter, P.M., Rousculp, M.D., and Adams, A.M. (2003) Mitigating risks, visible hands, inevitable disasters, and soft variables: Management research that matters to managers. *Academy of Management Executive*, 17, 46–61.

Huselid, M.A., Jackson, S.E., and Schuler, R. (1997) Technical and strategic human resource effectiveness as determinants of firm performance. *Academy of Management Journal*, 40, 171–188.

Ichniowski, C., Kochan, T.S., Olson, C., and Strauss, G. (1996) What works at work: Overview and assessment. *Industrial Relations*, 35, 299–333.

Johns, G. (1993) Constraints on the adoption of psychology-based personnel practices: Lessons from organizational innovation. *Personnel Psychology*, 46, 569–592.

Katzenbach, J.R. (2000) *Peak Performance: Aligning the Hearts and Minds of Your Employees.* Boston, MA: Harvard Business School Press.

Latham, G.P. and Latham, S.D. (2003) Facilitators and inhibitors of the transfer of knowledge between scientists and practitioners in human resource management: Leveraging cultural, individual and institutional variables. *European Journal of Work and Organizational Psychology*, 12, 245–256.

Lengnick-Hall, M.L. and Lengnick-Hall, C.A. (2003) *Human Resource Management in the Knowledge Economy.* San Francisco, CA: Berrett-Keohler.

Liker, J.K. (2003) *The Toyota Way.* New York: McGraw-Hill.

Micklethwait, J. and Wooldridge, A. (1997) *The Witch Doctors: Making Sense of the Management Gurus.* New York: Random House, Inc.

Mohrman, S.A., Gibson, C.B., and Mohrman, A.M. (2001) Doing research that is useful to practice: A model and empirical exploration. *Academy of Management Journal*, 44, 357–376.

O'Reilly, C.A. III and Pfeffer, J. (2000) *Hidden Value: How Great Companies Achieve Extraordinary Results with Ordinary People.* Boston, MA: Harvard Business School Press.

Pfeffer, J. (1994) *Competitive Advantage Through People.* Boston, MA: Harvard Business School Press.

Pfeffer, J. (1998) *The Human Equation: Building Profits by Putting People First.* Boston, MA: Harvard Business School Press.

Pfeffer, J. and Sutton, R.I. (2000) *The Knowing-Doing Gap: How Smart Companies Turn Knowledge into Action.* Boston, MA: Harvard Business School Press.

Roe, R.A. and van den Berg, P.T. (2003) Selection in Europe: Context, developments and research agenda. *European Journal of Work and Organizational Psychology*, 12, 257–287.

Ryan, A.M., McFarland, L., Baron, H., and Page, R. (1999) An international look at selection practices: Nation and culture as explanations for variability in practice. *Personnel Psychology*, 52, 359–391.

Rynes, S.L. and Quinn, T.C. (1999) Behavioral science in the business school curriculum: Teaching in a changing institutional environment. *Academy of Management Review*, 24, 808–825.

Rynes, S.L., Bartunek, J.M., and Daft, R.L. (2001) Across the great divide: Knowledge creation and transfer between practitioners and academics. *Academy of Management Journal*, 44, 340–356.

Rynes, S.L., Brown, K.G., and Colbart, A.E. (2002) Seven common misconceptions about human resource practices: Research findings versus practitioner beliefs. *Academy of Management Executive*, 16, 92–102.

Rynes, S.L., Trank, C.Q., Lauson, A.M., and Ilies, R. (2003) Behavioural course work in business education: Growing evidence of a legitimacy crisis. *Academy of Management Learning and Education*, 2, 269–283.

Terpstra, D.E. and Rozell, E.J. (1993) The relationship of staffing practices to organizational level measures of performance. *Personnel Psychology*, 46, 27–48.

Terpstra, D.E. and Rozell, E.J. (1997) Why some potentially effective staffing practices are seldom used. *Public Personnel Management*, 26, 483–495.

Terpstra, D.E. and Rozell, E.J. (1998) Human resource executives' perceptions of academic research. *Journal of Business and Psychology*, 13, 19–29.

Ulrich, D. (1997) *Human Resource Champions*. Boston, MA: Harvard Business School Press.

Waterman, R.H. (1987) *The Renewal Factor*. New York: Bantam Books.

Whitney, J. and Tesone, D.V. (2001) Management fads: Emergence, evolution and implications for managers. *Academy of Management Executive*, 15, 122–134.

Wright, P.M. and Boswell, W.R. (2002) Desegregating HRM: A review and synthesis of micro and macro human resource management research. *Journal of Management*, 28, 247–276.

Wright, P., McMahan, G.C., and McWilliams, A. (1994) Human resources and sustained competitive advantage: A resource-based perspective. *International Journal of Human Resource Management*, 5, 301–327.

Yancey, G., Wagner, S., Baxa, J., Alkouri, K., and Haugen, E. (2003) Is the dissemination of knowledge about industrial-organizational psychology too insulated? *Psychological Reports*, 92, 723–730.

Chapter 2

Human resources as a competitive advantage[1]

Ronald J. Burke

WHY HUMAN RESOURCES MATTER

Organizations today are facing challenges on several fronts in their efforts to remain competitive. These include the need to increase productivity, the prospects of expanding into global markets, new technological developments, responding to changes in the marketplace, containing costs, developing a skilled and flexible workforce and bringing about significant organizational change. These challenges are emerging in the context of changing needs of the workforce, changing attitudes in the broader society and heightened legal requirements (Capelli, 1999). These challenges are making it both more important and more difficult for organizations to be successful. There is now a greater emphasis on organizational results. Not surprisingly, more organizations are looking for ways to improve their performance (Ashkenas *et al.*, 1995; Galbraith *et al.*, 1993; Heskett *et al.*, 1997; Lawler, 1992; Lawler *et al.*, 1995; Nadler *et al.*, 1995; Pfeffer and Sutton, 2000; Tushman and O'Reilly, 1997).

The past decade has produced research evidence supporting the critical role human resource management plays in the success of an organization. This evidence has been generated in a variety of different types of organizations including manufacturing, professional services and health care (Becker *et al.*, 2001).

The human resources function has, for a number of reasons, been typically viewed by executives as peripheral to the successful performance of their organizations (Ulrich, 1997). HRM, as a course in most MBA programs is often not seen as useful as offerings in finance, marketing, or information technology. Yet, managers with full-time work experiences report that their major challenges involve people.

Pfeffer (1998) notes a downward performance spiral as organizations address real and pressing performance problems such as low profits, high costs, poor customer service and low stock prices. Typical organizational responses include staff layoffs, greater use of part-time and contract staff, a restriction of hiring and promotions, freezes or cutbacks and reduced investment in training and employee development. Employees respond, in turn, by reducing their job involvement, exhibiting lower job satisfaction, decreasing their effort, increased accidents and greater turnover. These individual behaviors have the effect of increasing the performance problems that led to the organizational responses in the first place. Thus, the downward spiral continues.

17

Some organizations do see increased profits in the short run through cost cutting efforts. In addition, cost cutting can be done in ways that minimize their impact on the long-term success of the organization. But these somewhat successful initiatives fall short of achieving peak performance.

There is considerable empirical evidence that the use of effective HRM practices increases firm performance. Why should this be the case? Performance increases because employees work *both harder and smarter* (Pfeffer, 1994, 1998). Employees work harder because of greater job involvement, greater peer pressure for results, and the economic gains based on high performance. Employees work smarter because they can use their knowledge and skill, acquired through training and development in the jobs themselves, in getting the work done.

In addition, effective HRM practices are likely to reduce the direct and indirect costs of employee grievances. Finally, performance benefits are likely to be seen in the elimination of jobs whose main responsibility is to monitor people whose main job, in turn, is to monitor other people. Such administrative overhead is costly, both in the salaries paid to those who hold such positions and in the diminished contributions from those being monitored. Trained, motivated, self-managed and broadly skilled staff can dramatically reduce administrative overhead costs.

The traditional views on competitive advantage have emphasized such barriers to entry as economies of scale, patent protection, access to capital, and regulated competition. More recent views have highlighted a different source of competitive advantage, a firm's human resources and human capital. New demands facing organizations as a result of heightened competition, globalization and technological advances have put a premium on creativity and innovation, speed and flexibility, as well as efficiency. The critical firm assets do not appear on a balance sheet but reside, instead, in people and management systems. The role of firm strategy, human resources and the role of HRM in firm performance is being rethought. Rather than seeing the HR function as a cost, the HRM system that supports a firm's strategy should be seen, instead, as an investment, a strategic lever for the organization in creating value (Wright and McMahan, 1992).

The 1990s witnessed a growth in research interest in examining the link between HRM strategies and practices and a firm's financial performance. Studies have shown a strong positive relationship between the two, and this relationship has been observed in studies of one firm, one industry and multiple industries (Becker and Huselid, 1998). Becker and Huselid have shown in three separate national surveys (over 2,400 firms) an economically significant impact on several measures of firm performance. They observed a link between changes in the sophistication of a firm's HR architecture and dollar change in market value per employee, suggesting three stages in influence of HRM practices on firm performance. The first stage represents the development of a professional HR capability. The second stage involves the development of HR excellence by the HR function but with a modest influence on firm performance. In the third stage, the HRM system achieves a dramatic impact on financial performance. The HRM system at this stage has both achieved operational excellence and is supportive (consistent with) the firm's strategic goals.

HRM practices influence employee skills through the acquisition and development of human capital. Effective recruiting and selection practices can provide the firm with highly

18

qualified applicants. Training and development opportunities contribute to increasing human capital. HRM practices can also increase levels of motivation through the use of perform- ance appraisals, pay-for-performance incentives and internal promotions systems based on merit. HRM practices can also influence the design of work so that highly motivated and skilled employees can use what they know in performing their jobs (Bailey, 1993).

In summary, the contributions of employees can have an impact on firm performance, and HRM practices can influence employee contributions through their effect on motiva- tion, skill and participation in decision-making. These employee contributions have been shown, in reviews of research findings, to have a financial impact.

Pfeffer writes (1998, p. xvi): "The returns from managing people in ways that build high commitment, involvement, and learning and organizational competence are typically on the order of 30 to 50 percent, substantial by any measure." He later adds (Pfeffer, 1998, p. 32): "substantial gains, on the order of 40 percent or so in most of the studies reviewed, can be obtained by implementing high performance management practices." HRM matters.

The sources of competitive advantage today are different than they may have been 20 years ago. Today, how firms manage their workforces is the major competitive advantage the organization, its employees and how they work. Pfeffer argues (1995) that HRM practices likely to be successful are *not* faddish, it is not hard to understand them or why they work, and they are not contingent on a firm's particular organizational strategy.

Although we are beginning to understand more about effective HRM practices, signifi- cant challenges remain in the application of this knowledge. First, it takes significant time to achieve a competitive advantage through the workforce. Organizations doing well may feel no need to change; organizations doing poorly may face immediate pressures, making them, too, unlikely to change. There also may not be enough communication of best- practice knowledge. In addition, managers may know something that researchers do not. Finally, some HRM practices may be risky and often fail.

HRM PRACTICES AND FIRM PERFORMANCE

There is considerable evidence that a range of HRM practices have been shown to reduce staff turnover. In addition, HRM practices have been found to be associated with organ- izational productivity. Finally, some work has explored the links between individual HRM practices and corporate financial performance (see Becker and Gerhart, 1996).

Huselid (1995) examined the links between systems of HRM practices and firm perform- ance in a sample of almost 1,000 US firms. He included 13 HRM practices which factor analysis then reduced to two factors: employee skills and organizational structures and employee motivation. His results showed that use of these HRM practices had an econom- ically and statistically significant effect on both intermediate employee outcomes (turnover, productivity) and short- and long-term measures of corporate financial performance. Little support emerged for a contingency perspective.

Arthur (1994) compared two HRM strategies in a study of 30 US steel mini-mills. One strategy emphasized control and attempted to reduce labor costs or improve efficiency by enforcing employee compliance with specific rules and procedures. The other strategy emphasized commitment and focused on developing highly motivated and committed employees through employee involvement in decision-making and training in group problem solving. He found that the commitment approach resulted in greater labor efficiency and lower scrap rates. Turnover was higher in the control-oriented mills, but their hiring and training costs were low. Turnover in the commitment-oriented mills, while lower, had a more negative effect on labor efficiency and scrap rates.

Banker *et al.* (1996a) undertook a longitudinal field study examining the impact of work teams on manufacturing performance. Both quality and labor productivity improved over time with the use of work teams.

Welbourne and Andrews (1996) examined the impact of HRM in enhancing the performance of initial public offering (IPO) companies. Two HRM variables, human resource value and organization-based rewards predicted initial investor reactions and long-term company survival. Rewards had a negative relationship with initial performance and a positive relationship with long-term survival.

Banker *et al.* (1996b), using a contingency framework, investigated the effects of an outcome-based incentive plan on sales, customer satisfaction and profit. Contingency factors included competitive intensity, customer profile and behavior-based control (supervisory monitoring). The outcome-based incentive scheme had positive relationships with the performance measures (intensity of competition, proportion of upscale customers) and negative relationship with level of supervisory monitoring.

Delaney and Huselid (1996), in 590 for profit and non-profit firms, found positive relationships between HRM practices (e.g., training, staffing selectivity) and perceptions of firm performance.

Davidson *et al.* (1996) found that the presence of an early retirement program, a strategic HRM response, was associated with favorable views of investors.

Schneider *et al.* (2003) reported the results of a study of the relationship between employee attitudes and organizational performance with both sets of variables measured at the organizational level of analysis. Employee attitude data from 35 companies over eight years were analyzed at the organizational level against financial returns (return on assets, ROA) and market performance (earnings per share, EPS) using cross-lagged analyses. Statistical significant relationships across various time lags were observed for three of the seven employee attitude measures. Overall job satisfaction and satisfaction with security were predicted by ROA and EPS more strongly than the reverse, though some of the reverse relationships were also significant. Satisfaction with pay had a reciprocal relationship with ROA and EPS.

Schneider and his colleagues integrate the literature on high performance work practices (HRM) with their findings as follows. HRM increases production efficiencies which, in turn, increases organizational financial and market performance which, in turn, increases pay and security to employees and a more positive company reputation, resulting in higher levels of employee positive outcomes (Cameron *et al.*, 2003).

Batt (2002), in a nationally representative sample of call centers, examined the relationship of HRM practices, employee quit rates and organizational performance. She found that quit rates were lower and sales growth higher in call centers that stressed high skills, employee participation in decision-making and in work teams, and HR incentives such as high pay and job security. Quit rates partially mediated the relationship between HRM practices and sales growth; call centers with lower quit rates indicated greater sales growth.

Carpenter *et al.* (2001) propose that CEOs with international experience create value for their organizations and themselves through their possession of a valuable and unique resource. They found that US multinationals performed better with CEOs with international assignment experience, particularly when this human capital was bundled with other organizational resources and capabilities.

Perry-Smith and Blum (2000), based on a national sample of 527 US firms, reported that organizations with more extensive work-family policies have higher perceived firm-level performance. In addition, there was partial support for the hypothesis that the relationship between work-family bundles and firm performance was stronger in older firms and firms employing a larger proportion of women.

Guthrie (2001) reported a positive association between the use of high-involvement work practices and employee retention and firm productivity. Interestingly, high turnover was associated with lower productivity when use of high involvement practices was high and with increased productivity when use of high involvement work practices was low.

Delery and Doty (1996) related seven HRM practices (internal career opportunities, formal training systems, appraisal measures, profit sharing, employment security, voice mechanisms and job definition) to measures of financial performance. They found that HRM practices (profit sharing, results-oriented appraisals, employment security) were significantly related to two financial performance measures.

Konrad and Linnehan (1995) considered the question of whether formalized human resources management structures promote goals of employment opportunity and affirm active action. They examined antecedents and outcomes of formalized HRM structures in over 100 organizations, measuring the presence of "identity conscious" and "identity blind" HRM structures. They report that identity-conscious structures were associated with some positive indicators of the employment status of women and people of color.

Terpstra and Rozell (1993) found that organizations using the employee selection processes recommended by industrial-organizational psychologists (validation studies, structured interviews, cognitive ability tests, validation of application form questions and investigation of the usefulness of different recruiting sources) enjoy superior performance (higher profit margins, higher annual growth in profit and higher annual sales growth). But few organizations use these processes.

EFFECTIVE HRM PRACTICES

Effective HRM practices are long-established and well-known, easy to understand what they are and why they work and are not contingent on an organization's strategy. Pfeffer (1994) lists 16 interrelated HRM practices, for example. No organization does all 16, or all 16 well. And an organization can do all 16 and fail because people are only one factor in the success of an organization. These are not easy to implement. Their implementation requires involvement, effort and responsibility of all employees. Some employees will resist, some may leave, some are used to and feel comfortable with low commitment and not using their minds.

Pfeffer's original list of HRM practices include the following:

- *Employment security* conveys a long-standing commitment of the organization to its people. Employees respond in kind.
- *Selectivity in recruiting* means you hire better people in terms of performance, signaling to all that high performance expectations exist and the organization is an excellent one.
- *High wages* attract more and better applicants who stay. Firms can be more selective in hiring and high wages signal that the organization values its people.
- *Incentive pay* shows that the organization values performance and shares performance gains with all its people.
- *Employee ownership* aligns the goals of people with managers and shareholders. Employees are more likely to take a long-term view of the company.
- *Information sharing* makes more people knowledgeable and powerful.
- *Participation and empowerment* pushes decision-making to lower organizational levels where hands-on experience resides.
- *Use of teams and job redesign* increases communication, coordination, disciplined effort, data collection and monitoring and peer supervision.
- *Training and skill development* increases problem-solving skills and ability to use knowledge.
- *Cross-utilization and cross-training* increase motivation and employment security.
- *Symbolic egalitarianism* increases *communication*, reduces "us" versus "them" attitudes and focuses people towards a common goal.
- *Wage compression* reduces competition, increases cooperation, and signals that all people matter.
- *Promotion from within* encourages training and development, increases the likelihood that managers understand the business, increases trust between management and employees and serves as a reward for good performance.
- *Long-term perspective* supports the necessary long-term commitment to implement effective HRM practices.
- *Measurement of the practices* suggests that HRM is important and provides information on how well these practices are being implemented.
- *An overarching philosophy* connects the individual HRM practices into a coherent system, offers a rationale explaining what the organization is doing and why, and supports experimentation to achieve effective HRM practices. A philosophy, a system of values or beliefs about what the organization holds about the basis of its success and its approach to HRM, ties all the individual practices together.

These 16 HRM practices are not fads but reflect long-standing ideas about how to manage people.

Pfeffer (1998) later listed seven broader HRM practices, not 16. He combined some and eliminated others that dealt with implementation. These seven were: employment security, selective hiring, self-managed teams and decentralization, high compensation contingent on performance, training, reduction of status differences, and the sharing of information.

O'Reilly and Pfeffer (2000) identified six HRM levers in common across eight outstanding organizations. These were: alignment of values, culture and strategy; hiring people for fit with the values and culture; investing in the training and development of all staff; widespread sharing of information; the use of team-based systems, and tying rewards and recognition to desired behaviors and results.

ALIGNMENT OF HRM PRACTICES

In their discussion of strategic HRM practices, several writers focus on alignment—the alignment of HRM practices with each other (internal consistency or alignment) and the alignment of HRM practices with an organization's strategy (external consistency or alignment).

Gratton and Truss (2003) propose a three-dimensional people strategy based on their work with several large UK organizations over a ten-year period. The three dimensions were: vertical alignment between people strategy and business goals; horizontal alignment between individual HR policies, and practices and an action or implementation dimension to capture the extent to which the people strategy impacts the day-to-day experiences of employees and the behaviors of first-line managers.

Pfeffer (1998) suggests that the alignment process start by examining the organization's particular strategy. The next step involves identifying a small number of critical competencies or behaviors that are needed to implement the strategy. A consideration of the various HRM practices that will support the demonstration of these competencies and behaviors is undertaken. The final step is a check to make sure these HRM practices are internally and externally consistent. Pfeffer provides an illustrative example of how a firm can assess external congruence and internal consistency.

Can the HRM practices observed in high performing firms be labeled as "best practices" or are they so specific to a particular firm that generalization across firms become meaningless—you will recall that Pfeffer (1998) proposed seven "best practices." These seven elements all emphasize the performance-enhancing aspects of the HRM system and each is part of an integrated high performance HRM system.

BEST PRACTICES VERSUS CONTINGENCY?

The internal fit perspective suggests that the use of an internally consistent system of HRM practices would be seen in better firm performance in all cases. This would lead to the identification of specific HRM practices leading to important firm outcomes. The contingency perspective, on the other hand, raises the question of whether any HRM practice can only be seen as "best" in the context of a particular firm's strategy, industrial sector or environment (Lepak and Snell, 1999).

It is also possible for evidence to support *both* a best practices and a contingency perspective. That is, some HRM practices and good internal fit may lead to high performance across all firms. But firms that tailor their HRM practices to their specific strategy, sector or environment may achieve additional performance gains.

Youndt *et al.* (1996) considered universal and contingency models of the HRM–performance relationship in manufacturing settings. Data were collected in 97 plants and generally supported a contingency approach to HRM. Human capital HR systems, linked with a quality manufacturing strategy, were associated with multiple dimensions of operational performance (employee productivity, machine efficiency, customer alignment).

The universal approach is the "best practices" perspective and implies a direct relationship between particular HR practices and performance. The universal approach documents the benefits of HRM across all contexts. The contingency approach suggests that an organization's strategy adds to (or detracts from) the impact of HR practices and performance. The contingency approach develops more situationally specific findings. These two approaches can be complementary, not competing views, that is, not mutually exclusive. In both cases, HRM policies and practices matter.

It is likely that bundles of HR practices have more impact on performance than individual practices, suggesting that internal consistency or fit among HR practices matters.

CASE STUDIES OF HRM PRACTICES

Becker and Huselid (1999) synthesize findings from five case studies carried out in firms known to be leaders in the management of people (Herman Miller, Lucent, Praxair, Quantum, Sears). The case studies are reported in Barber *et al.* (1999); Harris *et al.* (1999); McCowan *et al.* (1999); Artis *et al.* (1999); and Kirn *et al.* (1999). They draw three broad conclusions (Becker and Huselid, 1999, p. 287):

1   the foundation of a value-added HR function is a business strategy that relies on people as a source of competitive advantage and a management culture that embraces that belief;
2   a value-added HR function will be characterized by operational excellence, a focus on client service for individual employees and managers, and delivery of these services at the lowest possible cost; and
3   a value-added HR function requires HR managers who understand the human capital implications of business problems and can access or modify the HR system to solve those problems.

SOME KEY CONTRIBUTORS

Edward Lawler

Lawler (1996) builds on the writings on employee involvement, TQM, re-engineering, empowerment, learning and boundarylessness, and offers a broader new logic for organizing based on six principles. He believes that particular programs (e.g., TQM) can be successful but, by themselves, not be enough to make organizations effective in a highly competitive, global business environment. In addition, many programs are adopted as quick-fixes. Instead, Lawler advocates change from the ground up.

He contrasts six principles to organizing (Lawler, 1996, p. 22):

Old Logic Principle: Organization is a secondary source of competitive advantage.

New Logic Principle: Organization can be the ultimate competitive advantage.

Old Logic Principle:	Bureaucracy is the most effective source of control.
New Logic Principle:	Involvement is the most effective source of control.
Old Logic Principle:	Top management and the technical experts should add most of the value.
New Logic Principle:	All employees must add significant value.
Old Logic Principle:	Hierarchical processes are the key to organizational effectiveness.
New Logic Principle:	Lateral processes are the key to organizational effectiveness.
Old Logic Principle:	Organizations should be designed around functions.
New Logic Principle:	Organizations should be designed around products and customers.
Old Logic Principle:	Effective managers are the key to organizational effectiveness.
New Logic Principle:	Effective leadership is the key to organizational effectiveness.

These six new logic principles must be considered as a whole and form the basis of a broad approach to organizing and managing that involves changes to all systems and practices necessary for organizational effectiveness. Lawler goes on to illustrate how these principles can be implemented. Bringing about large-scale organizational changes is very difficult. The following are important factors in bringing about successful change. First, there must be a compelling business reason for change. Second, senior management must support and guide the change. Third, change must be seen as a long-term investment. Fourth, continuous experimentation and learning must be encouraged. Fifth, involve as many managers as possible in the change process. Sixth, start the change process in the most responsive areas; these spread it to other areas as requested.

Lawler (2003) titles a recent book *Treat People Right*. This sounds obvious and simple to do but, in reality, it is very difficult to do. Managers need to take action that is good for both people *and* organizations. Lawler calls the relationship between people and organizations when people are treated right a "virtuous spiral" in contrast to the downward spiral described by Pfeffer (1998).

This is not a feel-good approach. Treating people right is complex. Organizations must treat employees in ways that motivate and satisfy them; employees must behave in ways that help their organizations become more effective and high performing. This approach requires insightful, forward-looking leaders, skilled management, well thought out management structures, programs and policies designed to motivate employees to perform at peak levels.

It is commonly believed that there is a conflict between what is good for an organization and what is good for people. While sometimes true, when people are treated right the likelihood of such conflict is reduced. Lawler sees this as a two-way street. Organizations must adopt new attitudes and practices; employees have a responsibility in meeting goals of high organizational performance. Employees need to take responsibility for their knowledge, skills, development and performance. These efforts foster a virtuous spiral of success. When organizations value and reward people, those people are committed to performing well. As a result, the organization accomplishes more and it can then reward employees more and attract and retain more talented employees. This leads to even higher organizational performance. This involves developing a variety of HRM practices that motivate people to peak performance with accompanying rewards. Staff, in turn, are more committed to the organization and more responsible for their own behaviors (contribution, learning, development, etc.).

Seven principles for treating people right and creating a virtuous spiral

1   *Attraction and retention*: Organizations must create a value proposition that defines the type of workplace they want to be so that they can attract and retain the right people.
2   *Hiring practices*: Organizations must hire people who fit with their values, core competencies, and strategic goals.
3   *Training and development*: Organizations must continuously train employees to do their jobs and offer them opportunities to grow and develop.
4   *Work design*: Organizations must design work so that it is meaningful for people and provides them with feedback, responsibility and autonomy.
5   *Mission, strategies and goals*: Organizations must develop and adhere to a specific organizational mission, with strategies, goals and values that employees can understand, support and believe in.
6   *Reward systems*: Organizations must devise and implement reward systems that reinforce their design, core values and strategy.
7   *Leadership*: Organizations must hire and develop leaders who can create commitment, trust, success and a motivating work environment. Virtuous spirals are the ultimate competitive advantage—powerful and hard to duplicate.

John Katzenbach

Katzenbach (2000) studied energized workforces that achieved higher (peak) performance than their competitors, than similar workforces in other companies, than was expected, and better than the norm. They identified 27 companies that met his criteria.

They then spent considerable time in each, examining front-line workers, middle management and executive levels, resulting in intensive case studies. Objective performance data were assembled for each company. This included indicators of productivity, quality, customer service (where relevant) and employee turnover.

Although each organization took its own unique approach, some common themes were noted. They believed strongly in each employee. They captured their employees both emotionally and rationally. They also balanced a disciplined emphasis on worker fulfillment and organizational objectives. While good people management was important, these peak performing organizations went further in firing up their workforces.

Katzenbach expected these organizations to use similar approaches in achieving their success: in fact, they did not. Katzenbach identified five balanced paths to peak performance. These were:

1 mission, values and pride
2 process and metrics
3 entrepreneurial spirit
4 individual achievement
5 reception and celebration.

Some organizations combined two or more paths. Katzenbach suggests that these organizations did not deliberately create or decide on these paths but the paths emerged as senior managers tried to realize both organizational performance and fulfilled employees. Although these two objectives are basic to each of the five paths, organizations used a different set of practices and approaches; each formed a balanced path (or culture) that produces a highly motivated workforce that consistently achieves high performance. Katzenbach offers suggestions on how organizations can create and focus the energy of a workforce, how discipline can be developed and enforced to achieve consistently superior performance and how organizations can identify the best paths for them to pursue.

Jim Collins and Jerry Porras

Collins and Porras (1994) studied 18 outstanding and long-lasting companies (outperformed the stock market by a factor of 15) comparing them to one of their top competitors. Great companies embrace both extremes on a number of dimensions (e.g., visionary and futuristic/outstanding daily execution). They put profits after people and products. They retain a core ideology while changing practices, products and people. They set challenging and risky goals. They build very strong cultures. They promote from within. They resist the status quo and continually try to do better. They experiment, take action and make things happen. Mistakes are accepted as a necessary cost of doing outstanding business. Finally, they work continually to make sure all parts are as well aligned as is possible.

Visionary companies continue to be outstanding performers over long time periods, several generations of leaders and many product life cycles. Collins and Porras use the term visionary companies to distinguish companies that have been the best performers in their industries for decades.

Collins and Porras used vast amounts of financial data and written information (books, articles, case studies, company publications, video footage) on their 36 companies. The key question was what distinguished the visionary companies from the 18 comparison companies.

In the visionary companies, the building of the company, not the building of products, was the ultimate goal. Visionary companies put profits after people. Visionary companies lived with paradox (e.g., low cost and high quality, conservative and bold). Visionary companies retained a core ideology while pursuing programs and change. Visionary companies had "big hairy audacious goals." Visionary companies had cult-like cultures. Visionary companies tried lots of things, keeping what was useful. Visionary companies invested heavily in management development, believing strongly in promotion from within. Visionary companies were never satisfied with being good enough. Finally, visionary companies forged their core ideology and unique approaches to progress and peak performance into all aspects of the organization and into everything the organization did.

Much of the latest management writing can be described as buzzwords and fads trumpeted as new creative approaches. Most of these buzzwords are not new, having been practiced in outstanding organizations for decades. In addition, widely held assumptions about outstanding organizations were found to have questionable value.

Collins and Porras (1994), for example, list 12 shattered myths. These include: it takes a great idea to start a great company; visionary companies require great and charismatic visionary leaders; the most successful companies exist first and foremost to maximize profits; and visionary companies are great places to work, for everyone (Collins and Porras, 1994, pp. 7–9).

Jim Collins

Collins (2001) studied 14 companies that dramatically improved their performance and maintained these results for at least 15 years. These companies were matched with comparison companies that were unable to move from good to great. Data on these companies included financial information, interviews with many executives in the good to great companies, and published material on these 28 companies.

Similar to the earlier Collins and Porras (1994) study, the good-to-great companies were contrasted with those companies that failed to achieve greatness. As in the 1994 book, Collins found many of the myths were not supported. Thus, strategy did not separate the two groups of companies. Neither technology nor mergers and acquisitions made a difference. Good-to-great companies were not necessarily in great industries. Finally, bringing in celebrity leaders from the outside reduced the likelihood of moving from good to great.

But some factors did distinguish the two groups of organizations. Senior executives in the good-to-great companies invested in building the company and not themselves. This exhibited high levels of personal humility and professional resolve and fearlessness. Executives in good-to-great companies focused initially on recruiting the right people and removing the wrong people. Then efforts were made to build a superior executive team. Executives in good-to-great companies thrive on truth, dialogue and debate, and the facts. Good-to-great companies understood what they could excel at and what they could not. Good-to-great companies had a culture of discipline. Disciplined people engaged in disciplined thought, and then undertook disciplined action. Good-to-great companies used carefully selected technology as an accelerator of momentum. The changes that took place in these good-to-great companies were natural, evolving and cumulative processes over a long period of time. There was no single dramatic defining moment or program.

WHY DON'T ORGANIZATIONS EMPHASIZE HRM?

What is surprising, however, is the slow rate of diffusion of the use of HRM practices across organizations. A survey of US businesses showed that only 16 percent had at least one innovative practice in each of four major HRM policy areas (flexible job design, worker training, pay-for-performance compensation and employment security). A study of 3,300 US workplaces concluded that the use of high performance work systems was relatively rare. About one-third had tried a formal TQM program, and about one-quarter used bench-marking programs to compare their practices and performance with other organizations. The fact that it is difficult to specify the particular HRM practice that contributed to enhanced firm performance may be one more reason for the lack of diffusion.

Although the use of best HRM practices has increased, only a minority of firms use them. And, somewhat surprisingly, successful HRM practices are not necessarily the ones adopted; instead, firms often opt for those easiest to adopt. Practices adopted sometimes fail and more often are discontinued. Implementing such programs is difficult. Implementation needs to be monitored and approached in a planned and comprehensive way.

Pfeffer (1994, 1998) identifies several internal and external barriers to the use of effec-tive HRM practices. Four internal barriers are noted. First, CEOs touted as heroes are often those who succeed in the short term by destroying the human system rather than achieving long-term competitive advantage through people. Second, unproductive theories of human behavior in the workplace are endorsed. Employment relationships are couched in economic transaction terms rather than in human and social terms. Third, organizations use language that diminishes trust, cooperation and self-management. Fourth, managers are resistant to and cynical about the implementation of new HRM practices because of the past history of management practices in their companies (deskilling, fighting unions, management control). Among external factors, Pfeffer believes that labor laws, at least in North America, mitigate against organizational change. The legal system applicable to the employment relationship makes it harder to use people to competitive advantage.

There are also other internal sources of resistance to implementing HRM practices. These include: the loss of jobs, status and pay through the removal of hierarchy; the costs, bene-fits and uncertainty of change; inadequate measures of the benefits of change; and hiring man-agers from outside who do not understand ways to obtain competitive advantage through people in their new companies.

Pfeffer (1998, p. 132) finds the following sources of resistance to utilizing HRM best practices. Organizations desire to do what everyone else is doing and to follow the crowd—a problem is, the conventional wisdom is incorrect. There are managerial career pressures, derived from the need to "make the numbers" and to have a track record that makes one "mobile," pressures that create an emphasis on short-term financial results. There is a persua-sive belief in leadership and a tendency to overvalue things we have helped produce, making delegation difficult. There exist demands for accountability and reproducibility in results and decisions that destroy the benefit of expertise, which is inevitably dependent on tacit knowledge. Career trajectories—who gets promoted—all too often reward financial rather than human resource or people management. There is an excessive focus on measuring costs—often short-term costs at that—and neglecting to assess the returns of those costs and investments. The business press and management education touts "mean" or "tough" management. There exists a management education and training focus on finance and accounting rather than on human resources or organizational behaviour. There is a greater normative and economic value placed on being a skilled analyst, on knowing, compared to

29

the value placed on being able to manage people, on doing. Finally, the capital market primacy over other stakeholders and demands for short-term performance make long-term investments in people more difficult.

IMPLEMENTING EFFECTIVE HRM PRACTICES

It has been estimated that about three-quarters of all organizational change efforts fail. Ulrich (1997, p. 157) offers ten reasons why change efforts do not produce results:

1 Not tied to strategy
2 Seen as a fad or quick fix
3 Short-term perspective
4 Political realities undermine change
5 Grandiose expectations versus simple successes
6 Inflexible change designs
7 Lack of leadership about change
8 Lack of measurable, tangible results
9 Afraid of the unknown
10 Unable to mobilize commitment to sustain change.

Pfeffer offers some thoughts on bringing about change to achieve competitive HR advantage. Management must take responsibility for fixing those problems found to exist. Then strategic choice must be exercised. To what extent are the HRM policies and practices internally consistent? To what extent are the HR practices and policies externally consistent; that is, produce the skills and behaviors necessary to compete given the firm's strategy and the competitive environment it faces? People must feel a need for change, a need to do things differently. This can be assisted by data showing that current practices are not working, identifying ways in which evolving company strategy impacts on HRM, and seeking external stimulation through plant visits, other companies, seminars.

Ulrich (1997, pp. 158–159) summarized seven critical success factors for change. These are fairly widely known, yet most change efforts fail. Organizations and change agents have done a poor job of translating this knowledge into action:

- *Leading change*: having a sponsor of change who owns and leads the change initiative.
- *Creating a shared need*: ensuring that individuals know why they should change and that the need for change is greater than the resistance to change.
- *Shaping a vision*: articulating the desired outcome from change.
- *Mobilizing commitment*: identifying, involving and pledging the key stakeholders who must be involved to accomplish the change.
- *Changing systems and structures*: using HR and management tools (staffing, development, appraisal, rewards, organization design, communication, systems and so on) to ensure that the change is built into the organization's infrastructure.
- *Monitoring progress*: defining benchmarks, milestones and experiments with which to measure and demonstrate progress.

■ *Making change last*: ensuring that change happens through implementation plans, follow-through and on-going commitments.

How does one start?

First, senior management must establish a philosophy, goal or vision. This means publicly and repeatedly stating the importance to the organization's success. Senior management has a key role in developing an overarching philosophy or vision for their HRM initiatives. Second, it is critical to make some changes with immediate impact (immediate visible results generate support and widespread commitment to make going back almost impossible); to take action of some sort. Try experimenting. Finally, companies seriously committed to effective HRM practices use measurement of their efforts as a central feature of their efforts. Measurement serves several purposes. It puts attention on these practices. It provides feedback on the implementation of their HRM practices.

To the extent that organizations can unleash the hidden value within their people, they will increase their chances of success, particularly as knowledge and intellectual capital become more important. There is a sense that organizations today need new ways of functioning to be successful. As a recent advertisement stated: "There's just one problem with business as usual. It's business as usual."

NOTE

1 Preparation of this chapter was supported, in part, by the School of Business, York University. Joe Krasman assisted in the literature review; Louise Coutu prepared the manuscript.

REFERENCES

Artis, C.R., Becker, B.E. and Huselid, M.A. (1999) Strategic human resource management at Quantum. *Human Resource Management*, 38, 309–313.

Arthur, J. (1994) Effects of human resource systems on manufacturing performance and turnover. *Academy of Management Journal*, 37, 670–687.

Ashkenas, R., Ulrich, D., Jick, T. and Kerr, S. (1995) *The Boundaryless Organization: Crossing the barrier to outstanding performance*. San Francisco, CA: Jossey-Bass.

Bailey, T. (1993) Organizational innovation in the apparel industry. *Industrial Relations*, 32, 34–49.

Banker, R.D., Field, J.M. Schroeder, R.G. and Sinha, K.K. (1996a) Impact of work teams on manufacturing performance: A longitudinal field study. *Academy of Management Journal*, 39, 867–890.

Banker, R.D., Lee, S.Y., Potter, G. and Srinivasan, D. (1996b) Contextual analysis of performance impacts of outcome based incentive compensation. *Academy of Management Journal*, 39, 920–948.

Barber, D., Huselid, M.A. and Becker, B.E. (1999) Strategic human resource management at Quantum. *Human Resource Management*, 38, 321–328.

Batt, R. (2002) Managing customer services: Human resource practices, quit rates and sales growth. *Academy of Management Journal*, 45, 587–598.

Becker, B. and Gerhart, B. (1996) The impact of human resource management on organizational performance: Progress and prospects. *Academy of Management Journal*, 39, 779–801.

Becker, B.E. and Huselid, M.A. (1998) High performance work systems and firm performance: A synthesis of research and managerial implications. *Research in Personal and Human Resource Management*, 16, 53–101.

Becker, B.E. and Huselid, M.A. (1999) Strategic human resource management in five leading firms. *Human Resource Management*, 38, 287–301.

Becker, B.E., Huselid, M.A. and Ulrich, D. (2001) *The HR Scorecard: Linking People, Strategy and Performance*. Boston, MA: Harvard Business School Press.

Cameron, K., Dutton, J. and Quinn, R.P. (2003) *Positive Organizational Scholarship*. San Francisco, CA: Berrett-Koehler.

Capelli, P. (1999) *The New Deal at Work*. Boston, MA: Harvard Business School Press.

Carpenter, M.A., Sanders, W.G. and Gregersen, H.B. (2001) Bundling human capital with organizational context: The impact of international assignment experience on multinational firm performance and CEO pay. *Academy of Management Journal*, 44, 493–511.

Collins, J. (2001) *Good to Great*. New York: HarperCollins.

Collins, J.C. and Porras, J.J. (1994) *Built to Last: Successful Habits of Visionary Companies*. New York: HarperCollins.

Davidson, W.N., Worrell, D.L. and Fox, J.B. (1996) Early retirement programs and firm performance. *Academy of Management Journal*, 39, 970–984.

Delaney, J.T. and Huselid, M.A. (1996) The impact of human resource management practices on perceptions of organizational performance. *Academy of Management Journal*, 39, 949–969.

Delery, J.E. and Doty, D.H. (1996) Modes of theorizing in strategic human resource management: Tests of universalistic, contingency and configurational performance predictions. *Academy of Management Journal*, 39, 802–835.

Galbraith, J.R., Lawler, E.E. and Associates (1993) *Organizing for the Future: The New Logic for Managing Complex Organizations*. San Francisco, CA: Jossey-Bass.

Gratton, L. and Truss, C. (2003) The three-dimensional people strategy: Putting human resources policies into action. *Academy of Management Executive*, 17, 74–86.

Guthrie, J.P. (2001) High-involvement work practices, turnover, and productivity: Evidence from New Zealand. *Academy of Management Journal*, 44, 180–190.

Harris, B.F., Huselid, M.A. and Becker, B.E. (1999) Strategic human resource management at Prazair. *Human Resource Management*, 38, 315–320.

Heskett, J.L., Sasser, W.E. and Schlesinger, L.A. (1997) *The Service Profit Chain: How Leading Companies Link Profit and Growth to Loyalty, Satisfaction and Value*. New York: Free Press.

Huselid, M.A. (1995) The impact of human resource management practices on turnover, productivity, and corporate financial performance. *Academy of Management Journal*, 38, 635–672.

Katzenbach, J.R. (2000) *Peak Performance: Aligning the Hearts and Minds of Your Employees*. Boston, MA: Harvard Business School Press.

Kirn, S.P., Rucci, A.J., Huselid, M.A. and Becker, B.E. (1999) Strategic human resource management at Sears. *Human Resource Management*, 38, 329–335.

Konrad, A. and Linnehan, F. (1995) Formalized HRM structures: Coordinating equal opportunity or concealing organizational practices? *Academy of Management Journal*, 38, 787–820.

Lawler, E.E. III (1992) *The Ultimate Advantage: Creating the High Involvement Organization.* San Francisco, CA: Jossey-Bass.

Lawler, E.E. III (1996) *From the Ground Up: Six Principles for Creating New Logic Organizations.* San Francisco, CA: Jossey-Bass.

Lawler, E.E. III (2003) *Treat People Right.* San Francisco, CA: Jossey-Bass.

Lawler, E.E. III, Mohrman, S.A. and Ledford, G.F. (1995) *Creating High Performance Organizations: Practices and Results of Employee Involvement and Total Quality Management in Fortune 1000 Companies.* San Francisco, CA: Jossey-Bass.

Lepak, D.P. and Snell, S.A. (1999) The human resource architecture: Toward a theory of human capital allocation and development. *Academy of Management Journal*, 24, 31–48.

McCowan, R.A., Bowen, U., Huselid, M.A. and Becker, B.E. (1999) Strategic human resource management at Herman Miller. *Human Resource Management*, 38, 303–308.

Mohrman, S.A., Cohen, S.G. and Mohrman, A.M. (1995) *Designing Team-based Organizations: New Forms for Knowledge Work.* San Francisco, CA: Jossey-Bass.

Nadler, D.A., Shaw, R.B., Walton, A.E. and Associates (1995) *Discontinuous Change: Leading Organizational Transformation.* San Francisco, CA: Jossey-Bass.

O'Reilly, C.A. III and Pfeffer, J. (2000) *Hidden Value: How Great Companies Achieve Extraordinary Results with Ordinary People.* Boston, MA: Harvard Business School Press.

Perry-Smith, J.E. and Blum, T.C. (2000) Work-family human resource bundles and perceived organizational performance. *Academy of Management Journal*, 43, 1107–1117.

Pfeffer, J. (1994) *Competitive Advantage Through People.* Boston, MA: Harvard Business School Press.

Pfeffer, J. (1998) *The Human Equation: Building Profits by Putting People First.* Boston, MA: Harvard Business School Press.

Pfeffer, J. and Sutton, R.I. (2000) *The Knowing-Doing Gap: How Smart Companies Turn Knowledge into Action.* Boston, MA: Harvard Business School Press.

Schneider, B., Hanges, P.J., Smith, D.B. and Salvaggio, A.N. (2003) Which comes first: Employee attitudes or organizational financial and market performance? *Journal of Applied Psychology*, 88, 836–851.

Terpstra, D.E. and Rozell, E.J. (1993) The relationship of staffing practices to organizational level measures of performance. *Personnel Psychology*, 46, 27–48.

Tushman, M. and O'Reilly, C.O. (1997) *Winning Through Innovation: A Practical Guide to Leading Organizational Change and Renewal.* Boston, MA: Harvard Business School Press.

Ulrich, D. (1997) *Human resource champions.* Boston, MA: Harvard Business School Press.

Welbourne, T.M. and Andrews, A.O. (1996) Predicting the performance of initial public offerings: Should human resource management be in the equation? *Academy of Management Journal*, 39, 891–919.

Wright, P.M. and McMahan, G.C. (1992) Theoretical perspectives for strategic human resources management. *Journal of Management*, 18, 295–320.

Youndt, M.A., Snell, S.A., Dean, J.W. and Lepak, D.P. (1996) Human resource management, manufacturing strategy, and firm performance. *Academy of Management Journal*, 39, 836–866.

Chapter 3

The HR function in the new economy

Mark L. Lengnick-Hall and Cynthia A. Lengnick-Hall

A firm's human resources often are acknowledged as a crucial source of competitive value and among a firm's most important assets. This has never been more accurate than in the new knowledge economy. The knowledge economy erodes many familiar sources of competitive advantage (D'Aveni, 1994). Market characteristics make it unlikely that any firm can find a secure external position that offers a sustainable edge over rivals. Corporate boundaries, rather than national borders, define a firm's scope of activities. Substitutes for natural and technological resources are rapidly developed and made readily available, and technological advances are quickly replaced or so diffused that they become basic business requirements rather than sources of advantage. These diminished sources of dominance, coupled with relentless market shifts, suggest that a firm's internal resources and intangible capabilities are the primary source of value creation for the future, since they offer a more reliable and controllable foundation for strategy making (Grant, 1991). It is becoming clear that success in the knowledge economy will accrue to those organizations that are adept at creating *strategic capability*.

What is strategic capability? According to Saint-Onge (2001) strategic capability is the capacity to create value based on the intangible assets of the firm. A firm's tangible assets generally are well understood: they are readily visible, rigorously quantified, form an integral part of the balance sheet, can be easily duplicated, and depreciate with use. In contrast, intangible assets are less well understood. Intangible assets are invisible, difficult to quantify, not tracked through accounting, have to be developed in a path-dependent way over time—they cannot be obtained instantaneously, bought, or imitated—and they appreciate with purposeful use. Examples of intangible assets include technological know-how, customer loyalty, branding, and business processes. Tangible assets are necessary, but not sufficient, for gaining a competitive advantage in the knowledge economy because most tangible assets can be imitated or obtained through the market. It is the intangible assets that will make the difference to which firms succeed and which fail.

Some of the indicators of strategic capability include: a high level of business competency; a superior ability to detect, understand and direct what's going on in the marketplace (where preferences are shifting rapidly); the ability to transfer skills quickly and effectively across the organization, the ability to scale-up production to meet explosive demand, and quickly expand market reach; and the ability to generate new opportunities for the organization before the marketplace has discovered they are required. *Strategic capability* is a readiness for the present and an ability to adapt in the future.

Strategic capability is obtained through relationships where the creation, exchange, and harvesting of knowledge builds the individual and organizational resources and capabilities that enable a firm to provide superior value for customers. On their own, most resources offer limited competitive value. It is when resources from different categories (i.e., financial, technological, human, intangible) are combined and coordinated to create a bundle that is rare, valuable, difficult to imitate, and non-substitutable, that resources make the greatest strategic contribution (Barney, 1995). Combining bundles of resources through organizational processes can yield organizational and strategic capabilities. Organizational capabilities describe what a firm can do more effectively than its rivals. An *organizational capability* is the capacity to accomplish a specified task, outcome, or mission. Capabilities are integrated bundles of skills and accumulated knowledge that use organizational processes to coordinate and exploit the firm's assets. Therefore, resources are the foundation of a firm's capabilities, and capabilities are the primary source of competitive advantage. Successful firms typically make strategic investments in infrastructures and processes that link resources of various kinds to create capabilities. The longer and more complicated the string of activities needed to transform a bundle of resources into a capability, the more difficult it is for competitors to duplicate the accomplishment.

However, a sustained advantage requires a firm to be as varied, flexible, and changeable as the market in which it competes. The more turbulent, unpredictable, and diverse the marketplace, the more flexible, agile, and varied the organization needs to be in order to compete (Ferrier *et al.*, 1999). Therefore, an extensive repertoire of capabilities that create different kinds of value, coupled with organizational agility and versatility, are necessary to sustain desirable competitive results.

People play an essential role in realizing the benefits of resources, organizational capabilities, and strategic competencies. Building block resources typically are inert—they cannot create value without human intervention. Likewise, few resources can be bundled into capabilities or orchestrated into competencies without human contributions. A decision support system, for example, offers little value without a decision maker. Sophisticated cameras and unique special effects equipment are ineffective without the artists who create the movie. Human resources are the connective tissue of value creation.

The juxtaposition of a string of highly orchestrated, rare, and valuable organizational capabilities with the fluid, diverse, and often discontinuous market expectations characteristic of the knowledge economy, creates a dynamic tension that puts an additional premium on human factors. Most strategically valuable resources and capabilities are path dependent—building on prior actions and experiences and requiring investments over time to develop. Path dependency exploits tacit knowledge and, therefore, is dependent on human capital. In addition, most strategically valuable resources and capabilities are socially complex. Social complexity means value is realized through people working collaboratively, often in reciprocally interdependent ways that transcend formal job descriptions and reporting relationships. Social complexity builds on relationships and, therefore, is dependent on social capital. Both path dependency and social complexity reinforce consistency in patterns of behavior.

However, as noted previously, the fluid market of the knowledge economy requires agility and versatility. Knowledge management provides the foundation for achieving effective organizational flexibility and variety. Four processes lie at the core of knowledge management: generating knowledge, organizing knowledge, developing knowledge and distributing knowledge (March and Garvin, 1997). Each of these processes depends heavily on human contributions. Therefore, as with human capital and social capital, knowledge management is dependent on a firm's human resources.

Human capital, social capital, and knowledge management are foundation capabilities that can lead to competitive advantage in the knowledge economy if they are applied quickly, effectively, decisively, and toward the appropriate target. Rapid deployment is the orchestrating competency that transforms these three foundation capabilities into strategic advantage. As with human capital, social capital and knowledge management, rapid deployment is derived, primarily, from people in action.

The knowledge economy suggests that a new lens is needed for the human resource management (HRM) function in most organizations. People are at the heart of value creation in the knowledge economy, but the conventional ways in which many HRM professionals have viewed people is not focused on the types of contributions that will be crucial in this context. Many of the practices and perspectives traditionally found in HRM units are well suited to matching people to jobs and jobs to strategies, to motivating people to make a variety of contributions to value creation expertly and efficiently, and to responding to a firm's strategic intent. But, the knowledge economy requires a different kind of human resource management in which human resource (HR) professionals take the initiative in designing value creation options for their organizations. The focus of HRM in the knowledge economy should emphasize making it possible for people to leverage other types of resources to create capabilities, and to nurture core competencies within a context that rewards both consistency and innovation and values both persistence and flexibility (Quinn, 1991).

This chapter will describe how the HRM function is evolving and will continue to evolve to meet the demands of the knowledge economy. First, we will describe characteristics of the knowledge economy. Second, we will define new roles for the HR function. Third, we will provide an example of how one company has reshaped its HR function to meet the demands of the knowledge economy.

THE KNOWLEDGE ECONOMY

By the end of the twentieth century, there was a great deal of discussion about the "new economy." In contrast to the "old economy," the "new economy" describes aspects or sectors of an economy that are producing or intensely using innovative technologies, and rely heavily on information and other knowledge-based sources of value creation. This concept particularly applies to industries where people depend more and more on computers, telecommunications, and the internet, to produce, sell, and distribute goods and services. Articles and pundits proclaimed a new and transformed way of doing business and—to a large extent—they were correct. Now that we are several years past the peak of excitement, it is possible to reflect on what was hype and fad, and what was truly transformational and enduring.

37

The term knowledge economy probably better captures what is new and different about a marketplace that is becoming ever more dominant. The knowledge economy encompasses all jobs, companies, and industries in which the knowledge and capabilities of people, rather than the capabilities of machines or technologies, determines competitive advantage (Lengnick-Hall and Lengnick-Hall, 2003). Labor, materials, and money can be combined from locations dispersed across the globe, making it possible—for example—to have computer programmers in India and California working on developing the same software 24 hours a day, 7 days a week, and 365 days a year. Organizations and institutions are becoming increasingly interconnected—facilitating sharing information and forming ad hoc partnerships that can be created and dissolved to meet situational needs. Products and services can be quickly and cost effectively fitted to the individual needs of customers, using the methods of mass production coupled with the speed of information technology. The middleman standing between producers and customers can be largely eliminated due to more direct means of communication afforded by technology, allowing companies to deal directly and efficiently with each of their customers. The knowledge economy brings together disparate groups, blurring the boundaries between industries, organizations, units, and technologies. Finally, the knowledge economy places a premium on immediacy—business is transacted in real time, organizations continuously adjust to changing business conditions, and product life cycles become shorter.

Competition in the knowledge economy takes place on three levels (Doz *et al.*, 2001). *Competing on the sensing plane* means organizations will have to constantly search out new knowledge that could lead to the development of new products and services. *Competing on the mobilizing plane* means that once organizations have found useable knowledge, it must be marshaled to create a product or service. *Competing on the operating plane* means that knowledge must be focused to create and distribute the products or services. Competition at all three levels will require a combination of individual and organizational capabilities to learn and share knowledge rapidly and effectively.

The knowledge economy will have two important effects on HRM. First, HRM should not remain confined to its conventional activities of staffing, training and development, performance management, and so on. As with all other functional areas, HRM activities will be expected to demonstrate how they contribute to value-creation, create organizational capabilities that enable the firm to thrive in a fluid economy, and leverage the other activities and resources of the organization. HRM in the knowledge economy includes activities that overlap with other traditional business functions (e.g., finance, marketing, and strategy). HRM in the knowledge economy also includes new activities, such as knowledge management, that do not fit into one of the previous functional areas of HR concern. Finally, HRM is responsible for managing the capabilities that people create and the relationships that people must develop to enable organizations to compete.

The second important effect of the knowledge economy on HRM is that who does HRM will become the joint responsibility of the HR department, managers, and employees. Much of the administrative work is, and will continue to be, outsourced. In addition, HRM shares more of its work with managers and employees as developments such as e-HR (web-based manager and employee HR self-service) become more prevalent. A partnership orientation means that HR will need to contribute directly to activities traditionally relegated to line managers. In addition, employees will assume responsibility for many of the routine HR activities (e.g., benefits management) and those outside of HR will collaborate with HR professionals to select, develop, reward, and orchestrate the firm's human talent.

HUMAN RESOURCE MANAGEMENT AND STRATEGIC CAPABILITY

In the knowledge economy, organizations need to build strategic capability—the capacity to create value based on the intangible assets of the firm. Hubert Saint-Onge (2001) defines *strategic capability* as a readiness for the present and an ability to adapt in the future, and it consists of three components: human capital, structural capital, and relationship capital. *Human capital* is the know-how, skills, and capabilities of individuals in an organization—it reflects the competencies people bring to work (and take home). *Structural capital* is the organizational architecture and managerial processes that enable human capital to create market value—it represents organizational competencies that employees leave behind when they go home. *Relationship capital* is the interpersonal connections across members of the firm and relationships with suppliers, customers, and other firms that form the basis for cooperation and collaborative action. It is the interaction among human, structural, and relationship capital that produces strategic capability. However, strategic capability must be realized through action. Organizations that apply their strategic capabilities to meet the needs of customers will have a competitive advantage over their rivals who have capability, but act too little or too late.

The concept of strategic capability suggests that four composite elements are essential for creating an enterprise that has what it takes to thrive in the knowledge economy. One: expert, technologically sophisticated, and continuously improving human capital provides the elemental knowledge, skill, ability, and other characteristics that form the building blocks for more integrative capabilities. Two: rich, varied, and strategically oriented social capital (the capability for collective, collaborative action) provides the contextual web that enables an organization to combine, leverage, amplify, and share the ideas, competencies, and boundaryless interactions needed for integration and action. Three: the ability to effectively generate, organize, analyze, distribute, and apply knowledge provides the foundation and means for organization flexibility, adaptation, initiative, and direction setting. Knowledge management is the capability for organizational learning, unlearning, discovery, and choice. Four: an organizational competence for rapid, agile, decisive deployment of resources and capabilities is the enabling mechanism that translates organizational intent into strategic action. Combined, these four elements provide strategic capability for effective competition in the knowledge economy.

The logical extension of this thinking to HRM is that the knowledge economy offers the opportunity for HR to become a pivotal source of competitive advantage. The knowledge economy creates a watershed situation for HRM. If, as in the past, HR managers focus on conventional activities of staffing, compensation, training and development, and so forth, then the HR function is destined to become increasingly tangential to the core of a firm's strategic activities. If, however, HR capitalizes on the increasingly important role that people play in developing the resources, capabilities, and competencies that lead to strategic success, then HR will be poised to enhance its value to the organization.

Thus, an emphasis on strategic capability necessitates rethinking the HRM function. Rather than focusing on specific operational tasks, such as selection or training, the creation of strategic capabilities requires a broader perspective. This is similar to the reorientation toward core competencies in the strategic management field (Prahalad and Hamel, 1990). Rather than emphasizing products and markets, a strategy built around core competencies centers on harmonizing streams of technology and knowledge across organizational units to create integrative organizational capabilities. We propose that by forming the HRM function around common themes (Ulrich, 1999) or roles, organizations will be able to adapt better to the demands of the knowledge economy. Roles blend and extend conventional HRM functions in a way similar to that by which core competencies combine and broaden traditional distinct competencies of various business units. These HRM roles encompass more than traditional HRM practices. Roles provide direction and guidance, but do not lock the HR function into a specific set of activities.

To create strategic capability and effectively manage its three components of human capital, structural capital, and relationship capital, we propose that the HRM function will have three primary roles in the knowledge economy: Human Capital Steward, Knowledge Facilitator, and Relationship-Builder. To effectively capitalize on a firm's strategic capability, we add a fourth role—Rapid Deployment Specialist. The relationships among these roles are depicted in Figure 3.1.

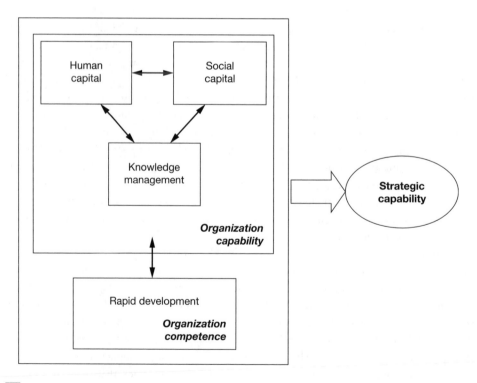

Figure 3.1 *Components of strategic capability*

40

FOUR NEW ROLES FOR HRM

HR roles provide a logical basis for constructing common themes that support an organization's strategic capability for thriving in the knowledge economy. Typically, roles are a more broad and adaptable concept than practices or jobs since they emphasize results rather than procedures. Roles reduce functional boundaries and conventional organizational borders since they describe outcomes that typically require diverse contributions. Roles facilitate adaptation and adjustment since they focus on ends rather than means. Since the knowledge economy requires capabilities that balance consistency with change, inventiveness with expertise, and individual interests with collective results, roles offer a useful approach to redefining an organization's HR contribution.

Human Capital Steward

Human capital is the knowledge, skills, abilities, and experience unique to an individual employee. The collective human capital of all of an organization's employees forms a unique intangible resource that distinguishes it from other organizations and provides the basis for strategic capability. The new role of Human Capital Steward requires accumulating, concentrating, conserving, complementing, and recovering the collective knowledge, skills, and abilities within an organization (Hamel and Prahalad, 1993). To thrive in the knowledge economy, organizations will need to develop a deep reservoir of talent—among both employees and external co-producers. HR professionals must develop both competencies and commitment among this diverse group of workers (Ulrich, 1998). The role of HR will focus on keeping the best minds and thinkers engaged.

A human capital perspective is different from the traditional (job-based) view of KSAOs (knowledge, skills, abilities, and other characteristics). In the traditional view of KSAOs, only those elements directly related to task performance on specific jobs are considered. However, in the human capital view, all of the various talents, attributes, capabilities, and insights a person brings to the workplace are included (non job-related as well as directly job-related). Thus, while an employee's music skills typically are not considered as directly relevant to effective performance for many jobs, musical talent may play a significant role in an individual's value-creating potential when considered in conjunction with the other KSAOs the employee brings to the workplace. Musical skills, for example, may allow an employee to design more creative solutions to a problem, or develop a habit of disciplined rehearsal, or may form the basis for relationships with other employees that facilitate the building of social capital. Non-traditional capabilities may enhance job performance in indirect, but quite valuable ways and thus contribute to strategic capability.

The second aspect of this role that differs from the conventional HR perspective is that of stewardship. Human Capital Steward prescribes a relationship between the organization and its employees in which the organization leads without dominating and facilitates followers without controlling them. Stewardship allows for a relationship between organizations and employees in which each makes significant, self-responsible contributions to organizational success (Daft, 1999). Stewardship metaphors commonly are used with natural resources, such as land, fish, and forests. These metaphors focus on preserving, conserving,

41

sustaining, growing, and developing the natural resources. Furthermore, these metaphors focus on the future and ensuring that the resources will be available and thriving beyond the current time horizon.

The stewardship concept acknowledges several key shifts in employment relationships that accompany the knowledge economy. Intellectual capital is not owned by the employer, but is bought and sold in human capital markets. Workers are volunteers or free agents since they control their intellectual capabilities. Workers also are investors, choosing where they will share their KSAOs and how long they will stay. They expect a return on their investment, too. This creates new challenges for attracting, motivating, and retaining volunteers and ensuring their identification with the firm. Despite circumstances in which market contracts often replace employment contracts, HR must ensure that the needed human capital is available, capable, effective, and grows in value. Stewardship is a pivotal shift in HR thinking. It is about being deeply accountable to others as well as to the organization, without trying to control, define meaning and purpose, or take care of them.

Stewardship requires a significant reorientation in HR thinking. First, it means basing relationships on a partnership assumption rather than a paternalistic, policing role. It reflects an understanding that partners have a right, and at times an obligation, to say "no" to each other. Partners are honest with each other. They don't hide information and they don't protect each other from bad news. Partners jointly are responsible for outcomes and for defining vision and purpose. To move toward a partnership orientation, HR needs to unlearn habits focused on imposing regulations or, conversely, on waiting for direction from corporate leadership.

Second, a reorientation toward stewardship means localizing decisions and power to make strategic capability everyone's responsibility. Everyone is responsible for thinking strategically, being on the alert for opportunities, providing early warning of problems, and responding to situational needs. Localized power also means that employees take ownership and responsibility for their own human capital development, and that HR facilitates, but does not control this process.

Third, stewardship means that core work teams are expected to build the organization. Teams define goals, maintain controls, and create a nurturing environment. Teams are expected to choose how they respond to changes in the marketplace or the work context. Teams design selection, compensation, appraisal, and training practices and are held accountable for the outcomes that result from these processes. HR responsibilities are more in the realm of mentor and teacher than supervisor. HR sets the parameters to ensure consistency and provides their expertise through education to expand the firm's competence (Block, 1993).

As a Human Capital Steward, HR contributes to strategic capabilities by developing, leveraging, renewing, and nurturing a firm's stock of knowledge, skills, abilities, interests, and talents. HR is there to help ensure that every individual is able to make value added contributions by identifying and cultivating individual competencies and capabilities. Moreover, HR contributes to the firm's strategic capabilities by ensuring that renewal and rejuvenation are on-going activities rather than episodic events. Resource flexibility, coordination flexibility, and adaptability over time are all important responsibilities. While initiatives might include many familiar training and development activities, human capital stewardship also includes creating a culture of continuous learning, inquiry, and personal responsibility for avoiding obsolescence. HR shapes the values and provides the contextual backdrop that enables people to take initiative and use their judgment in a flexible and fluid business setting. The role of HR is not to create a dependency between the employee and the HR unit, but to forge a partnership that leads to increased intellectual capital, enhanced commitment, greater awareness of opportunities to make a difference, and adaptability.

In addition, Human Capital Stewards contribute to strategic capabilities by creating a broad and adjustable pool of human talent. This requires the design of an appropriate mix of core, associate, and peripheral groups of employees, supplemented by flexhire workers, mediated services, contractors, customers, suppliers, and others willing to engage in co-production to improve productivity. An important part of the HR unit's contribution to strategic capabilities comes from transforming potential contributors into actual contributors. HR will need to devise broad, flexible, customized, and meaningful sets of incentive, reward, and appraisal systems to energize people to want to contribute their best and to look for opportunities to make a difference.

Relationship Builder

In an increasingly fast-paced and turbulent environment, more emphasis will be placed upon the relationships—or social capital—created and sustained among employees within and across organizations. Rather than building fixed assets on their balance sheets, companies will develop partnerships, oftentimes creating intense collaborators out of a company's fiercest rivals.

The role of Relationship Builder focuses on creating programs and practices that enable employees to encourage, facilitate, nourish, and sustain relationships among fellow employees, customers, suppliers, firms in complementary arenas, and at times, even rivals. The power of relationships lies in creating synergy within the organization and across the marketplace. Agile combinations of employees who have developed relationship networks can create more value for the organization than the mere sum of their individual contributions.

One of the lessons from the work on complex adaptive systems is that relationships hold the key to organizational resourcefulness and resilience (Pascale, 1999). The ways in which people interact substantially determine the extent to which the full benefits of their capabilities are realized by a firm. Thus, the creation of social capital through building relationships is a key factor for leveraging human capital and other resources to create strategic capability. The significance of social capital is demonstrated dramatically when firms attempt to implement sophisticated information processing systems. Social capital is essential for transforming the potential benefits of information technology systems into competitive reality (McDermott, 1999).

The relationship builder role is pivotal since both human capital and knowledge management are most effective in the context of an organizational community. Communities are more resilient and more adept at co-evolution with their surroundings than other types of social groupings (Peck, 1987). In communities, individual and collective interests are integrated by an allegiance to the firm as a whole. What does it take to build a community? Communication and relationships in communities go deeper than the typical "masks of composure" found in many workplaces. Communities are noted for their interdependence and mutual respect. They are intimate and invite disclosure through on-going verbal and nonverbal communication. Community members share a mutual concern and are committed to resolving problematic conditions faced by others in the web. Communities typically are populated by good organizational citizens (Bateman and Organ, 1983). Communities develop an allegiance to the whole enterprise that, in turn, enables them to balance both individual performance and collective action. Communities are the result of complex, genuine, and healthy relationships. When HR creates community relationships across the firm and beyond its borders, it provides a platform for leveraging resources, creating capabilities, and developing core competencies.

Communities are built around real needs and real work, so HR can make valuable contributions by clearly distinguishing value-added work from historical artifact activities within a firm (Brown *et al.*, 1994). A corollary contribution comes from ensuring that current definitions of value creation are well publicized. It is easy for an organization to become habituated to considering a particular competence as a source of competitive advantage even when the market no longer values this capability. HR must be vigilant in helping an organization unlearn obsolete assumptions and perspectives.

In addition, communities are built by shared experiences. Therefore, HR can create experiences in which individuals learn by doing together. For example, many of the technology tools for knowledge management offer important opportunities for enhancing the structural, cognitive, and relationship components of social capital (Nahapiet and Ghoshal, 1998). The structural dimension is the configuration of impersonal links between people and units. Data flows and network connections present a tremendous opportunity to enhance a firm's structural basis for building social capital. The relational dimension is the personal relationships people develop with each other across a history of interactions. These relationships include emotional responses such as respect and friendship that influence individual behavior. Technology implementation increases opportunities for new relationships to be developed by exchanging information about formerly tacit processes. However, counter to intuition, developing personal relationships in the presence of electronically mediated exchanges requires an increase, rather than a decrease, in face-to-face communication. For information technology to foster relational social capital, information exchanges must be used as a platform for developing direct human contact rather than as a substitute for face-to-face meetings. The cognitive dimension of social capital is the knowledge and language system providing shared representations, meanings, and interpretations among members of a network. Implementing a new organization-wide information system, such as enterprise resource planning, is an experience that is both personal and widely shared across a firm. This experience provides a powerful foundation for developing the cognitive dimension of social capital. Information technology is an omnipresent factor in the knowledge economy. HR can leverage the technology itself, and the implementation processes, as mechanisms for developing social capital.

One of the biggest challenges for creating communities in the knowledge economy is to be able to forge relationships to achieve the benefits of co-location without actual proximity. Periodic face-to-face contact must be rich and memorable. Virtual connections need to be constructed to share intimate, revealing, and significant ideas.

HR can contribute to a firm's ability to leverage its resources and develop strategic capabilities and core competencies by helping individuals build a strong web of relationships. Some of these, such as those within a *community of practice* (an informal association of people with something in common who share what they know and learn from others), should be quite "sticky" and enduring. Others should be fairly loose and more focused on particular types of transactions or events. In its various forms, social capital benefits an organization in many ways (Adler and Kwon, 2000). It helps workers find jobs and creates a richer pool of recruits. It facilitates inter-unit resource exchange and product innovation. Social capital facilitates the creation of intellectual capital since people are more likely to share tacit information and take intellectual risks in a supportive social environment. It facilitates cross-functional team effectiveness since social capital enables people to see situations from perspectives that are different from their own. It reduces turnover rates, since individuals are less likely to leave a firm if they have strong, positive social connections with their co-workers. It strengthens supplier relations, regional production networks, and inter-firm learning since social capital can be the foundation for multifaceted, multidirectional, mutually beneficial relationships that extend beyond transactional exchanges. Clearly, the ability to create social capital is a crucial organizational capability in the knowledge economy.

Knowledge Management Facilitator

It is not enough simply to hire talented employees and put them to work. Strategic capability requires a firm to be able to create and disseminate knowledge among its employees and often its customers, suppliers, and firms that make complementary products as well. This knowledge sharing can range from the mundane simple fix of a computer problem shared by an employee via e-mail, to the re-engineering of a process disseminated throughout all units in the organization via a training program, to ensuring that products purchased by other organizations make full use of a firm's product functionality. As Intel discovered, not only was it essential for its own employees to share technology advances among themselves, it was equally important for firms making the software and hardware that uses their microprocessors to incorporate new concepts in their products. Cutting-edge technology allows employees in the lower levels of organizations to seize opportunities and get breakthrough ideas to the market first. Language barriers are eroding as employees and freelancers anywhere in the world will soon be able to converse in numerous languages online without the need for translators.

HR can play a vital role in facilitating organization learning and knowledge sharing between employees, among departments, throughout the organization, and with external co-producers. This is not an easy capability to develop and it is closely linked with human capital and social capital. An important aspect of human capital stewardship is identifying people who want to learn. Employees need to be able to learn and unlearn continuously, to teach and to be taught. The organization must tap into all employees' knowledge as sources of innovation. HR can make an important contribution by identifying sources of employee knowledge and eliciting that knowledge from employees. A crucial responsibility is determining how to reward knowledge acquisition and sharing. Rewarding knowledge acquisition may be the easier challenge of the two since there are few answers for how to

45

get employees to share knowledge that they know, once shared, no longer provides them with a personal competitive advantage, and makes them expendable.

New knowledge must lead to new behaviors if it is to create strategic capability. Knowledge is of little use unless a firm is able to adjust its actions, decisions, and relationships to capitalize on the insight (Garvin, 1993). Knowledge management facilitation includes developing organizational capabilities that enable individuals to apply knowledge more adeptly, quickly, and creatively. Equally important, HR must help organizations strike a balance between productively focusing efforts on critical tasks while constantly incorporating new ideas.

Knowledge management and human capital stewardship inevitably are intertwined. Knowledge management develops the root source of organizational capabilities and competencies that comprise human capital. What people know, the skills they have honed, the observations that they can interpret, and the situations in which they can act effectively, comprise the capabilities and competencies of an organization. Several themes dominate effective knowledge management efforts: (1) expanding the data, intelligence, and information that is available, (2) facilitating access, sorting and interpretation so that information is useful for action, and (3) maintaining a rich diversity of ideas while seeking agreement on purposes.

Realizing these capabilities will require HR to orchestrate a complicated dance that requires both individual mastery and collective artistry. Knowledge management facilitation is not teaching people what they need to know—often the technical expertise and specialized information this requires is well beyond the scope of HR. Rather, the essential capability is ensuring that people know how to learn. This parallels the concept of personal mastery defined as "the capacity not only to produce results, but also to 'master' the principles underlying the way you produce results. It stems from your ability and willingness to understand and work with the forces around you" (Kleiner, 1994, p. 194). As facilitators of individual mastery, HR professionals are personal coaches (to customize a development investment), resource gatherers (to set the stage for learning), "tightrope spotters" (for when the learning becomes risky or uncomfortable), and appraisers (to provide feedback continuously regarding the clear competitive value of what is being mastered). Collective knowledge management requires a relationship orientation and, thereby, is linked to social capital as well as human capital.

The connection between knowledge management and strategic capability is extensive and visible. Effective knowledge management allows organizations to respond effectively to threats, problems, and other changes in the marketplace. Buckman Laboratories, for example, found that a customer needing a solution to a problem in France was able to get one from an associate in Monaco after receiving input from US associates and locating previous solutions and presentations on the K'netix knowledge network (Hackett, 2000). Another Buckman associate (i.e., employee) had a microbiological control problem that was solved by a colleague halfway around the globe who had a hobby—micro brewing—that involved controlling a similar organism. In both cases, rapid knowledge sharing led to more productive people who solved customers' problems quickly. This capability resulted in big gains for the company. Also in both cases, the synergies across the resources and organizational capabilities embedded in management, human capital, and social capital are obvious.

Each of these three roles—Human Capital Steward, Relationship Builder, and Knowledge

Management Facilitator—puts the greatest emphasis on organizational capacity, capability, and readiness. The final HR role needed in the knowledge economy emphasizes action. As Rapid Deployment Specialists, HR draws upon the firm's human capital, knowledge, and social capital to deliver performance quickly, efficiently, flexibly, and with superior effectiveness. For many in HR, this is a clear departure from the current perspective. Here the focus is on organization-level results. Evaluation of success is not based on whether HR did its part, but on whether the organization accomplished its strategic intent.

Rapid Deployment Specialist

The rapid pace and constantly changing environment that many organizations and industries confront creates another new challenge and new role for HRM: Rapid Deployment Specialist. The benefit from introducing new products to the market before competitors is short-lived. Technology, as well as a variety of ways to create value, allows competitors to meet or exceed such advantages almost instantaneously. Rather than creating and sustaining a long-term competitive advantage that is defended over time, many organizations in the knowledge economy, instead, will opt for short-term, in-and-out guerrilla-like tactics that allow them to take advantage of fleeting opportunities in the marketplace (D'Aveni, 1994). Once the advantage has been achieved, these organizations will move on to the next opportunity. Many whole companies intentionally will be ephemeral, formed to create new technologies or products only to be absorbed by sponsor companies when their missions are accomplished. Other firms will design their strategies around maneuverability to reflect their turbulent and unpredictable marketplaces.

Many firms are experiencing greater competitive aggressiveness as the total number of competitive actions (new market-based moves that challenge the status quo) increase (Ferrier et al., 1999). Persistent strategic success is likely to come from continuous and quite varied competitive activities. Firms that rely on a comparatively simple and narrow range of strategic initiatives increase their vulnerability to performance declines in aggressive and changeable markets. Dynamic competition is driven by the ability to move quickly, take decisive and unexpected action, and thereby confuse and slow the competitive response capabilities of rivals. Since the knowledge economy is characterized by aggressive, unprecedented, and quite varied value-creation activities, rapid deployment is a principal dimension of strategic capability.

Consequently, strategic capability requires competence in rapidly assembling, concentrating, and deploying specific configurations of human capital in order to achieve mission-specific strategic goals. Rapid deployment of human talent requires employees who are adaptable. Workers need to be adaptable, versatile, and tolerant of uncertainty to operate effectively in the constantly changing global market (Pulakos et al., 2000). The variety of conditions and situations that workers will need to adapt to is daunting: new people, new teams, novel and ill-defined problems, different cultures, new technology, challenging physical conditions, among others. Eight primary dimensions of adaptive performance have been identified and empirically tested (Pulakos et al., 2000). Adaptive employees react with appropriate and proper urgency in life threatening, dangerous, or emergency situations. They remain composed and cool under pressure, not overreacting,

47

managing frustration well, and acting as a calming and settling influence on others. Adaptive individuals are effective in solving atypical, ill-defined, and complex problems. They are able to act effectively despite uncertainty and ambiguity. Adaptive individuals anticipate, prepare for, and learn what is needed to perform future assignments. Adaptive individuals demonstrate interpersonal flexibility. Likewise, they demonstrate cultural adaptability— successfully integrating into a new culture or environment. Finally, these individuals adapt quickly and effectively to different physical conditions required in changing job/task environments. Identifying and fostering these dimensions is part of human capital development, but rapid deployment effectively uses these capabilities.

As customization and co-production become more prevalent, it becomes increasingly difficult to respond to local situations if the workplace remains fixed within the walls of a factory or corporate office. Technology advances enable people to telecommute or to take their work on the road. In the knowledge economy, work needs to become portable and this means developing a number of new skills within the workforce and new design mechanisms within the firm.

Reconceptualizing place to mean working together on a common issue rather than working in the same room, enables HR to rethink the ways in which location can allow people to contribute to a firm's competitive advantage. To transform physical location into psychological location, individuals with very different perspectives must be able to interpret and use many types of information effectively and toward a common purpose. Employees, and many who are external to a firm, will have direct access to real time information at multiple locations within a firm and in the field. Information transparency is a prerequisite for effective decentralized and autonomous decision making. For information to be transparent, not only does data need to be accessible in many locations, people need to know how to transform data that may be generated outside their sphere of expertise into effective choices and actions. This requires enterprise-based training and a clear understanding of organizational goals and metrics. A very dispersed workforce also means that a strong culture and a common passion, rather than rules or supervision, must provide the guidance system for autonomous choices and behaviors.

Quick response is also a direct source of strategic capability. From quick turnaround times for aircraft, to rapid response on insurance claims, to immediate commercialization of movie tie-ins, the ability to move quickly leads to greater resource utilization, lower costs, and customer loyalty. Speed also can improve accuracy. When an adverse drug reaction is detected immediately or when a claims agent can observe an accident scene before vehicles have been moved, the root source of a problem is easier to detect and fix, and it is less likely that a firm will respond to secondary symptoms. Speed can enable a firm to adjust its pace to meet market conditions. As firms move toward just-in-time production, all of those organizations along their supply chain must be able to adjust their processing speed to match that of the dominant player. As product customization becomes the industry standard, firms with quick development and production cycles will outperform those with slower internal responses. Many firms are just beginning to recognize the value of speed as an important strategic competence.

It is important to recognize that rapid deployment has a reciprocal interdependence with human capital development, relationship formation, and knowledge management. As a firm's cumulative competitive activity increases, new action repertoires, routines, and wisdom about how to carry out competitive moves also expand. In this way, these four roles work together to enhance strategic capability both immediately and into the future.

ORGANIZING THE HRM FUNCTION FOR THE KNOWLEDGE ECONOMY

With new roles to play in the knowledge economy, how should the HR function be organized? How do you organize without functions? How do you implement a broader, more role-based organizational structure for HR?

To contrast the dramatic changes in organizing the HR function, it is worthwhile to see how HR typically has been organized in the past and how it is evolving in the present. A traditional HR function compartmentalizes HR responsibilities—staffing, compensation, training and development, labor relations, etc. (see Figure 3.2). Determining where decisions on HR responsibilities are made depends upon the size of the organization and other considerations, such as business strategy. Some organizations centralize HR responsibilities at corporate headquarters; dispersed business units simply implement directives from headquarters. Some organizations decentralize HR responsibilities, allowing flexibility for business units to meet the particular needs of their situations. Some organizations combine both centralized direction with decentralized flexibility.

In the 1990s, cost and efficiency pressures stimulated some organizations to move toward a new "three-legged stool" model (Joinson, 1999). The "three-legged stool" consists of an administrative service center, a center of excellence, and HR business partners. Figure 3.3 depicts how Dell Computer Corporation organizes its HR function using this "three-legged stool" model. The *administrative service center* (Dell's Employee Resource Center) processes payroll, benefits, and other transactional activities. Its focus is on efficiency. Much of this work is delivered through employee and manager web-based self-service in some organizations. The *center of excellence* (Dell's Center of Competency) houses managerial expertise in areas important to the business. Its focus is on effectiveness. Experts in this function concentrate on design rather than transactions, and their customers are line managers. *HR business partners* (Dell's HR Generalists) are generalists who report directly to line managers in business units, and only indirectly to the HR department. Their focus is on providing tailored HR services to individual units. They serve as business consultants, aiding managers in the development and utilization of their human capital.

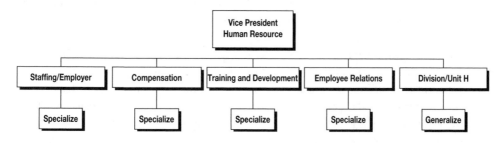

Figure 3.2 *Traditional HR function*

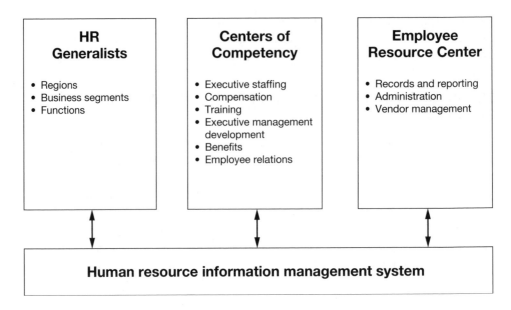

Figure 3.3 *Dell's HR function*

Neither the traditional HR function model nor the "three-legged stool" approach is adequate for meeting the demands of organizations in the knowledge economy. Both models still maintain a largely functional focus for HR activities. Both models focus on traditional HR activities and do not directly address issues of human capital, structural capital, and relationship capital. What is needed is a new way of organizing HR that integrates the management of all three forms of capital for the benefit of creating strategic capability. A Canadian financial services company provides a model for how the HR function can be organized to meet the challenges of the knowledge economy.

Clarica (formerly Mutual Life of Canada) has embraced many of the ideas discussed in this chapter. As a member of the Sun Life Financial group of companies, Clarica helps more than four million customers with their personal financial needs. Clarica has more than 8,000 employees at 90 locations in Canada and two in the US.

Their HR function is organized around three teams; each led by a *Practice Leader* (see Figure 3.4). The *Individual Capability Team* seeks to promote self-initiation and collective ownership. A key component of this team is the membership contract. The membership contract establishes the relationship between individuals and the organization as one of opportunity to develop and use capabilities rather than entitlement to a guaranteed future. Members include anyone who is involved in creating value for customers. *Membership Services* provides employees and managers with a three-tiered system for supporting their work. Tier 1 provides employees and managers the opportunity to conduct HR transactions through self-service on the corporate intranet and via e-mail. For issues that cannot be handled at Tier 1, Tier 2 provides employees and managers with a contact (e.g., by telephone) to facilitate resolution. Finally, at Tier 3, *Individual Capability Consultants* are available to intervene for the most complex situations.

50

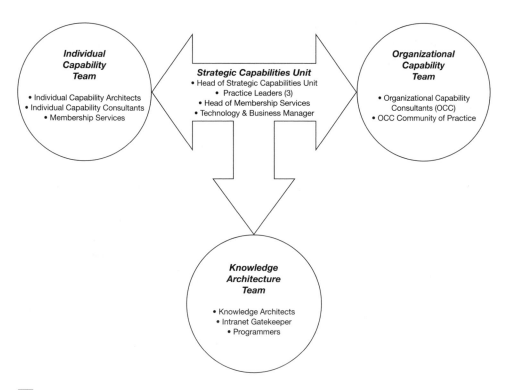

Figure 3.4 *Clarica's HR function*

The *Organizational Capability Team* consists of 12 *Organizational Capability Consultants* (OCCs). These consultants report to the leaders of their assigned business teams. The 12 OCCs form a community of practice that oversees the organization's approach to change and leadership development. OCCs focus on organizational-level issues of capability whereas the Individual Capability Team focuses on individual employee capability issues.

The *Knowledge Architecture Team* is responsible for providing all employees with the knowledge they need to learn in real-time to support colleagues and serve customers. This team, in collaboration with the various business areas, constantly updates the *knowledge depot*, which contains reference and learning materials. This team also is responsible for helping to create communities of practice through which knowledge is shared widely in the organization.

The *Strategic Capabilities Unit* is the organizational structure that links individual and organizational capabilities to the customer and the overall strategies of the firm. The *Head of the Strategic Capabilities Unit* oversees three *Practice Leaders* (for each of the three teams), the *Head of Membership Services*, and the *Technology and Business Manager*.

Some general principles can be derived for organizing the HR function in the knowledge economy. First, the HR function should reduce its role in managing the mundane, administrative tasks that do little to add value and further the perception of HR as primarily a clerical function. Outsourcing is one route for some of these activities. Web-based employee and manager self-service provide another means for accomplishing this goal. Second, the HR function should increase its role in creating and exploiting strategic capability. HR should collaborate actively in the design and administration of knowledge management systems. HR should provide nurturance and support for communities of practice and other forms of relationship building that generate social capital for the organization. Third, the HR function should organize around broader roles, such as those Clarica devised, in order to move away from a focus on tools and methods and move toward making value-added contributions to the strategic capability of the organization.

CONCLUSION

HR is at a crossroads in many organizations. It can be outsourced, automated, and relegated to a secondary support role. This is most likely to occur if HR professionals continue to see themselves primarily as deliverers of HR services. Alternatively, it can become a major player in the creation and realization of competitive advantage. This is most likely to occur if there is a fundamental shift in rethinking what purpose HR can serve in the organization, along with a transformation in how it is organized. Continuing to operate along principles and methods that were effective in the industrial era will lead to the declining importance of the HR function and an erosion of its ability to contribute directly to organizational effectiveness. However, rethinking the roles of HR in the knowledge economy will mean that, while the HR function may look quite different from what it was in the past, it may have a large and direct impact on the success of the organization.

REFERENCES

Adler, P. S. and S. Kwon, "Social capital: The good, the bad, and the ugly." In E. L. Lesser (ed.) *Knowledge and Social Capital: Foundations and Applications.* Boston, MA: Butterworth-Heinemann. 2000, pp. 89–115.

Barney, J. B., "Looking inside for competitive advantage." *Academy of Management Executive,* 9(4): 1995, 49–61.

Bateman, T. S. and D. W. Organ, "Job satisfaction of the good soldier: The relationship between affect and employee 'citizenship'." *Academy of Management Journal,* 26: 1983, 587–595.

Block, P., *Stewardship: Choosing Service Over Self-interest.* San Francisco, CA: Berrett-Koehler. 1993.

Brown, J., B. Smith, and D. Isaacs, "Operating principles for building community." In P. M. Senge, C. Roberts, R. B. Ross, B. J. Smith, and A. Kleiner (eds) *The Fifth Discipline Fieldbook: Strategies and Tools for Building a Learning Organization.* New York: Currency-Doubleday. 1994, pp. 525–529.

Daft, R. L., *Leadership: Theory and Practice.* Fort Worth, TX: Dryden. 1999.

D'Aveni, R. A., *Hypercompetition: Managing the Dynamics of Strategic Maneuvering.* New York: Free Press. 1994.

Doz, Y., J. Santos, and P. Williamson, *From Global to Metanational: How Companies Win in the Knowledge Economy.* Boston, MA: Harvard Business School Press. 2001.

Ferrier, W. J., K. G. Smith, and C. M. Grimm, "The role of competitive action in market share erosion and industry dethronement: A study of industry leaders and challengers." *Academy of Management Journal*, 42(4): 1999, 372–388.

Garvin, D., "Building a learning organization." *Harvard Business Review*, July–Aug. 1993, 78–91.

Grant, R. M., "The resource-based theory of competitive advantage: Implications for strategy." *California Management Review*, 22: 1991, 114–135.

Hackett, B., *Beyond Knowledge Management: New Ways to Work and Learn.* New York: The Conference Board, Inc. 2000.

Hamel, G. and C. K. Prahalad, "Strategy as stretch and leverage." *Harvard Business Review*, 71(2): Mar.–Apr. 1993, 75–85.

Joinson, C., "Changing shapes: As organizations evolve, HR's form follows its function." *HR Magazine*, Mar. 1999, 41–48.

Kleiner, A., "Mastery." In P. M. Senge, C. Roberts, R. B. Ross, B. J. Smith, and A. Kleiner (eds) *The Fifth Discipline Fieldbook: Strategies and Tools for Building a Learning Organization.* New York: Currency-Doubleday. 1994, p. 194.

Lengnick-Hall, M. L. and C. A. Lengnick-Hall, *Human Resource Management in the Knowledge Economy: New Challenges, New Roles, New Capabilities.* San Francisco, CA: Berrett-Koehler. 2003.

March, A. and D. A. Garvin, *A Note on Knowledge Management*, 9–398–031. Boston, MA: Harvard Business School Press. 1997.

McDermott, R., "Why information technology inspired but cannot deliver knowledge management." *California Management Review*, 1999, 103–117.

Nahapiet, J. and S. Ghoshal, "Social capital, intellectual capital, and the organizational advantage." *Academy of Management Review*, 23(2): 1998, 242–266.

Pascale, R. T., "Surfing the edge of chaos." *Sloan Management Review*, 1999, 83–94.

Peck, M. S., *The Different Drum.* New York: Simon and Schuster. 1987.

Prahalad, C. K. and G. Hamel, "The core competence of the corporation." *Harvard Business Review*, May–June 1990, 70–91.

Pulakos, E. D., S. Arad, M. A. Donovan, and K. E. Plamondon, "Adaptability in the workplace: Development of a taxonomy of adaptive performance." *Journal of Applied Psychology*, 85: 2000, 612–624.

Quinn, R. E., *Beyond Rational Management: Mastering the Paradoxes and Competing Demands of High Performance.* San Francisco, CA: Jossey-Bass. 1991.

Saint-Onge, H., *Strategic Capabilities Shaping Human Resource Management within the Knowledge-driven Enterprise.* www.konvergeandknow.com/articles/strategic.html, accessed November 1, 2003.

Sampler, J. L., "Redefining industry structure for the information age." *Strategic Management Journal*, 19: 1998, 343–355.

Ulrich, D., "Intellectual capital = competence × commitment." *Sloan Management Review*, Winter 1998, 15–26.

Ulrich, D., "Integrating practice and theory: Towards a more unified view of HR." In P. M. Wright, L. D. Dyer, and J. W. Boudreau (eds) *Strategic Human Resources Management in the Twenty-First Century* (supplement 4). New York: Elsevier. 1999.

Part II

New challenges for Human Resource Management

Chapter 4

An architectural approach to managing knowledge stocks and flows

Implications for reinventing the HR function

Shad Morris, Scott A. Snell and David Lepak

INTRODUCTION

Strategy tends to increasingly focus on how firms configure knowledge-based resources to create value. This is largely due to firms competing less on stable products and markets, and more on competencies, dynamic capabilities, new ideas, and innovation. Thus, scholars and executives alike are interested in how firms can enhance and exploit the knowledge embedded in their people, and other forms of intellectual capital. Such knowledge (often referred to as *knowledge stocks*) helps firms create competitive advantage through the effective use, manipulation, and transformation of various organizational resources required to perform a task (Nonaka, 1994; Kogut and Zander, 1992; Grant, 1996).

In addition to the importance of knowledge stocks, Dierickx and Cool (1989) noted that *knowledge flows* are vital for strategic renewal of new knowledge, as well as recombination of existing knowledge. In dynamic environments especially, the flow of knowledge both within and across firms is essential for innovation and continuous adaptation—leading to a more sustainable competitive position (Grant, 1996; Kogut and Zander, 1992; Nonaka and Takeuchi, 1995; Spender, 1996). Viewed this way, it is the configuration of knowledge stocks that provides a foundation for competitive advantage (Grant, 1996), but the renewal and recombination of those stocks that allow a firm to sustain that advantage (Grant, 1996; Teece *et al.*, 1997). This distinction can be important because, as Leonard-Barton (1995) pointed out, without continual knowledge flows to enhance and renew their strategic value, knowledge stocks can sometimes become the cause of rigidity rather than advantage.

These points at once highlight the importance of knowledge management for competitive advantage and make the boundary between strategic management and human resource management almost indistinguishable. Unfortunately, while HR is often on the "front line" in developing the knowledge base in organizations, it is almost never in a leadership role when it comes to creating competitive advantage. However, in today's environment, the assumption of people-embedded knowledge requires that we re-examine our approaches to HRM (Snell *et al.*, 2002).

In this chapter, our intent is to examine how different employees' knowledge stocks are managed within a firm and how—through their recombination and renewal—those stocks can create sustainable competitive advantage. To do this, we organize the chapter as follows. First, we discuss the notion of an architecture for managing human resources and review how the framework provides a foundation for studying alternative employment arrangements used by firms in allocating work. We review both the theoretical and empirical work done in this area and discuss how the HR architecture allows us to draw inferences about the form and function of an entire employment system within firms (cf., Becker and Gerhart, 1996; Nadler *et al.*, 1992). Second, we extend the architecture by examining how knowledge stocks (human capital) can be both recombined and renewed through the management of social capital. By identifying and managing different forms of social capital across employee groups within the architecture, HR practices can facilitate the flow of knowledge within the firm, which ultimately leads to sustainable competitive advantage. Finally, we discuss the relationships among HR practices designed to manage the human capital (knowledge stocks) relative to the HR practices designed to manage the social capital (knowledge flows).

AN ARCHITECTURAL PERSPECTIVE ON KNOWLEDGE STOCKS

Research dealing with strategic issues in HR has helped shift our attention toward firm-level issues related to managing people's knowledge stocks. Instead of focusing on particular HR practices that are used independently or in isolation, strategic human resource management (SHRM) typically looks more broadly at bundles of HR practices that are implemented in combination. For instance, many SHRM researchers (e.g., Arthur, 1992, 1994; Koch and McGrath, 1996; Kochan and Osterman, 1994; Lawler, 1992; Levine, 1995; Pfeffer, 1994) have supported high commitment and other types of high-involvement work systems that focus on making large investments in knowledge stocks to foster sustainable competitive advantage.

While more macro perspectives such as these help to draw the linkage to strategy, they do not offer much insight into how different knowledge stocks might contribute to firm advantage. As firms depend more upon employees who contribute in different ways based on differences in their knowledge (Grant, 1996), it is increasingly important to do two things: first, firms must recognize how they can best manage those differences. And second, they must recognize how they can best combine those differences. Generally speaking, these requirements reflect the dual imperatives of systems differentiation and integration (cf., Lawrence and Lorsch, 1973; March and Simon, 1958; Thompson, 1967).

Researchers have noted differences in employees' knowledge stocks and how employment sub-systems exist as a result (e.g., Baron *et al.*, 1986; Pinfield and Berner, 1994). For instance, Mangum *et al.* (1985), Doeringer and Piore (1971), and Cohen and Pfeffer (1986) all noted that many firms heavily invest in a core group of employees (often called knowledge-workers), while also maintaining a peripheral group of employees from whom they prefer to remain relatively detached. In fact, Osterman (1987) identified four patterns or types of subsystems based on the firm's decision-making process. These categories helped identify the different employment arrangements or modes that might exist within one firm.

Building on this research, Rousseau (1995) as well as Tsui *et al.* (1995) argued that not only do employment arrangements or subsystems differ, but also that the employment relationships or psychological contracts may differ as well. In general, firms might emphasize either a long-term, relational approach or a short-term, transactional approach for internal and external workers. Related research also exists that shows not only how employment arrangements and relationships might differ according to employees' knowledge stocks, but also how the actual HR practices might differ across these groups. Miles and Snow (1984), for example, were among the first to note that while companies may have HR practices that are standardized across the firm, many may very well be customized to fit the individual knowledge and skills of different employee groups. These ideas were later made more explicit in a framework by Lepak and Snell (1999, 2002) to show how HR practices might differ across employment groups based on their human capital.

The conceptual foundation of the architecture

An architectural perspective helps to link these differences and create an overall picture of how an organization's portfolio of knowledge stocks is managed. The architectural perspective, as purported by scholars such as Lepak and Snell (1999), Hitt *et al.* (2001), and Tsui, *et al.* (1995) provides a framework for examining how differences in human capital are likely to be accompanied by differences in employment as well as by variations in HR practices. Lepak and Snell identified two overarching dimensions of the architecture based on the characteristics of employee human capital: value and uniqueness.

The first dimension in the framework, human capital value, is determined by the accumulated knowledge and skills of employees that enable a firm to enact strategies that improve efficiency and effectiveness, exploit market opportunities, and/or neutralize potential threats (Barney, 1991; Porter, 1985; Ulrich and Lake, 1991; Wright and McMahan, 1992). Accordingly, value is derived from the ability of these knowledge stocks to increase the ratio of benefits to customers relative to their associated costs (i.e., value = benefits/costs). The second dimension, human capital uniqueness, refers to the extent to which knowledge and skills are specialized or firm-specific (e.g., Coase, 1937; Williamson, 1975). Unique human capital may consist of tacit knowledge or deep experience and understanding that cannot be found in an open labor market (Perrow, 1967). Accordingly, Becker (1976) mentioned that firms are more likely to make investments in firm-specific human capital that cannot be transferred to other firms.

By juxtaposing these two dimensions—value and uniqueness—it is possible to derive a matrix of four types of human capital: core, compulsory, ancillary, and idiosyncratic (Snell *et al.*, 1999). Each cell in the matrix differs in terms of employment modes and employment relationships (see Figure 4.1). Based on these different employment modes and relationships, the HR practice configurations are also likely to vary across each cell. Figure 4.2 summarizes four configurations of HR practices that are aligned with each type of employment found in a firm.

59

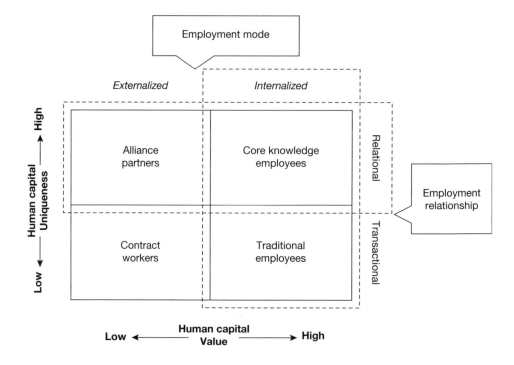

Figure 4.1 *Architectural perspective*

Core human capital

Based on their unique and valuable human capital, these employees tend to be employed internally and managed as core knowledge-workers. Their employment relationships tend to be long-term and focused on fostering organizational commitment and trust. The HR practices found among core employees are most likely to be associated with high-performance work systems (e.g., Huselid, 1995; Lawler *et al.*, 1995) that empower employees, encourage participation in decision making and discretion on the job. Likewise, many different long-term incentives (e.g., stock ownership, extensive benefits, or knowledge-based pay systems) may be offered to ensure that core employees receive continued and useful feedback and adopt a long-term orientation (Snell and Dean, 1992; Delany and Huselid, 1996). Such practices are designed to help firms maintain unique knowledge that leads to strategic advantage (Becker, 1976).

Compulsory human capital

Similar to core human capital, compulsory human capital is important for value creation and strategic advantage. For that reason, employment tends to be internalized. However, because this form of human capital is not unique (i.e., more transferable to other firms), organizations tend to de-emphasize development, and the employment relationship tends to adhere to a more traditional job-based orientation focused on immediate performance. As a result, managers are likely to rely more on a productivity-based HR configuration that

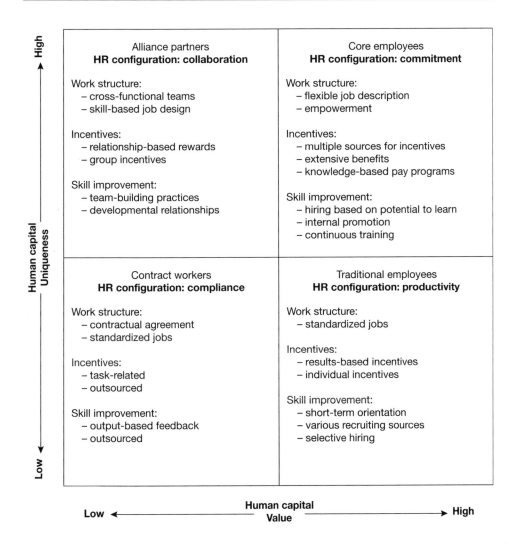

Figure 4.2 *HR practices from an architectural perspective*

focuses on standardized jobs and selecting people from the external labor market who can contribute immediately (cf., Koch and McGrath, 1996; Snell and Dean, 1992; Tsui *et al.*, 1995). Incentives for these employees tend to focus on efficiency and productivity through a results-based approach (Mahoney, 1989). Consistent with a productivity orientation firms are also less likely to expend money and time on long-term developmental performance appraisals but more likely to emphasize a short-term, results oriented component (Snell, 1992; Snell and Youndt, 1995).

Idiosyncratic human capital

Because their knowledge is not as central to value creation and strategy, employees with this type of human capital tend to be externalized. However, these external partners have specialized knowledge that is not easy to find in the market. As a consequence, long-term partnerships are likely to be fostered that preserve continuity over time, ensure trust among partners, and engender reciprocity and collaboration (Dyer, 1996). Thus, while there tends not to be investment in the human capital itself, there is substantial investment in the relationship with these individuals. Given the need for ongoing exchange, alliance partners are more likely to be managed by a collaborative HR configuration characterized by group incentives, cross-functional teams, and the like. Such practices ensure greater integration and stronger relationships with the firm and the partner employees (cf., Mathieu *et al.*, 1992).

Ancillary human capital

In cases where human capital is of less strategic value and not unique to the firm, employment is increasingly externalized (e.g., outsourced). Contract workers are similar to traditional workers in that they have a more transactional relationship with the firm (Rousseau and Parks, 1993), and in this case the scope of work tends to be limited and well defined. To manage these employees, firms are likely to implement HR practices that focus on worker compliance with preset rules, regulations, and/or procedures. For example, job descriptions are likely to be standardized and training and performance management, if conducted, is likely to be limited to ensuring that company policies, systems, and procedures are carried out (cf., Mahoney, 1989; Rousseau and Parks, 1993). In addition, compensation schemes for these employees are likely to be based on an hourly wage and the accomplishment of specific tasks or goals (Lepak and Snell, 2002).

Empirical evidence of the architecture

Based on theoretical implications of an architectural perspective, studies have been conducted to test the model empirically. For example, in a study of 206 cases from 148 publicly traded companies with over 200 employees, Lepak and Snell (2002) provided support for the notion that different types of employment are associated with variations in human capital value and uniqueness. Consistent with the strategy and economics literatures (Barney, 1991; Becker, 1976; Quinn, 1992; Williamson, 1975), these findings showed how workers with high degrees of strategic value tended to be internalized. Likewise, alliance partners and core employees were found to have more unique knowledge stocks than the other two cells, which was theorized based on Matusik and Hill's (1998) suggestion that firms invest more long-term (in terms of employment relationship and employment mode) in external and internal workers who are key in providing private or complex knowledge. The HR configurations found within each of these employment groups also vary. For example, commitment-based HR configurations were found to occur more often in core groups than any other employee group. Similarly, the compliance-based HR configuration was found to be significantly more prevalent in the contract employee group.

Lepak and Snell (2002) also noted several related points when looking at the HR function. First, typical job descriptions do not offer clear indicators of how employees are managed and their relationship to the firm. Specifically, a group of engineers in one firm might be called upon to utilize their general occupational training, while the same type of engineer in another firm may be asked to develop and utilize firm-specific competencies. The skills underlying the nature of these employees' contributions, rather than their job descriptions, would likely place them in different employment groups, suggesting that job descriptions do not neatly capture differences in employee contributions. Such findings argue for the importance of HR research to focus more on the characteristics of employees' human capital in determining how they are managed (cf., Ulrich and Lake, 1991; Stewart, 1997; Lepak and Snell, 1999), rather than relying exclusively on traditional HR systems focused on tasks and jobs. One of the broader implications of this research is that different employees are clearly managed in different ways. Lepak and Snell (2002) provide evidence that there is no single approach to HRM that tends to be used for all employees, nor perhaps should there be. However, simply showing differences across employees does not reveal much of an *architecture* in the sense of integrated design and function. Indeed, a fundamental premise of organizations is that individuals pool their talents and energies to achieve collective outcomes. To address this issue, Lepak *et al.* (2003) examined the various combinations of the four types of employment (core, traditional, alliance, and contract) and firm performance. Using an accounting-based performance indicator (return on equity, ROE) and a market-based performance indicator (market-to-book), they measured the relationships among the use of different employment modes and firm performance. Focusing on archival performance data, they were able to identify top-level executives to comment on their firm's overall use of each employment mode. The results of their study showed that firms that rely on both core employment and contract labor display higher performance than firms that rely on only one or neither of these employment modes. This finding supports arguments made by researchers such as Baron *et al.* (1986), Davis-Blake and Uzzi (1993), Lepak and Snell (1999), Matusik and Hill (1998), and Pinfield and Berner (1994), in that firms might benefit from the simultaneous use of both external and internal employment modes.

Conceptually, the underlying rationale for this benefit is that different employment modes afford firms different types of flexibility (Wright and Snell, 1998). With regard to internal employees, knowledge-workers provide organizations with a greater degree of resource flexibility—the ability to perform a wide assortment of tasks—compared to traditional employees. With regard to external or contingent workers, contract arrangements provide organizations with more coordination flexibility—the ability to adjust the number and types of skills in use—as compared to more long-term alliances. The benefits of these forms of flexibility are enhanced when knowledge-workers are used in conjunction with contract workers. At the same time, however, the combined use of alliances and traditional employment minimizes the benefits of flexibility and, as a result, was negatively associated with firm performance. In short, their findings indicate that there are multiple ways to improve performance via the use of knowledge-workers as well as contract labor, due to the realization of different types of organizational flexibility.

Interestingly, Lepak *et al.* (2003) found that, while traditional employees are the most widely used form of employment in firms, their effectiveness is dependent on the level of technological intensity as well as whether they are used in conjunction with core or contract employees. Thus, the benefits of traditional employment may be limited to when it is used in firms within more stable environments such as firms low in technological intensity, and when it is used in conjunction with knowledge-based or contract employees who provide enhanced organizational flexibility to offset their limited flexibility (Lepak *et al.*, 2003). Viewed in combination, these results provide support for Tsui *et al.*'s (1995) argument that there is no single best way to deploy employees to enhance firm performance and, more broadly, it shows the importance of examining employment systems through an architectural framework.

Implications for HRM

The aforementioned studies offer insight into how different knowledge stocks—or human capital—are managed and how they might affect firm performance. They also provide a model for managing the HR configurations in a way that is consistent with the uniqueness and value of employee knowledge and skills, employment mode, and employment relationship. In that regard, the architectural perspective offers a framework to understand how employees are managed in a firm based on their strategic contributions.

However, while focusing on knowledge stocks provides a foundation for understanding the role of human capital as a potential source of a firm's core competencies (Grant, 1996), knowledge flows are necessary for creating a firm's dynamic capabilities to renew and integrate knowledge (Teece *et al.*, 1997). Managing current knowledge and human capital is certainly an important component for an architectural model of HRM. However, managing the creation of new knowledge and shared knowledge may be equally important and, perhaps, more important to understand how to leverage existing knowledge for competitive success (Kang *et al.*, 2003). In the remainder of this chapter, we extend the architectural perspective to incorporate social capital as a critical component to managing the flow of knowledge between employees to serve as a source of competitive advantage.

AN ARCHITECTURAL PERSPECTIVE ON KNOWLEDGE FLOWS

Understanding how different knowledge stocks are configured and managed within a firm is a potentially important first step in understanding how configurations of people's human capital (knowledge stocks) can be a source of competitive advantage for firms. However, these points alone do not reveal much about how employee knowledge can be managed to combine and move knowledge across the organization as a whole to leverage knowledge as a source of future value creation and competitive advantage.

From the standpoint of organizational learning and innovation, the architectural framework needs to be augmented to reflect how knowledge flows across employees within firms (see Figure 4.3). Just as different employees are characterized as having different knowledge stocks, they are also likely to be characterized by different knowledge flows across employee groups. To date, there has been very little work that addresses how HR practices can facilitate the accumulation and integration of knowledge within, as well as across, firms (Leana and Van Buren, 1999). Yet, as we discuss below, the implications for strategic management in this capacity are very clear.

Managing knowledge flows through social capital

Scholars from a variety of perspectives have argued that social capital may play an important role in knowledge flows by providing a mechanism to share and combine the distributed

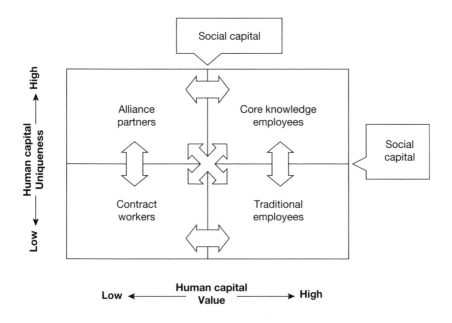

Figure 4.3 *The architecture of knowledge-exchange relationships*

knowledge among organizational members (e.g., Nahapiet and Ghoshal, 1998; Tsai and Ghoshal, 1998; Adler and Kwon, 2002; Tsai, 2002). These scholars posit three significant dimensions of social capital that facilitate knowledge flow—structural, affective, and cognitive. The *structural* dimension refers to the pattern of interpersonal networks as well as the strength of ties among related parties. Through social interactions, employees may gain access to other employees' knowledge that allows them to transcend structural boundaries within an organization as well as outside an organization to find what they need (Kanter, 1983). Second, the *affective* dimension refers to elements of trust and reciprocity. Simply stated, when there is trust in social interactions among employees, they may be more willing to share knowledge without worrying that they will be exploited (Bradach and Eccles, 1989). Third, the *cognitive* dimension of social capital refers to the shared understanding and mental models of how parties interact with one another, thus influencing the clarity and economy of communications among employees (Tsai and Ghoshal, 1998).

These three dimensions of social capital (structural, affective, and cognitive) are conceptually linked with parallel components of the architectural perspective (employment mode, employment relationship, and human capital). We discuss these below in order to reveal how social capital might facilitate knowledge flow within an architectural perspective (cf., Kang *et al.*, 2003).

Employment modes and the structural dimension

In addition to influencing the HRM practices used by organizations to acquire, build, and/or retain their human capital, employment modes also influence the opportunities and patterns of interactions among the four employee groups. For example, decisions regarding which employees are internalized versus externalized are likely to be directly related to the extent to which these different groups of employees are able, and likely, to interact. External employees have different organizational memberships so there may be relatively few formal mechanisms (e.g., shared organizational identity or shared geographic location) for frequent and dense interaction with internal employees. In contrast, internal employees (i.e., core and traditional) share membership in the same organization and are more likely to be co-located; thus, providing greater opportunity for frequent and redundant interactions than with external employee groups. This said, it is conceivable that while structural interactions among internal employees and various external groups may be developed over time, without strategic interventions they are likely to remain comparatively sparse and fail to fully develop as much as among employees within the same firm. Indeed, Dyer and Nobeoka (2000) found that strong and dense knowledge sharing networks were developed between internal employment groups at Toyota and their suppliers through strategic interventions supporting these types of relationships.

Employment relationships and the affective dimension

Beyond the structure of employment arrangements, employment relationships also affect the affective component among employees themselves (Rousseau, 1995). This establishes a direct link between employment relationships and the affective elements underlying social relations (cf., Kang *et al.*, 2003). For example, Lepak and Snell (1999) noted that when core employees and alliance partners collaborate in the utilization of their knowledge stocks, a synergistic value might be realized for both. Accordingly, external parties may develop dyadic trust (trust between individuals based on past interaction) to facilitate knowledge sharing and simultaneously suppress opportunistic behavior to withhold knowledge from one another (Kale *et al.*, 2000).

While dyadic trust may be found among internal employee groups, the type of trust most prevalent among internal employees is a more generalized trust (trust between individuals based on reciprocity expectations derived from shared norms or organizational identity). Whether traditional or core, Rousseau (1995) noted that most employment relationships that are internalized carry with them an expectation of conformity to norms. In these instances, individuals are more likely to accord respect and discretion to fellow employees based upon shared norms and identity. This means that there is less of a need for dyadic trust, which requires commitment and investment between the inter-acting parties. Furthermore, if the interacting employee groups represent different departments, functions, or business units of the firm, they may have a greater need for a more generalized trust that does not require large investments in the individual relationship, and that allows for maintaining a denser network than might be found between internal and external employees. Thus, there are two main types of trust that might exist across employee groups, and each may depend on the relationships those employees have with the organization.

Human capital and the cognitive dimension

Not only is it important for employees to interact and develop relationships, they also need to understand one another in order to share and apply each other's knowledge. As employees interact, they often develop a shared language of expertise, codes, and the like as well as how to communicate and exchange knowledge. One form of this shared cognitive dimension is referred to as common "component knowledge" (Matusik and Hill, 1998), which allows people to understand one another's domain knowledge deeply enough to transfer, assimilate, and apply it. For example, alliance partners tend to have specialized knowledge that, while perhaps not directly related, is complementary to a firm's core employees (Lepak and Snell, 1999). They jointly work with core knowledge-workers to conduct particular tasks or projects. Those common task experiences are likely to facilitate the development of common component knowledge between alliance partners and core knowledge employees over time (Cicourel, 1973; Brown and Duguid, 1991, 2001). The other shared cognitive dimension that can exist is known as common "architectural knowledge," which allows people of different specializations to understand how the different components fit together (Matusik and Hill, 1998). An example would be the interaction of knowledge-workers and traditional employees who are likely to share common architectural knowledge, which is most likely due to the fact that they both understand the processes and coordination mechanisms in the firm.

Thus, common component knowledge might be found or be more appropriate across certain employee groups, while common architectural knowledge is more likely found in other situations. In other words, both forms of shared cognition among employees contribute in different ways to the flow of knowledge.

Knowledge-exchange relationships in an architectural perspective

Because social capital is not one-dimensional, it is important to understand the patterns among structural, affective, and cognitive elements as they relate to facilitating knowledge flows. The challenge for HRM is to understand how these social capital dimensions should be related and managed to facilitate knowledge creation. Knowledge creation can be broken down into two separate categories: (1) the pursuit of new knowledge, which is often referred to as exploratory learning; and (2) the recombination or deepening of existing knowledge, or exploitative learning (March, 1991). Both types of knowledge creation are considered necessary, but require two separate forms of learning by the firm—thus creating a need for unique HR systems to manage each. Researchers focusing on knowledge creation have suggested that these two forms of learning may stem from two different types of activities: (1) entrepreneurial activities among employees that result in the creation of new knowledge; and (2) cooperative activities among employees that involve the refining and recombining of existing knowledge in new ways (cf., Schumpeter, 1934; March, 1991). While the notion of entrepreneurial and cooperative activities is fairly straightforward, the manner by which HRM may foster these two types of activities is less well understood. Kang *et al.* (2003) suggested that there are two dominant and distinct relational HR archetypes that facilitate or build upon the realization of entrepreneurial and cooperative activities among employees (see Figure 4.4).

67

Structural	Weak/sparse interactions (Granovetter, 1973; Burt, 1992)	Strong/dense interactions (Coleman, 1988; Krackhardt, 1992; Uzzi, 1997)
Affective	Resilient dyadic trust (Putnam, 1993; Leana and Van Buren, 1999)	Generalized trust (Sheppard and Tuchinsky, 1996; Jones and George, 1998; Lean and Van Buren, 1999)
Cognitive	Common component knowledge (Cohen and Levinthal, 1990; Grant, 1996; Matusik and Hill, 1998; Szulanski, 1995)	Common architectural knowledge (Nonaka, 1991; Weick and Roberts, 1993; Matusik and Hill, 1998)
	Entrepreneurial archetype	**Cooperative archetype**

Figure 4.4 *Knowledge-exchange relationships*

At one extreme, a *cooperative archetype* is designed to refine and recombine in new ways the existing knowledge stocks that are dispersed across different employee groups within an HR architecture. Essentially, a cooperative archetype focuses on linking and leveraging different sources of existing knowledge in ways that may stimulate new knowledge. These knowledge flow activities may be facilitated through specific, interrelated aspects of the social capital dimensions. With regard to the structural dimension of social capital, frequent interactions with numerous people in other employment groups may facilitate the exchange of knowledge necessary to stimulate new and creative ideas. With regard to the affective dimension of social capital, employee groups that share generalized trust—trust based on norms of reciprocity—are more likely to share personal knowledge, regardless of a direct personal relationship. Doing so enables the recombination and refinement of employee knowledge already in existence in or outside of the firm. With regard to the cognitive dimension of social capital, when employees share an architectural understanding of how things fit together, they are more likely to exploit and tweak existing knowledge or ways of doing things. This is because their focus is more on the big picture that allows them to look at minor improvements in terms of efficiency or more surface level changes that affect the interconnection of all the components.

Looking at the pattern among these three characteristics of social capital, it reinforces the notion of cooperative activities among employees. Thus, cooperative dimensions of social capital are logically consistent with the efforts of employees to refine and recombine existing knowledge among closely affiliated employee groups.

At the other extreme, the *entrepreneurial archetype* is designed to create knowledge through the exchange and combination of new knowledge from different employee groups. Whereas cooperative archetypes are utilized to realize the extension of existing knowledge into new possibilities, an entrepreneurial archetype is oriented toward the creation of new knowledge from disparate, and previously unrelated knowledge sources. Like the cooperative archetype, there are also specific aspects of social capital that facilitate this type of knowledge flow. First, the structural dimension of social interactions is based not on ongoing and frequent interactions but on sparse and non-redundant networks of employees, where they are in a better position to identify new and creative ways of linking these different sources of knowledge. Second, the social connections are based on dyadic trust among some of the parties rather than generalized trust over the whole unit. This means that people with dyadic trust relationships are able to share unique and new knowledge that might not normally be found in generalized trust relationships found through common employers. And finally, relationships among group members in this instance are more likely to have common component knowledge that allows them to combine deeper and more radically new knowledge. This more loosely connected system is consistent with the entrepreneurial requirements of an organization's efforts to share and develop novel and diverse knowledge stocks in new or unfamiliar domains.

The two archetypes discussed above are typically found within the HR architecture. Kang *et al.* (2003), for example, suggested that relationships among internal partners within an organization most likely reflect the characteristics of a cooperative archetype, while external partnerships more likely reflect the entrepreneurial archetype. More specifically, they argue that internal partnerships tend to be more structurally redundant, based on generalized trust and organization norms, connected and integrated not by common expertise, but by the architectural knowledge of organizational coordination. In contrast, connections with external partners typically are more sparsely populated and loosely connected networks, based on dyadic trust born through personal experience, and connected via common areas of expertise.

Human resource implications for knowledge flows

If we recognize that relational archetypes (social capital) play a fundamental role in facilitating knowledge flow, and that these two alternative archetypes involve fundamentally different employee behaviors, then it is likely that different HR practices will be appropriate for each (cf., Kogut and Zander, 1992; Kang *et al.*, 2003) (see Figure 4.5).

The theoretical development of alternative HR configurations takes into account several premises. First, HR practices typically focus on managing human capital (i.e., ways to develop and utilize individual skills and competencies that will enable the employee to optimally contribute to the firm) (e.g., Snell and Dean, 1992), while recent research shows the importance of managing the exchange relationship (social capital) between employees (Nahapiet and Ghoshal, 1998; Leana and Van Buren, 1999; Dyer and Nobeoka, 2000; Takeishi, 2001). Taking this into account, HRM researchers have discussed and identified various HR practices that are focused more on helping employees develop and utilize social relationships with each other rather than developing or utilizing their own skills (e.g., Batt

HR practices for knowledge				HR practices for knowledge flows		
Commitment	**Productivity**	**Collaborative**	**Contractual**	**Cooperative**	**Entrepreneurial**	
Work structure: – flexible job description	**Work structure:** – standardized jobs	**Work structure:** – cross functional teams – skill-based job design	**Work structure:** – contractual agreement – standardized jobs	**Work structure:** – team-based production – job rotations – expanded staffing patterns	**Work structure:** – flexible work design – temporary project teams – cross-functional teams	**Structural**
Incentives: – multiple sources for incentives – extensive benefits – knowledge-based pay programs	**Incentives:** – results-based incentives – individual incentives	**Incentives:** – relationship-based rewards – group incentives	**Incentives:** – task-related – outsourced	**Incentives:** – clan-fostering activities – communities of practice – multi-rater feedback – participative goal setting – rights of redress	**Incentives:** – individual incentives – pay-for-knowledge – pay-for-relationships	**Affective**
Skill improvement: – hiring based on potential to learn – internal promotion – continuous training	**Skill improvement:** – short-term orientation – various recruiting sources – selective hiring	**Skill improvement:** – team-building practices – developmental relationships	**Skill improvement:** – output-based feedback – outsourced	**Skill improvement:** – long-term employment – extensive orientation and socialization – mentoring – on-the-job training – group training	**Skill improvement:** – multiple career development – cross training – know-how-reports	**Cognitive**

Figure 4.5 *Extended HR practices for knowledge flow*

and Moynihan, 2002; Gant *et al.*, 2002; Gittell, 2000). In other words, while most HR practices might influence the way employees interact with one another, certain practices might be designed for, and directly encourage, employees to interact with others in a certain way. For example, HR practices applied to core employees may encourage them to develop more cooperative exchange relationships with employees in other groups.

Second, the configurational approach implies that HR practices reinforce and complement each other as a coherent system to improve organizational performance (Wright and Snell, 1991; Snell and Youndt, 1995; Huselid, 1995; Delery and Doty, 1996; Delaney and Huselid, 1996; Ichniowski *et al.*, 1997; Becker and Huselid, 1998; Guthrie, 2001). This means that there likely exists a group of practices that support one another in building exchange relationships that support both exploratory and exploitative learning.

Third, we argue that there are two distinct configurations of HR practices that are applicable to almost all possible exchange relationships within an architectural perspective and focus on managing across employee groups rather than managing all employees within a particular employee group. While certain exchange relationships across different employee groups might already exist within an organization's architecture, the two HR configurations we discuss may be strategically applied in conjunction with existing practices to create or enhance cooperative-type knowledge recombination or entrepreneurial-type knowledge renewal.

Related HR practices supporting relational archetypes (social capital) are complementary to—or supplemental to—HR practices designed to support human capital. In other words, these configurations of practices can usually be applied over the existing practices used to manage each employee group. Where applicable, by adding such practices to different employee groups, a firm may be able to facilitate greater knowledge flow. Specifically, for a certain knowledge-exchange relationship to be encouraged, the corresponding HR practices need to be applied to only one of the interacting groups. For example, a firm might apply cooperative HR practices to a certain group of core employees to encourage them to develop stronger relationships with their external alliance partners.

HR practices for the cooperative archetype

Researchers have proposed a wide array of HR configurations that are comprised of reinforcing HR practices that may lead to organizational performance. Despite their differences, a common theme is that an effective HR system must simultaneously focus on developing the skills of employees, motivating employees to use their skills via incentive systems, and provide a work environment that allows them to do so (MacDuffie, 1995). HR configurations geared toward the facilitation of cooperative knowledge-exchange relationships also consist of HR practices directly focused on work structure, incentive, and skill improvement practices consistent with the three dimensions of social capital.

Work structure. The structural dimension of frequent and dense connections found in cooperative exchange relationships may be developed and maintained by interdependent work structures. For example, team-based production that requires reciprocal interdependence among employee cohorts can help to enhance their interactions, which leads to mutual adjustment and close coordination (Delaney and Huselid, 1996; Gittell, 2000). Similarly, job rotations across employee groups can strengthen the ties and facilitate knowledge transfer. Dyer and Nobeoka (2000), for example, discussed how rotational schemes used by Toyota with their external suppliers encouraged knowledge sharing and strengthened their network ties (cf., Nonaka and Takeuchi, 1995; Gant et al., 2002). Another example of how interdependent work structures might influence dense connections is found in the expansion of staffing patterns to include external partners (Pennings et al., 1998).

Incentives. Generalized trust found in the affective dimension may be enhanced through clan-fostering activities that strengthen shared goals and values (Goold and Quinn, 1990; Snell, 1992). For example, selecting partners based on organizational fit or alignment with organization values helps to ensure that there are common motives and expectations across employee groups. Snell (1992) and Snell and Youndt (1995) found that this is especially important in those situations where behavioral protocols cannot be spelled out in advance. To support this, socialization programs and efforts to build communities of practice, reinforce the idea that partners stand to gain more by working together than they do operating in isolation.

71

Generalized trust may also be reinforced through performance management systems that emphasize collective achievements (Leana and Van Buren, 1999). For example, team-based appraisal systems and multi-rater (360 degree) feedback have been shown to strengthen the sense of contextual performance and mutual reliance (Day *et al.*, 2001). Similarly, participative goal-setting, rights of redress, formal grievance procedures, and the like, are all ways to more broadly enhance organizational support that encourages generalized trust (Gittell, 2000; Orlikowski, 2002; Wayne *et al.*, 1997).

Skill improvement. The cognitive aspect of cooperative exchange relationships may be developed through staffing practices that encourage different employee groups to focus on broader organizational issues. For example, long-term employment contracts, which not only increase commitment and loyalty, may also prevent premature endings to valuable learning networks (Dyer and Nobeoka, 2000).

Training and development practices also provide effective mechanisms to build broader architectural knowledge among different employee groups. Extensive orientation and socialization programs are typical development practices that help employees understand and internalize unique values, goals, history, and culture of the firm and share tacit knowledge including cognitive schema (Feldman, 1989; Nonaka and Takeuchi, 1995). Similarly, mentoring and on-the-job training enable them to build strong social and cognitive connections (Mullen and Noe, 1999; Gittell, 2000; Orlikowski, 2002). Other organizational development techniques such as group training can help to expand and integrate the mental models of different employee groups (cf., Wright and Snell, 1991; Nonaka, 1994).

HR practices for the entrepreneurial archetype

In contrast to the cooperative archetype, HR practices supporting entrepreneurial exchange relationships are geared toward creating an infrastructure that not only provides the flexibility needed for knowledge-exchange relationship creation, but the mechanisms that encourage and reinforce its development. Those HR practices include work structures that might facilitate structural aspects of social capital, incentives for affective dimensions, and skill development focusing on cognitive aspects of social capital.

Work structure. Certain work structures are likely to affect the structural aspects of entrepreneurial exchange relationships. For example, the design of flexible work structures and temporary project teams may help to engender diverse and transitory connections between different employee groups. In cases where jobs are broadly defined and allow for discretion and self-direction, employees are likely to build exchange relationships with a variety of partners in order to address problems and opportunities (Lepak and Snell, 1999; Gant *et al.*, 2002). Also, cross-functional teams provide employees with opportunities to interact with colleagues in different functions and practices and thus to access various knowledge domains and expertise within the firm (Clark *et al.*, 2002).

Incentives. Dyadic trust might be strongly influenced by the focus of incentive systems. For example, individual incentives may stimulate individuals' motives to build varied relationships of trust for exploratory learning (Edmondson, 1999). Accordingly, Leana and Van Buren (1999) noted that individual incentive systems might discourage social loafing or the free-rider effect (a problem inherent in group-based incentives). The potential advantages of individual incentives may be best leveraged when incentives are accompanied with the acquisition of knowledge or new ideas (e.g., pay-for-knowledge or pay-for-reputation), which may motivate core employees to acquire a broad set of knowledge and skills by various social connections within firms (Youndt *et al.*, 1996; Hargadon and Sutton, 1997; Gant *et al.*, 2002). These types of incentives may institutionalize an organizational culture emphasizing "creative abrasion" (Leonard-Barton, 1995), which stimulates conflicting ideas in order to productively link them to performance (Nonaka and Konno, 1998).

Skill improvement. Common component knowledge is a cognitive aspect of social relationships that might be developed through skill improvement practices. For example, multiple-career development practices (e.g., generalist or boundaryless careers) are often used to develop trans-specialist or multi-skill knowledge by helping employees to experience various job opportunities beyond the boundaries of a single expertise (Defillippi and Arthur, 1994). Such knowledge may also be enhanced through group training (Moreland and Myaskovsky, 2000) and cross-training or job rotations (Hargadon and Sutton, 1997). Such practices might encourage employees to develop a common area of interest or know-how with various other employee groups in order to share more complex knowledge outside of their traditional knowledge domains. Another example of how firms develop greater common component knowledge is through the development of archival-based mechanisms such as know-how reports and electronic databases to retain component-specific knowledge that improves transactive memory (i.e., shared knowledge of each other's expertise) (Takeishi, 2002).

By looking at how HR configuration might facilitate relational archetypes we can better understand the potential role HR plays in different knowledge-creation activities. Such practices might prove useful in developing or redirecting existing archetypes found within a firm.

CONCLUSION

The primary objective of this chapter was to create an integrative framework that brings together current thinking about knowledge stocks and flows and how they can be managed from an architectural perspective. Using the characteristics of human capital (value and uniqueness), we reviewed how employee knowledge stocks are identified and managed differently in the firm. Combining that with social capital theory, we extended the architectural perspective to show how knowledge stocks might be recombined and renewed through two distinct types of knowledge-exchange relationships. We also discussed two HR configurations that might specifically be applied to the development of these relationships.

This chapter also addressed the ongoing question of how the tensions of exploratory and exploitative learning might be balanced in a firm through HR practices. Part of this tension comes from the fact that management researchers have identified very few mechanisms (incentives, structures, etc.) to avoid what Levinthal and March (1993) describe as the "myopia of learning" where organizations feel that they can focus only on one or the other forms of knowledge-exchange activities. We presented a potential solution for future empirical research by arguing that firms might apply cooperative HR practices to one group of employees while simultaneously applying entrepreneurial HR practices geared toward another group of employees under the same organizational umbrella.

We believe that the framework offered in this chapter provides several avenues for future research. Obviously, the ideas presented in this chapter are conceptual and research is needed to determine the salience of the different social capital dimensions and how they correspond with the architectural dimensions of human capital, employment mode, and employment relationships. Related to this, while we anticipate that distinct HR systems are more appropriate for each type of knowledge-exchange relationship (cooperative and entrepreneurial), we do not know if differences in how firms structure their HR systems for each archetype translates into differences in employee and organizational performance. Moreover, when the focus is on managing knowledge flows in addition to knowledge stocks, there may be implications for different types of performance for each knowledge-exchange relationship. It may be the case that cooperative relationships are strongly related to some indicators of performance (e.g., product extensions, new market penetration), while entrepreneurial relationships are more strongly related to other performance metrics such as new markets and new products/services. Moreover, the relative level of performance may be enhanced (or diminished) based on the extent to which firms align their HR systems to realize cooperative or entrepreneurial archetypes These two exchange relationships, and their associated HR systems, are distinctly focused on different types of value creation and research is needed that examines how these configurations are uniquely related to important organizational outcomes.

Second, future research might also help understand whether the archetypes are exclusive to internal or external relationships. For instance, can one group of employees have both cooperative and entrepreneurial relationships? Based on social capital theory, we assume that more cooperative relationships will be found internally and more entrepreneurial types found with outside partners. Yet, other research has suggested that the opposite can actually happen. Dyer and Nobeoka (2000), for instance, found that relationships of cooperation, strong ties, and generalized trust were developed between Toyota core groups and their suppliers. Similarly, Uzzi (1997) showed how strong cooperative knowledge-exchange relationships between external business partners developed in the New York City garment industry. Thus, what is more common and what is more effective become two pertinent questions.

Third, as we assumed in this chapter that these practices might be applied simultaneously with existing practices, future research might address how these relationship-based HR practices might actually be implemented with existing practices and the possible effects of these overlaps. For example, do some of these relationship-based HR practices send conflicting messages to employees on what type of relations to value? Also, how cost effective is it to implement multiple HR practices within the firm? Likewise, are there compromises that need to be made in terms of taking out or adding in certain HR practices?

In conclusion, as firms turn more toward people and their knowledge stocks to create a competitive advantage, it is important to remember that the sustainability of these advantages may be dependent upon how they renew these stocks. Many avenues emerge when we view the dynamics of knowledge in a firm. The architectural perspective provides a focus and clarity to how both knowledge stocks and flows should be viewed and researched. Hopefully, this focus will offer greater understanding of the importance of people in today's organizations.

REFERENCES

Adler, P. S. and Kwon, S.-W. (2002) Social capital: Prospects for a new concept. *Academy of Management Review*, 27: 17–40.

Arthur, J. B. (1992) The link between business strategy and industrial relations systems in American steel minimills. *Industrial and Labor Relations Review*, 45: 488–506.

Arthur, J. B. (1994) Effects of human resource systems on manufacturing performance and turnover. *Academy of Management Journal*, 37: 670–687.

Barney, J. (1991) Firm resources and sustained competitive advantage. *Journal of Management*, 17: 99–120.

Baron, J. N., Davis-Blake, A., and Bielby, W. T. (1986) The structure of opportunity: How promotion ladders vary within and among organizations. *Administrative Science Quarterly*, 31: 248–273.

Batt, R. and Moynihan, L. (2002) The viability of alternative call center production models. *Human Resource Management Journal*, 12: 14–34.

Becker, B. E. and Huselid, M. A. (1998) High performance work systems and firm performance: A synthesis of research and managerial implications. *Research in Personnel and Human Resource Management*, 16: 53–101.

Becker, G. S. (1976) *The Economic Approach to Human Behavior*. Chicago: University of Chicago Press.

Becker, G. S. and Gerhart, B. (1996) The impact of human resource management on organizational performance: Progress and prospects. *Academy of Management Journal*, 39: 779–801.

Bradach, J. L. and Eccles, R. G. (1989) Price, authority, and trust: From ideal types to plural forms. *Annual Review of Sociology*, 15: 97.

Brown, J. S. and Duguid, P. (1991) Organizational learning and communities of practice: Toward a unified view of working, learning and innovation. *Organization Science*, 2: 40–57.

Brown, J. S. and Duguid, P. (2001) Knowledge and organization: A social-practice perspective. *Organization Science*, 12: 198–213.

Burt, R. S. (1992) *Structural Holes: The Social Structure of Competition*. Cambridge, MA: Harvard University Press.

Cicourel, A. V. (1973) *Cognitive Sociology*. Harmondsworth: Penguin Books.

Clark, M. A., Amundson, S. D., and Cardy, R. L. (2002) Cross-functional team decision-making and learning outcomes: A qualitative illustration. *Journal of Business and Management*, 8: 217–236.

Coase, R. H. (1937) The nature of the firm. *Economica*, 4: 386–405.

Cohen, W. M. and Levinthal, D. A. (1990) Absorptive capacity: A new perspective on learning and innovation. *Administrative Science Quarterly*, 35: 128–152.

Cohen, Y. and Pfeffer, J. (1986) Organizational hiring standards. *Administrative Science Quarterly*, 31: 1–24.

Coleman, J. S. (1988) Social capital in the creation of human capital. *American Journal of Sociology*, 94: 95–120.

Conner, K. R. and Prahalad, C. K. (1996) A resource based theory of the firm: Knowledge versus opportunism. *Organization Science*, 7: 477–501.

Davis-Blake, A. and Uzzi, B. (1993) Determinants of employment externalization: A study of temporary workers and independent contractors. *Administrative Science Quarterly*, 38: 195–223.

Day, E. A., Winfred, A., and Gettman, D. (2001) Knowledge structures and the acquisition of a complex skill. *Journal of Applied Psychology*, 86: 1022.

Defillippi, R. J. and Arthur, M. B. (1994) The boundaryless career: A competency-based perspective. *Journal of Organizational Behavior*, 15: 307–324.

Delaney, J. T. and Huselid, M. A. (1996) The impact of human resource management practices on perceptions of organizational performance. *Academy of Management Journal*, 39: 949–969.

Delery, J. E. and Doty, D. H. (1996) Modes of theorizing in strategic human resource management: Tests of universalistic, contingency, and configurational performance predictions. *Academy of Management Journal*, 39: 802–835.

Dierickx, I. and Cool, K. (1989) Asset stock accumulation and sustainability of competitive advantage. *Management Science*, 35: 1504–1513.

Doeringer, P. and Piore, M. (1971) *Internal Labor Markets and Manpower Analysis*. Lexington, MA: D.C. Heath.

Dyer, J. H. (1996) Does governance matter? Keiretsu alliances and asset specificity as sources of Japanese competitive advantage. *Organization Science*, 7: 649–666.

Dyer, J. H. and Nobeoka, K. (2000) Creating and managing a high-performance knowledge-sharing network: The Toyota case. *Strategic Management Journal*, 21: 345–367.

Edmondson, A. (1999) Psychological safety and learning behavior in network teams. *Administrative Science Quarterly*, 44: 350–383.

Eisenhardt, K. M. and Martin, J. A. (2000) Dynamic capabilities: What are they? *Strategic Management Journal*, 21: 1105–1121.

Etzioni, A. (1988) *The Moral Dimensions: Toward a New Economics*. New York: Free Press.

Feldman, D. C. (1989) Socialization, resocialization, and training: Reframing the research agenda. In I. L. Goldstein (ed.), *Training and Development in Organizations*. San Francisco, CA: Jossey-Bass.

Gant, J., Ichniowski, C., and Shaw, K. (2002) Social capital and organizational change in high-involvement and traditional work organizations. *Journal of Economics and Management Strategy*, 11: 289–328.

Gittell, J. H. (2000) Organizing work to support relational co-ordination. *International Journal of Human Resource Management*, 11(3): 517–539.

Goold, M. and Quinn, J. J. (1990) The paradox of strategic controls. *Strategic Management Journal*, 11: 43–57.

Granovetter, M. S. (1973) The strength of weak ties. *American Journal of Sociology*, 78: 1360–1380.

Grant, R. M. (1996) Toward a knowledge-based theory of the firm. *Strategic Management Journal*, 17(S2): 109–122.

Guthrie, J. P. (2001) High involvement work practices, turnover and productivity: Evidence from New Zealand. *Academy of Management Journal*, 44: 180–190.

Hargadon, A. and Sutton, R. (1997) Technology brokering and innovation in a product development firm. *Administrative Science Quarterly*, 42: 716–749.

Hitt, M. A., Bierman, L., Shimizu, K., and Kochhar, R. (2001) Direct and moderating effects of human capital on strategy and performance in professional service firms: A resource-based perspective. *Academy of Management Journal*, 44(1): 13–16.

Huselid, M. A. (1995) The impact of human resource management practices on turnover, productivity, and corporate financial performance. *Academy of Management Journal*, 38: 635–672.

Ichniowski, C., Shaw, K., and Prennushi, G. (1997) The effects of human resource management practices on productivity: A study of steel finishing lines. *The American Economic Review*, 87: 291–313.

Itami, H. (1987) *Mobilizing Invisible Assets*. Cambridge, MA: Harvard University Press.

Jones, G. R. and George, J. M. (1998) The experience and evolution of trust: Implications for cooperation and teamwork. *Academy of Management Review*, 23: 531–546.

Kale, P., Singh, H., and Perlmutter, H. (2000) Learning and protection of proprietary assets in strategic alliances: Building relational capital. *Strategic Management Journal*, 21: 217–238.

Kang, S.-C., Morris, S. S. and Snell, S. A. (2003) Relational archetypes, organizational learning, and value creation: Extending the human resource architecture. Working paper: CAHRS, Cornell University.

Kanter, R. M. (1983) *The Change Masters: Innovation for Productivity in the American Corporation*. New York: Simon and Schuster.

Koch, M. J. and McGrath, R. G. (1996) Improving labor productivity: Human resource management policies do matter. *Strategic Management Journal*, 17: 335–354.

Kochan, T. and Osterman, P. (1994) *The Mutual Gains Enterprise*. Boston. MA: Harvard Business School Press.

Kochan, T., Katz, H., and McKersie, R. (1986) *The Transformation Of American Industrial Relations*. New York: Basic Books.

Kogut, B. and Zander, U. (1992) Knowledge of the firm, combinative capabilities, and the replication of technology. *Organization Science*, 3: 383–397.

Krackhardt, D. (1992) The strength of strong ties. In N. Nohria & R. G. Eccles (eds), *Network and Organizations: Structure, Form and Action*. Boston, MA: Harvard Business School Press, pp. 216–239.

Lawler, E. E. (1992) *The Ultimate Advantage: Creating the High Involvement Organization*. San Francisco, CA: Jossey-Bass.

Lawler, E. E., Morhrman, S. A., and Ledford, G. E. (1995) *Creating High Performance Organizations: Practices and Results of Employee Involvement and Total Quality Management in Fortune 1000 Companies*. San Francisco, CA: Jossey-Bass.

Lawrence, P. R. and Lorsch, J. W. (1973) *Organization and Environment: Managing differentiation and integration*. Boston, MA: Harvard Business School Press.

Leana, C. R. and Van Buren, H. J. III (1999) Organizational social capital and employment practices. *Academy of Management Review*, 24: 538–555.

Leonard-Barton, D. (1995) *Wellsprings of Knowledge: Building and sustaining the sources of innovation*. Boston, MA: Harvard Business School Press.

Lepak, D. P. and Snell, S. A. (1999) The human resource architecture: Toward a theory of human capital allocation and development. *Academy of Management Review*, 24: 31–48.

Lepak, D. P. and Snell, S. A. (2002) Examining the human resource architecture: The relationship among human capital, employment, and human resource configurations. *Journal of Management*, 28: 517–543.

Lepak, D. P., Takeuchi, R., and Snell, S. A. (2003) Employment flexibility and firm performance: Examining the interaction effects of employment mode, environmental dynamism, and technological intensity. *Journal of Management*, 29: 681–703.

Levine, D. (1995) *Reinventing the Workplace: How Business and Employees Can Both Win*. Washington, DC: Brookings Institute.

Levinthal, B. and March, J. G. (1993) The myopia of learning. *Strategic Management Journal*, 14: 95–112.

MacDuffie, J. P. (1995) Human resource bundles and manufacturing performance: Organizational logic and flexible production systems in the world auto industry. *Industrial and Labor Relations Review*, 48: 197–221.

Mahoney, T. A. (1989) Employment compensation planning and strategy. In L. R. Gomex-Mejia (ed.), *Compensation and Benefits*, ASPA/BNA Series, no. 3. Washington, DC: Bureau of National Affairs.

Mangum, G., Mayall, D., and Nelson, K. (1985) The temporary help industry: A response to the dual internal labor market. *Industrial and Labor Relations Review*, 38: 599–611.

March, J. A. and Simon, H. A. (1958) *Organizations*. New York: Wiley.

March, J. G. (1991) Exploration and exploitation in organizational learning. *Organization Science*, 2: 71–87.

Mathieu, J. E., Tannenbaum, S. I., and Salas, E. (1992) Influences of individual and situational characteristics on measures of training effectiveness. *Academy of Management Journal*, 35: 828–847.

Matusik, S. F. and Hill, C. W. (1998) The utilization of contingent work, knowledge creation, and competitive advantage. *Academy of Management Journal*, 23: 680–697.

Miles, R. and Snow, C. C. (1984) Designing strategic human resource systems. *Organizational Dynamics*, 13: 36–52.

Moreland, R. L. and Myaskovsky, L. (2000) Exploring the performance benefits of group training: Transactive memory or improved communication? *Organizational Behavior and Human Decision Processes*, 82: 117–133.

Mullen, E. and Noe, R. A. (1999) The mentoring information exchange: When do mentors seek information from their protégés? *Journal of Organizational Behavior*, 20: 233–242.

Nadler, D. A., Gerstein, M. S., and Shaw, R. B. (1992) *Organizational Architecture: Designing for Changing Organizations*. San Francisco, CA: Jossey-Bass.

Nahapiet, J. and Ghoshal, S. (1998) Social capital, intellectual capital, and the organizational advantage. *Academy of Management Review*, 23: 242–256.

Nonaka, I. (1991) The knowledge-creating company. *Harvard Business Review*, 69(6): 96–104.

Nonaka, I. (1994) A dynamic theory of organizational knowledge creation. *Organization Science*, 5: 14–37.

Nonaka, I. and Konno, N. (1998) The concept of "Ba": Building a foundation for knowledge creation. *California Management Review*, 40(3): 40–54.

Nonaka, I. and Takeuchi, H. (1995) *The Knowledge-Creating Company*. New York: Oxford University Press.

Orlikowski, W. J. (2002) Knowing in practice: Enacting a collective capability in distributed organizing. *Organization Science*, 13: 249–273.

Osterman, P. (1987) Choice of employment systems in internal labor markets. *Industrial Relations*, 26(1): 48–63.

Pennings, J. M., Lee, K., and van Witteloostuijn, A. (1998) Human capital, social capital and firm dissolution. *Academy of Management Journal*, 41: 425–440.

Perrow, C. (1967) A framework for the comparative analysis of organizations. *American Sociological Review*, 32: 194–208.

Pfeffer, J. (1994) *Competitive Advantage through People*. Boston, MA: Harvard Business School Press.

Pinfield, L. T. and Berner, M. F. (1994) Employment systems: Toward a coherent conceptualization of internal labor markets. In G.R. Ferris (ed.), *Research in Personnel and Human Resource Management*, Vol. 12: 41–78.

Porter, M. (1985) *Competitive Advantage: Creating and Sustaining Superior Performance*. New York: Free Press.

Putnam, R. (1993) The prosperous community: Social capital and public life. *The American Prospect*, 13: 35–42.

Quinn, J. B. (1992) The Intelligent enterprise a new paradigm. *The Executive*, 6: 48–64.

Rousseau, D. M. (1995) *Psychological Contracts in Organizations: Understanding Written and Unwritten Agreements*. Thousand Oaks, CA: Sage Publications.

Rousseau, D. M. and Parks, J. M. (1993) The contracts of individuals and organizations. In L. L. Cummings and B. M. Staw (eds), *Research in Organizational Behavior*, vol. 15: 1–43.

Schumpeter, J. A. (1934) *The Theory of Economic Development*. Cambridge, MA: Harvard University Press.

Sheppard, B. and Tuchinsky, M. (1996) Micro-OB and network organizations. In R. Kramer and T. Tyler (eds), *Trust in Organizations: Foundations of Theory and Research*. Thousand Oaks, CA: Sage Publications, pp. 140–165.

Snell, S. A. (1992) Control theory in strategic human resource management: The mediating effect of administrative information. *Academy of Management Journal*, 35: 292–328.

Snell, S. A. and Dean, J. W. Jr. (1992) Integrated manufacturing and human resource management: A human capital perspective. *Academy of Management Journal*, 35: 467–504.

Snell, S. A. and Youndt, M. A. (1995) Human resource management and firm performance: Testing a contingency model of executive controls. *Journal of Management*, 21: 711–737.

Snell, S. A., Lepak, D. P., and Youndt, M. A. (1999) Managing the architecture of intellectual capital: Implications for strategic human resource management. In G. R. Ferris (ed.), *Research in Personnel and Human Resources Management*, 17(S4): 175–193.

Snell, S. A., Shadur, M., and Wright, P. (2002) Human resources strategy: The era of our ways. In M. A. Hitt, R. E. Freeman, and J. S. Harrison (eds), *Handbook of Strategic Management*. Oxford: Blackwell Publishing.

Spender, J.-C. (1996) Making knowledge: The basis of a dynamic theory of the firm. *Strategic Management Journal*, 17(S2): 45–62.

Stewart, T. A. (1997) *Intellectual Capital: The New Wealth of Organizations*. New York: Bantam Dell Doubleday.

Szulanski, G. (1995) Unpacking stickiness: An empirical investigation of the barriers to transfer best practices inside the firm. *Academy of Management Proceedings*: 437–442.

Takeishi, A. (2001) Knowledge portioning in the interfirm division of labor: The case of automotive product development. *Organization Science*, 13: 321–329.

Teece, D. J., Pisano, G., and Shuen, A. (1997) Dynamic capabilities in strategic management. *Strategic Management Journal*, 18: 509–534.

Thompson, J. D. (1967) *Organizations in Action*. New York: McGraw-Hill.

Tsai, W. (2002) Social structure of "coopetition" within a multiunit organization: Coordination, competition, and intraorganizational knowledge sharing. *Organization Science*, 13: 37–53.

Tsai, W. and Ghoshal, N. (1998) Social capital and value creation: The role of intrafirm networks. *Academy of Management Journal*, 41: 464–477.

Tsui, A. S., Pearce, J. L., Porter, L. W., and Hite, J. P. (1995) Choice of employee-organization relationship: Influence of external and internal organizational factors. In G. R. Ferris (ed.), *Research in Personnel and Human Resources Management*. Greenwich, CT: JAI Press: 117–151.

Ulrich, D. and Lake, D. (1991) Organizational capability: Creating competitive advantage. *Academy of Management Exccutive*, 7: 77–92.

Uzzi, B. (1997) Social structure and competition in interfirm networks: The paradox of embeddedness. *Administrative Science Quarterly*, 42: 35–67.

Wayne, S. J., Shore, L. M., and Liden, R. C. (1997) Perceived organizational support and leader-member exchange: A social exchange perspective. *Academy of Management Journal*, 40: 82–111.

Weick, K. E. and Roberts, K. H. (1993) Collective mind in organizations: Heedful interrelating on flight decks. *Administrative Science Quarterly*, 38: 357–381.

Williamson, O. E. (1975) *Markets and Hierarchies: Analysis and Antitrust Implications*. New York: Free Press.

Wright, P. M. and McMahan, G. C. (1992) Theoretical perspectives for strategic human resource management. *Journal of Management*, 18: 295–320.

Wright, P. M. and Snell, S. A. (1991) Toward an integrative view of strategic human resource management. *Human Resource Management Review*, 1: 203–225.

Wright, P. M. and Snell, S. A. (1998) Toward a unifying framework for exploring fit and flexibility in strategic human resource management. *Academy of Management Review*, 23: 756–772.

Youndt, M. A., Snell, S. A., Dean, J. W. Jr., and Lepak, D. P. (1996) Human resource management, manufacturing strategy, and firm performance. *Academy of Management Journal*, 39: 836–866.

Chapter 5

Managing people in global markets

Colette A. Frayne

Developments during the last decades of the twentieth century have produced what may be termed an era of globalization. As business has continued to globalize, one of the most challenging aspects has focused on how a firm manages its human resources to sustain a competitive advantage.

Scholars from several disciplines are addressing these issues—coming at them from the perspective of strategy, cross-cultural management, international business, organizational theory, sociology, and human resource management (HRM) (Evans *et al.*, 2003). It appears that the traditional boundaries between academic disciplines and functional areas (e.g., HRM and strategy) are becoming more highly integrated and that the globalization of business is having a significant impact on human resource management and organizational performance (Dowling *et al.*, 1999). This chapter presents an integration of various approaches to designing and delivering courses on the topic of international human resource management. The key role of the international human resource management professional, implications for training and development in organizational settings, and future challenges regarding managing people in global markets are presented.

APPROACHES TO INTERNATIONAL HRM

The field of international HRM is generally characterized by three broad approaches (Dowling *et al.*, 1999). Initial approaches in this area emphasized a cross-cultural approach to examining human behavior in organizations. Another approach studies comparative HRM practices within and across countries. A third approach focuses on various functional aspects of HRM in multinational firms. However, a recent undertaking by Evans, Pucik and Barsoux (2002) integrates the orientations of strategy, culture, and HRM and presents international human resource management from a general management rather than a functional perspective. These authors suggest using an organizational systems perspective and argue that we must consider implementation of various HRM strategies within a context of conflicting needs of the organization, such as local responsiveness versus global integration, coordination versus control, and short-term profitability versus long-term innovation. This orientation expands the traditional curricular focus to be more comprehensive and interdisciplinary, drawing on multiple theoretical perspectives and clearly promoting a general management view. The theoretical rationale draws upon fit and contingency theory, the resource-based view of the firm, different contextual schools (comparative management, institutional theories from political science), while building links to social capitalism and network theories, as well as theories of organizational learning (Evans *et al.*, 2003). This approach clearly fits with recent demands of scholars and practitioners that international HRM be interdisciplinary and focused on contributing to firm performance.

A course or seminar designed to teach students and managers about human resource management in international settings has been identified at different schools as well as within different organizational settings. The course is usually designed to introduce students to the nature of managing human resources in international, multinational, global, and transnational firms. The purpose of the course is to provide students with an in-depth understanding of the basic problems inherent in international HRM. The intention is to either prepare the students for further work in the field or to give them a sound basis for understanding the international corporate dimensions of their own careers—sometimes both. Utilizing Evans *et al.*'s (2003) framework, I developed a course entitled *Managing People in Global Markets*. The overall framework stipulates that the relationship between HRM and organizational performance must be separated into three different faces or roles; namely, "the builder," "the aligner," and "the navigator" who steers through the dualities confronting organizations today. This course, which is comprised of case studies, readings, videos, and projects, has been designed to reflect an integrative strategic approach to understanding and practicing international HRM. Adaptations of this course and its foundations have also been introduced in organizational settings in an attempt to develop an awareness and capability among line managers, senior managers, and professionals within the international human resource management division.

CONCEPTUALIZING AND DESIGNING A COURSE/SEMINAR IN INTERNATIONAL HUMAN RESOURCE MANAGEMENT

The *Managing People in Global Markets* course is designed for students of international management and general management, rather than for specialists in human resource management. The course is intended to introduce students to the major issues associated with managing people in the context of the global marketplace. The emphasis in the course is upon skill development. In this regard, an effective manager must evidence fluency in the theories and concepts required to achieve congruence between an organization, its environment, its organizational systems and structures, the key tasks that the organization has to perform, and the organization's human, technological, financial, and other resources. Yet, conceptual skills alone are not sufficient. An effective manager must also evidence the skills required to manage the task, people, structures, and systems, as well as the ability to apply those skills to complex situations. This course uses the case study method as a primary pedagogical approach, in an effort to create an environment conducive to active and participative learning, as opposed to more passive lecture-based instructional approaches.

Pedagogical objectives for the course

I have various objectives for this course:

- to facilitate students' understanding of the impact of cultural differences on the management of people in multinational organizations;
- to enhance students' ability to assess the impact of global conditions on the strategic management of human resources in the context of overseas subsidiaries, acquisitions, and joint ventures and alliances;
- for the student to compare and contrast critical human resource issues in the contexts of domestic and international operations and the stages of a firm's internationalization.

In order to increase students' awareness of the complexity of managing multinational operations, I continuously ask them to identify key environmental, strategic, and organizational variables that influence international operations, how these variables interact, and how these variables affect the management of an organization's human resource capabilities. This course was designed for graduate students and practicing managers, however, I am teaching it to an upper division undergraduate class. The course materials are complex and rigorous and certainly present challenges to any audience, particularly to undergraduates. After a discussion of the course, I will discuss adaptations of the course for organizational settings as well as the challenges faced as we continue to confront the multitude of challenges that are posed by the development of international human resource management professionals.

Outline of the course

The course is divided into four modules:

1 Historical Overview of HRM and Global Competition
2 Foundation Components of HRM
3 Aligning or Changing HRM Practices
4 Leveraging HRM Capabilities.

I use the term "module" to reflect focused learning on a specific topic within the overall course. These modules vary in length and depth, depending on the overall topic area being addressed, and are discussed in greater detail in the following sections. I use the term "course" when referring to my courses designed for university students; "seminar" when referring to modules offered through organizational settings.

Module 1: Historical Overview of HRM and Global Competition

Module 1 provides a historical overview of human resource management and global competition, building, aligning, and leveraging HRM capabilities. The overview seeks to establish the scholarly disciplines inherent to the design of the course, including HRM, strategy,

83

cross-cultural management, international business, international economics, and trade theory. The interdisciplinary nature of international HRM is distinguished from traditional HRM and the changing role of HRM in international organizations is highlighted. I have found the article by Harry Lane, "Implementing Strategy, Structure, and Systems" (Lane, 1999a) to be very useful for students in the beginning phase of this course. This reading provides students with a framework for assessing the various elements of an organization's design. This module also emphasizes the need for students to understand and assess the importance of cultural biases that may exist in an organization's normal modes of operation. Culture and context, central to the entire course, are presented so that students focus on being aware of the cultural assumptions underlying their systems and practices and the implications of their use in other countries and cultural contexts. The contextual issues considered extend beyond the realm of national/organizational culture and challenge the student to simultaneously balance these variables with the external context of the firm, its international context and stage of internationalization, the business strategy context, and the key structures, tasks, and mode of operation in the business environment. In this way, students are continuously challenged to examine the cultural and non-cultural contextual variables and their impact for the HRM context within the firm.

In organizational settings, the focus of this module requires each participant to understand the industry context within which the organization operates—a need to understand the changes in the environment that are affecting changes in the organizational strategy, structure, and systems of the firm. Key within designing this module is to challenge the participant to consider the critical link between a firm's and/or business unit's strategy and the "fit" of the other elements of an organization's design in relationship to the human resource management function. I often present the organizational design framework found in the Lane article as a basis for each participant to map the current organization and assess (within the elements of the framework) where changes in internationalization of the firm can result in subsequent changes needed in managing people. A critical analysis often gives managers insight into what type and level of employee is required in the international context and what "bench strength" the firm has when attempting to accomplish its key tasks.

Module 2: Foundation Components of HRM

Module 2 introduces the first face of building HRM—getting solid foundations of selection, development, and performance management into place. I use the *Lincoln Electric: Venturing Abroad* case to illustrate getting the basics of human resource management into place and ensuring internal coherence. This case has been used traditionally to show how human resource management can contribute to sustainable business performance. The largest manufacturer of welding equipment in the world, Lincoln Electric motivates its employees in the US through its incentive and performance appraisal system. The company enjoyed unrivaled growth and prosperity until it decided to embark on a bold strategy for internationalization, under the guidance of a management team that had never worked outside the US. The *Lincoln Electric: Venturing Abroad* case sets the foundation for the entire course by raising many important issues about how HRM contributes to organizational performance as a company goes international. Issues and concepts raised in the case include those of core competencies, culture-bound management practices, and the need to adapt, transfer, or create new systems as a company operates in one country versus another. Students get to see international acquisitions as a growth strategy, the duality of control versus coordination during the process of internationalization, and the overall importance of developing managers with international experience. I teach this case over a four-hour time block and complement the case study by showing a video of an interview with Lincoln Electric's former CEO, Donald Hastings, and NBC's Leslie Stahl from an excerpt of the television program, *Sixty Minutes* (CBS video). The video is excellent and brings the plant, the workers, and Cleveland, Ohio, into your classroom.

In organizational settings, this case also works well. The critical theme within this module is one of understanding "fit" between the elements of the organizational design model as well as the pragmatic issues of internal consistency between the human resource management function and the other strategic functions within the firm. Many of the firms that I have worked with internationally often appreciate the key learnings in this case: namely, the link between HR and performance in international firms; the "power" of strategy-structure-systems fit; the motivations, mentalities, and means of internationalization; and the complications when national confronts organizational culture.

Module 3: Aligning or Changing HRM Practices

Module 3 introduces the second face of "aligning HRM"—aligning or changing HRM strategy and internal practices so as to implement that business strategy effectively. The relationship of HRM with the organization's business strategy is key and is seen as a critical partnership. During this module, I emphasize the role of strategic HRM and the importance of "fit" with the external environment. I use the *Colgate-Palmolive: Managing International Careers* case to illustrate the critical issues of human resource management and career development as the firm's activities span nations and continents. Colgate-Palmolive, the US-based consumer products company best known for its toothpaste and detergents, has long emphasized overseas experience for its managers. In the 1980s, Colgate-Palmolive developed a comprehensive policy regarding expatriate assignments, that addresses many personal, financial, and logistical concerns. By the 1990s, a new problem emerged: dual careers and the reluctance of some prospective expatriates to accept these critical international assignments. By examining these topics, students are exposed to the many issues involved in the management of international careers, as well as to the impact of social and environmental trends driving the company to re-examine this policy and its emphasis on international experience as a prerequisite for promotion to top management. Can a firm with 65 percent of its sales in international markets, which sells consumer products that must be adapted to local tastes and customs, not alter its expectations that managers obtain international experience through these types of assignments? The case provides a rich discussion of expatriate management, dual careers, business strategy, and the link of HRM strategy, international markets, and competence development. I also teach this course over a four-hour time period and end with a brief lecture on dual careers and the critical role that expatriates can play for a global firm.

The issue of dual careers, as well as what constitutes dual career families/couples, is a key challenge facing organizations today. In a seminar setting, having managers share their

85

concerns regarding expatriate assignments and/or any type of international assignments has been a useful lens for participants to identify challenges that they and their employees face as the need to develop human resource talent often outpaces the developing global strategy being pursued. This module is often a foundation or basis for developing a multitude of training programs consistent with a firm's strategy and stage of firm internationalization. Recent work in China and the rest of the Asia Pacific region confirms that the need to identify, train, and maintain internationally skilled and minded talent remains a key challenge and often an obstacle to further growth and performance of many firms.

To further "round out" the module on aligning capabilities, I continue the examination of global staffing and the key role of expatriation management. The *Marconi Telecommunications in Mexico* case allows the students to study personal accounts of expatriation, adjustment, and repatriation in the context of a firm that has continued global expansion through acquisitions while, perhaps, outdistancing its ability to staff the acquired companies in Mexico, Chile, and other parts of Latin America. We once again revisit the systems framework provided in Module 1 by the Lane article and examine the role of "fit" between strategy and systems as Marconi embarks on a global strategy with implications for its human resource capabilities. Continuing with an examination of the systems model and the concept of "fit," the *ABB Poland* case provides a wonderful study for examining international strategy, structure, and staffing in acquisitions, as well as the need to manage change initiatives in the newly acquired Polish companies. The students struggle with issues of national versus organizational culture, how to implement changes, and how to maintain the matrix structure and mindset of ABB with a host of companies in an ex-Soviet bloc area. We conclude this module and the *ABB Poland* case analysis with a discussion of the challenges of transferring systems within another organizational entity—namely, international joint ventures—and we address the continued difficulty of adaptation versus creation of new systems to fit the strategy, culture, or administrative heritage of either the foreign parent company or the host country partner. Throughout this module, I introduce various regions of the world (e.g., Latin America, Poland, Russia, Southeast Asia) so that the students are continuously challenged to think about HRM practices in a context of country comparisons, issues of globalization and localization, and stages of the firm's internationalization. I expect that the students will prepare each case with a clear recognition of the country or region in which the case is depicted. I challenge the students to use current internet sources, newspapers, magazines, and Culturegrams to understand the HRM practices particular to the country/region of study. When we do the ABB Poland case, for example, I provide them with the article "Business Success in Eastern Europe: Understanding and Customizing HRM" by Kirizov, Sullivan and Tu. This article gives the students a good grasp of the disparate and complex factors that influence human resource practices in some of the former communist countries.

A key component of this module in organizational settings is the aspect dedicated to the Management of Change. Most of the seminars delivered involve the need for the strategic alignment of a firm's human resource management practices with the strategic focus and organizational structure of the firm. Many line managers are charged with implementation of new business strategies but often lack the skills required to effectively assess and implement the changes needed from a human resource management perspective. The Change framework provided in the ABB Poland case allows managers to assess the key elements for consideration during a change process, including the skills needed for an effective change agent and/or change team.

Module 4: Leveraging HRM Capabilities

:raging HRM capabilities. The emphasis in
ɔnal capabilities for competitive advantage.
ed by international organizations are high-
g-term profitability and global integration
e cases that I have selected for this module
ɔabilities. The *Bristol-Compressors, Asia Pacific*
e Asia-Pacific region and his Management
l quantity of managers in the region. Lack
ical problem for Bristol Compressors and
that balance training current managers,
iates. Continuing with the theme of lever-
ι China (*Mabuchi Motor Co., Ltd*); Vietnam
lucts International); and Korea (*LG Group:*
cases exposes the students to different
ɔabilities (e.g., managing, protecting, and
.g., training and development programs;
velopment, recruitment, and selection).
is supported with readings dealing with
ning the functional areas with the global

e the course with an integrative review
ɩnd learning points. To promote active
l learning session, I require the students
rom the course and to share these points
ning points promote active involvement
it also allows for additional concepts to
er depth and with further emphasis on

ct on the challenges as well as successes
key challenge for me is presenting each
s between the three faces of HRM in
n areas; namely, the activity, the focus,
face. For example, during the Building
place; the focus is on internal coher-
ɩnizational design perspective; and the
ents some time to understand each of
se four main areas throughout the selec-
uon of cases that I use. The key success for me in teaching this course is my preparation

and selection of the various cases for each of the modules as well as the corresponding readings and activities. Through the extensive use of relevant, current, and meaningful case studies, I find that the student leaves the course with a richer appreciation of the human resource management challenges that are involved in the process of internationalization. They also understand the need to operate in an increasingly global and complex environment where people are considered a precious and sustainable competitive advantage.

ORGANIZATIONAL FIELD PROJECT

As an additional integral means of applying concepts from the course, student groups are asked to complete a field project that examines in some detail the management challenges of globalization. The student team selects an organization on which to conduct this project, which incorporates analysis, critique, and recommendations. In order to place responsibility on the students for accessing and interpreting primary as well as secondary data sources for the chosen organization, interview and first-hand data are required in this project. The field project tests the students' deeper understanding of how an organization actually manages the global workforce and how well each of the students is able to integrate the materials and learning that we have collectively developed throughout the course. Most importantly, this project is intended to help the students internalize and integrate the issues discussed in the course in a practical, useful, and career-enhancing way. Past students have reported that they learned an enormous amount about the organization that they were interested in, as well as knowledge of current global management challenges. Critical skills of how to collect data, conduct analyses, and apply the knowledge that they have gained in this course are also important to project success.

I also use these projects within organizational seminars as a basis for managers to transfer their training learnings and outcomes back to the workplace. I use the same guidelines described above and also encourage the organization to allow these projects to be graded within some type of certificate program within the company. Upon completion of the field projects, presentations are given to the company's top management team as a basis for organizational learning and discussion. The field projects provide the managers with a practical and effective way to apply the knowledge generated during the seminar and a means to share that knowledge with colleagues within and across business units and functions.

PERSONAL LEARNING JOURNALS

Coupled with the field project, a final and perhaps potent form of organization learning resides in the requirement for each student to keep a personal learning journal as we proceed through the course. The purpose of this journal is to ask each student to reflect on the daily learning in the class and ask the question, "What does all of this really mean for me as I try to enhance my ability to effectively manage and work with others?" After each session, students are asked to draw upon the session's mix of cases, readings, role plays, discussions, simulations, etc., and apply these various instructional activities to their own personal learning objectives for the course as well as their ability to maintain and enhance their overall effectiveness as global managers. I ask the student to do this reflection after *each* class. The student, via integration and prioritization efforts, should strive to translate this reflection into *at least* one journal entry for each class session topic and activity. For example, if a class session consists of a case, a reading, discussion, and a lecture, the student will have at least four entries for that day. Each entry should reflect a significant discovery, insight, connection, guideline, observation, concern, or other kind of learning that integrates session context/experience with the student's own current/future managerial reality.

It is within these entries that students often reflect on another key aspect of culture, namely, individual variations and interpretations of their own cultural beliefs, norms, values, and perspectives. This activity often aids the student in making sense of the various challenges presented in the cases when national culture confronts organizational culture. Rather than broadly interpreting cultural differences and making generalizations across cultures and/or countries, students are able to personalize such learning based on individual cultural backgrounds and experiences. Three or four entries per class session, multiplied times 17 classes (based on a quarter system), means that the student should possess at least 50 entries by the end of the course. Based on a review and integration of the journal entries, each student is required to prepare an essay. The essay should reflect their ability to sort out, integrate, and interpret their own entire collection of entries throughout the course. This essay provides the students with the opportunity to synthesize their learning from this course and apply the learning to their personal managerial effectiveness and their career.

I strongly advocate the use of personal learning journals within organizational settings. Two of the organizations within the Asia-Pacific region have implemented learning journals throughout each training module conducted with the organization. Each manager is encouraged to review his/her journal every two weeks and monitor learning objectives and outcomes based on personal competencies and goals as well as those set within the framework of a performance appraisal and/or coaching session. During each session of the organizationally based module, I invite participants to share their learning points and describe how these learnings can enhance the development of international considerations of human resource management throughout the firm.

CONCLUSIONS

Managerial development is the single biggest challenge presented by increased globalization of firms and markets. Developing tomorrow's generation of global managers requires a need to develop a global mindset and the specific task of developing leaders for the future. These challenges only serve to heighten the need to conceptualize, design, and deliver courses on managing human resources in international firms that emphasize a broader perspective of what operating internationally involves. The course discussed in this chapter is one effort to meet this important educational and managerial challenge. Adaptation, modification, and transfer of this course throughout organizational communities has also enhanced our ability to develop a cadre of international managers and human resource management professionals responsible for ensuring the quality and abundance of talent required as firms continue to expand into global markets—developing as well as developed.

REFERENCES

Bartlett, C. (1998) *Lincoln Electric: Venturing Abroad*. Cambridge, MA: Harvard Business School. 398–095.

Black, S. and Morrison, A. (1998a) *HCM Beverage Company*. London, Canada: Ivey Publishing.

Black, S. and Morrison, A. (1998b) *LG Group: Developing Tomorrow's Global Leaders*. London, Canada: Ivey Publishing.

Culturegrams. Axiom Press. www.culturegrams.com

DiStefano, J. and Everett, D. (1999) *Building Products International—A Crisis Management Strategy*. London, Canada: Ivey Publishing.

Dowling, P., Welch, D., and Schuler, R. (1999) *International Human Resource Management: Managing People in a Multinational Context*. Cincinnati, OH: South-Western College Publishing.

Evans, P., Pucik, V., and Barsoux, J. (2003) *The Globalization Challenge: Frameworks for International Human Resource Management*. New York: McGraw-Hill Higher Education.

Frost, A. and Weinstein, M. (1998) *ABB Poland*. London, Canada: Ivey Publishing.

Goldstein, I. L. (1990) Training in work organizations. In M. D. Dunnettee and L. M. Hough (eds), *Handbook of Industrial and Organizational Psychology*. Palo Alto, CA: Consulting Psychologists Press, Inc., pp. 507–620.

Lane, H. (1999a) Implementing strategy, structure, and systems. In H. Lane, M. Maznevski, and J. DiStefano (eds), *International Management Behavior: Text, Readings, and Cases*. Cambridge, MA: Blackwell Publishers, pp. 181–205.

Lane, H. (1999b) *Marconi Telecommunications Mexico*. London, Canada: Ivey Publishing. 8A98C09.

Morrison, A. and Black, S. (1998a) *Black and Decker-Eastern Hemisphere and the ADP Initiative*. London, Canada: Ivey Publishing.

Morrison, A. and Black, S. (1998b) *Bristol Compressors, Asia-Pacific*. London, Canada: Ivey Publishing.

Rosenzweig, P. (1994) *Colgate-Palmolive: Managing International Careers*. Cambridge, MA: Harvard Business School. 394–184.

Sixty Minutes Video (1994) Lincoln Electric (November 8, 1992). CBS, Inc.

Chapter 6

How I stopped worrying and learned to appreciate the gaps between academic HRM and practice

Robert L. Dipboye

The academic work in Human Resources Management (HRM) has challenged many of the traditional HRM practices and has suggested alternative practices that can have substantial economic benefit to the organization. The research demonstrating these benefits is growing in quantity and sophistication. Moreover, the news is getting out to practitioners in the form of articles and books on best practices. Despite these encouraging developments, the impact of research and theory on the adoption and implementation of HR techniques is disappointing. There is a wide gap between HRM practice and academic HRM that is growing wider. In this chapter, I will consider several factors at the organizational and the individual/group level that can potentially account for these gaps. Although I advocate a greater use of academic HRM in industry, my thesis is that gaps can occur for good reasons. While academic HRM is quite functional at one level of the organization, practices that are contrary to research and theory are functional at other levels. Moreover, practice requires modes of thinking that differ from those required in theory and research. To narrow the gap, practice will require compromises between scientific rigor and intuition, and theory and research will need to incorporate a multi-level perspective.

ACADEMIC HRM

HRM has progressed as a field over the last century by applying an analytical model that is designed around a careful situational analysis and evaluated on the basis of rigorous scientific research. This is to be contrasted with the intuitive approach which is more informal, subjective, and particularistic and relies on the "gut feel" of the decision maker. Beyer and Trice (1982) described the rational process by which organizational research is utilized. This process starts with the identification of research that suggests useful applications. The organizational decision maker questions the validity of the finding and compares the support for the research and the associated application to the support that exists for alternative possibilities. A rational choice is then made among the alternatives on the basis of expected benefits and costs of each alternative, in which that alternative having the highest expected value is chosen for implementation. This first phase of the utilization process is the adoption phase. The second phase is implementation, which includes the diffusion of information on the intervention, actions to reduce attitudinal resistance, and evaluation of the intervention's effectiveness.

At the macro level, strategic HRM has emerged as a major approach to improving the competitive advantage of the firm (Baron and Kreps, 1999). According to this approach, the strategic objectives and plans of the firm dictate the goals and objectives for HRM. The role of HRM is to determine the human resources needed to support strategic objectives and to ensure that employees are selected, trained, evaluated, and rewarded in ways that further the achievement of business objectives. Strategic HRM is usually depicted as a linear, rational process that starts with the identification of goals that will guide human resource practices. HR programs are designed to achieve these goals and evaluated on the basis of how well they do in this regard. Another theme running through strategic HRM is that there is internal consistency among HR practices (Baron and Kreps, 1999; Huselid et al., 1997). Thus, the recruitment, compensation, performance appraisal, promotion, training, and other HR functions are designed and managed so that they work in concert to achieve the strategic objectives of the firm.

At the micro level, academic HRM is often described as beginning with a careful analysis of the work and the organization (Dipboye, 1994). An HR intervention is designed on the basis of the knowledge, skills, abilities, and other characteristics (KSAOs) that are identified as fulfilling the criteria that have been identified as important to the organization. HR interventions are chosen that previous theory and research has shown effective in achieving the desired objectives in situations such as faced by this organization. Programs are developed and implemented in a standardized, universal fashion. Finally, the HR program is evaluated on the basis of the criteria identified in the first step of the process and the program is revised or discarded on the basis of the results. The cycle then begins anew.

The research has shown that HRM does make a difference and can improve the effectiveness and profitability of organizations. For instance, Huselid et al. (1997) found that with every one standard deviation increase in the effectiveness of HRM, sales per employee increased 5.2 percent or $44,380. In another study Huselid (1995) found that increases in firm performance were associated with increases in high performance HR practices aimed at enhancing employee knowledge, skills, and abilities and increasing employee motivation through performance appraisals, pay-for-performance, and merit-based promotion. A one standard deviation increase in such practices was associated with a 7.05 percent decrease in turnover and, on a per employee basis, $27,044 more in sales (16 percent) and $3,814 more in profits.

The research addressing the impact on firm performance has given more attention to the mere presence of training, formal selection, and other HRM procedures rather than the specific types of HR methods used. Nevertheless, the findings are encouraging insofar as more effective firms appear to use formal HR programs similar to those recommended in the academic literature. The academic research has yielded a variety of specific tools and procedures that are of potential value in the traditional HRM functions. In staffing, the employer can choose from predictors that have been shown to be reliable, valid and useful (Schmidt and Hunter, 1998). In performance management, the research has shown how to measure performance in ways that are relevant to the job, free of contamination, and reliable (Borman, 1991). In training, the instructional systems model is often presented as a guide for designing, implementing, and evaluating training programs (Goldstein, 1990).

GAPS BETWEEN ACADEMIC HRM AND THE PRACTICE OF HRM

Despite the evidence to support the value of academic HRM, there are large gaps between what is proposed and actual practice. Strategic implementation of HRM does not appear to be widely practiced (Othman, 1995). Human resource often does not proceed in the rational fashion described above. Similar to the utilization of other workplace innovations, the adoption and implementation of HRM occurs ". . . in many different orderings, with omission, repetition, recyclings, and truncations" (Beyer and Trice, 1982, p. 597). HRM strategy, similar to other forms of strategic management is the outcome of the interplay of various forces (Storey and Sisson, 1993, p. 68) and emerges as a pattern in a stream of decisions (Mintzberg, 1994). In this process, practices often determine strategy rather than strategy determining practices (Brewster and Larsen, 1992). There is often conflict among multiple and incompatible interests and, rather than being a rational process, politics often determine the choice and implementation of HRM practices (Kochan and Dyer, 1993). The use of strategic HRM would imply that packages or bundles of procedures would be implemented that are consistent with strategic objectives of the firm. However, it is relatively rare to find that work practice innovations are actually implemented as systems (Ichniowski *et al.*, 1996).

Not only does HRM appear to stray from the strategic model but there is also evidence that the process in which specific HR practices are used in organizations fails to follow the planned process recommended in academic HRM (Dipboye, 1994). Contrary to the academic model, the adoption of particular training programs, selection procedures, and performance management interventions in organizations seldom start with a careful needs assessment or job analysis (Saari *et al.*, 1988). More often particular programs are adopted because they are in fashion and other organizations are using them. They are evaluated on the basis of subjective accounts such as the personal liking of trainees for the trainer or the intuitive impressions of managers. When evaluations are conducted, they are limited to short-term results and there is seldom a follow-up to see if there is any degree of institutionalization.

Many of the HRM practices that have received the greatest support in research are still not widely used (Colarelli, 1996). For example, the selection procedures that research has identified as the most valid (Schmidt and Hunter, 1998) are used less frequently than subjective evaluations of work experience (Wilk and Cappelli, 2003). The most frequently used technique is the unstructured interview which is also among the least valid (Colarelli, 1996; Friedman and Williams, 1982; Smith, 1991). Most organizations invest little or nothing in the training of employees (Labor letter, 1991; Office of Technology Assessment, 1990). Performance appraisals still suffer from many of the problems (e.g., trait-based ratings) that academics warned them about five decades ago (McGregor, 1957). The high performance work arrangements that have been touted in the academic literature have not found their way into most organizations. Pfeffer (1998) reported a study by the National Center on the Educational Quality of the Workforce of more than 3,300 establishments in which

93

it was found that "only 16 percent of U. S. businesses have at least one innovative practice in each of the four major HRM policy areas: flexible job design, worker training, pay-for-performance compensation, and employment security" (Pfeffer, 1998, p. 61). One sign of this is the continuing use of layoffs despite the evidence that they are not effective in improving the long-term effectiveness and profitability of the firm.

Consistent with the infrequent use of the processes and practices proposed in academic HRM, there seems to be little knowledge or appreciation of this work. HR managers, directors, and vice presidents in one survey were found to err substantially on a test of HR research findings (Rynes et al., 2002a, 2002b). This lack of knowledge on the part of HR professionals was not surprising given that less than 1 percent said that they usually read the literature and 75 percent said that they never read the academic literature. Another survey found that full-time practitioners placed less value on the empirical literature on teams than did academic practitioners with over six times more full-time practitioners than academics (31 percent vs. 6 percent) reporting that the only helpful source of information was the non-empirical literature (Offermann and Spiros, 2001). The lack of appreciation for the research literature does not seem limited to those without Ph.Ds. A survey of the membership of the Consulting Division of the American Psychological Association found that Ph.D. respondents ranked empirical studies only 7 out of 11 as useful to their consulting practice, and less important than their personal experience (O'Neill et al.,1998). In another survey, HR executives with Ph.Ds were more negative toward academic research than were those who did not have a Ph.D. (Terpstra and Rozell, 1998). While the readership of the academic literature is relatively small, the popular literature in management is booming. In their criticism of the management consulting industry, Micklethwait and Wooldridge (1997) estimated that over $750 million in business books are sold in the US each year but the managers who buy them fail to finish four in every five. And what is diffused in these venues is not the academic literature but more often the latest fad.

So far we have noted problems of diffusion and adoption in showing how HR practitioners are unfamiliar with, and fail to adopt, the suggestions of academic HRM. In many of the cases in which academic HRM is adopted, gaps between academic HR and the practice of HR still emerge in the implementation phase. Decision makers in organizations may be knowledgeable about HR research and theory and the interventions implied by this academic work. They may even be committed to using these interventions in their organizations, and take steps to incorporate the interventions in the organization. Nevertheless, there are several ways in which academic HR still fails in the process of implementation.

One type of failure is slippage in which the intervention that is implemented does not match what was intended. For example, many organizations purport to use behavioral or structured interviews but what they use in many cases appears far removed from the structured interview described in the research literature (Barclay, 2001). Another source of slippage is resistance to these procedures. Interventions that clash with the values of the organization, the culture, or the individual who implements the procedure seem likely to be resisted in a variety of ways. Benign neglect is, perhaps, the most common form of resistance, where those who are charged with implementing the procedure simply fail to do so. Resistance can also occur as those who implement the HR procedures go through the motions of doing so but undermine the procedure to others. And, of course, resistance can occur in more overt forms such as sabotage. The end result is that the procedure as actually used deviates from what was intended. Over time one might expect even further decay and deterioration. Evidence of this was provided by Latham and Saari (1984) who found a validity coefficient of only 0.14 in the prediction of performance from a situational interview, a level of validity that was much lower than is typically found for this type of procedure. The authors observed that:

> The original interviewers did not use the situational interview correctly. Rather than record and score the answer to each question, the original interviewers recorded nothing. They merely used the questions and the scoring guide to help them form an overall impression of the applicant.
>
> (Latham and Saari, 1984, p. 573)

THE TYPICAL EXPLANATIONS FOR THE GAPS

There are three common explanations for the gaps between academic HRM and HRM practice. Each of these explanations is based on the assumption that the research and theory in academic HRM should be adopted and implemented.

Failures of academics to communicate their research and theory to practitioners

By far the most common explanation for the gap is that academics have failed to communicate their work in a way that is understandable and persuasive. In support of this contention, there is some indication that lack of knowledge is a major reason that proven selection techniques are not used (Terpstra and Rozell, 1997). Rynes and Quinn (1999) report on a 1997 survey of MBA students that found that out of 12 disciplines, HR ranked twelfth in perceived importance to the curriculum and eleventh in perceived quality of teaching. From this perspective, academicians have a responsibility to ensure that their findings and theories are not only comprehended but potential users are motivated to use them.

The first step is to communicate in a language that practitioners can appreciate and understand. The academic literature is unlikely to be read because it is highly technical, is often focused on questions that are far removed from application, and is conveyed in highly specialized language. One example of this is the research on the "futility of utility" (Latham and Whyte, 1994). Communications of test validation results in terms of sophisticated utility analyses have been shown to have no effect, or even a negative effect, on managerial acceptance of the results (Latham and Whyte, 1994; Whyte and Latham, 1997). Managers are looking for solutions but the literature more often provides contingencies and areas for future research than stating in unequivocal language what should be done in specific situations. Framing HR problems in administrative terms rather than in technical terms when communicating to managers is one possible way to improve communication (Johns, 1993). Other suggestions are: expanding the use of qualitative methods, writing reports in plain language, and increasing contact between academics and practitioners (Offermann and Spiros, 2001; Rynes et al., 2001; Ford et al., 2003).

95

Failures to research the topics of importance to practitioners

Consistent with failures of communication, others have pointed to the type of research questions and topics that are addressed in the research (Campbell *et al.*, 1982; Lawler *et al.*, 1985). Research questions are posed on the basis of the literature and are aimed at addressing inconsistencies, ambiguities, or gaps in the previous academic research. What is often stressed is the theoretical foundation of the research questions that are posed and practical implications are relegated to minor comments in the discussion.

The critics would say that the academic research needs to focus more on the specific problems that are of concern to practitioners. To generate research that is more relevant to practitioners, researchers are urged to collaborate with managers and to engage in dialogue (Ford *et al.*, 2003). Such collaboration can allow the identification of "critical success factors" or those factors that are contained in the company's strategy and give it unique competitive advantage (Banks and May, 1999). Moreover, the gap between academics and executives can be bridged with research that not only has validity and verifiability but also deals with critical problems and has utility for the manager (Dossabhoy and Berger, 2002).

The education of practitioners is deficient

Still another common explanation points to failures in the education of practitioners. According to this rationale, users lack the proper education to enable them to understand, appreciate, and implement academic HR. In partial support of this contention, Rynes *et al.* (2002) found that the discrepancies between research findings and practitioners' beliefs were more pronounced when they lacked SPHR certification and did not read the academic literature. Another point is that those who must practice HRM should be taught behavioral skills that will allow them to implement HRM practices. The solution to the gap between academic and practical HRM is to educate practitioners so as to convince them of the value of academic HRM and prepare them to read the scholarly literature and how to translate this literature into practical applications. Of course, this is likely to require major changes in business school curricula, textbooks, and classroom teaching to make HRM research and theory more accessible and interesting (Rynes and Quinn, 1999).

A FUNCTIONAL APPROACH TO UNDERSTANDING THE GAPS BETWEEN ACADEMIC HR AND HR PRACTICE

The arguments that the gaps between practice and academic HRM reflect failures in communication, choice of research problems, and the education of practitioners are well taken but do not in my opinion capture the entire situation. These arguments assume that the prescriptions of academic HR are correct and that practice needs to be brought in line with these findings. I would like to raise another possibility—that these gaps exist for legitimate reasons and are not just the result of a lack of dissemination to practitioners or failures in implementation. What I propose is that deviations from the prescriptions of academic literature occur because they serve important functions of the organization that are not served by alternative approaches.

Functions served at the level of the organization

The organization and the environment in which it must operate set the context for HRM practices. A neglect of these macro contextual factors accounts, in part, for the failure of academic HRM to convince practitioners of its worth. In discussing these factors, I assume that there are decision makers at higher levels in the organization who decide on the HRM practices that organizations attempt to use. These decision makers may choose HRM approaches that deviate from academic HRM to cope with a turbulent environment, to provide a better fit with other cultures, to gain legitimacy in the eyes of important constituencies, to provide competitive advantage, and to reinforce and maintain the organizational system.

1 *Deviations from academic HRM can be functional in dealing with a turbulent environment.* In a post-industrial world in which there is turbulence, change, global competition, and uncertainty, the planned, rational approach is not always ideal. Kraut and Korman (1999) refer to the Five Delta Forces to capture the change and variety of the present world in which business organizations compete. These include changes in demographics (immigration, increased diversity of the work force), economics (e.g., competition at a global level, the rise of multi-national corporations), legal and regulatory (e.g., increased regulation in the form of discrimination but less in terms of competition), technology (e.g., increasing rate of innovation), and attitudes and values (e.g., increased emphasis among employees on work–family balance, decreased loyalty to the corporation). Techniques that achieve their intended consequences could prove dysfunctional when judged against how well the organization competes in the context of these changes. Traditional modes of HR in this turbulent environment have been described as having disadvantages compared to procedures that are unstructured and subjective in nature.

Evolutionary organizational theory provides a theoretical framework for understanding why academic HRM might be less than optimal in a turbulent environment. In the evolution of social systems, variation occurs and choices are made among social technologies some of which are retained (Colarelli, 1998, 1996). From an evolutionary perspective one could point to several potential advantages of selecting and retaining HRM practices that deviate from the prescriptions of academic HRM. According to Ashby's Law of Requisite Variety, there should be sufficient variation in the system to match the variation in the environment (Weick, 1979). Highly specific, standardized HR techniques are well suited to a highly predictable environment where labor markets are stable and there is little innovation and technological change. By contrast, HR techniques that are unstructured and intuitive have the advantage of matching the variation in the environment and the flexibility of these techniques allows for a quicker response and adaptation to change (Colarelli, 1998).

The changes under way in organizations and in their environments seem likely to widen the gap between academic HRM and the practice of HRM. As organizations restructure to increase their flexibility and competitiveness in a global economy, they are placing less emphasis on hierarchical relationships and providing a good fit of the individual employee to narrow sets of KSAOs. In the context of these changes, organizational decision makers may see HRM as a hindrance rather than an aid and, as a consequence, turn to management fads in a search for solutions that may evolve into legitimate management practices if they work (Gibson and Tesone, 2001). I am not arguing here for the abandonment of rational HRM practices. To the contrary, structured procedures for staffing, compensation, appraisal, and training improve productivity and more organizations should use them than is currently the case. Yet, the technical evidence in favor of these practices is unlikely to have much impact if researchers and theorists continue to ignore the organizational and environmental forces working against scientific approaches.

2   *Deviations from academic HRM can be functional in other cultures.* Academic HRM has origi-nated in the research in North America and England. Consequently, the best practices sup-ported in the HRM research may not fit other cultures. Evidence of this are the large variations across countries found in the use of selection procedures (Huo *et al.*, 2002; Levy-Leboyer, 1994) and self-managed work teams (Kirkman and Shapiro, 2001). Selection procedures used in universalistic cultures such as Australia, Portugal, Canada, and the Netherlands are more likely to report the use of structured interviews than in particularis-tic cultures such as Belgium, France, Greece, and Italy (Nyfield and Baron, 2000). In a par-ticularistic society, the interview is seen as a personal conversation rather than a test and practitioners are less likely to be receptive to attempts to structure the process. Organizations in universalistic countries are not only more likely to use structured interviews but are more likely to use objective data in rank-ordering candidates and more likely to do formal audits of the selection process. Other research has shown that organizations in cultures high in uncertainty avoidance were more likely to use a fixed set of interview questions and audit the selection process, while organizations in cultures high in power distance were less likely to use peers as interviewers (Ryan *et al.*, 1999). Other work suggests that high power dis-tance, being oriented, individualistic cultures will resist a high level of self-management more than those from a low power distance culture, doing-oriented, collectivistic culture (Kirkman and Shapiro, 1997). The cross-cultural work conducted so far supports the con-clusion of Huo *et al.* (2002) that: "The best international HR management practices ought to be the ones best adapted to cultural and national differences" (p. 42).

3   *Deviations from academic HRM can be functional for gaining legitimacy from important constituencies.* According to institutional theory, decision makers adopt organizational prac-tices through imitation of other organizations in the same environment (e.g., Abrahamson, 1991; DiMaggio and Powell, 1983; Meyer and Rowan, 1977; Scott, 1995; Tolbert and Zucker, 1983). The underlying motivation for imitation and conformity is to gain legiti-macy in the eyes of important constituencies. Just as an individual may manage impressions to gain the approval of those around them, institutional decision makers are driven to legit-imize their practices to stakeholders who control important resources. These attempts to gain legitimacy can include eschewing the practices endorsed by academic HRM and adopting the fads and fashions being used by the prestigious organizations. Thus, if the industry leaders are using a particular personality test to select their managers, decision makers in other organizations in that environment adopt this test, despite the lack of evidence to support it, in the pursuit of winning the approval of their stakeholders. When these industry leaders decide to move on to another fad, the decision makers drop the personality test and move on to the next fashion.

98

Several studies have demonstrated how specific HRM practices can constitute attempts to gain legitimacy in the particular environment in which they must compete. In one study, executives were more likely to be hired for top management teams if they were from large organizations and from organizations that had served as sources of executive recruits by other Fortune 500 firms (Williamson and Cable, 2003). Another study examined transfer of a quality management practice from the headquarters of a large, privately held US multinational corporation to its subsidiaries in ten countries in Europe, North and South America, and Asia (Kostova and Roth, 2002). When a subsidiary was located in an environment in which quality practices were frequently used, there were higher levels of implementation. A third study found that work–family practices were more likely to be adopted the more widespread this type of program in the organizational environment of the organization (Goodstein, 1994). Also, larger organizations were more likely to adopt these practices. It appears, then, that large firms not only serve as the model for the HRM practices of other firms, but the large firms are also expected to become the first to adopt the latest fad or fashion. Institutional theory does not imply that decision makers are necessarily in error in attempting to imitate other firms. Rather, imitation of less than ideal practices may serve the important function of maintaining the organization's reputation and position in its environment.

4   *Deviations from academic HRM can be functional in seeking competitive advantage.* The resource-based theory of the firm would suggest that organizations gain advantage by not only using HRM approaches that create value but also by using HRM approaches that are rare, are not easily imitated, and for which there are few substitutes (Barney, 2002). From this perspective one might expect that some HRM approaches that are less than ideal when judged on the basis of academic research still provide more competitive advantage because of their idiosyncratic characteristics. On the other hand, HR approaches that appear more effective from the research may not be used because they are too easily imitated. One reason that paper-and-pencil tests of ability are used less than one might expect on the basis of their demonstrated validity is that they are commercially available and easily obtainable by other firms. Some successful firms such as Southwest Airlines or Microsoft use selection procedures that are extravagant and inefficient compared to the more researched procedures in the academic literature. While possibly lacking the same level of psychometric qualities of the commercial tests, the uniqueness of their practices, perhaps, compensates for their deficiencies. Along these lines Wright *et al.* (1994) speculated that unstructured HR techniques might provide more competitive advantage. Even if some unstructured procedures have less value when judged on the basis of rigorous research, they may be good enough in this respect and superior in being rare, inimitable, and non-substitutable.

5   *Deviations from academic HRM can be functional in maintaining the organizational culture and system.* HRM is a subsystem embedded in a larger organizational system and culture. Attempts to implement HR technologies that are incongruent with the existing systems and the organizational culture create tension that is resolved, perhaps, through elimination or modification of the intervention. If implemented, an HR technology may succeed in achieving the goals that it was intended to achieve, but at the organizational level it may prove disruptive

99

and have negative consequences (Klein and Sorra, 1996). For example, the use of standard-ized tests for selection allows selection of employees with the necessary KSAOs for the job, but can clash in an organization in which employees are expected to possess values that fit the culture. On the other hand, an HR technique that is ineffective at the level of the job may be retained because it fits the system. Thus, reliance on on-the-job training by peers is less effective than a formal training program in developing the necessary KSAOs but could reinforce the culture of a team-oriented firm in which employees look out for one another. In these instances, deviation from what academic HR would suggest is in the interest of maintaining the system and communicating the core values of the culture.

Evidence of a striving for internal consistency is seen in research showing that HR prac-tices are used that are consistent with the culture of the organization (Robert and Wasti, 2002). Innovative human resource management practices appear more likely to improve business productivity if they are implemented as bundles or systems of internally consistent practices rather than as isolated practices (Ichniowski *et al.*, 1996, p. 326). According to the authors: "There are no one or two 'magic bullets' that are the work practices that will stimulate worker and business performance. Work teams or quality circles alone are not enough. Rather, whole systems need to be changed" (p. 322). On the other hand, one might speculate that attempting to implement a practice that appears effective in the research liter-ature but is inconsistent with the existing system could have harmful effects. From this perspective, one could speculate that rejection of innovative practices has value in main-taining the integrity of the organizational system. As an example, consider the potential impact of a 360-degree appraisal program in a traditional hierarchical organization. Although this type of appraisal program could be effective at one level, it could disrupt such an organ-ization and inflict irreparable harm on relationships among peers and between supervisors and subordinates. Leaving well enough alone is wise advice on some occasions where a degree of stability and effectiveness has been achieved using "less than ideal" methods.

FUNCTIONS SERVED AT THE LEVEL OF THE INDIVIDUAL PRACTITIONER OR THE GROUP

At the organizational level, deviations from academic HR may reflect the actions of deci-sion makers in their adoption of HR policies and techniques. At the level of the individual practitioner or the group the rejection or assimilation of academic HR occurs in the imple-mentation process. In others, those who have the responsibility of actually putting into practice HR techniques are faced with demands that lead them away from the dictates of academic HR. Again, these deviations can serve important functions.

1 *Deviations from academic HRM reflect the requirements of the practitioner task.* The deviations that are observed may reflect the demands of the tasks faced by academics as opposed to practitioners. There are fundamental differences in the cognitive, emotional, and behavioral demands of the work of a researcher in an academic setting and the work of a practitioner or a researcher in an applied setting (Boehm, 1980). The academic researcher can choose the problems that he or she wishes to address, and can exert considerable statistical and experimental control in the study of this problem. The academic researcher also has the

time to study the problem, is rewarded for conforming to the rigorous standards of science, and is not expected to generate solutions. By contrast, the practitioner is typically assigned the problem, has little control over events, and is expected to generate solutions within a relatively short period of time. Academics have the time and are rewarded for the careful time-consuming process that characterizes rigorous science, whereas those attempting to take an analytical approach are driven by political exigencies that force them to deviate from the ideal (Boehm, 1980).

Not only do the tasks of research and practice differ, but the type of thinking required of practitioners seems to fundamentally differ from the modes of thinking required of the academic. Aristotle contrasted the thinking required in generating knowledge and truth, with practicing, in which a person applies concepts to the real world. Performance in each domain is governed by a specific kind of thinking. The academic uses logic, observation, and mathematics to construct an understanding of a phenomenon. The HR practitioner must use what he called *phronesis* (practical understanding) which is characterized by intuition and a dialectical interaction with the situation. The practitioner acts on the situation, gains an understanding from the consequences of these actions, and then acquires an expanded understanding. Practice activity progresses through trial and error without coming to a final closure. Blanton (2000) suggests that the nature of the task requires practitioners to engage in dialectic thinking and problems arise when they try to think like scientists.

A variety of scholars have proposed similar differences in modes of thinking, but I will use Hammond's (1996) distinction between analytical and intuitive thought. Analytical thinking is "rule-based, controlled, effortful, slow, independent of context, asocial, and acquired through education." By contrast, intuitive thought is "associated, holistic, automatic, effortless, fast, highly contextualized, social, and acquired through experience." Intuition relies on experience whereas analytical thinking relies more on abstract logic, assigning the object to categories and then using rules to "explain and predict the object's behavior." In analytic thought the object is separated from the context through categorization and the application of impartial rules. In intuitive thought the relationship of the object to the context is central to understanding. Moreover, analytical thinking seeks the right answers whereas intuition is more accepting of conflict and ambiguity. Practitioners may not do what academics want them to because their task naturally draws them to a more intuitive mode of thinking whereas the nature of the research task draws the academic to a more analytical mode of thinking (Hammond *et al.*, 1987). To expect practitioners to adopt an analytical mode of thinking characteristic of academic HRM is not only unrealistic but could be dysfunctional for the effective performance of their tasks.

2   *Deviations from academic HRM allow fulfillment of role expectations.* Those who must practice human resource management in an organization not only perform tasks but also occupy roles defined by the expectations of others inside and outside the organization. With the changes occurring in organizations, these roles have changed markedly and in ways that depart from the traditional role of a functional expert in which an individual performs specific activities. The performance of this role requires expertise in specific HR functional areas such as wage and salary administration, interviewing, and the like. However, with the outsourcing of the functional role, internal human resource professionals are assuming other

non-traditional roles. Ulrich (1997, p. 23) has described how the roles of HR professionals have moved from:

1   operational to strategic;
2   qualitative to quantitative;
3   policing to partnering;
4   short-term to long-term;
5   administrative to consultative;
6   functionally oriented to business oriented;
7   internally focused to externally and customer-focused;
8   reactive to proactive;
9   activity-focused to solutions-focused.

Ulrich (1997) presents a two-dimensional model for HR roles in building a competitive organization. Four roles are defined in this framework. The strategic human resource role consists of activities involved in aligning HR and business strategy. The administrative expert role consisted of activities related to management of the infrastructure. The employee champion role consists of listening and responding to employees. Finally, the change agent role consists of the management of transformation and change.

Deviations from academic HRM may occur in the service of these non-traditional roles. For instance, some HRM departments are expected to generate revenue by contributing to the bottom line of the organization. This might occur in the form of marketing HR practices developed inside the organization to outside customers. The demands to sell a product may lead practitioners to focus more on what is saleable than what academic research and theory would suggest as the most effective. HR practices that are ineffective in achieving the goals of selecting, training, and motivating employees to perform better in their jobs, could be quite effective in fulfilling this entrepreneurial role.

3   *Deviations from the academic HRM allows the social construction of the technology.* The introduction of any technology is an occasion for social interaction in which those implementing the technologies attempt to make sense of the situation. As a consequence of a process of applying the rules and resources to the situation and the give-and-take that follows, there are likely to be deviations from what was originally intended (Weick, 1979). As described by Barley (1986, p. 80), a new technology disturbs the existing patterns of interaction and as a consequence can lead to "slippages . . . between the institutional template and the exigencies of daily life." Over time, these deviations can stabilize and become the routine. The social structure that emerges from these interactions stabilizes and imposes restraints on future interactions. This has been shown in the implementation of hard technologies (Barley, 1986), so that it should not be a surprise to find that softer technologies such as those in HRM may depart from academic HRM as they are enacted in the organization over time. Unlike hard technologies, however, HRM procedures not only impact the social structure but the technology itself is modified by this emergent structure (DeSanctis and Poole, 1994). Another way of stating this is that HR technology is socially constructed in the process of being implemented.

102

How might this account for the gaps between academic HRM and the practice of HRM? To the extent that the HR technology clashes with the established pattern of relationships, one might expect those implementing the procedure to modify it in the process of using it. For example, a highly structured interview requires that interviewers ask questions with no follow-up or elaboration. In an organization in which interviewers are accustomed to freewheeling interviews with little structure, one might expect that, in the process of implementing the interview, some slippage would occur. Over time, a modification to the interview emerges that is discrepant from the procedure as originally intended. Although the emergent interview structure departs from what was originally intended, the social construction of the interview allows a necessary adjustment to the existing patterns of behavior in the situation.

4   *Deviations from academic HRM meet the needs and values of the HRM practitioner.* What is often ignored is that HRM techniques are implemented by people with their own needs and values. Deviations from academic HRM can reflect attempts to find satisfaction in the performance of their jobs. A hallmark of many of the HRM techniques suggested in academic literature is that they are structured and relieve HRM practitioners of information-processing and decision-making responsibilities. An example would be a highly structured interview. Interviewers are given a list of questions that they must ask verbatim with no chance for follow-up and then evaluate the applicants on behaviorally anchored rating scales using guidelines. Given this type of interview, it is not surprising to find some interviewers who would find this quite boring. Indeed, it would lack many of the critical components of a motivating task according to Hackman and Oldham (1976): variety, identity, significance. Highly rational procedures are satisfying in some ways especially to the extent that they allow more accurate decisions with less effort, but they can be an intensely dissatisfying experience for those who must implement the procedures. In these situations, I would suggest that interviewers will deviate from original guidelines as they attempt to enrich their task.

It is also possible that HRM practitioners deviate from the dictates of academic HRM in the interest of fairness (Dipboye, 1995). While rational approaches are fairer in some respects (especially in terms of objectivity and consistency), intuitive approaches allow practitioners flexibility in compensating for past wrongs or correcting for bias. Consequently, deviations from the recommendations of academic HRM are in the interest of making what they believe are fair and just decisions (e.g., compensating in the evaluation of minority candidates for what they see as unfair disadvantages or advantages).

Deviations from academic HRM can be a vehicle for obtaining power and influence. According to resource dependence theory those groups and individuals who gain control over resources also gain power over others. HRM departments or personnel can acquire power over other departments to the extent they can control the flow of human resources into and through the organization (Cohen and Pfeffer, 1986). Resistance to academic HR and the use of unstructured, subjective procedures could be in the interest of exerting control over the HRM process. For instance, one could propose that training departments avoid many of the elements of the instructional systems model, especially needs analysis and evaluation, to avoid scrutiny of practices and to retain control over the training process. Similarly, line managers

103

can deviate from proposed HR procedures in the interest of maintaining control over the hiring, appraisal, and training of those who report to them (Pfeffer *et al.*, 1998).

The amount of power possessed by a unit or person can influence the consequences of implementing an HR procedure. For instance, Welbourne and Trevor (2000) found that the power of a department in a university influenced the position upgrades achieved on the basis of job evaluation results and concluded that political dynamics confounded the job evaluation measures. Nevertheless, the authors suggest that this political use of a rational procedure could be justified if it leads to resources that allow the department to perform better.

CONCLUSIONS

The academic work on HRM shows that organizations can benefit from implementing many of the findings of the scientific work in this field. Clearly, organizations need to incorporate more of the technologies and processes suggested in this research. Also, rigorous research is needed to evaluate those practices that are implemented. The rules of science are reasonably clear and there can be no deviation from these rules to produce a valid body of knowledge and to develop an understanding of behavior in organizations. When practitioners attempt to apply academic HRM to an organization, they confront the reality that research and theory do not always directly translate into applications. Moreover, the choice among practices is not always a matter of what's right and what's wrong in that HRM practices serve other functions in addition to those for which the practices were designed. But how is the gap between practice and academic HRM bridged? I would like to conclude with three suggestions.

HRM theory and research needs a multiple-level perspective

Increasing attention is being given to multiple level models of HRM. Wright and Boswell (2002) call for more research on the multi-level linkages using a two-dimensional typology in which HRM research is focused at either the individual/group level or organizational level and on single or multiple practices. Ostroff and Bowen (2000) distinguish strong HRM systems, where a situation is created in which there is little ambiguity, from weak systems in which the goals and routines implied by the systems are unclear. In the context of a weak HRM system, those implementing HR practices are likely to modify them in the interest of their own interpretations and needs, and effects at the individual and group level have effects at the organizational level. In a strong system, HR policies at the organizational level will shape individual and group level HR practices.

A clear implication of multi-level perspectives is that "what is good at one level may not be good at another, and goals of different subsystems are often in conflict" (Colarelli, 1998, p. 1048). As we have seen, HRM practices that are terrible in achieving objectives at one level may be highly successful in achieving objectives at other levels. For example, a training program that has little evidence of imparting the intended knowledge, skills, and abilities is adopted because other companies are using the program. A selection procedure that succeeds in the selection of employees who can perform their tasks, fails in providing a good fit to the organizational culture or in increasing creativity and innovation. A performance

104

appraisal procedure that effectively improves performance of tasks at the level of the individual disrupts cooperation at the group level and cross-functional cooperation at the organizational level. This does not mean that HRM practices that have been shown to be effective at the micro-level are necessarily ineffective at the macro-level or vice versa. Rather, what I am suggesting here is that academic HRM, to be practical, must take into account multi-level criteria in evaluating interventions and in the basic theory and research that underlies these interventions.

To be useful, HRM theory and practice must confront paradox

If a multi-level perspective is taken, it seems necessary to confront paradox in our HRM research, theory, and practice. This is different than the typical contingency thinking that has been used in dealing with inconsistencies in results. In other words, when confronted with mixed findings (e.g., a particular HRM works in some situations and not in others) is to search for moderator variables. Once identified these moderator variables allow the construction of theories that state the contingencies and, potentially, a set of rules for deciding which procedure or technique to use in various situations. These models typically are constructed at one level of analysis, however, and do not confront the paradox of different consequences simultaneously occurring at different levels from the same HRM intervention.

Paradox is defined as "contradictory, mutually exclusive elements that are present and operate equally at the same time" (Cameron and Quinn, 1988, p. 2). One can propose four possible psychological responses to a paradox (Peng and Nisbett, 1999). Denial is where the person cannot deal with it or pretends it does not exist. Discounting is where the person dismisses both items of information. Differentiation is where a comparison is made of both items of information and a decision is made as to which is correct. Previous research has shown that differentiation is often the way in which decision makers deal with paradox. After deciding on the correct alternative, persons often increase their preference for the alternative that they were inclined to believe at the beginning and decrease their preference for the other. Dialectical thinking is the fourth possible response. In this approach the individual tolerates the inconsistency and appreciates that both perspectives contain truth. Rather than discounting, denying, or differentiating, the contradiction is accepted and an attempt is made to reconcile or integrate the opposing elements.

Scientific research requires non-dialectical thinking in which hypotheses are subjected to empirical test. However, dialectical thinking seems required in the application and practice of HRM where individuals must confront mutually inconsistent truths. Multi-level research in academic HRM can help to identify the paradoxes but cannot help much in reconciling the contradiction. Systems involving hierarchically nested subsystems inevitably are characterized by conflict and paradox, and the HR practitioner, by necessity, must deal with multiple truths rather than rigidly deciding between positions. In the act of day-to-day practice, dialectical thinking is often preferable to scientific reasoning if only because it provides the basis for reconciliation and integrative solutions. For instance, the paradox of solutions with high technical quality failing whereas solutions with low quality succeed, is reconciled through recognition of the importance of employee acceptance.

105

In taking academic HRM into practice, there is a need for compromise between the rigors of science and unfettered intuition

There is a fundamental difference in the tasks of science and practice. Research necessarily draws the individual to analytical/logical thinking but when an attempt is made to use the findings of this research in the field, the user is naturally drawn to intuitive thinking. A possible solution is not to go to either end of the continuum but to maintain a balance between analysis and intuition in the form of what Hammond (1996) has called quasi-rationality. He observes that quasi-rationality "will bring imperfect reasoning, inconsistency, conflict, and inevitably, error, with its attendant injustices." Yet, as "error ridden as it may be, quasi-rationality emerges as a valuable form of cognition because it tries to avoid the irresponsibility of intuition as well as the fragility of analysis" (Hammond, 1996, p. 353). Lawler (1985, p. 10) suggested that practitioners need frames, not facts. Specifically:

> the best way to improve practice is not by producing facts but by producing frames, or ways of organizing and thinking about the world. A good case could be made that the most important products of the field of organizational behavior are simple, elegant frames, not findings or hugely complex, ugly, inelegant frames.

Kleinmuntz (1990) reviewed the overwhelming evidence in favor of using formulae to make decisions rather than relying on the intuition of the decision maker and concluded people will continue to use their intuition: "flawed as they may be, instead of formulas, is that for many decisions, inferences, choices, and problems there are as yet no available formulas" (p. 303). Even when they are available the costs of using them may outweigh the benefits.

I began by stating that scientific HR has striven to achieve a rational model characterized by careful analysis and scientific research. In so doing HRM has attempted to move away from a more intuitive approach that comes naturally to those who must practice HRM. Despite progress in developing a science of HRM, the gap between science and practice is widening. Rather than worrying about this gap, perhaps, HRM scholars need to address the legitimate reasons that practitioners must deviate from what is prescribed in the literature. So, in closing, I suggest in response to the gap between academic HRM and the practice of HRM that we should not backtrack to the comfort of intuition or impose a strictly analytical view. Instead, I suggest that we live with the tension associated with this gap and embrace the paradox that is associated with practice. As HRM scholars and practitioners we should seek creative compromises that incorporate the best of scientific HRM while maintaining the creativity and flexibility of intuitive approaches.

REFERENCES

Abrahamson, E. (1991) Managerial fads and fashion: The diffusion and rejection of innovations. *Academy of Management Review*, 16, 586–612.

Banks, C. and May, K. (1999) Performance management: The real glue in organizations. In A. I. Kraut and A. K. Korman (eds) *Evolving Practices in Human Resource Management: Responses to a Changing World of Work*. San Francisco, CA: Jossey-Bass, pp. 118–145.

Barclay, J. M. (2001) Improving selection interviews with structure: Organisations' use of "behavioural" interviews. *Personnel Review*, 30, 81–101.

Barley, S. R. (1986) Technology as an occasion for structuring: Evidence from observation of CT scanners and the social order of radiology departments. *Administrative Science Quarterly*, 31, 78–108.

Barney, J. B. (2002) *Gaining and Sustaining Competitive Advantage* (2nd edn) Upper Saddle River, NJ: Prentice Hall.

Baron, J. N. and Kreps, D. M. (1999) *Strategic Human Resources: Frameworks for General Managers*. New York: John Wiley and Sons.

Beyer, J. M. and Trice, H. M. (1982) The utilization process: A conceptual framework and synthesis of empirical findings. *Administrative Science Quarterly*, 27, 591–622.

Blanton, J. S. (2000) Why consultants don't apply psychological research. *Consulting Psychology Journal: Practice and Research*, 52, 235–247.

Boehm, V. R. (1980) Research in the "real-world": A conceptual model. *Personnel Psychology*, 33, 495–504.

Borman, W. C. (1991) Job behavior, performance, and effectiveness. In M. D. Dunnette and L. M. Hough (eds) *Handbook of Industrial and Organizational Psychology* (2nd edn) Palo Alto, CA: Consulting Psychologists Press, Inc., pp. 271–327.

Brewster, C. and Larsen, H. H. (1992) Human resource management in Europe: Evidence from ten countries. *International Journal of Human Resource Management*, 3, 409–434.

Cameron, K. S. and Quinn, R. E. (1988) Organizational paradox and transformation. In R. E. Quinn and K. S. Cameron (eds) *Paradox and Transformation: Toward a Theory of Change in Organization and Management*. New York: Ballinger Publishing Co., pp. 1–18.

Campbell, J. P., Daft, R. L., and Hulin, C. L. (1982) *What to Study: Generating and Developing Research Questions*. Beverly Hills, CA: Sage Publications.

Cohen, Y. and Pfeffer, J. (1986) Organizational hiring standards. *Administrative Science Quarterly*, 31, 1–24.

Colarelli, S. M. (1996) Establishment and job context influences on the use of hiring practices. *Applied Psychology: An International Review*, 45, 153–176.

Colarelli, S. M. (1998) Psychological interventions in organizations: An evolutionary perspective. *American Psychologist*, 53, 1044–1056.

DeSanctis, G. and Poole, M. S. (1994) Capturing the complexity in advanced technology use: Adaptive structuration theory. *Organization Science*, 5, 121–147.

DiMaggio, P. J. and Powell, W. W. (1991) The iron cage revisited: Institutional isomorphism and collective rationality in organizational fields. *American Sociological Review*, 48, 147–160.

Dipboye, R. L. (1994) Structured and unstructured interviews: Beyond the job-fit model. In G. R. Ferris (ed.) *Research in Personnel and Human Resources Management*, vol. 12, Greenwich, CT: JAI Press, pp. 79–124.

Dipboye, R. L. (1995) How politics can destructure human resources management in the interest of empowerment, support, and justice. In R. S. Cropanzano and K. M. Kacmar (eds) *Organizational Politics, Justice, and Support*. Westport, CT: Quorum Books, pp. 55–82.

Dobbins, G. H., Cardy, R. L., and Carson, K. P. (1991) Examining fundamental assumptions: A contrast of person and system approaches to human resource management. *Research in Personnel and Human Resources Management*, 9, 1–38.

Dossabhoy, N. S. and Berger, P. D. (2002) Business school research: Bridging the gap between producers and consumers. *Omega,* 30 (4), 301–314.

Eleftheriou, A. and Robertson, I. (1999) A survey of management selection practices in Greece. *International Journal of Selection and Assessment,* 7, 203–208.

Epstein, S., Pacini, R., Denes-Raj, V., and Heier, H. (1996) Individual differences in intuitive-experiential and analytical-rational thinking styles. *Journal of Personality and Social Psychology,* 71, 390–405.

Ferris, G. R., Hochwarter, W. A., Buckley, M. R., Harrell-Cook, G., and Frink, D. S. (1999) Human resources management: some new directions. *Journal of Management,* 25, 385–415.

Ford, E. W., Duncan, W. J., Bedeian, A. G., Ginter, P. M., Rousculp, M. D., and Adams, A. M. (2003) Mitigating risks, visible hands, inevitable disasters, and soft variables: Management research that matters to managers. *Academy of Management Executive,* 17, 46–61.

Friedman, T. and Williams, E. B. (1982) Current use of tests for employment. In A. K. Wigdor and W. R. Garner (eds) *Ability Testing: Uses, Consequences, and Controversies.* Washington, DC: National Academy of Sciences, pp. 99–169.

Gibson, J. W. and Tesone, D. V. (2001) Management fads: Emergence, evolution, and implications for managers. *Academy of Management Executive,* 15, 122–134.

Goldstein, I. L. and Patrice, G. (1990) Training system issues in the year 2000. *American Psychologist,* 45, 134–143.

Goodstein, J. D. (1994) Institutional pressures and strategic responsiveness: Employer involvement in work-family issues. *Academy of Management Journal,* 37, 350–383.

Griffith, T. L. (1999) Technology features as triggers for sensemaking. *Academy of Management Review,* 24, 472–489.

Guest, D. (1990) Human resource management and the American dream. *Journal of Management Studies,* 27 (4), 377–392.

Hackman, J. R. and Oldham, G. R. (1976) Motivation through the design of work: Test of a theory. *Organizational Behavior and Human Performance,* 16, 250–279.

Hammond, K. R. (1996) *Human Judgment and Social Policy: Irreducible Uncertainty, Inevitable Error, Unavoidable Injustice.* New York: Oxford University Press.

Hammond, K. R., Hamm, R. M., Grassia, J., and Pearson, T. (1987) Direct comparison of the efficacy of intuitive and analytical cognition in expert judgment. *IEEE Transactions on Systems, Man and Cybernetics,* 17, 753–770.

Heracleous, L. and Barrett, M. (2001) Organizational change as discourse: Communicative actions and deep structures in the context of information technology implementation. *Academy of Management Journal,* 44, 755–779.

Huo, Y. P., Huang, H. J., and Napier, N. K. (2002) Divergence or convergence: a cross-national comparison of personnel selection practices. *Human Resource Management,* 41, 31–44.

Huselid, M. A. (1995) The impact of human resource management practices on turnover, productivity, and corporate financial performance. *Academy of Management Journal,* 38, 635–672.

Huselid, M. A., Jackson, S. E., and Schuler, R. (1997) Technical and strategic human resource effectiveness as determinants of firm performance. *Academy of Management Journal,* 40, 171–188.

Ichniowski, C., Kochan, T. S., Olson, C. and Strauss, G. (1996) What works at work: Overview and assessment. *Industrial Relations,* 35, 299–333.

Johns, G. (1993) Constraints on the adoption of psychology-based personnel practices: Lessons from organizational innovation. *Personnel Psychology*, 46, 569–592.

Kirkman, B. L. and Shapiro, D. L. (1997) The impact of cultural values on employee resistance to teams: Toward a model of globalized self. *Academy of Management Review*, 22, 730–758.

Kirkman, B. L. and Shapiro, D. L. (2001) The impact of cultural values on job satisfaction and organizational commitment in self-managing work teams: The mediating role of employee resistance. *Academy of Management Journal*, 44, 557–570.

Klein, K. J. and Sorra, J. S. (1996) The challenge of innovation implementation. *Academy of Management Review*, 21, 1055–1071.

Kleinmuntz, B. (1990) Why we still use our heads instead of formulas: Toward an integrative approach. *Psychological Bulletin*, 107, 296–310.

Kochan, T. A. and Dyer, L. (1993) Managing transformational change: The role of human resource professionals. *International Journal of Human Resource Management*, 29, 145–166.

Kostova, T. and Roth, K. (2002) Adoption of an organizational practice by subsidiaries of multinational corporations: Institutional and relational effects. *Academy of Management Journal*, 45, 215–234.

Kraut, A. I. and Korman, A. K. (eds) (1999) *Evolving Practices in Human Resource Management*. San Francisco, CA: Jossey-Bass.

Labor letter (1991) *Wall Street Journal*, October 22, p. A1.

Latham, G. P. and Saari, L. M. (1984) Do people do what they say? Further studies on the situational interview. *Journal of Applied Psychology*, 65, 422–427.

Latham, G. P. and Whyte, G. (1994) The futility of utility analysis. *Personnel Psychology*, 47, 31–46.

Lawler, E. E. (1985) Challenging traditional research assumptions. In E. E. Lawler, A. M. Mohrman Jr., S. A. Mohrman, G. E. Ledford, T. G. Cummings, and Associates (eds) *Doing Research that is Useful for Theory and Practice*. San Francisco, CA: Jossey-Bass, pp. 1–17.

Levy-Leboyer, C. (1994) Selection and assessment in Europe. In H. C. Triandis, M. D. Dunnette, and L. M. Hough (eds) *Handbook of Industrial and Organizational Psychology*, vol. 4. Palo Alto, CA: Consulting Psychologists Press, pp. 173–190.

McGregor, D. (1957) An uneasy look at performance appraisal. *Harvard Business Review*, 35, 89–94.

Meyer, A. and Rowan, B. (1977) Institutionalized organizations: Formal structure as myth and ceremony. *American Journal of Sociology*, 83, 340–363.

Micklethwait, J. and Wooldridge, A. (1997) *The Witch Doctors: Making sense of the management gurus*. New York: Random House, Inc.

Mintzberg, H. (1994) *The Rise and Fall of Strategic Planning*. London: Prentice-Hall.

Mohrman, S. A., Gibson, C. B., and Mohrman, A. M. (2001) Doing research that is useful to practice: A model and empirical exploration. *Academy of Management Journal*, 44, 357–376.

Nisbett, R., Peng, K., and Choi, I. (2001) Culture and systems of thought: Holistic versus analytic cognition. *Psychological Review*, 108, 291–310.

Nyfield, G. and Baron, H. (2000) Cultural context in adapting selection practices across borders. In J. F. Kehoe (ed.) *Managing Selection in Changing Organizations: Human Resource Strategies*. San Francisco, CA: Jossey-Bass, pp. 242–270.

Offermann, L. R. and Spiros, R. K. (2001) The science and practice of team development: Improving the link. *Academy of Management Journal*, 44, 376–393.

Office of Technology Assessment (1990) *Worker Training: Competing in the New International economy* (OTA-ITE-457) Washington, DC: US Government Printing Office.

O'Neill, H. M., Pouder, R. W., and Buchholtz, A. K. (1998) Patterns in the diffusion of strategies across organizations: Insights from the innovation. *Academy of Management Review*, 23, 98–125.

Osterman, P. (1994) How common is workplace transformation and who adopts it? *Industrial and Labor Relations Review*, 47 (4), 173–188.

Ostroff, C. and Bowen, D. E. (2000) Moving HR to a higher level: HR practices and organizational effectiveness. In K. J. Klein and S. W. J. Kozlowski (eds) *Multilevel Theory, Research, and Methods in Organizations*: *Foundations, Extensions, and New Directions*. San Francisco, CA: Jossey-Bass.

Othman, R. B. (1995) Strategic HRM: Evidence from the Irish food industry. *Personnel Review*, 25 (1), 40–58.

Peng, K. and Nisbett, R. E. (1999) Culture, dialectics, and reasoning about contradiction. *American Psychologist*, 54, 741–754.

Pfeffer, J. (1998) *The Human Equation: Building Profits by Putting People First*. Boston, MA: Harvard Business School Press.

Pfeffer, J., Cialdini, R. B., Hanna, B., and Knopoff, K. (1998) Faith in supervision and the self-enhancement bias: Two psychological reasons why managers don't empower workers. *Basic and Applied Social Psychology*, 20, 313–321.

Robert, C. and Wasti, S. A. (2002) Organizational individualism and collectivism: Theoretical development and an empirical test of a measure. *Journal of Management*, 28, 544–566.

Ryan, A. M., McFarland, L., Baron, H., and Page, R. (1999) An international look at selection practices: Nation and culture as explanations for variability in practice. *Personnel Psychology*, 52, 359–391.

Rynes, S. L. and Quinn, T. C. (1999) Behavioral science in the business school curriculum: Teaching in a changing institutional environment. *Academy of Management Review*, 24, 808–825.

Rynes, S. L., Bartunek, J. M., and Daft, R. L. (2001) Across the great divide: Knowledge creation and transfer between practitioners and academics. *Academy of Management Journal*, 44, 340–356.

Rynes, S. L., Brown, K. G., and Colbert, A. E. (2002a) Seven common misconceptions about human resource practices: Research findings versus practitioner beliefs. *Academy of Management Executive*, 16, 92–104.

Rynes, S. L., Colbert, A. E., and Brown, K. G. (2002b) HR professionals' beliefs about effective human resource practices: Correspondence between research and practice. *Human Resource Management*, 41, 149–174.

Saari, L., Johnson, T. R., McLaughlin, S. D., and Zimmerle, D. M. (1988) A survey of management training and education practices in U.S. companies. *Personnel Psychology*, 41, 731–743.

Schmidt, F. and Hunter, J. E. (1998) The validity and utility of selection methods in personnel psychology: Practical and theoretical implications of 85 years of research findings. *Psychological Bulletin*, 124, 262–274.

Scott, R. (1995) *Institutions and Organizations*. Thousand Oaks, CA: Sage.

Scott, W. R. and Meyer, J. W. (1991) The rise of training programs in firms and agencies: An institutional perspective. In L. L. Cummings and B. M. Staw (eds) *Research in Organizational Behavior*, vol. 13, Greenwich, CT: JAI Press, pp. 297–326.

Smith, M. (1991) Recruitment and selection in the UK with some data on Norway. *European Review of Applied Psychology*, 41, 27–34.

Storey, J. and Sisson, K. (1993) *Managing Human Resource and Industrial Relations*. Buckingham: Open University Press.

Terpstra, D. E. and Rozell, E. J. (1997) Why some potentially effective staffing practices are seldom used. *Public Personnel Management*, 26, 483–495.

Terpstra, D. E. and Rozell, E. J. (1998) Human resource executives' perceptions of academic research. *Journal of Business and Psychology*, 13, 19–29.

Tolbert, P. and Zucker, L. (1983) Institutional sources of change in the formal structure of organizations: The diffusion of civil service reform, 1880–1935. *Administrative Science Quarterly*, 28, 22–39.

Ulrich, D. (1997) *Human Resource Champions: The next agenda for adding value and delivering results*. Boston, MA: Harvard Business School Press.

Weick, K. (1979) *The Social Psychology of Organizations*. Reading, MA: Addison-Wesley.

Welbourne, T. M. and Trevor, C. O. (2000) The roles of departmental and position power in job evaluation. *Academy of Management Journal*, 43, 761–771.

Whitney, J. and Tesone, D. V.(2001) Management fads: Emergence, evolution, and implications for managers. *Academy of Management Executive*, 15 (4), 122–134.

Whyte, G. and Latham, G. (1997) The futility of utility analysis revisited: When even an expert fails. *Personnel Psychology*, 50, 601–610.

Wilk, S. and Cappelli, P. (2003) Understanding the determinants of employer use of selection methods. *Personnel Psychology*, 56, 103–124.

Williamson, I. O. and Cable, D. M. (2003) Organizational hiring patters, interfirm network ties, and interorganizational imitation. *Academy of Management Journal*, 46, 349–359.

Wright, P. M. and Boswell, W. R. (2002) Desegregating HRM: A review and synthesis of micro and macro human resource management research. *Journal of Management*, 28, 247–276.

Wright, P., McMahan, G. C., and McWilliams, A. (1994) Human resources and sustained competitive advantage: A resource-based perspective. *International Journal of Human Resource Management*, 5, 301–327.

Part III

Human Resource Management, development and employee well-being

Chapter 7

The new organizational career
Too important to be left to HR?

Elizabeth F. Craig and Douglas T. Hall

In this chapter, we argue that career development will be an increasingly critical organizational competency for all firms in the twenty-first century, and it will be particularly critical for firms in businesses and sectors where employees' valuable and inimitable knowledge and skills are the source of competitive advantage. However, recent changes in the organization of work, employment, and careers have led to a reduction in career development activities in many organizations. We identify the social trends and organizational practices behind this decline and argue that it is because of these very trends that organizational career development must be reinvigorated, though not in its traditional centralized form. We not only see the old HR planning model of career development as obsolete, but we also question whether career development should even be the work of HR managers. Building from an identity commitment theoretical framework and leveraging several contemporary examples of business-based career learning, we propose a new model of Organizational Career Development (OCD) in which career development work is diffused throughout the organization and the function of corporate HR is to capture learning innovations.

TRENDS IN ORGANIZATIONS, CAREERS, AND ORGANIZATIONAL CAREER DEVELOPMENT

Contemporary social trends and recent changes in the organization of work and employment have affected the degree and nature of career development activities in organizations (see Table 7.1 for an overview of these changes). Sweeping economic, technological, and social changes during the last two decades have begun to transform how work is organized in modern society. The shift from an industrial to a knowledge economy, the globalization of markets, and the rapid proliferation of new technologies have dramatically increased the pace and unpredictability of change. In response, firms dismantled rigid hierarchies to enhance their responsiveness to new environmental demands. Through downsizing and restructuring, organizations eliminated layers of management and expanded the responsibilities of remaining employees. These societal changes had direct consequences for employment structures and practices in organizations. Gone are stability, vertical advancement, and employment security that defined industrial era careers. Greater flexibility, performance demands, and inter-firm mobility characterize twenty-first-century employment.

Table 7.1 The contexts of career development: past, present and future

	(1950–1990) Traditional	(1990–2010) Transitional	(2000–?) Emerging
Strategic/organizational context			
Dominant sector	Industrial/manufacturing	Service/information	Knowledge/experience
Product markets			
Pace of change	Stable, slow	Increasing, fast	Hyper competition
Competition	Predictable	Unsettlingly unpredictable	Predictably unpredictable
Organization form	Bureaucratic	Decentralized	Entrepreneurial
Boundaries	Clearly bounded	Permeable boundaries	Fluid boundaries
Strategic focus	Product-centric	Customer-centric	Employee-centric
Org. need vis-à-vis workforce	Stability	Functional flexibility	Individual adaptability
HR context			
Sourcing decisions	Make	Make and buy core, buy (outsource) non-core	
Orientation of HR function	Planning	Strategic	Leadership
Role of HR function	Human resource management	Strategic human resource management	Strategic human capabilities development
HR task/challenge	Efficient labor utilization	Efficient and effective human resource utilization	Strategic human resource engagement
Activities of HR	KSAs and job analysis to fit person to job	Competency models and assessments to fit person with organization	Matching employees' talents, growth needs and personal goals with the talent needs of the business
Workforce demographics and expectations	Homogeneous	Heterogeneous	Diverse
Employment relationships			
Nature of psychological contract	Relational	Transactional	Relational
Nature of relationship	Dependent	Independent	Interdependent
Time frame	Long-term	Short-term	Useful-term

Nature of exchange (i.e., inducement/contribution)	Employment security/loyalty	Employability/performance	Experience/engagement
Trust between organizations and individuals	High; one-way, top-down	Low	High; two-way, mutual
Basis for trust	Systems, policies, rules		Personal relations
Career context			
Nature	Organizational		Protean
Driver	Organization in organization context	Individual in market context	Individual in life context
Evaluation of success	Objective—organization	Objective—market	Subjective—person
Dominant career theme	Advancement in org. hierarchy		Meaningful contributions to personal and organizational missions
Organizational Career Development (OCD)			
Image of people	People as suppliers (of labor)	People as contractors (of work)	People as consumers (of career experiences)
Career development			
Goal	Skill acquisition	Competency accumulation	Continuous learning
Focus	Job-based	Organization-based	Person-based
Task	Acquisition of skills and knowledge required to do the current job and future jobs in ladder	Accumulation of general competencies required to do a variety of jobs in the organization	Build on a person's strengths and develop self-awareness and adaptability to maximize contributions to the organization's and the person's strategic plans
OCD paradigm	Mass production: generic development		Mass customization: customized development solutions
Scope of OCD activities	As needed	High performers	Across the board
Career development process	Top-down	Top-down in organization and individuals' own efforts	Collaborative
Role of operations/line managers	CONTROL through supervision and evaluation	COORDINATION through empowerment and expertise	COACHING through teambuilding and development
Role of corporate HR	Allocation	Rationalization	Innovation
Outcomes for individuals in organizations	Promotion/advancement		Significant contributions/learning and development

Significant shifts in labor market demographics are also creating new challenges for organizations. The workforce is aging and the proportion of women and minorities is increasing. These trends, combined with slowing growth in the labor force will require firms to implement practices that enhance development opportunities for older workers, low-skill workers, and workers needing flexible schedules (Deavers *et al.*, 1999). What's more, younger workers entering the labor force have career expectations and aspirations that are often different from and more diverse than those of previous generations. Workers who are currently in their twenties, for example, grew up in the information age. Their formative years dovetailed with the rise of the service and knowledge economies and the decline of manufacturing, widespread layoffs and downsizing accompanied by the elimination of "lifetime" employment, and a general era of rapid change and discontinuity (Howe and Strauss, 1992; Tulgan, 1995; Zemke *et al.*, 2000). These young adults entered the working world without expectations for lifetime employment or traditional organizational careers. To the contrary, these twentysomethings enjoy and expect choices in their work careers. This growing diversity in the workforce as a result of these demographic shifts precludes one-size-fits-all approaches to career development.

Together, these environmental shifts have permanently altered the context for relationships between companies and their workforces. For the latter part of the twentieth century, long-term employment relationships tied careers and career rewards to employees' physical and psychological attachment to organizations. Advancement, compensation, and benefits were linked to seniority and loyalty to the firm. These long-term employment relationships between employees and firms were mutually beneficial: firms retained a loyal corps of employees who identified with and internalized organizational goals, while employees enjoyed employment security and stability along with steadily increasing career rewards.

In recent years, increasingly competitive landscapes have demanded new approaches to employment relationships and careers. Employers have all but abandoned the traditional implicit employment contract in which company loyalty was exchanged for long-term employment security. Seeking greater flexibility, firms now offer "employability" rather than employment security (Kanter, 1989). Firms provide opportunities for employees to accumulate skills and experiences that enhance both their contributions to firm performance and their attractiveness in the labor market. Individuals are responsible for managing their own careers, building a portfolio of diverse competencies and experiences, often by moving between firms to exploit opportunities (Arthur and Rousseau, 1996; Handy, 1989).

As employment arrangements and careers become more market-driven than organization-based (Cappelli, 1999), careers become more defined by the individual rather than the organization (Hall, 1976, 2002) and the likelihood of building one's career within a single firm diminished. Traditional "careers of advancement" that were realized in a single organization have been replaced by "careers of achievement," which involve the development of personal reputation and professional skill via employment experiences in multiple organizations (Zabusky and Barley, 1996, p. 438; Kanter, 1989). Continuous learning and adaptability became the key to continued employment with a firm as well as to future employment opportunities.

This "new deal" at work is believed to have engendered a sort of "free agent" mentality on the part of many employees (Cappelli, 1999; Pink, 2001). Individuals have more freedom in, and responsibility for, defining their careers and giving meaning to various experiences

(Mirvis and Hall, 1996). When combined with robust economic conditions, this arrangement led many employees to strike some new deals of their own, changing employers frequently in response to sweetened offers and new professional challenges. Employers sometimes found themselves losing the very people they wanted to keep as what became known as the "War for Talent" intensified (Michaels *et al.*, 2001). But this is not purely a trend associated with tight labor markets. Rather, we believe that it represents a fundamental shift in employment relations that has far-reaching implications for career development and management in organizations.

As careers were decoupled from individuals' attachments to organizations, and as the possibility for inter-firm mobility increased, employers became wary of investing in employees' career development. Investments in anything beyond firm-specific skills were thought to be a losing proposition for organizations because investments in general skills and marketable competencies would increase employees' value in the external labor market and, presumably, their likelihood of leaving. Firms are loath to bear the burden of developing talent for other companies. Indeed, firms tend to view the purpose of development efforts as facilitating internal mobility and building "bench strength." Of the career development efforts in large US corporations, three-quarters are in the form of career development "programs" that target high potentials and future leaders (Gutteridge *et al.*, 1993). Yet, given the demands of knowledge work and the increased strategic importance of human capital (Bartlett and Ghoshal, 2002), investments in employee development should be a top priority for firms.

CAREER DEVELOPMENT IS BECOMING STRATEGICALLY MORE IMPORTANT

In this hyper-competitive economy increasingly driven by knowledge work, competitive success is often dependent upon the talents, knowledge, and skills of the workforce. Firms need more than mere flexibility in the deployment of the workforce, they need each employee to be continually adaptable on the job. In light of the demands for adaptability and responsiveness associated with the complex work and competitive environments of contemporary organizations, we would argue that a strong commitment to career development is one of the most important levers available to organizations for developing and maintaining competitive advantage. Where employees' capabilities are most strategically important for the firm (e.g., knowledge-based businesses), career development becomes evermore strategically critical.

From a strategic perspective, OCD is not merely a tool for enhancing employee capabilities and performance; it is also a powerful retention mechanism. Organizations can simultaneously engage employees in the pursuit of organizational goals and outcomes and encourage ongoing commitment to the firm by creating conditions for them to develop valuable skills and competencies that will enhance their employability. Despite firms' concerns about investing in the development of employees who have the potential to act as self-interested "free agents," research has actually found that individuals are more committed to firms when they "believe that they are being treated as resources to be developed rather than as commodities to buy and sell" (Gaertner and Nollen, 1989, p. 987). For example,

Galunic and Anderson (2000) showed that an insurance firm's investments in insurance agents' general development were associated with greater agent commitment to the firm. Where firms provide valuable opportunities for development, employees, rather than opportunistically "taking the training and running," are likely to be more committed to the firm than where such opportunities are lacking.

Our own research supports this view. A survey of more than 400 mid-level executives in a wide range of industries around the globe revealed that those who were satisfied with opportunities to enhance their employability in their current firms were much more committed and intended to stay with their companies longer than executives who were less satisfied with these opportunities (Craig et al., 2002). Further, the more executives saw opportunities within the company to realize their career aspirations, the more committed they were to their firms and the longer they intended to stay. Most interestingly, development opportunities were more strongly associated with commitment and intentions to stay than the provision of employment security and employment stability (Craig and Kimberly, 2004).

Hall et al. (2001) examined these issues in the context of managers in expatriate assignments. In the highly competitive market for global managers, there is a reason why some companies in the current protean, "free agent" economy are unwilling to make these investments in the development of their employees: they are afraid that investing in the employees' human capital will make them more attractive targets to other employers, who might hire them away. Isn't there a risk of betrayals and unhappy endings if the firm invests in keeping its employees employable and marketable? Hall et al.'s response was that there is a paradox at work here: for the best development and retention of your people, you have to be willing to let them go. That is, you have to accept the fact that if you invest in employees' development, not only will that make them more effective for your firm, but the visibility that comes from their success in high-profile developmental assignments will also put them on the "radar screen" of recruiters.

> But this is where the paradox comes in. Because of the short-term success that this international assignment has created for the person (as well as for the organization), the person will probably have high job satisfaction and a very positive attitude toward the company. We know that there is a positive, self-reinforcing commitment cycle, which goes like this (Hall, 1976; Hall and Foster, 1977):
>
> CHALLENGE → SUCCESS → SATISFACTION → IDENTITY GROWTH → INVOLVEMENT
>
> [And greater involvement feeds back and leads to the setting of more challenging goals, completing the cycle.] Thus, the more you focus on loading the assignment with characteristics and expectations that promote short-term protean success, the more likely you are to reap long-term rewards of increased involvement and retention.
>
> (Hall et al., 2001, p. 343)

Therefore, this psychological success cycle, showing how investments in challenging assignments can lead to success and greater involvement and commitment, adds detailed support to the conclusions of Craig and colleagues' (2002, 2004) survey of global executives. Given the increasing strategic implications of organizational career development suggested by this research, OCD models in organizations must be updated.

OBSOLESCENCE OF THE OLD HR PLANNING MODEL

In the past, corporate human resource planners have attempted to forecast future skill needs and then developed strategies and plans for either hiring or developing those skills. This approach is based upon the assumption that it is possible to know what HR skills will be needed at some point in future time. Historically, we have gone through phases where there have been dire forecasts about the coming shortage of engineers, nurses, teachers, technicians, or some other important group. Then this would be followed by major efforts to recruit more people from those groups or to train or retrain people in other career fields to work in those needed areas. And often the result would be that, by the time those people were hired or trained, the projected demand would not be there (Leibowitz *et al.*, 1986).

More recently, HR planning has taken the form of assessing individual competencies and modeling the competencies required by the organization. This approach was adopted to allow for greater adaptability and responsiveness by planning in terms of general capabilities rather than specific skill sets, yet the more general focus of this approach is its weakness as well as its strength. Lists of competencies to be developed ignore the larger picture of the person who is developing the competencies—are they the most appropriate competencies for a particular person to develop? How will the development of competencies enhance or perhaps diminish (see Kaplan and Kaiser, 2003) a particular person's effectiveness?

We would argue that this HR planning approach is even more problematic today than it was in the past. As changes have accelerated in technologies and markets, the half-life of an occupational skill set has shortened correspondingly. Hall and Mirvis (1996) have proposed that the original model of a career as a lifelong cycle of stages has been replaced with a series of short *learning cycles*, because of these rapid environmental changes. Each learning cycle contains a stage of exploration of new needs and opportunities, trial or experimenting with working in a new area, becoming established in the new area, and mastery of the new area. And then, at some point after mastery was achieved, the person would feel the need to start exploring his or her next move. Such a cycle might take three to five years to play out.

In this model of the career as learning stages, adaptation occurs through continuous learning. This is an ongoing acquisition of new skills, which happens as the person senses the need for updating, as opposed to a less frequent, massive reskilling process. In this new career environment then, instead of focusing on top-down corporate human resource planning, we need to focus on helping employees *learn how to learn*. Just as the current business environment demands that organizations unleash employee potential by empowering them and delegating authority and responsibility for meeting customer needs, a corollary of this empowerment is that the employee also needs to be given responsibility, autonomy, and resources for his or her own continuous learning and development.

What, then, is the new form of organizational career development process that will enable this kind of empowered self-learning by the individual employee? Hall (1986) has argued that, rather than trying to help employees develop specific skills, organizations need to help people develop two higher-level capabilities, or *metacompetencies*: self-awareness and adaptability. Self-awareness, which Goleman (1995) calls the first of the emotional competencies, is the ability to know and understand oneself, one's skills, one's emotions, one's values and interests, as well as to know how to engage in a process of ongoing self-assessment. Through this ongoing self-assessment, the person's self-awareness is regularly calibrated and checked against external reality.

But the ability to know oneself and one's strengths and limitations is not sufficient. The person must also be able to change and grow if her self-assessment suggests that there is a gap between the skills she has and those that the current work environment requires. This ability to change oneself in response to the demands of a changed environment is called adaptability (Morrison and Hall, 2002). And there are two components of adaptability—it requires the competence to change (adaptive competence, or "can do") as well as the motivation to change (adaptive motivation, or "will do").

Both metacompetencies are required for learning how to learn. If the person is high in self-awareness but not in adaptability, he could be caught in an endless cycle of introspection or self-analysis paralysis. This represents a form of resistance to change. And even if he were highly adaptable but not very self-aware, his adaptation would be merely reactive. This combination would result in chameleon-like behavior that does not really serve his interests. It might serve the interests of the employer, the customer, or whoever is making the demands, but it probably does not help the person make progress on his personal mission.

Our colleague Kent Seibert (personal communication) has used the metaphor of the Olympics to describe the futility of traditional long-term HR planning. He suggests that the position most employers are in regarding anticipating needed future skills is similar to a team that is trying to prepare for the Olympics eight or 12 years away, but an Olympics with a special twist. What if these Olympics were games in which it is not known what the events will be? And what if the events would be newly created activities, such as a combination of a 250-meter dash, a javelin throw with your nondominant hand, and a standing long jump—but the team coaches would not know about the nature of the events until the day before they were held? How would you prepare for such an uncertain and high-stakes event? You would probably want athletes with a wide range of general athletic skills who were: (a) very clear on their own strengths and limitations (i.e., self-awareness), and (b) highly adaptable. In our view, business leaders who are trying to prepare for a highly unpredictable world ten years hence are in this same situation. We simply do not have the luxury of knowing what specific competencies are going to be needed, so we have to help employees grow their metacompetencies.

A NEW MODEL OF ORGANIZATIONAL CAREER DEVELOPMENT (OCD)

Self-awareness and adaptability will enable people to maximize not only their own career outcomes, but also their contributions to their organization's strategic goals. Hence, organizations that design OCD systems around the goal of helping employees develop these metacompetencies will also benefit from increased skills and knowledge, engagement, and commitment in employees yielding direct benefits in terms of organizational effectiveness (i.e., performance, learning, adaptation). We leverage a social-psychological perspective rooted in identity theory (Burke and Reitzes, 1991; Foote, 1951) to model relationships between organizational career development capabilities and individual and organizational outcomes.

The essence of identity theory is that people are committed to identity "images," or notions of themselves in particular roles, and they seek validation of those identity images in their experiences and relationships. The idealized image of the self in a role motivates performance in that role and if the feedback from individuals' experiences and/or relationships verifies their views of themselves, they will experience "feelings of mastery and efficacy" and become committed to those situations and people providing the validation (Burke and Stets, 1999, p. 350). The more committed one is to a particular identity image, the harder the person will work to establish and maintain congruence between that identity image and the feedback (i.e., reflected appraisals) from a situation. Through this self-verification process, people become committed to particular lines of activity that validate their sense of self.

This process is compatible with the psychological success cycle described earlier, from the work of Hall (1976) and Hall and Foster (1977). It can be illustrated with the simple cycle shown in Figure 7.1. First we have challenging *experiences* and key *relationships* that stretch the person and result in a certain level of *performance* and success. Then this performance and the positive feelings generated from that success lead to *personal and attitudinal outcomes*, such as enhanced skills, new identity perceptions, heightened involvement, and increased commitment. And since these are such rewarding personal outcomes, they can *feed back* and lead the person to seek more of these *challenging experiences* and *relationships* in the future.

The cycle shown in Figure 7.1 represents a simple developmental process at the individual level. Now, we can ask where does the organization come in? Let us now add to

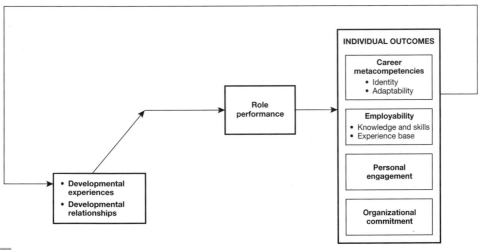

Figure 7.1 *Success cycle*

123

this model in Figure 7.1 the organizational influences—that is, the components of an Organizational Career Development process—that stimulate and reinforce this career development cycle. Figure 7.2 presents our multilevel model of the OCD process. The model integrates the individual development process (top boxes, Title case) with the organizational strategic management process (bottom boxes, UPPER case), highlighting the OCD levers and the mutually beneficial outcomes of personal engagement and organizational commitment (middle boxes, shaded).

Because people will work to establish and maintain situations and relationships that validate their sense of self, organizations can potentially influence the degree of engagement and commitment that results by structuring work experiences and relationships that resonate with the aspects of employees' identities to which they are most committed. According to this framework, if organizations fail to make an effort to align an employee's sense of self with his or her role in the organization, the feedback the person receives from the situation will not validate his or her identity. When a target identity is not validated, people will employ a number of strategies in an effort to re-establish themselves in situations and relationships that validate their sense of self. People will either change their behavior (e.g., intensify self-presentation of an identity image (e.g., Ibarra, 1999)), change the situation (to change feedback), or change the target identity. Thus, it is through a process of self-verification that people become (or fail to become) committed to and engaged in the situations and relationships present in their organization (Burke and Stets, 1999, p. 351).

If the essential career metacompetencies are self-awareness and adaptability, then the focus of OCD efforts must be helping employees develop those metacompetencies. To facilitate employees' self-learning and adaptability, organizations must develop capabilities in relationship development and experience structuring. The career process of the protean

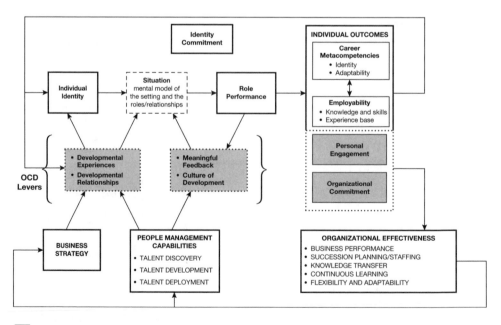

Figure 7.2 A multilevel model of organizational career development

career—learning how to learn—happens in the context of relationships and experiences that simultaneously stretch and support the employee (Kahn, 2002). This requires employees to experience considerable variety and challenge in their assignments, while receiving meaningful support and feedback from managers, coaches, team-mates and peers. Organizations must develop capabilities in structuring experiences that tap into employees' current strengths while stretching the employees and their understandings of their capabilities, and creating a culture of developmental relationships. The developmental experiences and relationships available in an organization provide the necessary context for the identity work (self-knowledge) that contributes to positive career outcomes (i.e., continuous learning and enhanced employability) and fuels employee engagement and commitment.

Organizations are able to influence the development of employee engagement and commitment through their capacity for structuring developmental experiences and supporting high-quality relationships. To the extent that the nature of experiences and relationships available to an individual are congruent with an important aspect of the person's sense of self (either current, desired, or ideal), he or she will experience positive emotions and become behaviorally committed to maintaining the attachment to the organization since it provides verification of the person's identity. Further, it is important that there is consistent feedback available to the person and that the feedback be meaningful and developmental. This provides employees who experience a lack of congruence the opportunity to change their behavior or their situation in an informed and thoughtful way, whereas distorted or hollow feedback might lead an employee to change the situation (i.e., leave the organization) unnecessarily.

SHOULD THIS WORK BE THE WORK OF HR?

In our view, this new development work is too important and too dynamic to be left to the Human Resources organization alone. It needs to be done in the midst of the dynamic business environment of the line units that come in contact with the customers and the clients of the firm. There are several reasons why the new career development should be based in the line organization. First, since 70 to 80 percent of development occurs on the job (Hall, 2002; McCall Jr. and Hollenbeck, 2002), you need to bring learning to the person rather than the other way around. People are much more motivated to learn when they have a *need to learn* that is created by some job requirement that they do not currently know how to perform. And second, there may not be time to take the person away from the job and put her in a classroom for a formal one-week training program. Most importantly, although the skills for acquiring the metacompetencies can be taught in formalized learning opportunities, most real learning about oneself and one's skills around change takes place experientially, real time, on the job, in developmental experiences and relationships.

But if these two ideas are valid, why doesn't more development occur naturally in work settings? This is where the Human Resources function comes in. Without having some sort of formal process by which coaches and other helpers assist the person in marshaling the resources that he needs to acquire new information, skills, and perspectives on the job, on-the-job learning just may not happen. At best, without learning resources, learning becomes hit-or-miss. The person might learn the minimum necessary to enable him to perform the

125

job but little more. Also, without a formal process, employees and organizations do not "capture" their learning in a way that would permit it to become *organizational* learning. And without a "capture" process, the person would probably be unaware of just what he had learned, and the learning thus might not be available to the person in the future. The learning might slip away like water running through sand.

Thus, we are advocating a sharing of responsibility for career learning between the HR organization and the line unit. The line organization pursues the attainment of business results and, in the process, learning happens. Employees are required to learn in order to perform. And HR captures the lessons of on-the-job learning, helps the individual realize the learning and incorporate it into her identity, and spreads the learnings across the organization. HR also keeps track of what the employee has learned in an employee database that is used for planning that employee's future assignments in ways that match the employee's developmental and career goals with the organization's goals and the business needs. This database captures not only the skills acquired or the competencies developed, but also the nature of the experiences in which employees have utilized those competencies, creating a platform for organizational learning through knowledge transfer within the organization.

AN IMMODEST PROPOSAL

Our OCD model is a dynamic one—over time, both the individual and the organization adapt and learn. Organizations must develop two OCD metacompetencies for successful adaptation and learning to occur at the firm level: *diffusion* and *capture*.

Diffusion: the operational role

First, the development work described above must be diffused through the organization. Line managers will need competencies in experience structuring. This means creating job assignment and management succession systems that place people in jobs that will stretch them in skill areas that have high competitive value for the company. It also will require providing employees with support for their training, learning, and development. These job assignments have to be made in a way that balances the personal development needs of the employee and the strategic needs of the business. The result of this experience structuring system will be greater alignment of the employee and the business—greater employability security for the employee and higher adaptability for the organization.

Similarly, organizations need to establish capabilities in relationship development throughout the organization. This means it must create systems and structures that support the creation of developmental relationships and networks and also support relational work— such as training in feedback and coaching techniques, integration of coaching and dialogue skills into performance management systems, etc. Ultimately, in the competitive marketplace it is going to be those organizations that establish the development and management of high quality relationships as a core competency of the firm that will be most able to attract, develop, and retain the best employees (e.g., Hoffer Gittell, 2002).

Since most development happens where the work is, operations managers, supervisors, team leaders, and co-workers will be the front line coaches in this model. The old managerial roles of controlling employees through supervision and evaluation, and coordination through empowerment and expertise, give way to coaching, employee development, and team building. Line managers need to be able to differentiate among employees and customized sequences of work experiences that stretch each employee. They must also be adept at nurturing sets of relationships to ensure adequate and meaningful feedback and support for employees.

Capture: the strategic role

Meanwhile, corporate HR will be responsible for ensuring the strategic management of the firm's human capital and capturing and transferring local learning innovations throughout the organization. What this means, first and foremost, is that the senior HR team must be clear on the overall business strategy and direction of the firm, so that they can deduce what kinds of human talents will be needed in the future. This means having a good sense of business acumen, as well as facility in translating business needs into human capital requirements.

Next, this means that HR has the responsibility for creating the systems and structures to facilitate these operational activities that we have just described. It means providing training for managers in how to hold good developmental career coaching sessions with employees, training in how to make assignments challenging, and training in how to make staffing decisions that include employee development as an explicit consideration. It also means creating a transparent job search and staffing system (probably on the company's intranet) that would permit employees to identify and apply for their next assignment and enable hiring managers to assess and select the best applicants for their open positions. Part of this system would be a talent assessment system that would make it easy for managers who are not HR specialists to assess the experience and competencies of the applicants.

Note that all of these systems and structures serve to develop the self-awareness and adaptability (the metacompetencies) of employees. On line resources for self-assessment and job search help people to get clearer on their own interests, past experiences, values, and skills. Good coaching from a supervisor can provide good reality-based feedback on personal capabilities, which adds to self-knowledge. And systems that promote developmental job experiences and relationships definitely enhance the employees' adaptability, as they increase their personal capabilities for dealing with new and challenging situations.

SOME EXAMPLES OF BUSINESS-BASED CAREER LEARNING

IBM

The reader may be thinking that these ideas sound pretty abstract and conceptual, short on practicality. What does this new kind of career learning process look like in practice? One place where we have seen it in practice is IBM, which went through a near-death experience in the 1990s. This technology giant has shed its dinosaur image (although it jokingly named its new mainframe T-Rex) and has moved to a more streamlined, decentralized HR presence. In addition to having traditional functions such as benefits delivered direct to the employee through their PCs (Think Pads, of course), they now deliver learning in the same way. Each line of business has its own "Learning Partner," who reports to the head of that business, with a dotted line to the corporate head of HR, Randy MacDonald. The Learning Partner develops e-learning programs around major organizational or technology changes, convenes learning seminars (face to face and on line), and collaborates in making key job assignments and in the management development/succession planning process. A rich array of e-learning resources is made available to each employee through his or her personal web site so that employees may engage in real-time learning as their jobs require. Having such a strong HR presence for learning within each business unit would not be possible without a strong corporate HR function to organize it and back it up. But, on the other hand, even this strong central HR unit would not be able to deliver its services without having HR "on the ground" in the businesses.

New Zealand public agency

One of the more subtle responsibilities of HR is its role as custodian of a *developmental culture* in the organization. An example here is a public sector organization in New Zealand in one of the country's largest cities. This is an organization that has undergone several rounds of restructuring and downsizing over the last ten years, as New Zealand's economy made the difficult transition from a planned economy to a market economy (Arthur *et al.*, 1999).

As Lips-Wiersma and Hall (2004) report, this organization has a very strong organizational career development process (as indicated by employee interviews, which indicate high levels of organizational support for their development). However, ironically, the organization does not have particularly explicit career development *programs*. Instead, this career development happens through a number of everyday business processes that are part of the basic fabric or culture of the organization. And these processes, in addition to accomplishing the daily tasks of the agency, also happen to have very potent and positive impacts on employee career development. Lips-Wiersma and Hall (2004) term these activities "career development practices," and they include: Developing Potential (explicit valuing of employee talent), Strategic Utilization (making staffing decisions based on development needs as well as performance requirements), Employability (explicit attention to continuous learning), Diversity (valuing and utilizing differences as a very conscious daily process), Nurturing the Culture (explicit valuing of the employee, building employee empowerment, collaborative decision making, team processes, giving voice to employee needs), and Communication/Information Management (transparency in decisions, clearly communicating how employees are valued, providing good information on availability of training and job assignment opportunities).

What is remarkable about these career development practices is precisely how unremarkable they are. They are just part of the way the agency does business. But, collectively, they constitute a developmental culture. Similar career developmental cultures are found in companies that are well known as good places to work but that do not have unusually complex career development programs—e.g., Southwest Airlines, Johnsonville Foods, Dell Computer, and Hewlett-Packard (Stayer, 1990; Karaevli and Hall, 2002).

Semco

One company that has taken the idea of alignment between individual careers missions and business strategies further than most is Semco, a $160 million Brazilian company that is involved in a range of businesses. The CEO, Ricardo Semler, would balk at the idea of defining or putting boundaries on the business. As he explains: "rather than dictate Semco's identity from on high, I've let our employees shape it through their individual efforts, interests, and initiatives" (Semler, 2000, p. 3). Working from the assumption that freedom inspires performance, Semco's employees ("Associates") decide for themselves what work they will do and how they will do it. This approach has led this one-time manufacturing firm into providing services and even into internet businesses, all without a strategy for doing so. Because employees are entrepreneurs encouraged to seek opportunities to contribute to the business in ways that leverage their strengths and engage their interests, the business ends up being defined by the employees. This degree of customized career development is possible because of the creative, performance-oriented culture and the lack of structures and systems of control that tend to inhibit productive relationships. Again, this is not about a career development "program"—it is how Semco works. And, the evidence suggests that Semco's developmental culture enhances retention. The turnover rates have been less than one percent each year.

CONCLUSIONS

This proposed model of OCD stands in distinct contrast to prior approaches in two significant ways. First, the image of people is different. The approach we advocate requires a significant shift in managerial mindsets. Unlike prior eras in which people were viewed as suppliers of labor or independent contractors of work, the new approach portrays people as consumers of career experiences. Organizations will be attractive to individuals to the extent that they can provide people with meaningful career experiences—those that enable continuous learning and enhance ongoing employability. Mindful of the unfeasibility of a standardized "mass production" approach to career development given these aims, we suggest firms move toward a "mass customization" approach to OCD (see also Kimberly et al., 2001). While a mass production approach may remain appropriate for some traditional training tasks such as skill learning, learning how to learn requires a much more customized, experiential approach. Development efforts in such an approach are focused on a unique person, rather than any person in a particular job or the set of people in an organization. Customized development solutions that take into account the whole of employees' talents, goals, and lives replace cookie-cutter development models.

A second important distinction between this approach to OCD and traditional development in organizations is the location and reach of the OCD efforts. Development is diffused throughout the organization. It must take place systematically, across the board, rather than occurring on an as needed basis or for high potentials only. And, it must be the joint responsibility of employers and employees. It cannot be imposed by "corporate," nor can organizations abdicate responsibility and leave it to individuals. It must be a collaborative process between employees, line managers, and HR professionals. While leadership support is crucial for making OCD a strategic priority for an organization, the development work must be woven into the work, values, and culture of the organization.

We have argued that by engaging employees' unique strengths and leveraging their knowledge and skills firms can enhance individual and organizational outcomes. Effective talent management underlies a firm's ability to achieve and sustain a competitive advantage through people. Organizations that make people management a strategic priority and cultivate capabilities in managing people, specifically in discovering, developing and deploying talent, will be at a distinct advantage in the contemporary context.

REFERENCES

Arthur, M. B., Hall, D. T., and Lawrence, B. S. (eds) (1989) *Handbook of Career Theory*. New York: Cambridge University Press.

Arthur, M. B., Inkson, K., and Pringle, J. K. (1999) *The New Careers: Individual Action and Economic Change*. Thousand Oaks, CA: Sage Publications.

Arthur, M. B. and Rousseau, D. M. (eds) (1996) *The Boundaryless Career: A New Nmployment Principle for a New Organizational Era*. New York: Oxford University Press.

Bartlett, C. A. and Ghoshal, S. (2002) Building competitive advantage through people. *MIT Sloan Management Review*, 43(2): 34–41.

Burke, P. J. and Reitzes, D. C. (1991) An identity theory approach to commitment. *Social Psychology Quarterly*, 54: 239–251.

Burke, P. J. and Stets, J. E. (1999) Trust and commitment through self-verification. *Social Psychology Quarterly*, 62: 347–360.

Cappelli, P. (1999) *The New Deal at Work*. Boston, MA: Harvard Business School Press.

Craig, E. and Kimberly, J. (2004) The social organization of managerial employment and executives' attachments to firms. Working Paper, Boston University School of Management.

Craig, E., Kimberly, J., and Bouchikhi, H. (2002) Can loyalty be leased? *Harvard Business Review*, 80(9): 24.

Deavers, K. L., Lyons, M. R., and Hattiangadi, A. U. (1999) *The American Workplace 1999: A Century of Progress – a Century of Change*. Washington, DC: Employment Policy Foundation.

Foote, N. N. (1951) Identification as the basis for a theory of motivation. *American Sociological Review*, 26: 14–21.

Gaertner, K. N. and Nollen, S. D. (1989) Career experiences, perceptions of employment practices, and psychological commitment to the organization. *Human Relations*, 42: 975–991.

Galunic, D. C. and Anderson, E. (2000) From security to mobility: Generalized investments in human capital and agent commitment. *Organization Science*, 11: 1–20.

Goleman, Daniel. (1995) *Emotional Intelligence*. New York: Bantam Books.

Gutteridge, T. G., Leibowitz, Z. B., and Shore, J. E. (1993) A new look at organizational career development. *Human Resource Planning*, 16(2): 71–84.

Hall, D. T. (1976) *Careers in Organizations*. Glenview, IL: Scott, Foresman and Company.

Hall, D. T. (1996) Protean careers of the 21st century. *Academy of Management Executive*, 10(4): 8–16.

Hall, D. T. (2002) *Careers In and Out of Organizations*. Thousand Oaks, CA: Sage Publications.

Hall, D. T. and Foster, L. W. (1977) A psychological success cycle and goal setting: Goals, performance, and attitudes. *Academy of Management Journal*, 20: 282–290.

Hall, D. T. and Associates (eds) (1986) *Career Development in Organizations*. San Francisco, CA: Jossey-Bass.

Hall, D. T., Guorong Zhu, and Aimin Yan (2001) Developing global leaders: To hold on to them, let them go! *Advances in Global Leadership*, 2: 327–349.

Handy, C. (1989) *The Age of Unreason*. Boston, MA: Harvard Business School Press.

Hoffer Gittell, J. (2002) *The Southwest Airlines Way: Using the Power of Relationships to Achieve High Performance*. New York: McGraw-Hill.

Howe, N. and Strauss, W. (1992) The new generation gap. *The Atlantic Monthly*, December: 46–54.

Ibarra, H. (1999) Provisional selves: Experimenting with image and identity in professional adaptation. *Administrative Science Quarterly*, 44: 764–791.

Kahn, William A. (2002) Managing the paradox of self-reliance. *Organizational Dynamics*, 30(3): 239–256.

Kanter, R. (1989) From climbing to hopping: The contingent job and the post-entrepreneurial career. *Management Review*, 78(4): 22–27.

Kaplan, R. E. and Kaiser, R. B. (2003) Developing versatile leadership. *MIT Sloan Management Review*, Summer: 19–26.

Karaevli, A. and Hall, D. T. (2002) Growing leaders for turbulent times: Is succession planning up to the challenge? *Organizational Dynamics*, 32: 62–79.

Kimberly, J. R., Bouchikhi, H., and Craig, E. F. (2001) The customised workplace: A Copernican revolution or a romantic fantasy? *European Business Forum*, 6: 12–13.

Kram, K. E. (1985) *Mentoring at Work: Developmental Relationships in Organizational Life*. Glenview, IL: Scott, Foresman and Company.

Leibowitz, Z. B., Farren, C., and Kaye, B. L. (1986) *Designing Career Development Systems*. San Francisco, CA: Jossey-Bass.

Lips-Wiersma, M. and Hall, D. T. (2004) Organizational career development is *not* dead: The role of HRM in integrating careers into an organizational change framework. Technical Report, Department of Management, University of Canterbury, Christchurch, New Zealand.

McCall Jr., M. W. and Hollenbeck, G. P. (2002) *Developing Global Executives: The Lessons of International Experience*. Boston, MA: Harvard Business School Press.

Michaels, E., Handfield-Jones, H., and Axelrod, B. (2001) *The War for Talent*. Boston, MA Harvard Business School Press.

Mirvis, P. H. and Hall, D. T. (1994) Psychological success and the boundaryless career. *Journal of Organizational Behavior*, 15: 365–380.

Mirvis, P. H. and Hall, D. T. (1996) Psychological success and the boundaryless career. In M. B. Arthur and D. M. Rousseau (eds), *The Boundaryless Career: A New Employment Principle for a New Organizational Era*. New York: Oxford University Press, pp. 237–255.

131

Morrison, R. F. and Hall, D. T. (2002) Career adaptability. In D. T. Hall, *Careers In and Out of Organizations.* Thousand Oaks, CA: Sage Publications, pp. 205–233.

Nicholson, N. (1996) Career systems in crisis: Change and opportunity in the information age. *Academy of Management Executive*, 10: 40–51.

Pink, D. H. (2001) *Free Agent Nation: How America's New Independent Workers are Transforming the Way We Live.* New York: Warner Books.

Semler, R. (2000) How we went digital without a strategy. *Harvard Business Review*, September–October: 22–29.

Stayer, R. (1990) How I learned to let my workers lead. *Harvard Business Review*, November–December: 38–46.

Thompson, C., Koon, E., Woodwell Jr., W.H., and Beauvais, J. (2002) Training for the next economy: An ASTD state of the industry report on trends in employer provided training in the United States. Product #790201. New York: ASTD.

Tulgan, B. (1995) *Managing Generation X.* Santa Monica, CA: Merritt Publishing.

Zabusky, S. E. and Barley, S. R. (1996) Redefining success: Ethnographic observations on the careers of technicians. In P. Osterman (ed.), *Broken Ladders: Managerial Careers in the New Economy.* New York: Oxford University Press.

Zemke, R., Raines, C., and Filipczak, B. (2000) *Generations at Work: Managing the Clash of Veterans, Boomers, Xers, and Nexters in Your Workplace.* New York: Amacom.

Chapter 8

Aligning work teams and HR practices

Best practices

Eduardo Salas, Mary P. Kosarzycki, Scott I. Tannenbaum, and David Carnegie

During the past 20 years, corporate America has increasingly adopted the use of teams as a means by which to achieve organizational objective. Teams are created when the goals are difficult, when the tasks are interdependent, and when the stakes are high. Teams are now much embedded in corporate America. For example, in 1987, a study by the Center for Effective Organizations reported that 28 percent of responding Fortune 1,000 companies employed at least one self-managed work team (SMWT). By 1999, the number of survey respondents using teams had more than doubled to 72 percent (Lawler *et al.*, 2001). There seems no end to this trend as we enter the twenty-first century. And so work teams have become an integral component of organizational life.

Smaller organizations have also adopted teams. *Training* magazine's 1992 Industry Report (Gordon, 1992) surveyed the use of teams by organizations with 100 or more employees. Of the 82 percent of the survey respondents that reported using teams, four team types were widely used: permanent work teams (45 percent), one or more self-managed teams (35 percent), temporary project teams (30 percent), and permanent, cross-functional teams (18 percent). Clearly, organizations often employ multiple team structures concurrently.

In addition to showing that the use of teams is widespread, the survey findings underscore the point that different types of team structure are used to accomplish various organizational objectives. For example, teams can improve customer satisfaction, service and product quality, and productivity (Gross, 1997). Teams can also make companies more responsive to changes in the business environment (Anon, 2002). Teams can make organizations be safer (Salas *et al.*, 2001). Organizations also believe that using teams can lead to improved employee morale and satisfaction, a stronger link between pay and performance, and increased staffing flexibility (Gross, 1997).

Once these potential benefits have been identified, organizations primarily implement teams through either a top-down or bottom-up approach. Top-down teams are those that are mandated by the strategic imperatives of the organization. For example, a customer-oriented organization may believe that teams are the best means by which to gain competitive advantage through delivery of enhanced customer service and support. In such cases, an organization may systematically restructure to make teams the building blocks of the organization. In contrast, bottom-up teams result from an analysis of deficiencies at group- or department-levels. For example, a production department may create temporary problem-solving teams to identify operational changes that would reduce waste. Bottom-up teams tend to be implemented throughout the organization in a more piecemeal, "as needed" fashion. However, as noted above, various types of teams may be operating concurrently to achieve different objectives.

In any case, no organization can successfully shift from individual-based to team-based activities without providing the teams with some form of support, such as compensation and performance management systems that encourage teamwork behaviors (Hackman, 1994). The traditional source of such performance drivers is the Human Resource (HR) function. Of course, the exact degree and nature of the support will vary according to whether the proposed team-based activities are temporary and local in nature or permanent and pervasive across the organization.

Early team research tended to be descriptive, seeking to create taxonomies of different team structures and concerned with such issues as determining the ideal size and composition of teams (Sundstrom et al., 1990; Salas et al., 2004). Recently, however, interest has shifted to the role and responsibilities undertaken by the HR function in designing and sustaining teams (Mohrman et al., 1995). The shift in focus is partially attributable to the changing role of HR. Once viewed as merely a provider of administrative support, today the role of HR is expanding to that of strategic partner. Proactive HR systems add value by aligning the organization's employees, its human capital, with the organization's strategic goals. A strong human capital–strategy alignment improves the organization's ability to successfully implement its strategy (Becker et al., 2001; Miller and Cardy, 2000).

The purpose of this chapter is to identify, discuss, and suggest specific HR "best practices" that evolved as organizations reacted to the increased prevalence of teams. In addition to reviewing empirical and case-based team literature, we conducted a small study. We asked organizational insiders to candidly describe their experiences with teamwork and to discuss how closely the HR practices within their respective organizations matched the "best practices" suggested by the team literature. Using a semi-structured interview, we spoke with both HR and operations-level managers employed by a variety of domestic and international service organizations (advertising, financial services, insurance, medical testing, and telecommunications). The purpose of the study was to uncover the types of issues that HR and other managers were experiencing as they attempted to implement or manage teams to accomplish organizational goals. The specific research question being addressed was whether organizations were doing anything differently (in terms of HR practices) because of using teams or because of increasing teamwork and collaborative requirements.

We will describe theoretical arguments and empirical evidence for the involvement of HR and suggest HR best practices that maximize the viability of teams. We will begin by reviewing the HR function vis-à-vis organizational strategy.

TRADITIONAL HR SYSTEMS

The traditional approach to people management focuses on individual employees performing specific jobs within an organizational setting (Jackson and Schuler, 1995). Traditionally, an individual works at a job, which is seen as a collection of tasks. The individual job typically requires little or no collaborative behavior although the employee may interact with others to some degree. Individuals are recruited as single entities and proceed through a selection process designed to discover how well the individual's knowledge, skills, and abilities reflect the requirements of the job's tasks. Rarely are teamwork skills and ability or desire to work with others assessed. The orientation and socialization of a new employee are also individual in nature, and typically focus on acquainting new hires with their new duties. Traditionally, training emphasizes the development of task work, and not team work, skills. The performance appraisal system is also consistent with the individual nature of jobs. In keeping with the solitary performance of job tasks, teamwork and collaborative skills are seldom assessed.

Finally, the compensation system is usually focused on providing individual rewards that recognize and reinforce individual performance. Outstanding individuals are often eligible to receive performance bonuses or recognition awards. The emphasis on individual rewards often fosters a spirit of competition and the recognition by employees that helping others may come at the expense of their personal profit (McHugh and Bennett, 1999). Helping others in the organization (for example, through organizational citizenship behaviors) may be valued informally, but is infrequently formally recognized. These traditional HR practices fit within an organizational culture in which the vision, as communicated by executive management and formal organizational communications, urges employees to do their individual best to help the organization reach its goals.

If traditional HR systems support individual behaviors and performance, then how should HR practices be changed to support teamwork? We next define and discuss teams and teamwork.

TEAMS AND TEAMWORK

A team can be defined as "a distinguishable set of two or more people who interact, dynamically, interdependently, and adaptively toward a common and valued goal/objective/ mission, who have each been assigned specific roles or functions to perform" (Salas *et al.*, 1992, p. 4). Members of *work groups* typically are less dependent upon one another (i.e., less task interdependence) than are *team* members. We can think of teams as fitting into one of five major team types: action and negotiation teams, advice and involvement teams, production and service teams, self-managing teams, and project and development teams (Cohen and Bailey, 1997; Sundstrom *et al.*, 1990). However, certain knowledge, skills, and attitudes (KSAs) that support teamwork are common to successful performance in virtually all work teams.

Over the years, researchers have identified a number of teamwork KSAs which are necessary in various degrees to support all forms of team structures (Salas and Cannon-Bowers, 2000). There appears to be a core set of teamwork competencies that cut across various team structures. And research has identified these key elements (see Salas *et al.*, 2004). Effective teamwork requires that employees exhibit the following behaviors and/or cognitions: adaptability, mutual performance monitoring, back up, motivating team members,

135

team leadership, closed-loop communication, shared understanding, collective orientation, and mutual trust. For successful teamwork to occur, team members must hold a shared mental model about their team-mates, their task requirements and their environment. Teamwork is a set of interrelated behaviors, actions, and decisions that yield a shared and valued outcome. For example, effective teamwork can lead to performance improvement (see Salas *et al.*, 2004).

Organizations are increasingly recognizing that teamwork skills are critical to the success of different types of teams, and that transportable teamwork skills are valuable to the organization because they allow greater staffing flexibility. A vice president of a Fortune 500 company who participated in our study remarked, "I see more emphasis toward teamwork and collaboration practices and less emphasis on team structure."

HOW WELL DO TRADITIONAL HR PRACTICES SUPPORT TEAMS?

The traditional HR system described earlier is ill-equipped to support and sustain team-based work units. As outlined above, the traditional job holder is not asked about team work preferences or experiences when interviewed, is selected for the ability to perform narrow job tasks, performs work-related activities mostly alone, is evaluated for technical and not teamwork skills, is compensated for individual performance that either ignores or minimizes the importance of helping others, and receives technical but not teamwork training.

For organizations that have strategic imperatives for implementing a team-based structure or that recognize that increased collaboration by employees both within and across departments is essential to attain organizational goals, traditional HR practices are insufficient and, indeed, may be counterproductive. Team members are interdependent and require additional teamwork skills, as well as process skills (planning, decision-making); along with a compensation system that promotes line-of-sight behaviors with team and organizational goals.

A related question might be, "How well can teams flourish without support from HR practices?" A manager of a mid-sized services firm shared with us that his organization's management was indifferent to the benefits of using teams and refused to support the teams through organizational practices. However, the manager highly values team-based outcomes, and encourages team-oriented behavior within his unit primarily by verbal reinforcement and informal rewards. He reports that collaborative behaviors are exhibited, but adds that "it is an uphill battle" and requires ongoing effort.

HR "BEST PRACTICES" TO SUPPORT TEAMS

Traditional HR functions include recruiting/selection, training, performance appraisal or performance management, compensation, supervision, culture, and communication. Below we describe the most common ways by which some organizations adapt the traditional functions to align them with a team-oriented approach to work performance. After each section, we offer a few suggestions for best practices that we can extract from the literature.

Table 8.1 *Best practices*

Recruiting and hiring	Use selection tools that assess teamwork skills.
	Seek personnel with a collective orientation (i.e., value being in a team).
	Involve team members during the selection process, when appropriate.
	Ensure that new team members have a "mentor."
Training	Identify the teamwork-related competencies of team members.
	Train intact teams when possible.
	Use team building to clarify roles.
	Use team training to provide teamwork KSAs.
	Evaluate team training.
Compensation	As team members become more interdependent, increase rewards for teamwork behaviors and reduce rewards for individual performance.
	Be sensitive to team members' preferences for seeking individual rewards.
	Reward team members for acquiring (and applying) teamwork-related skills.
	Design the reward system to reflect the nature and purpose of the team, for example, a project team charged with reducing inefficiencies could be rewarded through a gain-share approach.
	Both cash and non-cash incentives can encourage collaborative behaviors.
	Recognize that the compensation system may require ongoing fine tuning.
Performance management	Include teamwork competencies on performance management evaluation instruments.
	Solicit input from team members for the performance management process, for example, via 360-degree feedback.
Team leaders	Select, train, and reward team leaders who will consistently model teamwork and collaborative behaviors.
	Hold team leaders accountable for developing their teams.
	Ensure that team leaders have the necessary interpersonal and coaching skills.
Climate and culture	Send a consistent message that teamwork is recognized and valued, e.g., via newsletters, speeches, meetings.
	Articulate and clearly communicate a vision that collaborators are valued more than superstars and explain how and why teamwork contributes to the organization's bottom line.
	Ensure that supervisors, managers, and executives consistently model teamwork behaviors.

Recruiting and hiring practices

Teams can affect recruiting and hiring practices in two ways. First, the content of recruiting and hiring activities can be expanded to include some form of assessment about teamwork. Because some individuals prefer working alone and being compensated as an individual, organizations moving toward a team-based structure should screen for work preferences to avoid assigning those with a strong "individual contributor" mindset to work on teams (Campion and Higgs, 1995). Recruiters and interviewers can pose questions that assess teamwork orientation, preferences for working closely with others, and experience with teams in previous jobs. For example, Unisys selects team members who have demonstrated the ability and skills to work successfully on customer-focused teams in the past (Gross, 1997). Some researchers (see Werbel and Johnson, 2001) argue that while traditional job analysis focuses on maximizing person–job fit, the interdependencies among team members require a broader approach that emphasizes the need to develop and support interpersonal interactions known as person–group fit.

Second, members of teams can be partially or totally involved in selection and recruitment processes. For example, some organizations, such as Johnsonville Foods Co., allow self-managed work teams to control their own hiring (Lublin, 1995).

There has been little research examining within-team orientation, socialization, or mentoring (Eby, 1997). However, available research indicates that individual team members who are mentored possess higher levels of such KSAs as communication, problem solving, goal setting, conflict resolution, and planning (Hartenian, 2003). Mentoring helps new team members become socialized more quickly, which enables them to contribute more quickly and reduces the risk of their becoming alienated from the team (Reinertsen, 2000). The socialization process can be accelerated if new members are immediately given a meaningful role, assigned a sponsor, and given frequent feedback.

Recruitment and hiring—best practices

1   Use selection tools that assess teamwork skills.
2   Seek personnel with a collective orientation (i.e., value being in a team).
3   Involve team members during the selection process, when appropriate.
4   Ensure that new team members have a "mentor."

Training practices

To support teamwork, HR can offer training not only on technical skills, but on key teamwork skills (Anon, 2002). Teamwork skills training is important both to remedy individual deficiencies and to emphasize that such skills are an important part of meeting organizational goals. As stated previously, there are general teamwork skills. These skills are adaptability, closed-loop communication, team leadership, back-up behavior, interpersonal relations, and conflict resolution skills (Salas and Cannon-Bowers, 2000). While team training can be offered, some organizations have taken a more indirect approach. For example, one of our interviewees indicated that individual teamwork skills training courses were not offered, because the organization believed that integrating teamwork content into every other type of training, for example, technical and process training, sent employees a clearer message about the value of teamwork to the organizations.

For teams that need their members to support or back-up each other during busy times members can be prepared through cross-training on other team members' job duties (Campion and Higgs, 1995). The literature has identified other instructional strategies that can be implemented when appropriated and needed (see Salas and Cannon-Bowers, 2000). These strategies have yet to see their way to corporate America. Team building remains the strategy of choice. However, a recent meta-analysis showed that team building helps only in clarifying roles and does not have effect on performance (Salas et al., 1999). Corporate America and HR practitioners could benefit from the work conducted in aviation and the military. In fact, the aviation and military communities have been the biggest users of team training approaches, and have had some successes (see Salas et al., 1999).

Training—best practices

5   Identify the teamwork-related competencies of team members.
6   Train intact teams when possible.
7   Use team building to clarify roles.
8   Use team training to provide teamwork KSAs.
9   Evaluate team training.

Compensation practices

The HR practices that most directly influence whether team members exhibit teamwork are, without doubt, those related to the compensation system. A compensation system that only rewards individual performance is not consistent with sustaining teamwork (Lublin, 1995) because the compensation system tells employees which behaviors will be rewarded and which will be punished (Salas et al., 2004). If the system strictly reinforces individualistic behavior, without any consideration for collaboration or collective goals, then teamwork behaviors will be inhibited.

A team-based compensation system can be 100 percent team based (for example, for self-managed work teams) or it can be a mix of individual and team-based methods and practices. Even if the system is mostly individual based, it is still possible to reward some elements of team orientation. The organization needs to pay attention to its unique circumstances when designing the team-based compensation system. For example, some types of teams (for example, project teams) may have members who are superstars or key individuals who contribute above and beyond the efforts of most of the team members. If so, the organization may choose to offer individual-recognition awards in addition to team pay incentives (Lublin, 1995). For example, SMWT teams may not want to be responsible for allocating individual bonuses, and the responsibility would need to be shifted back to management (Lublin, 1995).

139

Various types of team rewards are possible. We will describe three major ones (Anon, 1999). First, team members can receive *skills-based pay* for developing team-oriented skills, such as adaptability, or for completing cross-training in multiple functional areas. A second way is *gain sharing*, with either equal pay for all members of a team, or in which individuals who exceed the quota are given additional increases while those who contribute less see either no increase or an appropriately reduced bonus. This approach is particularly suitable for short-lived project teams. Finally, *team-incentive* pay can take many forms. This approach is suitable for temporary and ongoing teams. The same objectives, such as cost reduction, customer satisfaction, and team profitability are applied to each team member. For example, Johnsonville Foods Co. permits its self-managed work teams to allocate monthly cash profit-sharing bonuses, based on written customer satisfaction feedback and progress toward previously set objective goals (Lublin, 1995). Other criteria can include conformance to budgets or meeting deadlines (Krotz, 2003).

Cash incentives can be an effective way to create desired behavior. For example, one survey participant recounted how a large financial institution offered a $50,000 bonus every year for three years to the department that exhibited the best teamwork behavior. After three years, the incentive was discontinued because the desired behavior had been embedded throughout the organization. Non-cash incentives can also encourage employees to engage in teamwork and collaborative behavior (Krotz, 2003). Award ceremonies are popular, and merchandise, T-shirts, plaques, and certificates can be displayed as a visible reminder of the importance of teamwork. However, care must be taken to ensure that the incentive is producing the teamwork behaviors desired and not becoming an end in itself (Krotz, 2003).

An important question that needs to be addressed by organizations that plan to implement teams is the timing of the switch from an individual- to a team-based compensation system. Some argue that compensation systems should be designed to elicit team behavior before teams are formed (Tudor *et al.*, 1996), while others advocate a year-long wait-and-learn approach (Anon, 1997). In either case, the effort required by the organization can be intensive. For example, R. R. Donnelley and Sons Co., a Chicago-based commercial printer, invested two years in designing a team-pay program for its self-directed teams before putting it into practice. The organization wanted to avoid inter-team competition (Lublin, 1995).

Compensation — best practices

10 As team members become more interdependent, increase rewards for teamwork behaviors and reduce rewards for individual performance.
11 Be sensitive to team members' preferences for seeking individual rewards.
12 Reward team members for acquiring (and applying) teamwork-related skills.
13 Design the reward system to reflect the nature and purpose of the team, for example, a project team charged with reducing inefficiencies could be rewarded through a gain-sharing approach.
14 Both cash and non-cash incentives can encourage collaborative behaviors.
15 Recognize that the compensation system may require ongoing fine tuning.

Performance management practices

Like reward systems, performance evaluation systems inform employees about the kinds of behaviors that are valued by the organization. If a performance appraisal system explicitly assesses teamwork, it emphasizes its importance (Murphy and Cleveland, 1995). Two changes can be made to traditional performance systems to support teamwork requirements. First, the content of the appraisal form can be changed to include dimensions that emphasize teamwork and collaborative behaviors as well as teamwork competencies (Gross, 1997; Heathfield, 2001).

Second, 360-degree feedback can be used to support team member development (Gross, 1997; Heathfield, 2001; Anon, 1996). Because team members have different information about a member's performance than do supervisors or managers, they may be able to supplement a supervisor feedback. Further, because team member ratings can be pooled, rating biases (such as halo effect) can be reduced (Liden *et al.*, 2001). While 360-degree ratings are not a substitute for other performance management practices, they can be a useful developmental tool. However, care must be taken in using 360-degree feedback for personnel decisions rather than simply providing developmental feedback (Anon, n.d.).

Performance management — best practices

16 Include teamwork competencies on performance management evaluation instruments.
17 Solicit input from team members for the performance management process, for example, via 360-degree feedback.

Team leaders

Depending on their purpose and structure, some types of teams require team leaders. As coaches or team leaders, supervisors and managers can positively affect team morale, provide and encourage social support, and encourage positive inter-team communication and cooperation (Campion and Higgs, 1995). Team leaders who model desirable teamwork behaviors can affect the way team members behave. Smith-Jentsch *et al.* (2001) demonstrated that team leaders are a powerful influence on team member behavior. In her study, Smith-Jentsch and her colleagues arranged for two groups to witness a brief, staged interaction between a team leader and a confederate in which assertive behavior was either reprimanded or rewarded. In spite of having just received training on how to communicate assertively, those in the group that witnessed the reprimanded behavior failed to demonstrate their newly learned skills during a subsequent exercise. Therefore, supervisors should also be held accountable for team development (Anon, 2002). The input of supervisors should be part of the planning and implementation stages of teamwork training.

In situations where teams are self-managed or autonomous, team members assume many of the responsibilities of supervisors and the supervisors act as coaches. For example, Johnsonville Food Co. allows SMWTs to recruit, hire, train, and fire team members with line supervisors assuming the role of coaches (Lublin, 1995). In some cases, team members may be unwilling to accept the responsibility for certain activities, such as disciplining a fellow team member whose behavior is substandard. There may also be legal issues with discipline and terminating team members, which a supervisor may have the training to anticipate (Liden et al., 2001).

Organizations should select team leaders who have the knowledge, skills, and ability to develop their team. For example, project team leaders should be chosen for cross-functional experience, belief in importance of teamwork, and interpersonal skills (Jassawalla and Sashittal, 2001). They found that teams with the highest levels of teamwork were managed by team leaders who encouraged communication and information sharing and were capable of developing self-directed teams, such as by developing team members' team process and interpersonal skills. Team leaders need to be skilled in conflict resolution, coaching, and communication (Caminiti and Sookdeo, 1995). Team leaders can be taught to facilitate or lead periodic team debriefs to enhance the team's effectiveness (Tannenbaum et al., 1998). Team leaders should be chosen, trained, and rewarded consistent with the purpose of the teams they will be leading.

Team leader — best practices

18 Select, train, and reward team leaders who will consistently model teamwork and collaborative behaviors.
19 Hold team leaders accountable for developing their teams.
20 Ensure that team leaders have the necessary interpersonal and coaching skills.

Organizational climate and culture

Moving from an individual-based work structure to a team-based structure requires a major cultural change (McHugh and Bennett, 1999). Team effectiveness depends on a supportive organizational context and a climate that supports teamwork (Krotz, 2003). The climate is influenced by the signals that organizational leaders send about what behaviors are expected and about how the organization will explicitly recognize and reward those behaviors (Holland et al., 2000). For example, if the organization shows that team players are valued more than a lone wolf, no matter how well he or she produces, then teamwork behaviors are reinforced (Heathfield, 2001). If executives communicate clearly and explicitly that teamwork is expected, then the organizational climate toward teamwork will reinforce desired behaviors (Heathfield, 2001). In addition to expressing what behaviors are important, executives should communicate why they are valuable, that is, senior management should communicate a clear vision about the purpose of the teams to the organization (Holland et al., 2000). Most importantly, leaders must create in a way that is consistent with the message being communicated.

Respondents to our survey overwhelmingly endorsed the importance of a teamwork-oriented culture for sustaining teamwork. An executive at a large New York-based credit union said: "All members of the organization are held to a teamwork focus. Teamwork is important to every position." The manager of an operating unit of an international advertising group agreed: "There is a mix of people with different backgrounds, Indian, European in the organization, but the organization has a strong corporate team culture; everybody buys into it." A manager at a major telecom. company expressed similar opinions, stating that the role of management was to "remove barriers between various organizations to make it easier to work together and provide encouragement that everyone needs to work together as one organization."

An organization's culture shapes employees' perceptions about the types of behaviors that are expected, accepted, and rewarded (Schein, 1996). How, then, does an organization communicate how much it values teamwork and collaborative behavior on the part of its employees? A teamwork culture is made visible to employees through the organization's communication system (Krotz, 2003). HR functions often assume at least some responsibility for communications or for advising managers and supervisors (Campion and Higgs, 1995).

Data from our informal interviews support the notion that the most teamwork-focused organizations integrate all communications: written, verbal, and symbolic, into a consistent message that permeates all HR practices. In whatever form, communications help employees recognize how their efforts contribute to the organization's goals which, in turn, gives them a shared purpose on which to focus their efforts (Salas et al., 2003).

Team-based successes, for example, productivity figures over time and anecdotes illustrate the prevalence and value of teamwork. They can send powerful messages that teamwork is good for the organization and important enough to be recognized in organizational communications such as the intranet and internal communication newsletters. Further, furnishing teams with "line of sight" information between their work and the organization's bottom line provides reinforcement. Regular surveys soliciting employee feedback on how effectively they perceive teams are operating and, equally important, how to improve them, is another visible means of supporting teamwork. Of course, surveys with no visible follow-up can generate apathy over time.

Organizational climate and culture—best practices

21 Send a consistent message that teamwork is recognized and valued, e.g., via newsletters, speeches, meetings.
22 Articulate and clearly communicate a vision that collaborators are valued more than superstars and explain how and why teamwork contributes to the organization's bottom line.
23 Ensure that supervisors, managers, and executives consistently model teamwork behaviors.

THEORETICAL JUSTIFICATION FOR ALIGNING HR PRACTICES AND TEAMWORK

"There is nothing," Kurt Lewin said, "so practical as a good theory." His 1951 proposal is still timely today. Not only does a good theory explain relationships among different variables, but it also allows predictions about expected behavior. In this case, the Human Capital Theory is an appropriate guideline for understanding the role of the HR function toward teams. According to Becker (1993), human capital describes employees' productive capabilities. Skills, knowledge, and experience contribute economic value by allowing organizations to be adaptable and productive (Jackson and Schuler, 1995). A corollary is that employees need to cooperate in order for human capital's potential value to be fully achieved. Organizations can increase the value of their human capital through the use of HR practices (Delaney and Huselid, 1996). To the extent that HR practices are used appropriately, the value derived from the practices offsets their associated costs and the anticipated return exceeds the cost (Jackson and Schuler, 1995). The clear implication is that HR practices that increase human capital provide economic benefit to the organization.

ALIGNMENT OF HR SYSTEMS AND TEAMWORK

Since the publication of Huselid's (1995) influential article on the impact of HR practices on organizational performance, there is general agreement that a strong relationship exists between corporate performance and HR practices, (Becker *et al.*, 2001; Overall, 2003; Youndt *et al.*, 1996). In fact, research has shown that human capital practices that contribute to a "collegial, flexible workplace" have a nine percent impact on market value (Pfau and Kay, 2002). Consensus is growing that an organization's success depends on effective human capital and that HR should assume a more strategic focus (Lawler and Mohrman, 2000; Walker, 1999).

As a result, most researchers and practitioners have been placing a greater emphasis on Strategic Human Resource Management (SHRM), which recognizes that as organizations employ more knowledge-workers, assume a team-based structure, and strive for adaptability and flexibility, they need a workforce strongly aligned with organization strategy to ensure that strategies can be executed successfully (Treen, 2000). The role of the HR function is to assist an organization's executives to ensure consistency between the organizational business strategy and the human resources management systems, and with research-based best practices (Gross, 1997; Treen, 2000; Ulrich, 1997).

HR practices are more effective if they complement each other as part of a systemic, integrated approach (Balkin and Montemayor, 2000; Hackman *et al.*, 2000; Morgan, 2001). This integration is critical for a number of reasons. First, coherent HR practices have a stronger effect on employees than do unrelated practices. "Employees do not respond to specific human resource policies and practices in isolation. They attend to and interpret the entire array of information available and from this they discern cultural values and behavioral norms" (Jackson and Schuler, 1995, p. 247). Our survey respondents agreed. According to the vice president of HR of a large credit union in New York State, "teamwork is considered so vital to organizational performance that it is woven into all aspects of HR practices." The vice president of a Fortune 500 company agreed: "None of the HR practices alone is enough."

Another rationale for integrating HR practices is to achieve cost savings (Youndt *et al.*, 1996). Although initial costs may be high because of the need to design and develop new practices, doing so ensures that employees will receive a consistent message about the behaviors and results that the organization values. Furthermore, inconsistent HR systems result in disruption and counterproductive behavior when employees circumvent systems to maximize their own outcomes (Campion and Higgs, 1995).

The approach taken by HR to accommodate the use of teams can range from adopting a single team-oriented practice (such as a team-based compensation system) to attempting

144

to design a constellation of team-supportive practices (integrating selection, training, appraisal, and compensation). In most cases, organizations are reluctant to make a comprehensive and simultaneous substitution of all related HR practices (Pil and Macduffie, 1996). Instead, they may evaluate the impact of implementing one or two new practices, and attempt an evolutionary process of changing practices (Pil and Macduffie, 1996). Pil and Macduffie point out that such an approach fails to take advantage of complementariness between HR practices and work systems (see Becker and Gerhart, 1996; Ichniowski and Shaw, 1999). They comment that if new work practices are complemented by HR practices, performance is improved incrementally by both the new work practices and the HR practices. Further, if adoption of the new practice depends on the presence of the complementary practice, then without the presence of the complementary HR practice, the new work practice may be dropped. For example, team-based performance is rarely successful in the presence of a strict individual-based compensation system.

Our informal telephone survey data revealed a pattern. The more importance that executive management gave to teamwork, the more likely it was that HR practices emphasized teamwork and was integrated. Further, if respondents indicated that the strategic plan called for teamwork as a means by which to achieve organizational goals, the emphasis given to teamwork in HR practices was noticeably greater. In several cases, organizations shed their traditional hierarchical structure and changed to a matrix or team-based structure. Those with whom we spoke also tended to report greater revenues as a result of the reorganization.

TAILORING "BEST PRACTICES"

When asked about the effort involved in changing to a team-oriented organizational structure, the HR director of an international financial services organization remarked: "It is simple to say that teamwork is important, but difficult to execute."

There is no "silver bullet" for designing HR practices that will support teams. One reason is that each organization is unique and needs to tailor any best practices appropriately. The nature and design of teams differ according to their purpose, level of interdependence, and task complexity (Campion and Higgs, 1995; Scott and Einstein, 2001). Also, contextual organizational factors, such as culture, values, strategy, morale, HR and financial capability, market position, and technology, influence whether and how best practice practices or processes can be implemented (Fitz-enz, 1997; Morgan, 2001). Any generic system is likely to ignore important team differences (Scott and Einstein, 2001). Organizations that try to implement best practices used by a competitor run the risk of failure because using best practices requires more than "copying and pasting" (Fitz-Enz, 1997; Treen, 2000). Organizations should remain flexible about work team designs, and be willing to modify them as needed (Campion and Higgs, 1995).

CONCLUSIONS

Both research evidence and case studies convincingly argue that effective team-based structure and attitudes toward teamwork do not occur in isolation. They require an integrated HR system with each subsystem (such as communication, selection, training, appraisal) consistently reinforcing (or at least not inhibiting) the organization's focus on teams and teamwork. Trying to align teamwork with HR reward systems is more complex than just managing steady change. It is an environment where HR policies meet workplace reality, and although clarity of purpose is craved it is rarely articulated. The challenge for HR professionals is to evaluate various specific HR practices and modify them in a manner appropriate to the organization's unique dynamic circumstances.

REFERENCES

Anon (n.d.) 360-Degree Feedback Overview, *VMCI*. Online, available at www.vmci.nl/doc/360_Degree_Feedback_Overview.pdf (accessed July 28, 2003).

Anon (1996) The network discusses: Team size, pay, performance, and awards, *Compensation and Benefits Review*, 28(2): 6–17.

Anon (1997) Paying for teamwork: Winning compensation strategies, *Getting Results . . . for the Hands-on Manager: Plant Edition*, 42(4): 6–8.

Anon (1999) When teamwork is a must, compensation should follow suit, *Timely Business Tips*, CPA Associates International. Online, available at www.cpaai.com/timely_tips_archives/june_28_1999.html (accessed July 28, 2003).

Anon (2000) Teamwork: What makes teams go and what to watch out for, *HRZone*, February. Online, available at www.hrzone.com/articles/team_variables.html (accessed July 28, 2003).

Anon (2002) Five case studies on successful teams, *HR Focus*, 79(4): 18–20.

Balkin, D. B. and Montemayor, E. F. (2000) Explaining team-based pay: A contingency perspective based on the organizational life cycle, team design, and organizational learning literatures, *Human Resource Management Review*, 10(3): 249–269.

Becker, B. and Gerhart, B. (1996) The impact of human resource management on organizational performance: Progress and prospects, *Academy of Management Journal*, 39(4): 779–801.

Becker, B. E., Huselid, M. A., and Ulrich, D. (2001) *The HR Scorecard: Linking People, Strategy, and Performance.* Boston, MA: Harvard Business School Press.

Becker, G. S. (1993) *Human Capital: A Theoretical and Empirical Analysis, with Special Reference to Education*, 3rd edn. Chicago, IL: University of Chicago Press.

Caminiti, S. and Sookdeo, R. (1995) What team leaders need to know, *Fortune*, 131(3): 93–97.

Campion, M. A. and Higgs, C. A. (1995) Design work teams to increase productivity and satisfaction, *HR Magazine*, 40(10): 101–105.

Cohen, S. G. and Bailey, D. E. (1997) What makes teams work: Group effectiveness research from the shop floor to the executive suite, *Journal of Management*, 23(3): 239–290.

Delaney, J. T. and Huselid, M. A. (1996) The impact of human resource management practices on perceptions of organizational performance, *Academy of Management Journal*, 39(4): 949–969.

Eby, L. T. (1997) Alternative forms of mentoring in changing organizational environments: A conceptual extension of the mentoring literature, *Journal of Vocational Behavior*, 51(1): 125–144.

Fitz-enz, J. (1993) The truth about "best practice", *Human Resource Planning*, 16(3): 19–27.

Fitz-enz, J. (1997) Highly effective HR practices, *HR Focus*, 74(4): 11–13.

Gordon, J. (1992) Work teams—How far have they come?, *Training*, 29(10): 59–65.

Gross, S. E. (1997) When jobs become team roles, what do you pay for?, *Compensation and Benefits Review*, 29(1): 48–51.

Hackman, J. R. (1994) Trip wires in designing and leading workgroups, *The Occupational Psychologist*, 23: 3–8.

Hackman, J. R., Wageman, R., Ruddy, T. M., and Ray, C. L. (2000) Team effectiveness in theory and in practice. In G. L. Cooper, E. A. Locke, and R. J. Burke (eds), *Industrial and Organizational Psychology: Linking Theory with Practice*. Malden, MA: Blackwell Publishers, pp. 109–129.

Hartenian, L. S. (2003) Team member acquisition of team knowledge, skills, and abilities, *Team Performance Management*, 9(1): 23–30.

Heathfield, S. M. (2001) How to build a teamwork culture: Do the hard stuff, *Human Resources, About.com*. Online, available at www.humanresources.about.com/library/weekly/aa122001a. htm (accessed July 28, 2003).

Holland, S., Gaston, K., and Gomes, J. (2000) Critical success factors for cross-functional teamwork in new product development, *International Journal of Management Reviews*, 2(3): 231–259.

Huselid, M. A. (1995) The impact of human resource management practices on turnover, productivity, and corporate financial performance, *Academy of Management Journal*, 38(3): 635–672.

Ichniowski, C. and Shaw, K. (1999) The effects of human resource management systems on economic performance: An international comparison of U.S. and Japanese plants, *Management Science*, 45(5): 704–721.

Jackson, S. E. and Schuler, R. S. (1995) Understanding human resource management in the context of organizations and their environments, *Annual Review of Psychology*, 46: 237–264.

Jassawalla, A. R. and Sashittal, H. C. (2001) The role of senior management and team leaders in building collaborative new product teams, *Engineering Management Journal*, 13(2): 33–40.

Krotz, J. (2003) Reward your employees for teamwork, *Microsoft bCentral*. Online, available at www.bcentral.com/articles/msnfeature/jun03_03.asp (accessed July 28, 2003).

Lawler, E. E. III, and Mohrman, S. A. (2000) Beyond the vision: What makes HR effective?, *Human Resource Planning*, 23(4): 10–20.

Lawler, E. E., III, Mohrman, S. A., and Benson, G. (2001) *Organizing for High Performance: Employee involvement, TQM, Reengineering, and Knowledge Management in the Fortune 1000: the CEO Report*, San Francisco, CA: Jossey-Bass.

Liden, R. C., Wayne, S. J., and Kraimer, M. L. (2001) Managing individual performance in work groups, *Human Resource Management*, 40(1): 63–72.

Lublin, J. S. (1995) Executive pay (a special report)—my colleague, my boss: As more companies divide workers into self-managed teams, they try to link pay to team performance. It isn't easy, *Wall Street Journal*, R4.

McHugh, M. and Bennett, H. (1999) Dream on: Team work from the confines of the bureaucratic cage, *Strategic Change*, 8(4): 189–203.

Miller, J. S. and Cardy, R. L. (2000) Technology and managing people: Keeping the "Human" in human resources, *Journal of Labor Research*, 21(3): 447–461.

Mohrman, S. A., Cohen, S. G., and Mohrman, A. M. Jr. (1995) *Designing team-based organizations: New forms for knowledge work.* San Francisco, CA: Jossey-Bass.

Moreland, R. L. (1999) Transactive memory: Learning who knows what in work groups and organizations. In L. L. Thompson, J. M. Levine, and D. M. Messick (eds), *Shared Cognition in Organizations: The Management of Knowledge.* Mahwah, NJ: Erlbaum, pp. 3–31.

Morgan, J. P. (2001) HR practices for high-performance organizations, *Foundation for sustainable economic development.* Online, available at www.fsed.org/researchprojects/project3a.html (accessed July 28, 2003).

Murphy, K. R. and Cleveland, J. N. (1995) *Understanding Performance Appraisal: Social, organizational, and Goal-based Perspectives.* Thousand Oaks, CA: Sage Publications.

Overall, S. (2003) Time to reflect on HR's influence, *Personnel Today*, September 2: 11.

Pfau, B. and Kay, I. (2002) The hidden human resource: Shareholder value, *Optimize*. Online, available at www.optimizemag.com/issue/008/pr_culture.htm (accessed July 28, 2003).

Pil, F. K. and Macduffie, J. P. (1996) The adoption of high-involvement work practices, *Industrial Relations*, 35(3): 423–456.

Reinertsen, D. (2000) How to make new team members become productive quickly, *Electronic Design*, 48(25): 58.

Salas, E. and Cannon-Bowers, J. A. (2000) The anatomy of team training. In S. Tobias and J. D. Fletcher (eds), *Training and Retraining: A Handbook for Business, Industry, Government, and the Military.* New York: Macmillan Reference, p. 317.

Salas, E., Bowers, C. A., and Edens, E. (eds) (2001) *Improving Teamwork in Organizations: Applications of Resource Management Training.* Mahwah, NJ: Lawrence Erlbaum Associates.

Salas, E., Dickinson, T. L., Converse, S. A., and Tannenbaum, S. I. (1992) Toward an understanding of team performance and training. In R. W. Swezey and E. Salas (eds), *Teams: Their Training and Performance.* Norwood, NJ: Ablex, pp. 3–30.

Salas, E., Kosarzycki, M. P., Tannenbaum, S. I., and Carnegie, D. (2003) Principles (and advice) for understanding and promoting effective teamwork in organizations. In R. J. Burke and C. L. Cooper (eds), *Leading in Turbulent Times: Managing in the New World of Work.* Malden, MA: Blackwell Science Inc., pp. 95–120.

Salas, E., Kosarzycki, M. P., Tannenbaum, S. I., and Carnegie, D. (2004) Principles and advice for understanding and promoting effective teamwork in organizations. In R. Burke and C. Cooper (eds), *Leading in Turbulent Times: Managing in the New World of Work.* Malden, MA: Blackwell, pp. 95–120.

Salas, E., Rozell, D., Mullen, B., and Driskell, J. E. (1999) The effect of team building on performance: An integration. *Small Group Research*, 30(3): 309–329.

Schein, E. H. (1996) *Organizational Culture and Leadership.* San Francisco: Jossey-Bass.

Scott, S. G. and Einstein, W. O. (2001) Strategic performance appraisal in team-based organizations: One size does not fit all, *Academy of Management Executive*, 15(2): 107–116.

Seaman, R. (1997) Case study: Rejuvenating an organization with team pay, *American Management Association, Compensation and Benefits Review*, 29(5): 25–30.

Smith-Jentsch, K. A., Salas, E., and Brannick, M. T. (2001) To transfer or not to transfer? Investigating the combined effects of trainee characteristics, team leader support, and team climate, *Journal of Applied Psychology*, 86(2): 279–292.

Sundstrom, E., De Meuse, K. P., and Futrell, D. (1990) Work teams: Applications and effectiveness, *American Psychologist*, 45(2): 120–133.

Tannenbaum, S. I., Smith-Jentsch, K. A., and Behson, S. J. (1998) Training team leaders to facilitate team learning and performance. In J. A. Cannon-Bowers and E. Salas (eds), *Making Decisions Under Stress : Implications for Individual and Team Training*. Washington, DC: APA, pp. 247–270.

Treen, D. (2000) Strategic human resources, *Ivey Business Journal*, 64(3): 62–67.

Tudor, T. R., Trumble, R. R., and Diaz, J. J. (1996) Work-teams: Why do they often fail?, *S.A.M. Advanced Management Journal*, 61(4): 31–40.

Ulrich, D. (1997) *Human Resource Champions: The Next Agenda for Adding Value and Delivering Results*. Boston, MA: Harvard Business School Press.

Walker, J. W. (1999) Is HR ready for the 21st Century?, *Human Resource Planning*, 22(2): 5–7.

Werbel, J. D. and Johnson, D. J. (2001) The use of person-group fit for employment selection: A missing link in person-environment fit, *Human Resource Management*, 40(3): 227–240.

Youndt, M. A., Snell, S. A., Dean, J. W. Jr., and Lepak, D. P. (1996) Human resource management, manufacturing strategy, and firm performance, *Academy of Management Journal*, 39(4): 836–867.

Chapter 9

Innovations in diversity management

Advancement of practice and thought

Mark D. Agars and Janet L. Kottke

As predicted (*Workforce 2000*, Johnston and Packer, 1987), the new workforce is here. Never have so many challenges *and* opportunities faced organizations as those posed by the diverse workforce. In response, diversity management has become a critical component of human resource management (HRM).

Diversity management is a relatively young field of HRM and its brief history—roughly 40 years—reveals a constant evolution and innovation of ideas and practice. In essence, a review of innovations in the field of diversity management could constitute a comprehensive historical review. Although not quite so ambitious, this chapter provides a brief review of critical historical points, and a highlighting of key themes and innovations that have emerged over the last ten years as organizational efforts to address diversity have come to represent the HRM practice of *diversity management*.

Diversity management takes many forms in practice, but can be defined as an organization's active investment in the integration, development, and advancement of individuals who in the collective, represent the heterogeneity of the labor force, and in the development of organizational strategy, culture, policies, and practices that support interpersonal respect, communication, and individual, team, and organizational performance in a diverse environment. Diversity management is necessarily inclusive, and requires efforts across HRM responsibilities and in all aspects of organizational functioning. The value of conceptualizing diversity management as a comprehensive set of processes (rather than a single policy or intervention) is now recognized (cf., Agars and Kottke, 2004; Cox, 2001). This perspective represents an important innovation in our *thinking* about diversity management, and so we begin our presentation of innovations in HRM practice related to diversity management by highlighting its emergence.

BEGINNINGS

Modern forms of diversity management evolved from affirmative action (AA) and equal employment opportunity (EEO) programs. In response to the Civil Rights Act of 1964, Executive Order 11246, and other social and governmental pressures, numerous human resource management practices were implemented in the 1970s and 1980s (Konrad and Linnehan, 1995). These AA and EEO programs were attempts to increase the presence of underrepresented groups, typically women and minorities. Unfortunately, many of these practices were symbolic or found to be illegal or improperly implemented. Consequently, the integrity and fairness of AA programs has often been called into question (Konrad and Linnehan, 1999; Kravitz and Platania, 1993). There is clear evidence, however, that AA and EEO practices made a positive impact on the presence and pay of underrepresented groups (Blau and Beller, 1988; Fosu, 1992). Though diversity management is much more than affirmative action (Yakura, 1996), these programs laid the groundwork for contemporary diversity management, and their limitations are the impetus for qualitatively different approaches to diversity.

In 1990, Roosevelt Thomas argued that affirmative action as an independent approach to workforce diversity was limiting and outdated. He believed that the landscape had changed such that, "the realities facing us are no longer the realities affirmative action was designed to fix" (Thomas, 1990, p. 107). He suggested, and subsequent research confirmed, that AA programs would foster perceptions of unfairness (Konrad and Linnehan, 1999) and the stigmatization of its beneficiaries (Heilman *et al.*, 1997). His call was for a fundamental transformation of diversity efforts from individual AA and EEO programs to active diversity management. This transformation represents an important innovation in our approach to diversity and, more specifically, this shift in perspective represents the birth of the modern HRM practice of diversity management. Others in the field echoed Thomas, and argued for organizations to rethink their approach to diversity and, specifically, to actively *manage* diversity (Cox, 1991; Kandola, 1995; Powell, 1993). Although initial ideas were limited on details for how organizations should achieve this desired end-state, the sentiment was consistent: AA and EEO programs needed to be replaced by proactive and comprehensive efforts to manage diversity.

Although some perceived the emergence of diversity management to be a fad, it is clear today that it is not (Ivancevich and Gilbert, 2000). Diversity management has swelled to a $300 billion a year industry (Flynn, 1998), which, by the year 2001, was present in over 75 percent of *Fortune 1000* companies (Daniels, 2001). This growth is evident not only in the resources allocated to diversity management efforts but, more importantly, in the innovative ideas and practices those resources have produced. Since 1990, thousands of articles have been written about diversity management programs in one form or another, and several texts review the area (Cox, 1994, 2001; Chemers *et al.*, 1995; Stockdale and Crosby, 2004). There is no doubting the impact diversity management has had on the development of organizational thought and practice.

THE BUSINESS CASE FOR DIVERSITY MANAGEMENT

Innovations are driven by purpose, and some have argued that the business case for diversity management has not been made (cf., Hansen, 2003; Kochan *et al.*, 2003). Others perceive efforts falling under the "diversity management" rubric to be unnecessary, unfair practices, or glorified AA programs. Among professionals, a legitimate criticism of diversity management is the absence of hard metrics to illustrate the impact of programs on meaningful organizational outcomes (Hansen, 2003). Although research linking diversity management to business outcomes is limited (see Frink *et al.*, 2003; Richard *et al.*, 2003), such links are not the only means to making the business case. Immigration and demographic data, as outlined in Census 2000, reveal an increasingly diverse country.Over 15 percent of the population reports having a disability, women now make up more than 50 percent of the MBA student population, the baby boomers are aging, and there is increased awareness of sexual orientation and class. Significant changes are already taking place in society and the workplace (Hays-Thomas, 2004; Holvino, 2002) and accepting the data as an illustration of the societal and workforce diversity, strong arguments for the importance of managing diversity emerge on the basis of the inevitable reality of considerable differences among people entering the workforce.

Further reason to manage diversity is found in the review by Williams and O'Reilly (1998) of the research examining the relationship between diversity and performance. Although there remains much we do not know about the underlying processes, their review reveals that diversity does impact processes, functioning, and performance, and in many contexts, this impact is a negative one. These findings underscore the need for organizations to identify and develop best ways of managing diversity.

IDENTIFYING INNOVATIONS

The history of HRM provides sufficient examples of practices that emerged, became popular despite a lack of theory or rigorous evaluation, and ultimately proved limited. Diversity management is *not* a fad, *nor* is it a short-term reality. It is critical, however, that innovations in the field be based on relevant and available knowledge of organizations. One limitation that has plagued the diversity management field has been the lack of comprehensive theoretical and systems-based approaches (Agars and Kottke, 2004; Triandis *et al.*, 1994). This limitation has meant that most innovations have been practice driven. Although we discuss and praise meaningful innovations that have emerged over the last decade, we recognize that sound HRM practices are grounded in theory.

SYSTEMS- AND THEORY-BASED APPROACHES

System theory (Katz and Kahn, 1978) argues that organizations are complex systems, and pushing or pulling on one part of the system affects another. Implementing a change in one part of the system without consideration for its effects on another part of the system is likely to lead to unexpected consequences. Even well-intentioned efforts to embrace diversity will fail if these efforts ignore the inevitable structural connections within the organization. Unfortunately, the practice of diversity management rarely presents the opportunity to appraise an organization's entire input-throughput-output system. Rather, practitioners are often restricted to working with only one or two elements of the system. The full picture must be in view, however, if diversity efforts are to be conceptualized properly and if they are to succeed.

153

INNOVATIONS

Our review of innovations focuses on examples that represent significant elements of a system and therefore are likely to improve significantly the organization's odds of diversity success. We define an innovation in HRM (diversity management) as one that introduces a novel approach, practice, or perspective that advances the cause of diversity in organizations. Specifically, an innovation, whether in organizational practice or in thought, enhances the ability of an organization to successfully manage workforce diversity. We have reviewed dozens of programs to highlight best practices, and we organize our examples of innovations around the HRM practices that have received the greatest attention in the advancement of diversity management practice.

Recruiting

Fundamental to diversity management is ensuring that the managerial pipeline is fueled by a diverse representation of individuals. Organizations have recognized this need, and many companies have developed programs designed to populate the pipeline with diversity. In some cases, these "diversity initiatives" are simply re-labels of older, existing AA programs. Other companies, like IBM (Shum and Moss, 2002) and Best Foods (White, 1999a; Osland et al., 2002), have used their AA plans as starting points and embraced diversity by identifying, through task forces, the barriers to recruiting minorities and women. In response to task force recommendations, for example, IBM instituted several family-friendly policies including flexible work schedules. Family-friendly policies have been used by organizations to attract applicants who might otherwise not have considered the organizations for employment (Allen et al., 2000; Galinsky et al., 1996).

Other innovations tied to recruiting have emphasized community partnerships. Continental has developed alliances with a number of minority associations (e.g., Organization of Black Airline Pilots, Black Flight Attendants of America, Hispanic MBA Association) that were instrumental in attracting minority candidates. To retain recruits, Continental instituted pay bonuses linked to teamwork, implemented diversity goals for each business division, and began training to address and prevent potential conflicts based on differences in the workplace. Continental has made Fortune's 100 list of Best Companies to Work For and the Hispanic Business's list of Best Places to Work for Latinos (Fitzerald, 2001). Other companies such as Northwestern Mutual (Van Grinsven, 1998), Pacific Bell (Johnson and O'Mara, 1992), and Charles Schwab (Mattis, 2002) have enhanced their college recruiting programs. Charles Schwab's recruitment program places graduating college seniors in training programs and develops leadership skills in business school students, then rotates them through field and corporate placements. Women now comprise 39 percent of Schwab's previously exclusively male workforce (Mattis, 2002). Other organizations have developed internships (Consolidated Edison, Mattis, 2002; Chubb, Tomlinson, 1992; Corn Products Refining, Scott, 1993) or scholarship awards (Medical Center at UCSF/SFSU Nursing, Spicer et al., 1994) targeting underrepresented groups to serve their recruiting goals. In the public sector, fire departments have held exercise programs for interested applicants to help attract and qualify applicants from underrepresented groups (Knutson and Noce, 1992).

The ability to recruit and retain a diverse workforce is a first and necessary step for diversity management. Although these initiatives have primarily targeted entry-level positions, they exemplify the array of strategies intended to increase access for traditionally underrepresented populations.

Structural support

Top management support

Active involvement of top management, demonstrated through statements, behaviors, or initiatives, is key to successful diversity management. The CEO of Eastern Bank in 1990 publicly announced that his vision for the bank included valuing diversity (Zane, 1998). In subsequent annual talks to employees, he revised and amplified his vision, and further demonstrated his support by attending a diversity-training workshop. The shift in vision led to organizational restructuring (flatter, less hierarchical structure) and intensive diversity training for employees. *DiversityInc*, which conducts an annual survey to identify the top 50 US companies for their diversity practices, named JP Morgan number 1 in 2002 (Cole, 2002; Frankel, 2002). JP Morgan's CEO does not simply pay lip service to diversity goals. He chairs JP Morgan's Corporate Diversity Council, prepares the report of the Corporate Diversity Council meetings, emails employees about diversity regularly, and meets with executives annually regarding their progress on diversity initiatives.

Other leaders have created distinct units responsible for promoting diversity. Georgia Power, in response to a racial discrimination lawsuit, designated a Senior Vice President of Diversity who reports directly to the CEO. The CEO also appointed managers dedicated to developing solutions to potential discrimination (James and Wooten, 2001). Core States Financial Corp (acquired in 1998 by First Union Corp) began a culture change friendly to diversity in 1990. One of the first moves made by the company's CEO was to create an office of diversity that answered directly to the CEO. The purpose of this office was to coordinate a diversity consulting group to train middle managers who would, themselves, become internal diversity training consultants. Known as Change Management Consultants (CMCs), they serve as facilitators for "learning labs" in which senior managers learn change management skills and apply those skills to their own business units. The office of diversity was eventually phased out when the responsibility for diversity change management shifted to the middle managers (Hyater-Adams and Frost, 1998), an important sign that the CEO's mission had permeated the organization. At Chevron (now ChevronTexaco), the CEO asked business units to incorporate diversity goals into their strategic plans (Stuller, 1995), both demonstrating top management support of diversity management, and encouraging accountability to diversity initiatives throughout the organization.

Top management support is critical to the success of HRM initiatives, and diversity management is no exception. Without top-level support, the message of importance is not going to be heard and, as the above examples illustrate, the involvement of top management creates many opportunities for innovations and, ultimately, for the success of diversity management efforts.

Diversity councils

Typically, diversity councils are composed of company volunteers who work as internal consultants with business units, helping those business units identify potential problems, detecting barriers to recruiting or retaining women and minorities, supporting training or events, and making recommendations to top management.

Amoco set up its first diversity advisory council (DAC) in 1993. This DAC was chaired by Amoco's CEO and was comprised of volunteers from Amoco's US operations. This initial DAC reported to the company's board of directors and was to identify shortfalls in the achievement of the strategic management of diversity at Amoco. Eventually, Amoco instituted DACs across its worldwide operations (40 as of 1997) (Watson, 1997). Other organizations that have incorporated diversity councils are GrandMet (owner of Pillsbury and Burger King; Greenslade, 1991), Hewlett Packard (Conklin, 2001), IBM (Shum and Moss, 2002), JP Morgan (Cole, 2002), and Northern States Power (Weidenfeller, 1992).

Diversity councils have the potential to exemplify important principles underlying successful diversity management: accountability, integration of resources across levels, and top management support. In addition, they also permit valuable feedback from ground troops to the leadership.

Mentoring programs

Mentoring is one of the most popular ways to provide support for minorities, particularly women. While not a comprehensive solution to the slow advancement into managerial and executive ranks (Scandura and Baugh, 2002), mentoring is a critical developmental marker differentiating those who advance into the top levels and those who do not (Burke, 2002).

The Bank of Montreal, in 1990, developed a strategic plan that targeted women and minorities for upgrades in skills and advancement. The mentoring program was one of several initiatives undertaken by the Bank of Montreal as part of its Workplace Equality Program, a program that has netted the Bank of Montreal a Catalyst award and the HR Development Canada Annual Merit Award (Jafri and Isbister, 2002). Before implementing its mentoring program, Bank of Montreal reviewed the literature, contacted consultants, and determined the infrastructure necessary to support the program. Key sponsors among the Bank executives were sought in advance of implementation of a pilot program in which protégés and mentors were carefully matched. Managers of protégés were consulted and were involved in the protégés' developmental plans. The process of mentoring was monitored by external consultants and through separate small group meetings for protégés and mentors. Surveys sent to protégés, their managers, and mentors revealed that all reported significant benefits. Protégés had more extensive networks and a better understanding of bank operations. Mentors reported a greater sense of teamwork and collegiality. Managers reported that protégés better understood what was required to succeed. The Bank of Montreal viewed the pilot as successful and implemented it bank-wide (Gray et al., 1995; Martinez, 1995).

Texas Commerce Bank has implemented a mentoring program with similar characteristics to the Bank of Montreal, aimed at ethnic minorities (Sadri and Tran, 2002). As part of its Advancement of Women Initiative, Procter and Gamble assigns junior level women to senior level managers, not as protégés but as mentors with the goal of educating the mostly male executive ranks on how their behavior affects women and others (White, 1999b).

Mentoring programs are widely used in organizations as a key developmental tool for future organizational leaders. Such efforts have a long history of providing essential development, access to networks, and other growth opportunities (Burke, 2002). Historically, one of the great limitations for non-majority members has been that access to mentors was restricted. The work done by these organizations demonstrates that innovations in diversity management may come, quite simply, by ensuring that vital HRM practices are accessible to all employees.

Support groups and networking

Many companies have chartered groups for minorities (Conklin, 2000). These groups provide opportunities for employees who share similar background or situational characteristics, to meet on company time, provide support for each other, and network. Microsoft sponsors employee resource groups for a broad range of employee groups including African-Americans, women, Hispanics, gays, lesbians and transgenders, deaf and hard of hearing, single parents, dads, and Hellenic (Microsoft, 2003). Sodexho, a worldwide food and facilities management conglomerate, implemented networking groups with an aim to help historically underrepresented group members to be exposed to, and mentored by, top management as well as to provide developmental opportunities (Anonymous, 2003).

Much like having a mentor, gaining access to both formal and informal networks within an organization and throughout an industry is essential to employee growth and advancement and has other benefits such as recruiting (Mattis, 2002). Networks provide social support, but also access to important professional opportunities. Researchers have noted that non-majority organizational members have not historically shared the same access to these critical HRM functions (Ibarra, 1995). The most effective innovations not only provide support, but also access to the most important organizational players.

Supportive policies and practices

Aimed initially at women with children, many companies began implementing family-friendly policies to attract and retain good employees. More recently, these flexible work scheduling and benefits options have become part of companies' diversity packages. Companies discovered that these policies attract and retain a broad range of workers. These flexible policies include part-time permanent work schedules, telecommuting or working from home, and "family-friendly" benefit plans. The Bank of Montreal, already mentioned for its mentoring program, has implemented flexible workweeks, job sharing, and "people care" days (hours or days off with pay for scheduling necessary events) (Jafri and Isbister, 2002). The Bank of Montreal (Jafri and Isbister, 2002), IBM (Shum and Moss, 2002), and Northern States Power (Weidenfeller, 1992) provide extended leaves of absence, with IBM granting among the most generous, at up to three years. Northern States Power cooperated with other employers to sponsor a school and childcare center close to the job site, a benefit attractive to working parents. Finally, Xerox (Sherter, 1996) provides a one-time mortgage assistance payment and extended health care for any member of the employee's household.

Evidence suggests that many family-friendly or work-life initiatives have a positive impact on attitudes, turnover, and performance outcomes in organizations (Lobel, 1999). Though, as with all diversity management components, success requires support from management, a supportive culture, and must address the specific needs of the organizational members (Rosin and Korabik, 2002).

Training

"Diversity training" is an inclusive label applied to a broad array of interventions including sensitivity workshops (Chevron, Stuller, 1995; Corn Products Refining, Scott, 1993), internships taken by managers (UPS, Darden, 2003) or students (Mt Sinai, Butts, 2001) in impoverished geographic regions, one-day cultural immersion events replete with food and festivities (Hebrew Home for the Aged, Lee and Baltazar, 2001), and skill development for working with people who are different (Eastern Bank, Zane, 1998; Pacific Gas and Electric, Johnson and O'Mara, 1992).

Diversity training programs have evolved during the past 20 years, much as our understanding of diversity has evolved. Early diversity training focused either on raising awareness of issues salient to women and minorities (e.g., Exxon, Sheridan, 1994) or was aimed at women and minorities through career development efforts (Price Waterhouse, Toner, 1996; Procter and Gamble, Neff, 1998). Later programs targeted other members of the organization: white males and managers. Some of these programs may have been counter productive in that they engendered hostility and allegations of political correctness over business necessity (Arai et al., 2001; Von Bergen et al., 2002). More recently, companies have begun to integrate diversity training into existing training or to implement within a broader scale change effort.

Introduction to diversity training is what most companies mean by basic training and is present in about 40 percent of US companies (Arai et al., 2001). Such training overviews the changing demographics of the labor force, how diversity differs from AA, persistent stereotypes, and why diversity is important to business success. The primary goal is to educate the organization's workforce and make it aware of the organization's goals regarding diversity.

Corn Products Refining (CPR) implements focused awareness training. In small group multi-day retreats, demographically mixed groups role-play and discuss their experiences with the company from their perspectives as a Canadian male, an African-American woman, and so forth (Scott, 1993). An external evaluation conducted after the training suggested that women and minorities felt CPR was more welcoming of their views. Others who have used this type of training include Chevron (Stuller, 1995), Exxon (Sheridan, 1994), GrandMet (Greenslade, 1991), and Kinney Shoes (Santora, 1991).

Skills-based training is exemplified by Chemical Group of Monsanto's consulting pairs technique (Galagan, 1993; Laabs, 1993). Consulting pairs are trained volunteers who have undergone 13 days of training of awareness of cultural, gender, and ethnic differences, conflict resolution, and consulting techniques. Two volunteers form a consulting team who facilitate discussion for an employee–boss pair. Bosses and employees can clear the air regarding underlying differences—that may be related to differences on the basis of color or gender—with help from consultants. After implementation, turnover of minorities and women dropped. Intensive, week-long skills-based training is used also by Pacific Gas and Electric (Johnson and O'Mara, 1992) to prepare internal consultants and managers for approaching diversity.

McDonald's Hamburger University represents a well-crafted use of integrated diversity planning (Flynn, 1996). Hamburger U educates employees from crew to management on how best to serve the customer, regardless of the region of the world in which that customer may reside. Attendees of Hamburger U have undergone diversity training since the 1970s (Solomon, 1993). Training emphasizes community involvement, and operators are expected to get to know the neighborhoods of their franchises and to develop ties to local associations and schools. By focusing attention on the local community, McDonald's staff typically resembles the diversity of the local community.

Diversity training is the most common diversity initiative and has one of the longest histories. As with any form of training, environment and management support are critical if the wisdom and skills developed in training are to extend to the workplace (Tracey *et al.*, 1995). Ultimately, the success of training as a diversity management technique depends on its integration with system-wide processes, supportive top management, and organizational culture.

Measurement of results

To measure progress, one needs a metric by which to evaluate it. The simplest metric is a headcount: how many women and minorities have been hired or promoted after the diversity initiative. Several organizations monitor turnover rates among women and minorities (Procter and Gamble, White, 1999b; Monsanto, Laabs, 1993). In addition to these measures, Grand Met checks performance appraisal ratings, acceptance rates of job offers, and grievance rates and their outcomes (Greenslade, 1991). More sophisticated measures may include group performance through team performance appraisals and bonuses. Sears (White, 1998) has developed a Total Performance Index (TPI) that tracks employee attitudes, customer satisfaction, upward mobility of women and minorities, retention rates, numbers of employees completing the diversity training, complaints and litigation, purchases from minority- and women-owned business, and diversity of its vendors. This dazzling array of indicators Sears uses is consistent with its system approach to diversity. A further benefit of developing measures, especially those related to performance, is that people pay close attention to what gets measured.

Accountability

Too many organizations espouse diversity management without developing the systems and support necessary to make it an effective HRM strategy. Holding decision-makers accountable demonstrates organizational commitment. At the Bank of Montreal, which initiated a plan in 1990 targeting the progression of women in the executive ranks, managers are held accountable via the performance appraisal. Managers at Eastern Bank are evaluated on their performance appraisals by how well they have demonstrated an ability to "work success-fully across demographics." Annual performance reviews at Northern States Power include how well the employee has created an environment for diversity and how well he or she is meeting department goals for diversity. The accountability at some companies is written into business plans (e.g., Chevron, Stuller, 1995; Security Pacific, Shea and Okada, 1992) or is incorporated into a "scorecard" (Bell South, Raphael, 2002) that measures not only headcount within the company but how well the executive or business unit is using minority-based suppliers (e.g., Sears, White, 1998).

As with developing indicators of diversity success, tying those indicators to rewards leads to accountability. At the individual level, when leaders, managers, and employees are held accountable for their support of diversity management, efforts are taken seriously and, ultimately, are more successful. Accountability also provides guidance for continued development. Similarly, organization-level accountability fosters the development of prac-tices and the support and vision of top management.

Integrated system-based programs

Clearly, many organizations are making strides toward implementing practices to support diversity by focusing on important elements necessary to organizational change. Next, we describe Sandia Labs' culture change to refocus its business and remedy an unhealthy climate. Sandia Labs serves as an exemplar of a system-wide diversity initiative.

Sandia National Labs, owned by Lockheed Martin, and operated for the US Department of Energy, has a highly educated and historically white, male workforce. Sandia had complied with AA and EEO mandates and had provided basic diversity training to its employees, but a Department of Labor survey conducted in the early 1990s uncovered a hostile work environment at the Livermore plant. In response, Sandia embarked upon wholesale culture change that was well integrated into the entire organization, directed attention to business performance, and tied diversity to broader business issues. Sandia first created a diversity-planning department that focused change on all levels: individual, team, management, and organization. The plan that unfolded had top-level management support, sufficient financial resources, and willing staff. Three events during the first 15 months prepared Sandia for culture change: (1) 50 employees participated in an intensive three-day diversity training to become diversity champions and internal consultants; (2) 15 employees attended a diversity program to develop an HR conference on diversity for 200 top leaders of Sandia; and (3) each division created its own diversity council that met and identified barriers to high performance and inclusion. In the ensuing months, diversity champions, top leadership (VPs) and diversity councils worked in concert to develop action plans. The HR Division at Sandia developed a wide range of practices, including family-friendly poli-cies and support for new networking groups such as a gay and lesbian affinity group, and inserted a new competency, managing diversity, into managers' performance appraisals. The payoffs of these initiatives became evident during subsequent reorganizing and down-sizing. Top leaders who had been sensitized to people issues during the diversity programs communicated effectively, respected input from employees, and developed a more humane process for separating employees from the organization. Five years after the initial program launch, a Corporate Diversity Team (CDT), representing every level of the organization, directed the transition from HR to divisions (Learson, 1998).

Sandia's experience with wholesale culture change demonstrates the challenges and potential for addressing diversity. Considerable effort was necessary, from all levels of the system, to create a new environment friendly to diversity. One of the unexpected benefits of developing a system friendly to diversity was that the organization became a better place to work, for everyone.

Summary/review of best practices

We've identified innovations in best practices that span the spectrum of HRM responsibilities. We see innovative practices in recruitment, training, leadership, and measurement. We see the value of integrating ideas across function and through the organizations although, we note, the practice of such integration is limited. Recruitment and retention of a diverse workforce is possible by making the organization a more attractive place to work with family-friendly policies. Moreover, top management must not only support diversity initiatives, but also participate actively and meaningfully in promoting the diversity efforts. Finally, tying desired diversity outcomes to reward systems makes the planned changes consequential.

RECOMMENDATIONS FOR THEORY AND PRACTICE INNOVATIONS IN DIVERSITY MANAGEMENT

Our review of "best-practices" in diversity management represents the evolution beyond AA and EEO programs to the active management of workforce diversity. These practices exemplify important themes, demonstrate the most promising ideas, or epitomize systemic approaches to what is a complex organizational phenomenon. We conclude with recommendations to direct future innovations in the area. Using two comprehensive models of diversity management, Agars and Kottke's (2002) Model of Full Integration, and Cox's (2001) Change Model for Work on Diversity, we present four theory- and four practice-based directions for continued innovation.

Comprehensive approaches to diversity management

Common to future innovations should be the recognition that diversity management is a comprehensive and systemic phenomenon. Therefore, guidance for innovation can be found in recently developed comprehensive models of diversity management. Cox's (2001) Change Model for Work on Diversity and Agars and Kottke's (2002) Model of Full Integration represent, respectively, a practice-based and theory-based approach to comprehensive organizational change related to the management of diversity. In providing recommendations, we discuss elements of each model to support our assertions. For a complete explication of each model, please see the original sources.

161

Future innovations from theory and thought

Both models identify diversity management as an organizational-level change-based process. Similarly, others have argued that diversity management requires *organizations* to develop a learning orientation (Dass and Parker, 1999; Thomas and Ely, 1996). Learning organizations are adaptive, focused on the continuous improvement of work processes and people, and embracing of change. These perspectives conceptualize diversity management as an organizational-level phenomenon. Such approaches are underrepresented in HRM practices in managing diversity, though empirical evidence suggests such approaches are critical (Kochan *et al.*, 2003; Williams and O'Reilly, 1998).

> Recommendation #1: Diversity management must be conceptualized as an organizational-level, change-based phenomenon.

Cox (2001) emphasizes the importance of leadership's role in establishing and communicating a vision around diversity management. Agars and Kottke (2002) highlight the role of leadership in forming and supporting a vision and culture, and in the modeling of behaviors in support of diversity management. Most leadership theories, however, were developed prior to the diversity management explosion and, consequently, are ill-equipped to address diversity management (Chrobot-Mason and Ruderman, 2004). Although elements of some theories (e.g., Leader-Member Exchange theory) may serve leaders well, the emergence of diverse environments and the impact that differences may have on leader perceptions require innovations in our approach to leadership. In addition, concepts such as "diversity competency" and "multi-cultural intelligence" have been proposed to relate to successful functioning and, more importantly, successful leadership in a diverse environment (Offerman and Phan, 2002). This possibility has implications for innovations across HRM practices in recruitment, selection, assessment, training, and retention of leaders.

> Recommendation #2: Theories of leadership must accommodate the challenges presented by a diverse work force.

The Model of Full Integration (Agars and Kottke, 2002) identifies four underlying individual processes as instrumental. We identify perceptions of utility, fairness, and threat, as well as social cognitive processes as potential facilitators of, or obstacles to, managing diversity. HRM practices targeting diversity management must consider the impact these perceptions have on receptivity to diversity management and the impact those efforts may have on these perceptions, which, in turn, produce critical behaviors and attitudes. Others (Agars, 2004; Austin, 1997) demonstrate the importance of cognitive processes (e.g., schemas, scripts, and stereotypes) associated with group membership, and the impact they have on organizational processes. Employee acculturation also has implications for diversity management, especially in light of immigration trends. In sum, individual perceptions and cognitive processes underlie diversity management and have the potential to facilitate or impede efforts.

162

Recommendation #3: Diversity management practices must identify ways to monitor and incorporate key individual perceptions and cognitive processes.

Diversity management must necessarily be incorporated into organizational strategy (Agars and Kottke, 2004; Cox, 2001). Strategy provides guidance and vision, and leads to the development of key policies and practices. The absence of diversity management goals within an organization's strategy reveals a lack of support, a lack of seriousness, and undermines HRM practices intended to address diversity (Dansky *et al.*, 2003).

Recommendation #4: The role of diversity management in organizational strategy must be clarified and codified.

Recommendation for innovations from organizational practice

To date, most diversity management efforts have been limited to race, ethnicity, and gender, with minimal consideration of other demographic classifications such as age, disability, sexual orientation, class, and obesity. Less-visible forms of diversity (e.g., values) may also be critical to understanding how diversity affects organizational performance (Harrison *et al.*, 1998). Although expansion of "diversity" is required, Konrad (2003) astutely cautions that we must be careful not to equate "diversity" with "individual differences" or the importance of managing diversity will be lost.

Recommendation #5: HRM practice needs to develop inclusive but meaningful definitions of diversity.

Although we search for unified themes in diversity management with generalizable implications, our review of practices reveals the importance of context. Agars and Kottke (2002) predict that historical or environmental factors can impact diversity management efforts at each stage of development. Cox (2001) argues that the pace of development in each key area will differ depending on context. Kochran *et al.* (2003) reviewed the impact of diversity on business performance and found context to play a "crucial" role. Similarly, a comprehensive review of the research examining the impact of group diversity on performance found inconsistency explained, in part, by organizational differences (Williams and O'Reilly, 1998). Context matters, and universal solutions are rarely adequate. Each organization faces a unique constellation of constraints such as different histories, different workforces, unique environments and communities.

Recommendation #6: The unique conditions faced by an organization must be identified and considered in the development and implementation of diversity management efforts.

Cox (2001) identifies measurement as a critical component of the diversity management process as it allows for planning, development, and accountability. Agars and Kottke (2002) stress measurement process throughout the change process as a means of identifying

163

minority representation, attitudinal and performance baselines, assessing organizational growth, and identifying and communicating successes or failures in achieving desired goals. Although some examples of internal benchmarking exist (cf., Mattis, 2002), the common business practice of external benchmarking is not frequently utilized when developing diversity management practice. Available metrics in diversity are limited, and often not reflective of hard business outcomes (Hansen, 2003).

> Recommendation #7: HR practice must develop broader benchmarking and identify best practices, measurement, and accountability.

As diversity management efforts become more comprehensive and rigorous, and practices are developed to demonstrate its effectiveness through key metrics and ties to hard business outcomes, effective communication of the importance of diversity management becomes critical. The identification and recognition of best practices in diversity management such as the Catalyst award, *Fortune* Best Companies lists, and *DiversityInc* recognition, reward organizations for their efforts and challenge others to strive for excellence. They also provide information to the business community about the importance of diversity management, but more are needed.

> Recommendation #8: The future of innovations in diversity management must include a mechanism for its effective and meaningful communication to business leaders.

CONCLUSION

The previous ten years has produced many substantive innovations in the HRM practice of diversity management. Our understanding of diversity has greatly improved, and our approaches to diversity have evolved to become inclusive, dynamic, and increasingly comprehensive. Diversity management *is* here to stay. We look with great anticipation to the next ten years of innovations in Human Resource *Diversity* Management. Best-practice innovations are critical, and we believe with greater attention to models (e.g., Agars and Kottke, 2002; Cox, 2001; Holvino *et al.*, 2004) significant innovations are yet to come.

REFERENCES

Agars, M.D. and Kottke, J.L. (2002) An integrative model of diversity. Paper presented as part of M. Agars and J. Kottke (Chairs). *Integrating theory and practice in gender diversity initiatives.* Symposium to be presented at the 17th Annual Conference of the Society for Industrial and Organizational Psychology (April). Toronto, Canada.

Agars, M.D. and Kottke, J.L. (2004) Models and practice of diversity management: A historical review and presentation of a new integration theory. In M. Stockdale and F. Crosby (eds), *The Psychology and Management of Workplace Diversity.* Oxford: Blackwell Publishers.

Agars, M.D. (2004) Reconsidering the impact of gender stereotypes on the advancement of women in organizations. *Psychology of Women Quarterly*, 28, 103–111.

Allen, T.D., Herst, D.E.L., Bruck, C.S., and Sutton, M. (2000) Consequences associated with work-to-family conflict: A review and agenda for future research. *Journal of Occupational Health Psychology*, 5, 278–308.

Anonymous (2003) Rohini Anand: Leading Sodexho's commitment to a globally diverse workforce. *Nation's Restaurant News*, 37(6) (February 10), 24.

Arai, M., Wanca-Thibault, M., and Shockley-Zalabak, P. (2001) Communication theory and training approaches for multiculturally diverse organizations: Have academics and practitioners missed the connection? *Public Personnel Management*, 30(4), 445–455.

Austin, J.R. (1997) A cognitive framework for understanding demographic differences in groups. *International Journal of Organizational Studies*, 5, 342–359.

Blau, F.D. and Beller, A.H. (1988) Trends in earnings differentials by gender 1971–1981. *Industrial and Labor Relations Review*, 41(4), 513–529.

Burke, R.J. (2002) Career development of managerial women. In R.J. Burke and D.L. Nelson (eds), *Advancing Women's Careers*. Oxford: Blackwell Publishers, pp. 139–160.

Butts, G. (2001) Mount Sinai School of Medicine responds to the call for diversity in medicine. *Diversity Factor*, 9(3), 27–30.

Chemers, M.M., Oskamp, S., and Costanzo, M.A. (1995) *Diversity in Organizations: New Perspectives for a Changing Workplace*. Thousand Oaks, CA: Sage.

Chrobot-Mason, D. and Ruderman, M.N. (2004) Leadership in a diverse workplace. In M. Stockdale and F. Crosby (eds), *The Psychology and Management of Workplace Diversity*. Oxford: Blackwell Publishers.

Cole, Y. (2002) Learn from the winners: What makes a top company for diversity? *DiversityInc*, 1(1), 12–15, 17–27.

Conklin, W. (2000) Employee resource groups: A foundation for support and change. *Diversity Factor*, 1(9), 12–25.

Conklin, W. (2001) Conversations with diversity executives. *Diversity Factor*, 10(1), 5–14.

Cox, T. (1991) The multicultural organization. *Academy of Management Executive*, 5, 34–47.

Cox, T. (1994) *Cultural Diversity in Organizations: Theory, Research & Practice*. San Francisco, CA: Berrett-Koehler.

Cox, T. (2001) *Creating the Multicultural Organization: A strategy for capturing the power of diversity*. San Francisco, CA, CA: Sage.

Daniels, C. (2001) Too diverse for our own good? *Fortune*, 144, 116.

Dansky, K.H., Weech-Maldonado, R., De Souza, G., and Dreachslin, J.L. (2003) Organizational strategy and diversity management: Diversity-sensitive orientation as a moderating influence. *Health Care Management Review*, 28(3), 243–253.

Darden, C. (2003) Delivering on diversity leadership: A walk in the other guy's shoes. *Executive Speeches*, 17(6) (June/July), 20–25.

Dass, P. and Parker, B. (1999) Strategies for managing human resource diversity: From resistance to learning. *Academy of Management Executive*, 19, 68–80.

Fitzerald, K. (2001) Diversity turns airline around. *Advertising Age*, 72(8) (February 19), S6-S7.

Flynn, G. (1996) McDonald's serves up HR excellence. *Personnel Journal*, 75(1), 54–55.

Flynn, G. (1998) The harsh reality of diversity programs. *Workforce*, 77(12), 26–30.

Fosu, A.K. (1992) Occupational mobility of black women, 1958–1981: The impact of post-1964 antidiscrimination measures. *Industrial & Labor Relations Review*, 45(2), 281–294.

Frankel, B. (2002) Top companies for diversity: Our methodology. *DiversityInc*, 1(1), 16–18.

Frink, D.D., Robinson, R.K., Reithel, B., Arthur, M.M, Ammeter, A.P., Ferris, G.R., Kaplan, D.M., and Morrisette, H.S. (2003) Gender demography and organization performance: A two-study investigation wit convergence. *Group & Organization Management*, 28(1), 127–147.

Galagan, P.A. (1993) Trading places at Monsanto. *Training & Development*, 47(4), 44–47.

Galinsky, E., Bond, J.T., and Friedman, D.E. (1996) The role of employers in addressing the needs of employed parents. *Journal of Social Issues*, 52, 111–136.

Gray, J.D., Lee, M.J., and Totta, J.M. (1995) Mentoring at the Bank of Montreal. *HR, Human Resource Planning*, 18(4) 45–49.

Greenslade, M. (1991) Managing diversity: Lessons from the US. *Personnel Management*, 23(12), 28–32.

Hansen, F. (2003) Diversity's business case: Doesn't add up. *Workforce*, 82(4) (April), 28–32.

Harrison, D., Price, K., and Bell, M. (1998) Beyond relational demography: Time and the effects of surface- and deep-level diversity on work group cohesion. *Academy of Management Journal*, 41, 96–107.

Hays-Thomas, R. (2004) Why now? The contemporary focus on managing diversity. In M. Stockdale and F. Crosby (eds), *The Psychology and Management of Workplace Diversity*. Oxford: Blackwell Publishers.

Heilman, M.E., Block, C.J., and Stathatos, P. (1997) The affirmative action stigma of incompetence: Effects of performance information ambiguity. *Academy of Management Journal*, 40, 603–625.

Holvino, E. (2002) Class: "A difference that makes a difference" in organizations. *Diversity Factor*, 10(2), 28–34.

Holvino, E., Ferdman, B.B., and Merrill-Sands, D. (2004) Creating and sustaining diversity and inclusion in organizations: Strategies and approaches. In M. Stockdale and F. Crosby (eds), *The Psychology and Management of Workplace Diversity*. Oxford: Blackwell Publishers.

Hyater-Adams, Y. and Frost, D.D. (1998) Partnership for change at CoreStates Financial Crop. *Diversity Factor*, 5(4), 42–47.

Ibarra, H. (1995) Race, opportunity, and diversity of social circles in managerial networks. *Academy of Management Journal*, 38, 673–703.

Ivancevich, J. and Gilbert, J. (2000) Diversity management: Time for a new approach. *Public Personnel Management*, 29, 75–93.

Jafri, N. and Isbister, K. (2002) A decade of diversity. In R.J. Burke and D.L. Nelson (eds), *Advancing Women's Careers*. Oxford: Blackwell Publishers, pp. 37–50.

James, E.H. and Wooten, L.P. (2001) Managing diversity. *Executive Excellence*, 18(8), 17–18.

Johnson, R.B. and O'Mara, J. (1992) Shedding new light on diversity training. *Training & Development*, 46(5), 44–51.

Johnston, W.B. and Packer, A.H. (1987) *Workforce 2000*. Indianapolis, IN: Hudson Instiutute.

Kandola, R. (1995) Managing diversity: New broom or old hat? In C.L. Cooper and I.T. Robertson (eds), *International Review of Industrial and Organizational Psychology: Vol. 10.* London: Wiley, pp. 131–167.

Katz, D. and Kahn, R.L. (1978) *The Social Psychology of Organizations.* New York: Wiley.

Knutson, L. and Noce, J. (1992) Cultural diversity is a hot program at fire department. *The American City & County,* 107(10), 48.

Kochan, R., Bezrukova, K., Ely, R., Jackson, S., Joshi, A., Jehn, K., Leonard, J., Levine, D., and Thomas, D. (2003) The effects of diversity on business performance: Report of the diversity research network. *Human Resource Management,* 42(1), 3–21.

Konrad, A.M. (2003) Defining the domain of workplace diversity scholarship. *Group & Organization Management,* 28(1), 4–17.

Konrad, A. and Linnehan, F. (1995) Race and sex differences in line managers' reactions to equal employment opportunity and affirmative action interventions. *Group and Organization Management,* 20, 408–438.

Konrad, A.M. and Linnehan, F. (1999) Affirmative action: History, effects, and attitudes. In G.N. Powell (ed.), *Handbook of Gender and Work.* Thousand Oaks, CA: Sage, pp. 429–474.

Kravitz, D.A. and Platania, J. (1993) Attitudes and beliefs about affirmative action: Effects of target and of respondent sex and ethnicity. *Journal of Applied Psychology,* 78, 928–938.

Laabs, J.J. (1993) Employees manage conflict and diversity. *Personnel Journal,* 72(12), 30–34.

Learson, B.E. (1998) Sandia National Laboratories influencing organizational culture change through line ownership of diversity. *Diversity Factor,* 6(4), 33–39.

Lee, J. and Baltazar, V. (2001) Celebrate and educate. *Nursing Homes,* 50(12), 27–28.

Lobel, S.A. (1999) Impacts of diversity and work-life initiatives in organizations. In G.N. Powell (ed.), *Gender and Work.* Thousand Oaks, CA: Sage.

Martinez, M.N. (1995) Equality effort sharpens bank's edge. *HRMagazine,* 40(1) 38–43.

Mattis, M.C. (2002) Best practices for retaining and advancing women professionals and managers. In R.J. Burke and D.L. Nelson (eds), *Advancing Women's Careers.* Oxford: Blackwell Publishers, pp. 309–332.

Microsoft (2003) Employee resource groups. Online, available at: www.microsoft.com/diversity/dac.asp. (accessed October 23, 2003).

Neff, J. (1998) Diversity. *Advertising Age,* 69(7) (February 16), S1–2.

Offermann, L.R. and Phan, L.U. (2002) Culturally intelligent leadership for a diverse world. In R. Riggio, S. Murphy, and F. Pirozzolo (eds), *Multiple Intelligences and Leadership.* Mahwah, NJ: Lawrence Erlbaum Associates.

Osland, J.S., Adler, N.J., and Brody, L.W. (2002) Developing women as global leaders: Lessons and sense making from an organizational change effort. In R.J. Burke and D.L. Nelson (eds), *Advancing Women's Careers.* Oxford: Blackwell Publishers, pp. 15–36.

Powell, G. (1993) Promoting equal opportunity and valuing cultural diversity. In G. Powell (ed.), *Women and Men in Management.* Thousand Oaks, CA: Sage, pp. 225–252.

Raphael, T. (2002) Diversity lives at BellSouth. *Workforce,* 81(1) (January), 18.

Richard, O., McMillan, A., Chadwick, K., and Dwyer, S. (2003) Employing an innovation strategy in racially diverse workforces: Effects on firm performance. *Group & Organization Management,* 28(1), 107–126.

Rosin H.M. and Korabik, K. (2002) Do family-friendly policies fulfill their promise? An investigation of their impact on work-family conflict and work and personal outcomes. In D. Nelson and R. Burke (eds), *Gender, Work Stress, and Health*. Washington, DC: APA.

Sadri, G. and Tran, H. (2002) Managing your diverse workforce through improved communication. *Journal of Management Development*, 21, 227–237.

Santora, J.E. (1991) Kinney Shoe steps into diversity. *Personnel Journal*, 70(9), 72–77.

Scandura, T.A. and Baugh, S.G. (2002) Mentoring and developmental relationships. In R.J. Burke and D.L. Nelson (eds), *Advancing Women's Careers*. Oxford: Blackwell Publishers, pp. 161–173.

Scott, S.C. III. (1993) Vive la difference. *Financial Executive*, 9(6) (November/December), 44–47.

Shea, S. and Okada, R.K. (1992) Benefiting from workforce diversity. *The Healthcare Forum Journal*, 35(1), 23–25.

Sheridan, J.H. (1994) Dividends from diversity. *Industry Week*, 243(17) (September 19), 23–25.

Sherter, A. (1996) Xerox financial assistance program aims to help employees balance work, family. *Employee Benefit Plan Review*, 51(6), 44–46.

Shum, M. and Moss, J.W. (2002) IBM: A case study in affirmative action best practices. *Diversity Factor*, 10(2), 10–14.

Solomon, C.M. (1993) McDonald's links franchises to the community. *Personnel Journal*, 72(3), 61–63.

Spicer, J.G., Ripple, H.B., Louie, E., Baj, P., and Keating, S. (1994) Supporting ethnic and cultural diversity in nursing staff. *Nursing Management*, 25(1), 38–41.

Stockdale, M.S. and Crosby, F.J. (2004) *The Psychology and Management of Workplace Diversity*. Oxford: Blackwell Publishers.

Stuller, J. (1995) Doing what comes unnaturally. *Across the Board*, 32(6), 27–30.

Thomas, D. and Ely, R. (1996) Making differences matter: A new paradigm for managing diversity. *Harvard Business Review*, 74: 79–90.

Thomas, R.R. (1990) From affirmative action to affirming diversity. *Harvard Business Review*, 68: 107–117.

Tomlinson, J.M. (1992) The diverse work force: Valuing differences at Chubb. *The Human Resources Professional*, 4(2), 47–50.

Toner, B. (1996) One terrific place to work. *CA Magazine*, 129(8), 33–35.

Tracey, J.B., Tannenbaum, S.I., and Kavanaugh, M.J. (1995) Applying trained skills on the job: The importance of the work environment. *Journal of Applied Psychology*, 80, 239–252.

Triandis, H.C., Kurowski, L.L., and Gelfand, M.J. (1994) Workplace diversity. In H.C. Triandis, M.I. Dunnette, and L.M. Hough (eds), *Handbook of Industrial and Organizational Psychology*. Palo Alto, CA: Consulting Psychologists Press, pp. 767–827.

Van Grinsven, M.T. (1998) Diversity and the new millennium. *LIMRA's MarketFacts*, 17(3), 42–43.

Von Bergen, C.W., Soper, B., and Foster, T. (2002) Unintended negative effects of diversity management. *Public Personnel Management*, 31(2), 239–251.

Watson, P. (1997) Diversity challenge. *People Management*, 3(9) (May 1), 30–32.

Weidenfeller, N. (1992) Celebrating diversity. *Public Utilities Fortnightly*, 129(12) (June 15), 20–22.

White, M.B. (1998) Work × shop = profit measuring change at Sears. *Diversity Factor*, 7(1), 7–10.

White, M.B. (1999a) Bestfoods: Satisfying a global appetite. *Diversity Factor*, 7(4), 23–28.

White, M.B. (1999b) Organization 2005: New strategies at P&G. *Diversity Factor*, 8(1), 16–20.

Williams, K.Y. and O'Reilly, C.A. (1998) Demography and diversity in organizations: A review of 40 years of research. In B. Staw and L. Cummings (eds), *Research in Organizational Behavior*, vol. 20. Greenwich, CT: JAI Press.

Yakura, E. (1996) EEO law and managing diversity. In E. Kossek and S. Lobel (eds), *Managing Diversity: Human Resource Strategies for Transforming the Workplace*. Cambridge, MA: Blackwell.

Zane, N. (1998) The discourses of diversity: The links between conversation and organizational change. *Diversity Factor*, 7(1), 29–35.

Chapter 10

HRM and downsizing

Wayne F. Cascio

In a 1993 paper, "Downsizing: What Do We Know? What Have We Learned?" I argued that the presumed economic benefits of employment downsizing, such as lower expense ratios, higher profits, increased return-on-investment, and boosted stock prices, often fail to materialize. Likewise, many anticipated organizational benefits do not develop, such as lower overheads, smoother communications, greater entrepreneurship among employees, and increases in productivity. I also have argued that human resources (HR) professionals have been heavily involved in implementing employment downsizing, but not nearly as involved in influencing executives at the strategic level, when decisions about restructuring strategies are debated and decided. Today, it seems appropriate to make a similar argument, despite numerous articles that have appeared in the interim that reinforce the same points about the economic and organizational effects of employment downsizing (Appelbaum *et al.*, 1999b; Cascio *et al.*, 1997; Gowing *et al.*, 1998; Morris *et al.*, 1999).

In a recent study (Rynes *et al.*, 2002), HR practitioners were presented with the following "true or false" item: "If a company feels it must downsize employment, the most profitable way to do it is through targeted cuts rather than attrition." The correct answer is "true," yet only 54 percent of HR practitioners answered the item correctly. This is but one of several gaps in understanding about the economic, psychological, and managerial effects of downsizing. This chapter summarizes some recent research findings on the subject of downsizing, it presents several myths about downsizing, along with the true facts, and it emphasizes responsible restructuring as an alternative approach. Finally, the chapter concludes with some recommended steps for restructuring. Let us begin by defining our terms.

DOWNSIZING DEFINED

In everyday conversation, the term "downsizing" is often used as a synonym for "layoffs" of employees from their jobs. Downsizing is commonly the result of a broader process of organizational restructuring, which refers to planned changes in a firm's *organizational* structure that affect its use of people. Such restructuring often results in workforce reductions that may be accomplished through mechanisms such as attrition, early retirements, voluntary severance agreements, or layoffs. Layoffs are a form of "downsizing," but it is important to note that downsizing is a broad term that may include any number of combinations of reductions in a firm's use of assets—financial, physical, human, or information assets. When referring to reductions in the numbers of people in an organization, therefore, it is appropriate to use the term "employment downsizing."

Employment downsizing is not the same thing as organizational decline. Downsizing is an intentional, proactive management strategy, whereas decline is an environmental or organizational phenomenon that occurs involuntarily and results in erosion of an organization's resource base. As an example, the advent of digital photography, disposable cameras, and other imaging products signaled a steep decline in the demand for the kind of instant photographic cameras and films that Polaroid had pioneered in the 1940s. On October 12, 2001 Polaroid was forced to declare bankruptcy.

RATIONALE FOR EMPLOYMENT DOWNSIZING

What makes employment downsizing such a compelling strategy to firms worldwide? The economic rationale is straightforward. It begins with the premise that there really are only two ways to make money in business: by cutting costs or by increasing revenues. Which are more predictable, future costs or future revenues? Anyone who makes monthly mortgage payments knows that future costs are far more predictable than future revenues. Payroll expenses represent fixed costs, so by reducing payroll through employment downsizing, other things remaining equal, a firm should reduce its overall expenses.

Reduced expenses translate into increased earnings, and earnings drive stock prices. Higher stock prices make investors and analysts happy. The key phrase is "other things remaining equal." In practice, however, other things often do not remain equal, and therefore the anticipated benefits of employment downsizing do not always materialize. As an example, consider just some of the direct and indirect costs associated with employment downsizing:

Direct costs	Indirect costs
Severance pay, in lieu of notice	Recruiting and employment costs of new hires
Accrued vacation and sick pay	Low morale, risk-averse survivors
Supplemental unemployment benefits	Increase in unemployment tax rate
Outplacement	Lack of staff when economy rebounds, training and retraining
Pension and benefit payouts	Potential lawsuits from aggrieved employees
Administrative processing costs	Heightened insecurity, reduced productivity
Costs of rehiring former employees	Loss of institutional memory and trust in management

EXTENT AND SCOPE OF EMPLOYMENT DOWNSIZING IN THE UNITED STATES

According to the US Department of Labor, about two million people a year, every year since 1996, are affected by employment downsizing. In 2001, for example, companies announced almost a million job cuts in the three months after the terrorist attacks of September 11. Many firms conduct multiple rounds of employment downsizing in the same year, as ongoing staff reductions become etched into the corporate culture. On average, two-thirds of firms that lay off employees in a given year do so again the following year.

LAYOFFS IN COUNTRIES OTHER THAN THE UNITED STATES

The phenomenon of layoffs is not limited to the US. Asia and Europe have been hard-hit as well. Japan's chip and electronics conglomerates have shed tens of thousands of jobs in the past year as the worldwide information-technology slump and fierce competition from foreign rivals have battered their bottom lines. High-profile firms such as Hitachi, Fujitsu, NEC, Toshiba, Matsushita Electric Industrial, and Sony have cut deeply, as has Mazda in automobile production (*South China Morning Post*, 2002a; Kunii, 2001; Larimer, 2001; Shirouzu, 2000). In mainland China, more than 25.5 million people were laid off from state-owned firms between 1998 and 2001. Another 20 million are expected to be laid off from traditional state-owned firms by 2006 (*South China Morning Post*, 2002b).

The incidence of layoffs varies among countries in Western Europe. Labor laws in countries such as Italy, France, Germany, and Spain make it difficult and expensive to dismiss workers. In Germany, for example, all "redundancies" must by law be negotiated in detail by a workers' council, which is a compulsory part of any big German company and often has a say in which workers can be fired. Moreover, setting the terms of severance is tricky, because the law is vague and German courts often award compensation if workers claim they received inadequate settlements. In France, layoffs are rare. As an example, consider that now-bankrupt appliance maker Moulinex, once considered an icon of French industry, repeatedly tried to restructure in 2001, but was blocked by the French Socialist government because its cost-cutting plans included layoffs. At present, even if companies offer generous severance payments to French workers, as both Michelin and Marks & Spencer did in 2001, the very announcement of layoffs triggers a political firestorm (Matlack, 2001; Winestock, 2002).

ECONOMIC CONSEQUENCES OF EMPLOYMENT DOWNSIZING

In a series of studies that included data from 1982–1994, 1995–2000, and 1982–2000, my colleagues and I examined financial and employment data from companies in the Standard & Poor's 500 (Cascio *et al.*, 1997; Cascio and Young, 2003; Morris *et al.*, 1999). The S&P 500 is one of the most widely used benchmarks of the performance of US equities. It represents leading companies in leading industries, and consists of 500 stocks chosen for their market size, liquidity, and industry-group representation. Our purpose was to examine the relationships between changes in employment and financial performance. We assigned companies into one of seven mutually exclusive categories based upon their level of change in employment and their level of change in plant and equipment (assets). We then observed the firms' financial performance (profitability and total return on common stock) from one year before to two years after the employment-change events. We examined results for firms in each category on an independent as well as on an industry-adjusted basis.

In our most recent study, we observed a total of 6,418 occurrences of changes in employment for S&P 500 companies over the 18-year period from 1982 through 2000. As in our earlier studies, we found no significant, consistent evidence that employment downsizing led to improved financial performance, as measured by return on assets or industry-adjusted return on assets. Downsizing strategies, either employment downsizing or asset downsizing, did not yield long-term payoffs that were significantly larger than those generated by Stable Employers—those companies in which the complement of employees did not fluctuate by more than ±5 percent.

This conclusion differs from that in our earlier analysis of the data from 1982 to 1994. In that study we concluded that some types of downsizing, namely, Asset Downsizing, do yield higher ROAs than either Stable Employers or their industries. However, when the data from 1995–2000 are added to the original 1982–1994 data, a different picture emerges. That picture suggests clearly that, at least during the time period of our study, it was not possible for firms to "save" or "shrink" their way to prosperity. Rather, it was only by growing their businesses (Asset Upsizing) that firms outperformed Stable Employers as well as their own industries in terms of profitability and total returns on common stock. With respect to the total returns on common stock, Asset Upsizers generated returns that were 41 percent higher than those of Employment Downsizers, and 43 percent higher than those of Stable Employers, by the end of Year 2.

IS EMPLOYMENT DOWNSIZING ALWAYS WRONG?

It might appear from the research results described above that firms should never downsize employees. In fact, many firms have downsized and restructured successfully to improve their productivity. They have done so by using layoffs as part of a broader business plan. As examples, consider Sears Roebuck & Company and Praxair, Inc. In January 2001, Sears cut 2,400 jobs as part of a restructuring that included closing 89 stores and several smaller businesses. Shares rose 30 percent in six months. Praxair, Inc., a $5 billion supplier of specialty gases and coatings, cut 900 jobs in September 2001, in response to the economic slowdown. At the same time, however, it also announced initiatives designed to pull it out of the slump, including two new plants for products where demand was on the rise. The result? The value of its shares rose 30 percent in three months.

In the aggregate, the productivity and competitiveness of many firms has increased in recent years. However, the lesson from our analysis is that firms cannot simply *assume* that layoffs are a quick fix that will necessarily lead to productivity improvements and increased financial performance. The fact is that layoffs alone will not fix a business strategy that is fundamentally flawed. Thus, when Palm, Inc. trimmed 250 jobs in an effort to cut costs after a delayed product launch slowed demand, shares lost nearly half their value in one day and never recovered. In response, Palm's Chief Financial Officer, Judy Bruner, noted: "There were a lot of questions about the viability of the business" (Lavelle, 2002, p. 78).

In short, employment downsizing may not necessarily generate the benefits sought by management. Managers must be very cautious in implementing a strategy that can impose such traumatic costs on employees, both on those who leave as well as on those who stay (Cascio, 1993, 2002a). Management needs to be sure about the sources of future savings, and carefully weigh those against *all* of the costs, including the increased costs associated with subsequent employment expansions, when economic conditions improve.

MYTHS VERSUS FACTS ABOUT EMPLOYMENT DOWNSIZING

Unfortunately there are many tantalizing myths that surround employment downsizing. Unless they are debunked, the mistakes of the past are bound to be repeated. While a complete treatment of such myths is beyond the scope of this chapter, we do consider eight of the most prevalent ones in the sections that follow. For a more complete treatment, see Cascio (2002b).

Myth #1—Jobs are secure at firms that are doing well financially.
Fact—Preemptive layoffs by large firms are common.

Today's job cuts are not solely about large, sick companies trying to save themselves, as was often the case in the early 1990s (e.g., IBM, Sears). They are also about healthy companies hoping to reduce costs and boost earnings by reducing head count (e.g., Goldman Sachs and AOL). They are about trying to pre-empt tough times instead of simply reacting to them. These layoffs are radical, preventive first aid (Morris, 2001). On the other hand, small companies, especially small manufacturers, tend to resist layoffs because they are trying to protect the substantial investments they made in finding and training workers (Ansberry, 2001).

Myth #2—Downsizing employees boosts profits.
Fact—Profitability does not necessarily follow downsizing.

Data presented earlier from the S&P 500, 1982–2000 (Cascio and Young, 2003), showed clearly that profitability, as measured by the return on assets, does not necessarily follow downsizing, even as long as two years later. Survey data support this conclusion. Thus, the *2001 Lay-offs and Job Security Survey*, conducted by the Society for Human Resource Management, reported that only 32 percent of respondents indicated that layoffs improved profits. Even massive staff cutbacks at firms such as Eastman Kodak, Apple Computer, and AT&T have not produced increased earnings years later (Quinones, 1998).

Myth #3—Downsizing employees boosts productivity.
Fact—Productivity results after downsizing are mixed.

The American Management Association surveyed 700 companies that had downsized in the 1990s. In 34 percent of the cases, productivity rose, but it fell in 30 percent of them (Cravotta and Kleiner, 2001). These results are consistent with those reported in another study of 250,000 manufacturing plants by the National Bureau of Economic Research. That study concluded that the productivity-enhancing role of downsizing has been exaggerated. While some plants did downsize and post healthy gains in productivity, even more (including many of the largest facilities) managed to raise output per worker while *expanding* employment. They contributed about as much to overall productivity increases in manufacturing as did the successful downsizers (Business Week, 1994).

> Myth #4—Downsizing employees has no effect on the quality of products or services.
>
> Fact—For most employers, downsizing employees does not lead to long-term improvements in the quality of products or services.

In the wake of decisions that affect them, such as those involving pay, promotions, or layoffs, employees often ask: "Was that fair?" Judgments about the fairness or equity of procedures used to make decisions, that is, procedural justice, are rooted in the perceptions of employees. Strong research evidence indicates that such perceptions lead to important consequences, such as employee behavior and attitudes (Colquitt *et al.*, 2001; Kanovsky, 2000). When employees feel that they have not been treated fairly, they may retaliate in the form of theft, sabotage, and even violence (Greenberg, 1997). Now, in an extended example, we will consider how poor labor relations can affect product quality— with tragic consequences.

Two Princeton University economists analyzed Bridgestone/Firestone tire production at the firm's Decatur, Illinois plant (Krueger and Mas, 2002). When a previous contract expired on April 1, 1994, employees worked for three months without a contract before going on strike. In negotiations, Bridgestone/Firestone broke with its industry by moving from an 8-hour to a 12-hour shift that would rotate between days and nights, as well as cutting pay for new hires by 30 percent, cutting wages for most job classifications by $5.34 per hour to about $12 per hour, reducing incentive pay for piecework, cutting two weeks of vacations for senior workers, and requiring hourly workers to contribute to their healthcare costs. The United Rubber Workers union that represented the workers proposed that the company follow the master pattern agreement set with Goodyear, which called for no wage increases other than cost-of-living adjustments. It is noteworthy that the company insisted on such large concessions during a period when the overall economy was growing.

Using replacements, the company imposed 12-hour shifts and kept production going. The union workers surrendered in May 1995, returning under the terms originally demanded by Bridgestone/Firestone. Although the strike officially ended in May 1995, the labor dispute continued until a final settlement was reached in December 1996. For nearly three years, therefore, from April 1994 to December 1996, union workers at the Decatur plant either were on strike or working without a contract. During this period tires were produced by 1,048 replacement workers, union members who crossed the picket line, management, and recalled strikers.

The Princeton analysis is compelling because three different sets of data all point the same way. Firestone tires made in Decatur during the labor strike were 376 percent more likely to prompt a complaint to the National Highway Transportation Safety Administration than tires made at two comparison plants. The two plants were Firestone's nonunion plant in Wilson, North Carolina and its unionized plant in Joliette, Quebec, which had a 1995 strike but did not use replacement workers. At times of labor peace, Decatur tires were 14 percent *less* likely to prompt a complaint.

Second, customers with tires made in Decatur during the dispute were more than 250 percent as likely to seek compensation from Firestone for property damage or injury blamed on faulty tires than were customers of tires made there during more peaceful times. Third, tires made in Decatur during the labor dispute did worse on laboratory stress tests that Firestone conducted when the tires were produced, than those made at other times or at other plants. The consequences were lethal, for the report concluded that more than 40 lives were lost as a result of the excessive number of problem tires produced in Decatur during the labor dispute.

Apparently, the problem tires were not the result of production by inexperienced replacement workers. Rather, it appears that it was something about the chemistry between the replacements and the recalled strikers. Why? Analysis of monthly tire production revealed that there was no surge in problem tires when replacement workers were making them, adjusting for lower production volumes. The problems were with tires made in 1994 following tough company demands on the union, and again after the strikers returned in May 1995 without a contract to work alongside workers who had crossed the picket line.

CONSEQUENCES OF INEQUITABLE TREATMENT

There is a simple lesson to be learned in all of this. When employees feel that they are not respected, and not being treated fairly and with dignity, managers should expect "push back" and resistance. Conversely, procedurally fair treatment has been demonstrated to result in reduced stress (Elovainio *et al.,* 2001) and increased performance, job satisfaction, commitment to an organization, and trust. It also encourages *organizational citizenship behaviors* or OCBs—discretionary behaviors performed outside of one's formal role that help other employees perform their jobs or that show support for and conscientiousness toward the organization (Colquitt *et al.,* 2001). OCBs include behaviors such as the following (Borman and Motowidlo, 1993):

- Volunteering to carry out activities that are not formally a part of one's job.
- Persisting with extra enthusiasm or effort when necessary to complete one's own tasks successfully.
- Helping and cooperating with others.
- Following organizational rules and procedures, even when they are personally inconvenient.
- Endorsing, supporting, and defending organizational objectives.

   Myth #5—Since companies are just "cutting fat" by downsizing, there are no adverse effects on those who remain.

   Fact—For the majority of companies, downsizing has had adverse effects on morale, work load, and commitment.

It has often been said that employee morale is the first casualty in a downsizing. Survey data bear this out. Right Associates found that 70 percent of senior managers who remained in downsized firms reported that morale and trust declined. Study after study has found similar results (Appelbaum *et al.*, 1999a; Kets de Vries and Balazs, 1997; Mirvis, 1997). A recent national survey found the following among survivors: feel overworked (54%), are overwhelmed by work load (55%), lack time for reflection (59%), don't have time to complete tasks (56%), and have to multi-task too much (45%) (Business Week, 2001b).

Between 1993 and 1995 an Australian bank, identified simply as Onebank, implemented a "restructuring improvement program" (yielding the ominous acronym RIP). Its objective was to improve the bank's competitiveness by reducing costs, instigating a sales culture, and installing new technology. RIP eliminated 350 branches and 10,000 employees, although 4,500 new jobs were created in the central processing sites. RIP involved a "spill and fill" process in which all staff lost their jobs and had to compete for the jobs remaining in the new structure. It was like a giant game of musical chairs, with about 20 percent fewer chairs than people.

An academic's survey of the bank's middle managers (to which a remarkable 80 percent responded) revealed an almost complete turnaround in attitudes toward their careers. The survey found a decline in the managers' commitment at all levels: to their job, to their branch or department, and most of all, to Onebank and its goals. This was true even though 83 percent considered RIP essential for the long-term future of the bank and 76 percent said they were fully committed to making it a success.

How had the restructuring changed the nature of the managers' jobs? More than 30 percent of the managers said they now had more staff reporting to them, 64 percent had increased responsibility, 69 percent had a wider range of duties, 77 percent worked longer hours, 83 percent experienced increased stress, and 85 percent had an increased work load overall.

Against all that, however, only 37 percent said they'd received a salary increase. Is it any surprise that 49 percent felt a decreased sense of commitment to Onebank or that 64 percent experienced decreased job satisfaction? Asked about their level of commitment and their views on working for the bank, the managers offered eight positive and 390 negative comments (Gittins, 2001).

> Myth #6—The number of employees let go, including their associated costs, is the total cost of downsizing.
> Fact—In knowledge-based or relationship-based businesses, the most serious cost is the loss of employee contacts, business forgone, and lack of innovation.

Knowledge-based organizations, from high-technology firms to the financial-services industry, depend heavily on their employees—their stock of human capital—to innovate and grow. Knowledge-based organizations are collections of networks in which interrelationships among individuals, that is, social networks, generate learning and knowledge. This knowledge base constitutes a firm's "memory." Because a single individual has multiple relationships in such an organization, indiscriminate, non-selective downsizing has the potential to inflict considerable damage on the learning and memory capacity of organizations.

Empirical evidence indicates that the damage is far greater than might be implied by a simple tally of individuals (Fisher and White, 2000).

When one considers the multiple relationships generated by one individual, it is clear that downsizing that involves significant reductions in employees creates the loss of significant "chunks" of organizational memory. Such a loss damages ongoing processes and operations, forfeits current contacts, and may lead to forgone business opportunities. Which kinds of organizations are at greatest risk? Those that operate in rapidly evolving industries, such as biotechnology, pharmaceuticals, and software, where survival depends on a firm's ability to innovate constantly.

> Myth #7—Violence, sabotage, or other vengeful acts from laid-off employees are remote possibilities.
>
> Fact—They are less remote than you think, and the consequences may be severe.

The *2001 Lay-offs and Job Security Survey*, conducted by the Society for Human Resource Management, reported that 93 percent of companies have not experienced workplace violence. However, the most common precipitator of workplace violence is a layoff or firing (Burlingame, 2001; Neuman and Baron, 1998).

Violence disrupts productivity, causes untold damage to those exposed to the trauma, is related to workplace abuse of drugs or alcohol and absenteeism, and costs employers millions of dollars (Business Week, 2001a). In a stressed-out, downsized business environment, people are searching for someone to blame for their problems. With the loss of a job or other event the employee perceives as unfair, the employer may become the focus of a disgruntled individual's fear and frustration. Under these circumstances, some form of workplace aggression, that is, efforts by individuals to harm others with whom they work, or have worked, or their organization itself, is likely (Adams, 2001; Neuman and Baron, 1998).

In France, laid-off workers at bankrupt household-appliance maker Moulinex SA threatened to blow up their factory if their demands for more severance pay were not met. A sign in black marker at the entrance to the plant said it all: "Money or BOOM!" Their demands were met. The French labor ministry and the unions agreed on a deal to give workers who were with Moulinex for more than 25 years a severance bonus of 12,200 euros (about $10, 785) and the rest of the workers 4,600 to 7,600 euros (about $4,050 to $6,690) (Carreyrou, 2001; Matlack, 2001).

Among white-collar workers, the cyber saboteur has emerged as a new threat among disgruntled ex-employees. Recently axed workers have posted a company's payroll on its intranet, planted data-destroying bugs, and handed over valuable intellectual property to competitors. Although exact numbers are hard to come by, computer security experts say it is fast becoming the top technical concern at many companies. The FBI estimates the cost of the average insider attack at $2.7 million (Business Week, 2001c).

> Myth #8—Training survivors during and following layoffs is not necessary.
>
> Fact—Training survivors is critical to success subsequently.

The American Management Association survey on corporate downsizing, job elimination, and job creation clearly supports this conclusion. In firms where training budgets increased after downsizing, 63 percent reported that productivity increased over the long term, and 69 percent reported that profits increased. In firms where training budgets decreased after downsizing, only 34 percent reported that productivity increased over the long term, and only 40 percent reported that profits increased. A similar pattern also emerged over the short term.

One explanation for these results is that two-thirds of reported job eliminations are connected to organizational restructuring or business process reengineering. Workers who receive training are far more likely to improve their productivity, which, in turn, leads to increases in profits (American Management Association, 1996).

EFFECT OF DOWNSIZING ON EMPLOYEE ATTITUDES AND BELIEFS

Restructuring, including downsizing, often leads to predictable effects—diminished loyalty from employees. In the wave of takeovers, mergers, downsizings, and layoffs over the past 15 years, millions of workers have discovered that years of service mean little to a struggling management or a new corporate parent. This breach of the unwritten rules that constitute the "psychological contract" between employer and employee leads to a rise in stress and a decrease in satisfaction, commitment, intentions to stay, and perceptions of an organization's trustworthiness, honesty, and caring about its employees (Gutknecht and Keys, 1993; Kleinfeld, 1996; Lester *et al.*, 2003; Schweiger and DeNisi, 1991). Indeed, our views of hard work, loyalty, and managing as a career will probably never be the same.

THE PSYCHOLOGICAL IMPACT OF DOWNSIZING ON VICTIMS AND SURVIVORS

Downsizings exact a devastating toll on workers and communities. Lives are shattered, people become bitter and angry, and the added emotional and financial pressure can create family problems. "Survivors," workers who remain on the job, can be left without loyalty or motivation. Their workplaces are more stressful, political, and cutthroat than before the downsizing. Local economies and services (e.g., human services agencies, charitable organizations) become strained under the impact to the community. Survivors often experience "burnout"—a gradual process of loss during which the mismatch between the needs of the person and the demands of the job grows ever greater. Research indicates that each person expresses burnout in a unique way, but the basic themes are the same (Maslach and Leiter, 1997):

- *An erosion of engagement with the job*. What started out as important, meaningful, fascinating work becomes unpleasant, unfulfilling, and meaningless.
- *An erosion of emotions*. The positive feelings of enthusiasm, dedication, security, and enjoyment fade away and are replaced by anger, anxiety, and depression.
- *A problem of fit between the person and the job*. Individuals see this imbalance as a personal crisis, but it is really the workplace that is in trouble.

180

RESPONSIBLE RESTRUCTURING—AN ALTERNATIVE APPROACH

In 1995 I wrote a publication for the US Department of Labor entitled, *Guide to Responsible Restructuring* (US Department of Labor, 1995). As I investigated the approaches that various companies, large and small, public and private, adopted in their efforts to restructure, what became obvious to me was that companies differed in terms of how they viewed their employees. Indeed, they almost seemed to separate themselves logically into two groups. One group of firms, by far the larger of the two, saw employees as *costs to be cut*. The other, much smaller group of firms, saw employees as *assets to be developed*. Therein lay a major difference in the approaches they took to restructure their organizations:

- *Employees as costs to be cut*—these are the downsizers. They constantly ask themselves: "what is the minimum number of employees we need to run this company? What is the irreducible core number of employees the business requires?"
- *Employees as assets to be developed*—these are the responsible restructurers. They constantly ask themselves: "How can we change the way we do business, so that we can use the people we currently have more effectively?"

The downsizers see employees as commodities—like paper clips or light bulbs—interchangeable and substitutable—one for another. This is a "plug-in" mentality: plug them in when you need them, pull the plug when you no longer need them. In contrast, responsible restructurers see employees as sources of innovation and renewal. They see in employees the potential to grow their businesses. Here is one example of responsible restructuring. For more on this approach, see Cascio (2002a, 2002b).

CHARLES SCHWAB & COMPANY

This organization used downsizing as a last resort. At the same time, it was reinventing its business. Here is why restructuring became necessary.

At the end of the second quarter of 2001, Schwab's commission revenues were off 57 percent from their peak 15 months earlier. Overall revenue was down 38 percent, losses totaled $19 million (US), and the stock had dropped 75 percent from its high. Something had to give. How did the company respond? It took five steps *before* finally cutting staff (Bernstein, 2001; Vogelstein, 2001):

- When Schwab first saw business begin to deteriorate the year before, it put projects on hold and cut back on such expenses as catered staff lunches and travel and entertainment. Management went out of its way to explain to employees the short-term nature of these cuts (Boyle, 2001).
- As it became clear that more savings were needed, top executives all took pay cuts: 50 percent each for the company's two CEOs, 20 percent for executive vice-presidents, 10 percent for senior vice-presidents, and 5 percent for vice-presidents.
- It encouraged employees to take unused vacation and to take unpaid leaves of up to 20 days.

181

- Management designated certain Fridays as voluntary days off without pay for employees who didn't have clients to deal with.
- Only after the outlook darkened again, at the end of the first quarter of 2001, did the firm announce layoffs—2,000 out of a workforce of 25,000. Even then the severance package included a $7,500 "hire-back" bonus that any employee will get if he or she is rehired within 18 months. It also included between 500 and 1,000 stock options, cash payments to offset the increased costs of health-care insurance for laid-off employees, and a full range of outplacement services (Jossi, 2001). Further, everyone being laid off, nearly 5,000 people by the end of September, 2001, is eligible for a $20,000 tuition voucher paid for by the founder himself. That could cost him as much as $10 million.

Over the past decade or so, Schwab & Company has a lengthy record of product innovation. Perhaps its greatest innovation appeared to be one of the gutsiest moves of the 1990s—offering online trading in a bigger and better way than anyone else, even though it meant cutting commission rates by more than half. The result? In early 2000 Schwab could boast of having generated a better 10-year return for investors than Microsoft!

Today, however, the company is reinventing its business model. Sure, it is cutting costs by making its website easier to use, thus cutting down on expensive phone traffic, and it is raising fees for customers who don't trade very often and are unprofitable for the firm. But its biggest bet—where it thinks the bulk of its future revenue will come from—will be a radical new approach to winning and keeping business. The firm that was founded on the principle that it would never tell customers what stocks to buy is about to do just that— but with an ingenious twist.

The plan is to have computers analyze customers' portfolios, compare them with a computer-generated list of Schwab-recommended stocks for that investor's risk profile, and then convey that message to the client. When the objective analysis is supplemented with research reports from partner Goldman Sachs, plus occasional access to a salaried investment specialist, the company feels this will fill in the final gap in what will be a complete set of services for virtually every investor (Business Week, 2002).

Schwab is practicing responsible restructuring. How? At the same time that it is demonstrating by its actions that it sees its employees as assets to be developed, it is developing business concept innovations that will allow it to generate new customers and new streams of revenue in order to grow its business. There is much to be learned from this approach. Here are nine issues to consider as part of any restructuring effort:

1 *Carefully consider the rationale behind restructuring.* Invest in analysis and consider the impact on those who stay, those who leave, and the ability of the organization to serve its customers.

2 *Consider the virtues of stability.* In many cases, companies can maintain their special efficiencies only if they can give their workers a unique set of skills and a feeling that they belong together. Best companies to work for understand that. Thus, 80 of the 100 companies that made *Fortune's* 2002 list of "The 100 Best Companies to Work For" avoided layoffs in 2001; 47 of them even have some kind of official policy

barring layoffs! Consider stockbroker Edward Jones, the Number 1 firm on the list. Although it was hit particularly hard by the gloomy stock market, it responded by cutting back bonuses. None of its 25,000 employees got the ax. Said Jones's CEO, John Bachmann: "We want to build the kind of relationship with workers that makes them willing to go the extra mile. You can't do that if you get rid of them whenever times are rocky." The lesson is simple: no matter how rough the economy, retaining top talent is a huge issue. In fact, losing key people during downturns can be disastrous (Levering and Moskowitz, 2002).

3 *Before making any final decisions about restructuring, executives should make their concerns known to employees and seek their input.* Make special efforts to secure the input of "star" employees or opinion leaders, for they can help communicate the rationale and strategy of restructuring to their fellow employees, and also help to promote trust in the restructuring effort.

4 *Use restructuring as an opportunity to address long-term problems.* Unless severe overstaffing is part of a long-term problem, consider alternatives to layoffs first, and ensure that management at all levels shares the pain and participates in any sacrifices employees are asked to bear. The approach of Charles Schwab and Company illustrates this nicely.

5 *If layoffs are necessary, be sure that employees perceive the process of selecting excess positions as fair and make decisions in a consistent manner.* Make special efforts to retain your best performers, and provide maximum advance notice to terminated employees. Provide as much personal choice to affected employees as possible.

6 *Communicate regularly and in a variety of ways in order to keep everyone abreast of new developments and information.* Executives should be visible, active participants in this process, and be sure that lower-level managers are trained to address the concerns of victims as well as survivors.

7 *Give survivors a reason to stay, and prospective new hires a reason to join.* As one set of authors noted, "People need to believe in the organization to make it work, but they need to see that it works to believe in it" (Kets de Vries and Balazs, 1997). Providing a stable, predictable employment relationship that honors the psychological contract is a powerful attraction to join and to stay at an organization.

8 *Train employees and their managers in the new ways of operating.* As we have seen, evidence indicates clearly that firms whose training budgets increase following a restructuring are more likely to realize improved productivity, profits, and quality (American Management Association, 1996; Appelbaum *et al.*, 1999).

9 *Examine carefully all management systems in light of the change of strategy or environment facing the firm.* These include workforce planning, recruitment and selection, performance management, compensation, and labor relations.

Managing a restructuring process is not easy, but it need not be synonymous with "employment downsizing." The real challenge is to downsize expenses without downsizing people. To do that, two ingredients are essential: (1) be aware of current research findings with respect to employment downsizing in order to avoid some of the common gaps between research and practice; (2) adopt a management philosophy that views people as assets to be developed rather than simply as costs to be cut.

183

REFERENCES

Adams, J. T., Workplace deaths decline, coworker homicides rise, *HRMagazine*, Feb., 2001, 12.

American Management Association, *Corporate Downsizing, Job Elimination, and Job Creation: Summary of Key Findings*, AMA Survey. New York: American Management Association, 1996, pp. 1–11.

Ansberry, C., Private resources: By resisting lay-offs, small manufacturers help protect economy, *The Wall Street Journal*, July 6, 2001, A1, A2.

Appelbaum, S. H., A. Everard, and L. T. S. Hung, Strategic downsizing: Critical success factors, *Management Decisions*, 37 (7), 1999a, 535–552.

Appelbaum, S., H. S. Lavigne-Schmidt, M. Peytchev, and B. Shapir, Downsizing: Measuring the costs of failure, *Journal of Management Development*, 18(5), 1999b, 436–463.

Bernstein, A., America's future: The human factor, *Business Week*, August 27, 2001, 118–122.

Borman, W. C. and S. J. Motowidlo, Expanding the criterion domain to include elements of contextual performance. In N. Schmitt and W. C. Borman (eds), *Personnel Selection in Organizations*. San Francisco, CA: Jossey-Bass, 1993, pp. 71–98.

Boyle, M., How to cut perks without killing morale, *Fortune*, February 19, 2001, 241–242, 244.

Burlingame, J., Lay-off methodologies: Downsizing with grace, *Trajectory*, October 2001, 1. Boston, MA: Deloitte & Touche.

Business Week, Why pink slips don't necessarily add up to productivity hikes," July 4, 1994, 20.

Business Week, After the shooting stops, March 12, 2001a, 98–100.

Business Week, Too much work, too little time, July 16, 2001b, 12.

Business Week, Revenge of the downsized nerds, July 30, 2001c, 40.

Business Week, Schwab versus Wall Street, June 3, 2002, 64–70.

Carreyrou, J., In France, labor resorts to radical tactics, *The Wall Street Journal*, November 19, 2001, A13.

Cascio, W. F., Downsizing: what do we know? What have we learned? *Academy of Management Executive*, 7, 1993, 95–104.

Cascio, W. F., Strategies for responsible restructuring, *Academy of Management Executive*, 16(3), 2002a, 80–91.

Cascio, W. F., *Responsible Restructuring: Creative and Profitable Alternatives to Layoffs*. San Francisco, CA: Berrett-Kohler, 2002b.

Cascio, W. F. and C. E. Young, Financial consequences of employment-change decisions in major U. S. corporations: 1982–2000. In K. P. De Meuse and M. L. Marks (eds), *Resizing the Organization*. San Francisco, CA: Jossey-Bass, 2003, pp. 131–156.

Cascio, W. F., C. E. Young, and J. R. Morris, Financial consequences of employment-change decisions in major U. S. corporations, *Academy of Management Journal*, 40(5), 1997, 1175–1189.

Colquitt, J. A., D. E. Conlon, M. J. Wesson, C. O. L. H. Porter, and K. Y. Ng, Justice at the millennium: A meta-analytic review of 25 years of organizational justice research, *Journal of Applied Psychology*, 86, 2001, 425–445.

Cravotta, R. and B. H. Kleiner, New developments concerning reductions in force, *Management Research News*, 24(3/4), 2001, 90–93.

Elovainio, M., M. Kivimaki, and K. Helkama, Organizational justice evaluations, job control, and occupational strain, *Journal of Applied Psychology*, 86, 2001, 418–424.

Fisher, S. R. and M. A. White, Downsizing in a learning organization: Are there hidden costs? *Academy of Management Review*, 25, 2000, 244–251.

Gittins,R., Survivors of downsizing count the cost, *Sydney Morning Herald*, August 1, 2001, 12.

Gowing, M. K., J. D. Kraft, and J. C. Quick, *The New Organizational Reality*, Washington, DC: American Psychological Association.

Greenberg, J., *The Quest for Justice on the Job*. Thousand Oaks, CA: Sage, 1997.

Gutknecht, J. E. and J. B. Keys, Mergers, acquisitions, and takeovers: Maintaining morale of survivors and protecting employees, *Academy of Management Executive*, 7(3), 1993, 26–36.

Jossi, F., Laying off well, *HRMagazine*, July 2001, 48.

Kanovsky, M., Understanding procedural justice and its impact on business organizations, *Journal of Management*, 26, 2000, 489–511.

Kets de Vries, M. F. R. and K. Balazs, The downside of downsizing, *Human Relations*, 50(1), 1997, 11–50.

Kleinfeld, N. R., The company as family no more, *The New York Times*, March 4, 1996, A1, A8–A11.

Krueger, A. B. and A. Mas, *Strikes, Scabs, and Tread Separations: Labor Strife and the Production of Defective Bridgestone/Firestone Tires*. Online, available at: www.irs.princeton.edu (accessed) January 11, 2002.

Kunii, I., Under the knife, *Business Week*, September 10, 2001, 62.

Larimer, T., Worst-case scenario, *Time*, March 26, 2001, 54–56.

Lavelle, L., Swing that ax with care, *Business Week*, February 11, 2002, 78.

Lester, S. W., J. R. Kickul, T. J. Bergmann, and K. P. De Meuse, The effects of organizational resizing on the nature of the psychological contract and employee perceptions of contract fulfillment. In K. P. De Meuse and M. L. Marks (eds), *Resizing the Organization*. San Francisco, CA: Jossey-Bass, 2003, pp. 78–107.

Levering, R. and M. Moskowitz, The best in the worst of times, *Fortune*, February 4, 2002, 60.

Maslach, C. and M. P. Leiter, *The Truth About Burnout: How Organizations Cause Personal Stress and What to Do About it*. San Francisco, CA: Jossey-Bass, 1997.

Matlack, C., The high cost of France's aversion to layoffs, *Business Week*, November 5, 2001, 56.

Mirvis, P. H., Human resource management: Leaders, laggards, and followers, *The Academy of Management Executive*, 11(2), 1997, 43–56.

Morris, B., White-collar blues, *Fortune*, July 23, 2001, 98–110.

Morris, J. R., W. F. Cascio, and C. E. Young, Downsizing after all these years: Questions and answers about who did it, how many did it, and who benefited from it, *Organizational Dynamics*, 27(3), 1999, 78–87.

Neuman, J. H. and R. A. Baron, Workplace violence and workplace aggression: Evidence concerning specific forms, potential causes, and preferred targets, *Journal of Management*, 24, 1998, 391–419.

Quinones, E., Massive staff cutbacks no guarantee of profits, *The Denver Post*, February 9, 1998, 3C.

Rynes, S. L., K. Brown, and E. Colbart, Seven common misconceptions about human resource practices: Research findings versus practitioner beliefs, *Academy of Management Executive*, 16, 2002, 92–102.

Schweiger, D. M. and A. S. DeNisi, Communication with employees following a merger: A longitudinal field experiment, *Academy of Management Journal*, 34, 1991, 110–135.

Shirouzu, N., Leaner and meaner: Driven by necessity—and by Ford—Mazda downsizes, U.S.-Style, *The Wall Street Journal*, January 5, 2000, A1, A10.

Society for Human Resource Management, 2001 Lay-offs and Job Security Survey. Alexandria, VA: Author, December 2001. Available at www.shrm.org/surveys/results.

South China Morning Post, Hitachi decides another 4,000 workers in Japan must go, January 31, 2002a, 1.

South China Morning Post, China warns of 20 million urban jobless, April 30, 2002b, 1.

US Department of Labor, *Guide to Responsible Restructuring*. Washington, DC: US Government Printing Office, 1995.

Vogelstein, F., Can Schwab get its mojo back? *Fortune*, September 17, 2001, 93–98.

Winestock, G., A reticent European right balks on labor, *The Wall Street Journal*, June 21, 2002, A6, A7.

Chapter 11

Well-being and health

What HRM can do about it

Marc J. Schabracq

INTRODUCTION

This chapter reviews how HRM can contribute to the well-being and health of employees. As there are hardly any thorough and relevant empirical effect studies available, it restricts itself to descriptions of possible interventions and methods. It just gives an overview of what organizations themselves do and can do to promote the health and well-being of their employees. Most examples are taken from the Dutch situation. The approach is characterized by the following elements and guidelines.

Primarily, it is a management task and responsibility to look after the employees' health, well-being and satisfaction. To this end, they have to know the employees involved, as well as their possibilities and limitations. Moreover, managers have to spend sufficient attention, time and money on the employees in their care. All this can be—and most of the time is—part of the normal task package of line managers. However, many line managers have other priorities, as they are primarily busy with external affairs, which often interfere with paying sufficient attention to internal affairs.

When line managers are unable to fulfill this task properly, special so-called co-managers can be appointed whose primary task consists of looking after the internal affairs of the department in question (see also Co-management: a possible approach, p. 202). If co-managers are appointed, all of them together can form a project team that occupies itself with the more systemic determinants of employees' well-being and health in that organization. In addition, such a team is a logical candidate when it comes to careful implementation of necessary changes in general (Schabracq, 2001).

Learning about potential problems and solutions of experienced health and well-being is a matter of questioning employees about it. In bigger organizations, interviewing employees is not sufficient. Here, this may imply doing periodical audits about these issues as well (Schabracq *et al.*, 2001). These are not only ways of gathering the right information, but also a matter of building support for possible interventions.

Problems with health and well-being have a significant signaling function. Frequent problems can be used as an indication of more systemic causes. These may have other undesired effects as well, which may have severe consequences for the organization. So, people who become ill in certain situations or circumstances can be considered as a kind of human mine canary, the bird that was used in coalmines to detect firedamp (Schabracq *et al.*, 2001).

Often—and certainly in times of scarcity of personnel—turn-over is a better indicator of employees' well-being and health than sick leave and work disability. When many employees leave, this may well be an indication of a poor working climate and management.

Preventing problems with well-being and health is to be preferred over curing, while it also better to strive for positive outcomes than to counteract negative outcomes (Ofman, 1995; Schabracq, 2003a). It is obviously more pleasant to spend money and effort to maximize effectiveness, pleasure and development than to counteract all kinds of unnecessary problems.

Interventions should be tailored, as much as possible, to individual employees' needs and desires. To realize this guideline, it is essential to ask these employees to give their input about the status quo, its causes and options for improvement, and to make as much use of these as possible. Workshops can be a good medium for this.

In solving organizational problems one should concentrate on solving the problem that causes the main constraint first (Goldratt, 1990), because this brings about the biggest improvement. The next intervention can focus on what causes the main constraint then, and so on. An alternative course is to solve the easiest problem first—picking the low hanging fruits—in order to get a quick success.

Real leadership is one of the most important means to prevent problems with well-being and health. Compared to management, real leadership is more about developing a vision—in the long and short term—and designing the organization, and less about controlling the everyday course of affairs. Leadership is about realizing in both of its meanings: making things happen as well as reflecting about them. In this second meaning, leadership is about learning, wisdom and a clear moral perspective. Actualizing a functional reality, its first meaning, implies that the resulting organization is—or should be—relatively free from alienation and stress.

The relevant existing HRM interventions are your main instruments here. However, they should be used more consistently for all age groups, as HRM now focuses mainly on employees under 40 (Schabracq, 2003a).

The way organizations deal with well-being and stress will become a critical strategic factor in global competition (Schabracq and Cooper, 2000). This is mainly a matter of the unprecedented acceleration of change we presently have to cope with. So, it is becoming increasingly important for any organization to develop its own competence to deal with change and the stress resulting from it in order to survive. Being completely dependent on external consultants for this crucial competence is simply becoming too risky.

As the main objective of HRM consists of simultaneous development of the goals of the organization and its employees in such a way that both parties profit optimally, taking care of employees' well-being and health is a logical element of consistent HRM. Within the HRM frame of reference, good employees—the human capital—are considered to be the main asset of the organization. From this point of view, it is only logical to take care of this human capital as well as possible. It is self-evident that exposing these employees needlessly to stress and other threats to their health and well-being would be foolish capital destruction.

Within HRM, investing in their own employees is the usual approach. In order to safeguard employees' well-being and health and to prevent them encountering needless problems in this respect, HRM disposes of an appropriate arsenal of techniques and methods.

188

The main difference with more traditional forms of HRM consists of applying this arsenal with more precision and consistency than usual. Though this costs time, attention and money (Doeglas and Schabracq, 1992), the outcome may be that the organization becomes more effective, is troubled less by stress phenomena and probably lives longer (de Geus, 1997).

This chapter first examines the possible role of leadership in preventing problems in the area of well-being and health (see below, pp. 189–192). The general approach (see pp. 192–193) sketches the approach itself. Short descriptions of HRM interventions that can be of help here can be found on pp. 194–200. The positive outcomes of such an approach and some of its inherent problems are discussed on pp. 200–201 and 201–202 respectively. Finally, the concept of co-management, which can help to solve some of the problems, is described on pp. 202–204.

LEADERSHIP

Employees' well-being and health depend to an important degree on the extent to which their managers realize a functional reality. Such a reality should be sufficiently orderly, offer the right degree of social embedding and be compatible with individual goals and values. As such, it is safe, free from alienation and stress, and so predictable that it can be dealt with in a self-evident, everyday way not demanding extra attention (Schabracq, 2003b; Schabracq and Cooper, 2003). This implies realizing the following four conditions (Parsons, 1937; Schabracq, 2002):

- Clear goals that are shared and supported by all employees.
- A good embedding of the organization or department in its environment, with good relations with all relevant parties.
- Good social relations between functional units as well as individual employees, and a good working climate.
- Patterns of activity that can be performed in a self-evident, everyday way not demanding extra attention.

An important leadership task within this framework consists of following normal moral standards such as decency, fairness, honesty, respect and mindfulness. Only then, is it possible to maintain a functional emotional climate. Some training or coaching in these issues may be needed. One reason is that it is not always self-evident to everybody that these standards contribute significantly to employees' well-being. Another is that it is not always easy to pay sufficient attention to these standards. However, guarding the emotional climate is, and should be, one of the most important managerial tasks, as there are many ways in which a leader can make a difference in preventing or counteracting unnecessary stress. All of these can be part of some leadership course. Though these issues may appear self-evident, flaws in this respect are among the most prominent causes of problems with well-being and health in a work context.

A real leader should engage, for example, in the following activities:

- Displaying the right social skills necessary to communicate an inspiring vision in such a way that it all appeals to and is subscribed by all involved (Schabracq, 2002).

189

- Knowing enough about the core-business of the department. It has been a real fad— and in many places it still is—to appoint managers who are supposed only to manage, as if this could be completely separated from what the department is about.
- Protecting employees from external threats as far as possible and introducing them to external parties they need to know to develop and maintain a functional reality (Schabracq, 2002).
- Paying sufficient attention to the department and being actively involved with its relational sides in order to maintain functional relations between functional units as well as individual employees. Though this may sound simple, managers are tempted to be preoccupied with all the appeals of the outside world that are all so very important (Schabracq, 2002). This also implies being focused on recognizing and overcoming interpersonal problems such as stereotyping, conflict, isolation, bullying and scapegoating (Adams, 1992).
- Giving employees emotional support, if needed.
- Staying long enough in the same job. Organizational policies that prescribe forced job rotation after a short period of time are useful for management trainees, but are murder when it comes to good management. Staying too long in the same job, on the other hand, can be inadequate too, as this may lead to rigidity and a too one-sided approach.
- Abstaining from the urge to leave one's mark in the department just for the cause of impressing the higher management and one's colleagues, or—in more general terms— refraining from treating the department exclusively as a "leg up" to a next job.
- Respecting your employees and overcoming your own prejudices and stereotypes towards them about their sex, age, ethnic or regional background, etc. (Kaye and Jordan-Evans, 1999).
- Paying attention to, acknowledging and rewarding good performance and not exclusively focusing on correcting sub-standard performance (Kaye and Jordan-Evans, 1999). Not living up to this guideline is very common and gives rise to complaints from employees in most organizations.
- Focusing on realizing the right conditions to allow the employees to perform well: the principle of subsidiarity (Handy, 1994), which essentially comes close to realizing a functional reality.
- Trying to act fairly and making that clear, that is, making the point of not acting out of self-interest, favoritism or nepotism.
- Refraining from sexual relations with one's subordinates, as this interferes with the normal communication patterns and the division of power and easily leads to abuse.
- Gathering enough knowledge about the department's or team's past (from different sources!) and the problems that occurred in it (Ryan and Oestreich, 1988).
- Recognizing employees' stress symptoms as such, looking for systemic causes in the organization and their work, and doing something about them (Schabracq and Cooper, 2001).
- Really putting problems on the agenda and discussing these in a constructive, problem-solving way in work progress meetings and in individual talks with the people with whom one has these difficulties (Ryan and Oestreich, 1988).

- Informing employees as early as possible about approaching radical changes that affect them, such as, for example, a merger, a reorganization, a change in their jobs, replacement and lay-off.
- Discussing things periodically during works progress meetings, especially in times of change. To prevent needless worrying and rumors, it is useful to explicitly ask about rumors during these meetings and to comment on these as openly as possible.
- Coaching. This implies helping with setting goals, planning, pointing out pitfalls and giving advice if necessary (Schabracq, 1998a). A Dutch study showed that managers tend to be overly optimistic about their own coaching skills and practices (Donders and Stoker, 2002).
- Regularly interviewing employees about their individual functioning, professional development and further career, and, if needed, offering training, further coaching or mentoring.
- Being reserved about implementing changes, that is, no changes for the sheer purpose of change in itself.
- Implementing changes in such a way that the resistance these may evoke is dealt with appropriately, while the occurrence of stress and alienation is prevented (Schabracq et al., 2001).
- Bringing bad news in such a way that the recipients get all the room they need to express their emotions.
- Being focused on recognizing and overcoming difficulties at the level of tasks and jobs, such as over- and under-load (Schabracq et al., 2001).
- Keeping in touch with ill employees, preparing their return to the department or team and investing extra time and attention in them after their return.
- Giving extra time and attention to employees who have experienced a traumatic event. Here, it is especially important to let them talk about what they have gone through and to find out whether referral to a specialist is necessary (Kleber and Van der Velden, 2003).

In order to develop some of the above-mentioned skills, it may help to enter a good leadership course that pays attention to such issues. A good alternative may be to have some professional coaching by an external expert (Schabracq, 1998a). A coach may help to set goals and may act as a listening ear, sparring partner, devil's advocate, individual trainer, psychotherapist, organizational consultant and adviser. At all times, however, the manager remains entirely responsible for his or her own decisions and interventions. The coach is just an independent discussion partner from outside the organization without other interests within the organization. Seeking a coach is not a sign of weakness, but a matter of wanting to perform optimally and develop oneself.

Though all the above-mentioned issues matter in creating appropriate working conditions without unnecessary risks for health and well-being, it is especially important for managers to get some extra training in social skills and stress prevention.

Social skills programs for managers should focus on increasing their sensitivity as well as their authenticity. Keywords are leadership and team building. To create the proper conditions for optimal performance, motivation and learning possibilities, as well as to bring about an atmosphere of good social support, managers need to master the following skills:

191

- Listening skills, such as empathizing, "reading" non-verbal behavior, interviewing, tracing underlying assumptions, delaying immediate responses, responding appropriately to intense emotions, recognizing and acknowledging individual differences, as well as moral sensitivity. Mastering all of these skills presupposes sufficient self-knowledge.
- Other coaching skills, such as internal congruence (being undivided, see Laborde, 1987), showing approval and disapproval, positive re-labeling, helping to make choices, goal-setting and delegating.
- Social skills to lead groups, such as making use of individual differences in order to accomplish synergy, negotiating, generating "win-win" solutions and conflict management, and appropriately leading workshops and other meetings.

All this is a matter of instruction, discussion and, foremost, much exercise and role-playing, with each other or with actors, while the trainees also serve as observers.

Training in stress prevention focuses on the following outcomes:

- Being able to notice stress risks and reactions of employees earlier and better.
- Acquiring a conceptual framework to talk about stress, overcoming the taboo of talking about stress at work and talking more easily about it with one's employees.
- Knowing about stress effects and their costs.
- Some knowledge about interventions as well as about what not to do.
- Implementing some interventions in one's own department.
- Dealing with crises and traumatic events.
- Knowledge about options of referral.
- Dealing with one's own stress sources and reactions, and being a role model in this respect.

A stress audit in the manager's own organization or department offers a good occasion for such a program. Here, too, it is important to get plenty of practice, in role-playing and in real life, and to get and give lots of feedback.

All in all, accomplishing all these leadership tasks is far from simple and it is quite justified to ask whether all this can be realized by one person, who is also responsible for the bottom line of the department.

THE GENERAL APPROACH

Problems with employees' well-being and health can be a good occasion to talk with these employees to find out what is going on and what can be done about it. The employees' suggestions are crucial here, because they are the experts on their own well-being and have the greatest interest in improving things. Inviting them several times explicitly to comment and making them responsible—"It is your work!"—as well as actually doing something about it—or, better still, letting them do something about it—is a logical and effective method. Beforehand, it should be made clear that not all suggestions can be realized. This approach is especially appropriate to find out about potential bugs in a recently implemented change: "Initially, all kinds of things will go wrong and it is your task to monitor what exactly goes wrong and devise better solutions." This element proved to be very successful in interventions in some Dutch non-profit organizations. Apart from interviews and informal individual talks, meetings about work progress are an appropriate context for this.

In bigger organizations, it makes sense to audit employees' well-being, experienced health, and work satisfaction periodically with the help of a questionnaire. Here, too, the focus is on exploring possible problems and solutions in this area. Departments and teams that experience problems can then be scrutinized in more detail by interviewing key informants about what is going on (Cox et al., 1993).

A special form of audit—partly a workshop, in fact—is the so-called "acceleration room." All members of a department sit around a table behind laptops, which are connected in a network. Their scores are pooled automatically and projected on the wall by a beamer. This allows for immediate reactions and leads to a lively and remarkably open discussion. As they can answer these questions anonymously and, therefore, without fear of possible negative consequences, this approach is especially appropriate for organizations where employees would otherwise feel unsafe answering such questions. In this way, this approach proved to be useful in a Dutch province administration.

If needed, a workshop can be organized. A workshop is a meeting of an existing group to solve a certain problem. It is led by one or two facilitators, the person responsible for the audit and, maybe, an HR professional or an external consultant. Usually, it takes place somewhere outside the organization and takes from half a day to two consecutive days. Most workshops are preceded by interviews with key participants. The objective of a workshop is to reach agreements and take decisions about the problem at hand. This results in a division of tasks, each with a definite time path, which is all recorded in writing. Participants can put themselves forward for tasks and roles that appeal to them. In this way, the participants make use of their mutual differences and complement each other, so that synergy may evolve.

In workshops, the objective of the session is pointed out first. This objective can be used by the facilitators as a criterion of the relevance of individual contributions—"How does this point relate to our objective?"—to guard the workshop's progress. Also, it is made clear beforehand that—for several reasons, among them financial considerations—not all solutions can be accepted. The next step consists of coming to a common, shared definition of the problems and their importance and causes. If there is agreement on these issues, the group tries to find solutions, which they then can try to improve during several rounds. This may involve some brainstorming techniques, as well as other exercises and games.

In this approach, it is essential that employees raise matters themselves. Also, they have to think for themselves, make their own choices and devise their own solutions. It is also important that employees take responsibility for their own destiny in matters of their own development and future, especially during radical organizational change. Sometimes, it is necessary to provide employees with some extra tools. A self-management program can be of help here (see pp. 194–200).

Of course, the group members cannot solve all problems by themselves, but they can solve some and they can point out directions to solve others. Here, the whole arsenal of HRM methods and techniques can be deployed.

HRM INTERVENTIONS

Taking employees' health and well-being as our objective, career and job policies can be used to attain a better person–job fit and to realize further personal and professional development. In all organizations where personnel are an important factor, these policies can be appropriate. Such a policy should be applied as much as possible in an individualized way, in order to make the best of everybody's individual talents, motives and life stage. This applies also to job redesign. Individualization here means that the employees in question are actively involved in the decisions about the design and implementation of the interventions. We examine shortly the following interventions:

- Selection
- Career policy
- Job rotation and replacement
- Secondment, projects and sabbaticals
- Outplacement and lay-off
- Training and coaching
- Job redesign.

Selection

The organization can use the selection procedure to create an optimal point of departure for new employees with respect to health and well-being. Something similar applies to assessment procedures for employees who have already been working for the organization for some time. In both cases, this may involve interviews, psychometric tests and forms of self-assessment, such as writing an autobiography. Usually, selection and assessment are about determining skills, abilities and potential for further development. However, from the perspective of health and well-being, there are more options in this respect.

A first objective consists of getting to know the expectations of the candidates about the job, further possibilities and the organization, and providing them with realistic information about these issues. This helps them to adjust possible unrealistic expectations. The reason to stress this point is that too high expectations form an important source of stress and burnout. This demands serious honesty from the organization, as many organizations tend to exaggerate their positive aspects.

Another important point is mapping training needs, as well as personal interests and preferences, in order to find out how and in what direction employees can and want to develop themselves. Also, it is important to get an idea of their attitude to work, colleagues and the organization: what they do and don't want in this respect; what they do and don't allow and compel themselves to do. Last, it is also important to determine whether somebody fits into the organization, even when there is no intention at all to develop a pure culture of clones in this respect.

Another part of the procedure is establishing how people deal with change and stress, as well as assessing their specific vulnerabilities in this respect. In addition to interviewing them about critical events, this can be done by filling in specific measurement scales. These are used, for instance, for the recruitment of airplane pilots (Schrader, 2003) and air traffic control personnel (Kaden, 2003). Another possibility consists of designing specific assessment situations, in which candidates are observed while they are exposed to relevant stress sources. A strange example is the use of a chair with legs of unequal length by an American, Admiral Rickover, who made job candidates sit in this chair when he interviewed them, to test their composure and coping qualities.

Using selection to find out about all the issues mentioned above implies that during the selection procedure, real face-to-face contact with the candidates is necessary, and that this should not be a matter of just taking a set of paper and pencil tests. Though an external selection agency can play a role, it does not make sense to outsource the whole procedure.

Career policy

In order to enable employees to develop in a way that is optimally attuned to both their own needs, talents and values, as well as to the organizational ones, the organization tries to meet individual training needs and develop individual talents in such a way that it benefits the organization as well. The organizational interest here lies in retaining good personnel, optimizing their motivation and output, and developing them professionally, so that they can take over the organizational key positions when needed. This implies enabling employees, in time, to prepare and make their next career steps. Coaching, mentoring—that is, a form of coaching by a more experienced, often older colleague—and training can be very useful here (see Training and coaching, pp. 197–199).

It means also that, from time to time, the parties involved have a closer look at the employee's present options, skills and further training needs. This can consist of periodical interviews about issues such as individual progress, problems, expectations, options, well-being, training needs, career issues, etc. The employee having proper insight into what the organization is about and wants to accomplish—its mission and vision—and the policies stemming from these is crucial as well. Only then, is it possible to really shape one's own career in a proactive way.

A good example of such an approach can be found at DSM, a Dutch chemical company. They talk about "stream policy" (Osse, 1999). The essence consists of creating individual career paths during so-called "stream sessions." An employee stays at least three years in one job, and then moves on to the next one. Career moves are not necessarily vertical.

Job rotation and re-placement

Job rotation, changing jobs from time to time as a structural element of personnel policy, can contribute to professional development. As such, it is a normal part of management trainee programs as practiced by many big companies. Moreover, it may help to prevent the problems stemming from doing the same job for too long (see Schabracq, 2003c). An additional advantage is that, if needed, people can be employed in a more flexible way as they have acquired a broader competence. The outcomes are highest when the different jobs are related in some way: changing merely for the sake of change often makes no sense and usually is not motivating. Also, for some transitions, on-the-job training or a specific training course may be necessary.

195

Re-placement, changing jobs on a more incidental basis, for instance to a job with different work pace and job demands, sometimes helps to attain a better person–job fit, for instance when a job has become too heavy or does not offer sufficient challenges any more. Another reason can be that somebody is not so popular in a department and wants to start with a clean slate elsewhere.

Many big companies have a special department to further mobility and employability within the organization. These centers give information about vacancies and options for additional training and education and provide some personal guidance. Sometimes (for instance at ABN-AMRO and IBM in the Netherlands), these are housed in separate buildings, to guarantee confidentiality and privacy, while sometimes confidentiality is deemed less important than openness and mutual responsibility, for instance at ING and Nedlloyd. Some smaller organizations have instituted joint mobility centers, as have some Dutch trade organizations and governmental institutions.

Secondment, special projects and sabbaticals

Seen from the perspective of career policy, job change also can be of a more temporary nature.

The first option is seconding employees in other organizations temporarily. These other organizations can be clients or suppliers, though research institutes or universities can also be likely candidates. In the non-profit realm, this has taken the form of exchange programs between related organizations such as different municipalities, ministries or schools in order to learn from each other. Secondment can greatly contribute to the professional development of the employee involved, but both organizations may also profit. The employee can act as a consultant or a "liaison officer" and pass information, knowledge and wishes between both organizations, to the profit of both sides. For example, somebody from a supply firm can help a client organization to develop new products or improve old ones by using other products of the supplier, or by making new use of old ones. On the other hand, it can also become clear to the employee in question that the client firm needs products with different specifications than the existing ones, which is important information for the supplier.

Another option is becoming a member of a temporary project team to develop and realize a certain goal that is important to the organization. Within such a project, participating employees can develop and broaden their specific skills and knowledge by learning from each other and from going through the process. Also, they can extend their social network. Some organizations are based almost completely on working in serial as well as parallel projects (which, for that matter, may not be the best way to prevent stress).

A last option here is a sabbatical, i.e. allowing an employee to spend several months or a year on purposes of personal reorientation or additional education or training. This option is becoming increasingly popular.

My own research indicates that, at least in a professional organization such as a university, secondment, special projects and sabbaticals are among the most powerful interventions for the good with respect to motivation and job satisfaction (Meyer and Schabracq, 2000).

196

Outsourcing, outplacement and lay-off

For different reasons, organizations and individual employees sometimes have to go their different ways. One particular form of this is outsourcing. This implies that a part of the organization that is no longer seen as part of the core business becomes an independent organization. The original organization may maintain complete or partial ownership, there may be a management buy-out or the outsourced department is sold to a third party. In all cases, the new organization may extend its client base while still catering to the original organization as well. Examples are training departments of KLM that were turned into independent training firms. Another variant is establishing a new consulting firm outside the original organization where well-trained, mostly older employees can work when there is not enough work for them inside the original organization. IBN-Sernet is a good example here (Thunnissen *et al.*, 2000).

However, new organizations are often not a real option. Lay-off then may become the only possibility. In such cases, it is wise to invest in employees' employability by offering training programs or investing in a different way in their professional future, and helping them to find a good job elsewhere. When lay-off is inevitable, the organization, generally speaking, should act so that those directly involved experience the least possible pain and disadvantage. This may also involve special workshops to vent the emotions in order to set those involved free for entering a new future. This is happening right now in one of the Dutch ministries, which has to downsize considerably.

This is not only a matter of simple decency to these employees. It gives also an important signal to the personnel that remain employed. A considerate approach can prevent the latter group from experiencing feelings of guilt, loss of faith in the organization and de-motivation, the so-called survivors' syndrome. To this end, special workshops for the remaining departments and teams can be provided, which explore these emotions and set new goals. Comparable workshops for managers who have to fire all these people and then have to guide the remaining people are very useful too.

Training and coaching

In order to promote employees' health and well-being, different kinds of coaching and training programs for individual employees can be helpful. Here, too, the outcomes are determined by the degree to which the program is tailored to the individual employees' wishes and needs. So participation always has to be based on agreement with, or a request from, the individual employees involved. In principle, all these kinds of education should be open to employees of all age categories, including the oldest.

Training may be purely directed at the job content, or be more general in nature. So, there are very specific ergonomic training programs in construction and nursing or programs to learn about new machines or software (Osse, 1999). On the other hand, training may consist of a form of general education to equip somebody better for a new career move. These kinds of training and education are most prominent in Scandinavia (Butler, 2001; Thunissen *et al.*, 2000), where the government is very much involved in such projects. In the UK too, initiatives such as "Investors in People" and the "Individual Learning Account

Centre" are supported by the government. In addition, training programs also may be about somewhat "softer" assets, such as social skills and personal growth.

All of these programs can have positive effects on employees' health and well-being. Some programs, however, aim more explicitly at improving employees' well-being and health. We briefly examine the following programs:

- Training in personal effectiveness or assertiveness.
- Training in time-management.
- Training in self-management and employability.
- Training in stress management.

Training in personal effectiveness or assertiveness

Problems with guarding your own autonomy and integrity in work settings form an important threat to your well-being and health. Training programs in personal effectiveness or assertiveness focus on dealing in a better way with questions and demands of clients, superiors or colleagues. Learning goals may be:

- saying no to clients, superiors or colleagues (or avoiding saying "yes indeed" to new exciting projects for which no time is available);
- sticking to one's own priorities and limits;
- counteracting task disturbances;
- explaining one's own dilemmas and impossibilities;
- dealing with stereotyping;
- dealing with scapegoating and harassment;
- coping with one's own anger and preventing unneeded conflicts.

Time management

Time management programs focus on formulating clear and realistic goals and setting priorities (important/unimportant; urgent/not urgent), as well as on phasing, grouping and shielding tasks. This enables one to dedicate oneself to what really matters, as well as to delegate and not to spend time on less relevant activities. This is primarily a matter of becoming aware of what is important and what is not. In addition, trainees learn about causes of unnecessary time loss and may practice all kinds of methods to minimize these. The latter vary from fixed procedures for routine activities and referral, to less time-consuming ways of handling visitors, mail, telephone, e-mail etc. All this can help to push back all kinds of task disturbances and stress (for example, Yukl, 1990).

Self-management and employability

Courses in self-management and employability focus on developing new options for employees of different age groups to become more effective, motivated and creative in their jobs, career and further life. This should lead to more effective steering of one's own life and career. In such training programs, trainees determine their basic themes, motives and talents. They then set goals for their different life realms and learn how to make and execute plans to realize these goals. An additional outcome of such a program may consist of being able to cope with change more adaptively: the trainees teach themselves to deal with changes in a "standardized" way. This gives them more influence on the way change takes place, while it decreases their resistance and stress. It also enables them to influence the result of the change, in a way that they like best (for example, Schabracq, 2003a).

Stress management

Stress management training programs focus on coping with stress, and stress prevention (for example, Schabracq and Cooper, 2001). The outcomes are partially similar to those of training programs for managers. In addition, such programs may aim at the following outcomes:

- Making time-out for regular recuperation, reflection and planning.
- A healthier lifestyle.
- Keeping a stress diary to get more insight into one's own stress sources and reactions.
- Tracing and adapting one's own suppositions underlying one's stress reactions.
- Some knowledge about goal-setting, time-management and planning.
- Some skill in personal effectiveness and thought-stopping (a technique from behavioral therapy to stop unproductive, recurring thoughts).
- Some knowledge of, and skill in, one or more of the many ways to bring about mental quiet, such as breathing techniques, relaxation exercises, guided fantasies, running, etc.
- Applications of "mental quiet," such as:
  - relaxation, refreshing or centering;
  - asking oneself questions ("focusing");
  - motivating oneself, as well as setting goals for oneself.
- Methods to prepare difficult tasks.

Job redesign

Another important issue is to design and redesign jobs in such a way that they become attuned to what individual employees are able and willing to do. To prevent stress, these jobs have to enable employees to remain motivated, work effectively, develop themselves and not become isolated. There are all kinds of methods of job redesign to improve all jobs in an organization following standard principles (Kompier, 2003). Though these principles may be of importance as general guidelines, it is, nevertheless, preferable to tailor job redesign to the needs of the individuals involved. This is, again, a matter of good communication. Examples of directions for job redesign are making jobs more diverse (in order to prevent fatigue or physical wear-and-tear) or complete, allowing more autonomy in job performance, and providing more opportunities for social interaction.

A good example of making jobs more diverse in order to prevent wear-and-tear, as well as allowing for more autonomy is a project in the municipality of Groningen (NL), where

199

the jobs of road mender and gardener were combined into the single post of neighborhood manager. Being responsible for a certain city area, they operate in autonomous couples in a little vehicle, learning from each other and preventing knee trouble for the road menders, which is a very prominent complaint in that profession (as road menders do a lot of their work on their knees) (Schabracq, 1998b; Osse, 1999). Good examples of all kinds of job redesign projects are to be found in Kompier *et al.* (1996)

OUTCOMES

To the degree that the approaches sketched above are successful, they may have all kinds of positive outcomes for the organization in the following areas:

- The primary outcome consists of a reduction of stress complaints and a higher level of well-being and health.
- Another effect is that employees are more thoroughly socialized by the organization. As a result, they may identify themselves with it, so that being a member of that organization becomes a part of their own identity. This implies that they come to see the organization's interest as their own. As such, this can be reflected in increased motivation and commitment.
- Moreover, people who work with more pleasure, motivation and commitment want to do a good job and are willing to do something extra. This makes them more effective and productive, while the quality of what they do and make tends to improve as well. This implies fewer errors, resulting in lower costs for quality control and repair, while the expenses associated with such errors have increased considerably. In addition, employees tend to make more effective use of all kinds of chances and opportunities that are important to the organization's survival. These self-steering abilities become more and more important.
- People who are motivated to do their work well are, generally speaking, also more attentive and creative, and learn more. As a result, they develop better individual mastery and collective effectiveness.
- Another effect may be that employees are in a better mood and generally interact in a better way. This prevents conflicts and disturbed relationships between employees and between departments, which, in turn, contributes to a better working climate and smoother collaboration.
- A similar effect may be that the employees are able to develop better relations and communication with clients, suppliers, sister organizations and government.
- An organization with a good working climate, few stress complaints and high work satisfaction is an attractive employer. This decreases the risk of turn-over of good employees, in whom the organization has invested much.
- A good working climate and few stress complaints among employees positively influence the corporate image. It indicates that the organization is serious about its corporate values on well-being and health. This has become increasingly important, both with respect to clients and relationships with the government, as well as to hiring new personnel. An additional point is that young, well-educated employees, more and more, are making a point of working for a company that has more to offer in this area.

- The policies sketched above make and keep employees broadly employable, also at an older age. This prevents the dangers of staying too long in one job and the build-up of unbridgeable gaps in training and education.
- In the longer run, this approach leads to a group of well-informed and knowledgeable potential managers who can take up key positions in their organization. In this way, the organization is not dependent on scarce and expensive outsiders, who have no special bind with the organization and have to be fully introduced to its specific expertise and culture.
- A final outcome is that in this way the organization can develop its own core competencies and corporate style, tailored to its own niche of clients and products. Essentially, this is a feature of a "learning organization" (Mintzberg *et al.*, 1998).

Overall, all these effects positively influence the corporate results, leading to greater shareholder satisfaction and a satisfied management that encourages the employees to go on in this way, etc. This starts up a positive spiral, which Reichheld (1996) calls the "loyalty effect," a phenomenon characteristic of successful companies. Similar arguments are described in "The customer comes second" by Rosenbluth and McFerrin Peters (1992) and "The living company" (1997) by de Geus. Essentially, the same kind of reasoning applies to the body of thought behind "organizational health" and the "healthy organization." Though all of this may sound overly optimistic, such a positive spiral is a well-documented phenomenon, even though many of us may work in organizations where such a spiral is not very prominent.

PROBLEMS

The success of the approach described above is heavily dependent on the time, information and attention that the organization wants to give to its employees. The main problem here is that in most organizations, the line manager is responsible for all those tasks described above. However, much of this often gets stuck in paper rules, good intentions and lip service. Most managers are simply too busy with technical problems or external matters to occupy themselves deeply with their employees. Also, their heart often is not primarily in "people tasks." They are not selected for these matters, it usually is not the reason why they wanted their present job and, most importantly, it is not an important evaluation criterion for their job performance. Some of them might be helped by a training program in this respect, but it is unlikely that this will really affect the way most of them work, as their other tasks will still absorb them too much.

If things are like this, it is to be preferred that somebody else takes up this task, preferably somebody of some influence. However, this implies a major change in the organization and its division of power, which probably will evoke intense reactions and resistance.

For several reasons, it would not be easy for most present HR officers to take up such tasks. As it is, they usually are staff members not used to taking responsibility for the everyday affairs of a department. Apart from the need of an attitude change from the HR officer, it also might lead to a power struggle with the department manager, which the

HR officer is unlikely to win. Moreover, HR officers usually know little of the technicalities of the actual work and are also too far removed from employees to know them well personally. All this means that in bigger organizations these tasks, preferably, should not be left to the central HR department.

CO-MANAGEMENT: A POSSIBLE APPROACH

What is co-management?

In order to solve the problems of making managers or HR officers responsible for the employees' well-being and health, it is a logical step to design a new job to take care of this, the one of co-manager. Generally speaking, the co-manager works at two levels: in the individual departments as well as in a team of other co-managers, at a level above the individual departments.

First, co-managers are responsible for the performance, collaboration, well-being and professional development of the employees of one or more departments. This demands close collaboration with the actual managers. The specific power relation between manager and co-manager can vary. In some organizations, the co-manager holds the higher position. This is the case, for instance, in the Research and Development Department of the Visual Displays Division of one of the big electronic multinationals. However, in most cases the original manager is leading, while the co-manager acts as a kind of minister of internal affairs. Examples are to be found in some national armies, hospitals, a merchant bank, a chemical industry and a law firm. In some instances, co-managers are being seconded by a specialized agency on a temporal basis to get things organized in client organizations.

Second, the co-managers of the different departments form a special team that concerns itself with the same issues from a higher level, either divisional or corporate. The team members here act as each others' sounding board and together approach relevant issues at a more strategic level. In this context, they can devise audits about well-being, map bottle-necks and think about solutions. Next, they can centrally initiate and guide improvement projects. Though, initially, they can benefit from some supervision of an external expert, they gradually develop themselves into a team of specialists in this respect, with an important advisory role towards their top management as well.

Another important co-management task is shaping and guiding the implementation of radical changes in organizations. This task, in particular, makes co-management important at a strategic level. The ability to deal with change adaptively threatens to become a major constraint in the survival and further development of many organizations (Schabracq and Cooper, 2000). This is about the way in which organizations are able to prevent such changes, and the stress generated by them, interfering with an orderly course of affairs. Moreover, dealing with change in such a way can become part of the core competence of the organization, a part of the unique expertise that the competition cannot copy. This also indicates why, preferably, co-managers should be organizational employees, and not external consultants. Their role is simply too strategically important and too central to the organizational objectives.

Advantages and pitfalls

All in all, the idea of co-management is a logical consequence of the body of thought of HRM. As such, it may contribute to all the positive consequences mentioned in the section on Outcomes, pp. 200–201. This, in itself, can be sufficient reason to implement it. However, there may be some additional positive effects. Apart from helping an organization to deal better with change and a turbulent environment, co-management enables line managers to spend more time on their original core tasks. Also, it opens up for managers the option of more "normal" working hours and, possibly, even of a part-time job. This would also make a management career much more attractive to many women. Moreover, co-management allows the organization to make better use of good HR officers, while it also contributes to organizational policies for management development, employability and senior employees.

The most obvious pitfalls of co-management are issues such as power struggles, conflicts and being played against each other. This is often a matter of sliding back into "old" familiar ways of functioning, personal as well as organizational ones. Solutions can be found in better communication, with or without the help of an external facilitator, while the success of it all is heavily dependent on a careful implementation.

Implementing co-management

Successfully implementing co-management implies a serious form of cultural change, with all its accompanying shifts in responsibility and power. As such, implementation will always involve a kind of jolt in the organization. A good implementation implies that all parties should get the necessary information, time and attention to familiarize themselves with it and develop forms of adaptation. In the implementation stage, the following steps have to be taken, preferably guided by some external expert:

- Establishing to what extent it is realistic to implement co-management in the organization. This concerns the compatibility of the approach with the existing culture, the available means and time, and the presence of sufficient good candidates for the co-manager role.
- Getting sufficient support and commitment from the top management to implement co-management. To this end, it is necessary that the highest level gets a clear picture of the nature and implications of co-management, both for the whole organization and their own functioning as role models. One or more workshops about the subject by an expert can be useful in this respect.
- Appointing responsibility for the implementation to one of the highest level managers, preferably a volunteer with a positive attitude to the project.
- Making a plan and time path for the implementation.
- Communication of the intended implementation to the line managers and, subsequently, to the rest of the organization.
- Selection of the co-managers. Of course, the line managers in question are involved in the procedure. As inside candidates have the great advantage of knowing the organization, co-managers, preferably, are recruited from the pool of managers, HR officers and other professionals within the organization. The focus here is on

203

volunteers who have the right feel for such matters. However, sometimes it is appropriate to choose one or two "fresh" outsiders who have some experience in this area and can act as protagonist. For two reasons, it usually makes sense to include some older employees. First, they know the organization and its culture very well. Second, some of them have developed the cognitive skills that I have described elsewhere under the denominator of wisdom (Schabracq, 2003d), which essentially consists of dealing with, as well as giving form and meaning to, the radical changes that life forces upon us. Apart from motivation and affinity with the job, good social skills, good general intelligence and experience with functioning at a higher organizational level are important selection criteria. Some expertise in the department's business is useful, but not necessary per se. The main guideline here is that they should be able to act as good sparring partners for the line managers.

- Training the selected candidates. A short educational program deals with the nature of the job and issues such as stress, stress management and organizational diagnosis and change. It also involves training in the social skills needed for coaching, advising, leading workshops, recognizing and discussing stress reactions, and conflict management. Subsequently, they mainly learn by practice on the job and by regular group supervision sessions.
- Introduction of the co-managers in their own departments, by individual talks with the line manager and all employees involved, followed by a workshop with the departments in question to clarify mutual role expectations.
- A short course of joint coaching of manager and co-manager.
- Intervision (i.e. mutual supervision of colleagues) at regular time intervals about occurring problems.
- Conducting specific improvement projects and accompanying occurring change projects.
- Evaluation.

CONCLUSION

This chapter examined what HRM can do for optimizing employees' well-being and health. The described approach demands some organizational changes, but for most organizations this does not imply a total break with the past. The approach is primarily about a more consistent HRM policy, and willingness to follow up its implications. Of course, this implies expenses. However, when we take the positive outcomes for the organization and the usual costs of ill-conducted organizational changes into account, this is probably money well-spent.

REFERENCES

Adams, A. (1992) *Bullying at Work: How to Confront and Overcome it.* London: Virago Press.

Butler, R.N. (2001) *Lifelong Learning in Norway: An Experiment in Progress.* New York: International Longevity Center USA.

Cox, T., Griffith, A. and Randall, R. (1993) A Risk Management Approach to the Prevention of Work Stress. In M.J. Schabracq, J.A.M. Winnubst and C.L. Cooper (eds) *The Handbook of Work and Health Psychology*. Chichester: J. Wiley & Sons, pp. 191–206.

Doeglas, J.D.A. and Schabracq, M.J. (1992) *Transitiemanagement (Transition management)*. *Gedrag en Organisatie* (*Behavior and Organization*), 5, 448–466.

Donders, M. and Stoker, J. (2002) Woorden, weinig daden (Words, few deeds). *De gids voor personeelsmanagement* (*The Guide for HRM*), 81 (9), 17–22.

Geus, A. de (1997) *The Living Company*. New York: Longview.

Goldratt, E. (1990) *What is This Thing Called Theory of Constraints and How Should it be Implemented*. Croton on Hudson NY: North River Press.

Handy, C. (1994) *The Age of Paradox*. Boston, MA: Harvard Business School Press.

Kaden, D. (2003) *Omgaan met werkdruk bij luchtverkeersleiding* (Coping with Work Pressures in Air Control), unpublished manuscript. Amsterdam: University of Amsterdam.

Kaye, B. and Jordan-Evans, S. (1999) *Love 'em or Lose 'em: Getting Good People to Stay*. San Francisco, CA: Berrett-Koehler.

Kleber, R.L. and Van der Velden, P.G. (2003). Acute Stress at Work. In M.J. Schabracq, J.A.M. Winnubst and C.L. Cooper (eds) *The Handbook of Work and Health Psychology*. Chichester: J. Wiley & Sons, pp. 367–382.

Kompier, M.A.J. (2003) Job Design and Well-Being. In M.J. Schabracq, J.A.M. Winnubst and C.L. Cooper (eds) *The Handbook of Work and Health Psychology*. Chichester: J. Wiley & Sons, pp. 429–454.

Kompier, M.A.J., Gründemann, R.W.M., Vink, P. and Smulders, P.G.W. (eds) (1996) *Aan de slag* (*Get Going*). Alphen aan de Rijn, Netherlands: Samsom.

Laborde, G.Z. (1987) *Influencing with Integrity*. Palo Alto, CA: Syntony Publishing.

Meyer, J. and Schabracq, M.J. (2000) *Ouder wetenschappelijk personeel: situatie, beleving en scenario's* (*Older Scientific Personnel: Situation, Experience and Scenarios*), internal publication. Amsterdam: University of Amsterdam.

Mintzberg, H., Ahlstrand, B. and Lampel, J. (1998) *Strategy Safari*. London, etc.: Prentice Hall.

Ofman, D.D. (1995) *Bezieling en kwaliteit in organisaties* (*Inspiration and Quality in Organisations*). Cothen, Netherlands: Servire.

Osse, P. (1999) *Doorlopende banen* (*Continuing Jobs*). Amsterdam: FNV Pers.

Parsons, T. (1937) *The Structure of Social Action*. New York: McGraw-Hill.

Reichheld, F.F. (1996) *The Loyalty Effect*. Boston, MA: Harvard Business School Press.

Rosenbluth, H.F. and McFerrin Peters, D. (1992) *The Customer Comes Second*. New York: W. Morrow and Cy.

Ryan, K.D. and Oestreich, D.K. (1988) *Driving Fear out of the Workplace*. San Francisco, CA: Jossey-Bass.

Schabracq, M.J. (1998a) *Management Coaching*. Deventer, Netherlands: Kluwer Bedrijfsinformatie.

Schabracq, M.J. (1998b) *Medewerkers van boven de veertig* (*Employees over Forty*). Deventer, Netherlands: Kluwer Bedrijfsinformatie.

Schabracq, M.J. (2001) *De HRM-functionaris (The HRM Officer)*. Praktijkboek gezond werken (*Manual of Healthy Working*). Maarsen, Netherlands: Elsevier I 2.2–1–12.

Schabracq, M.J. (2001) *De HRM-functionaris (The HRM Officer). Praktijkboek gezond werken* (*Manual of Healthy Working*). Maarsen, Netherlands: Elsevier I 2.2–1–12.

Schabracq, M.J. (2002) *Leiderschap is teamwerk (Leadership is Teamwork). De gids voor personeelsmanagement* (*The Guide for HRM*), 81 (12), 17–20.

Schabracq, M.J. (2003a). *De droomfabriek* (*The Dream Factory*). Utrecht: Kosmos.

Schabracq, M.J. (2003b) Organisational Culture, Stress and Change. In M.J. Schabracq, J.A.M. Winnubst and C.L. Cooper (eds) *The Handbook of Work and Health Psychology*. Chichester: J. Wiley & Sons, pp. 37–62.

Schabracq, M.J. (2003c) Issues of the Second Career Half. In M.J. Schabracq, J.A.M. Winnubst and C.L. Cooper (eds) *The Handbook of Work and Health Psychology*. Chichester: J. Wiley & Sons, pp. 333–348.

Schabracq, M.J. (2003d) Policies and Strategies for the Second Career Half. In M.J. Schabracq, J.A.M. Winnubst and C.L. Cooper (eds) *The Handbook of Work and Health Psychology*. Chichester: J. Wiley & Sons, pp. 349–365.

Schabracq, M.J. and Cooper, C.L. (2000) The Changing Nature of Work and Stress. *Journal of Management Psychology*, 15, 227–241.

Schabracq, M.J. and Cooper C.L. (2001*). Stress als keuze. Werkboek persoonlijk stressmanagement* (*Stress as a Choice. Workbook for Personal Stress Management*) Schiedam: Scriptum.

Schabracq, M.J. and Cooper, C.L. (2003) To be me or not to be me: About alienation. *Journal of Counselling Psychology*, 16, 53–79.

Schabracq, M.J., Cooper, C.L., Travers, C. and Maanen, D. van (2001) *Occupational Health Psychology: The Challenge of Workplace Stress*. Leicester: British Psychological Association.

Schabracq, M.J., Maassen van den Brink, H., Groot, W., Janssen, P. and Houkes, I. (2000) *De prijs van stress* (*The Price of Stress*). Amsterdam: Elsevier.

Schrader, K. (2003) *Stressbestendigheid, coping en onderbelasting*. (Resistance to Stress, Coping and Task Under-load), unpublished manuscript. Amsterdam: University of Amsterdam.

Thunnissen, M.A.G, Thijssen, J.G.L. and Lange, W.A.M. de (2000) *Beleid zonder management?* (*Policies Without Management?*). Tilburg: OSA-publicatie A174.

Yukl, G.A. (1990) *Skills for Managers and Leaders*. Englewood Cliffs, NJ: Prentice-Hall.

Part IV

Human Resource Management and organizational effectiveness

Chapter 12

HRM in service

The contingencies abound

Lisa H. Nishii and Benjamin Schneider

INTRODUCTION

In the majority of Western countries, services account for the largest share of gross domestic product and are a major source of employment (Dicken, 1998). A recent estimate states that in the US, services-producing industries account for at least 67 percent of the GDP and over 80 percent of US employment (McCahill and Moyer, 2002; Bureau of Labor Statistics, 2003). As an example, consider the restaurant section of services in the US: it has $420 billion in sales, accounts for 6.6 percent of economic activity, and has more than 11.5 million workers (Day, 2003). In addition to customers in the US, the customers for whom these services are being produced are becoming increasingly multicultural. The volume of US commercial services exports doubled during the period 1990–2002, totaling $292 billion by the year 2002, and accounting for over 4 million jobs in the US (Bureau of Economic Analysis, 2003; Office of the US Trade Representative, 2003). Even within the domestic market, customers are becoming increasingly diverse: by the year 2050, less than 53 percent of the US population will be Caucasian; 16 percent will be Black, 23 percent will be of Hispanic origin, 10 percent will be Asian and Pacific Islander, and 1 percent will be Native American (US Census Bureau, 2001). In fact, after 2030, the Caucasian population will begin to decline in size while the minority ethnic populations will continue to grow at ever-faster rates.

Despite the rapid growth in the diversity of service consumers—both abroad and domestically—theoretical developments regarding this diversity in the service world have lagged far behind those that have characterized the world of manufacturing. With regard to international services, Knight (1999) conducted a review of the literature and concluded that there is an alarming paucity of research on international services management despite the importance of services in the global economy. A large proportion of the research that has been conducted on international services has focused on marketing issues rather than human resource management (HRM) issues. This means that little is known about the cross-cultural applicability of service HRM theories, which have hitherto been developed and tested almost exclusively within the West (mostly within the US context). Similarly, there has been little research on the HRM implications of the growing diversity of service consumers within the US domestic market. Again, much of the research focuses on the challenges associated with simultaneously marketing services to a multicultural customer base, with little or no work focusing on the implications of these challenges for HRM in service firms.

Thus, the purpose of our chapter is to introduce a preliminary discussion of the HRM implications of both increased internationalization and domestic diversity for service firms. We begin by presenting a brief synthesis of the services management literature that has been established to date. Readers will note in the synthesis that a number of contingencies with regard to HRM practices have already been introduced, especially via definitions of what constitutes service and the role of customers in service production and delivery. We then discuss the potential cross-cultural applicability of these services management principles abroad, and when doing so, we focus primarily on the aspects of services management theories that are laden with Western cultural principles. Next, we discuss parallel challenges faced by service firms as a result of increased diversity within the domestic marketplace and we conclude with some thoughts about the necessity to more explicitly explore the contingent nature of HRM practices.

SERVICES MANAGEMENT, WITH A FOCUS ON HRM

The world of services marketing is little more than 30 years old, and those of services operations management (OM) and services HRM are, perhaps, 25 years old. The three together are referred to generically as services management. A number of texts have appeared integrating these three disciplines to gain increased understanding of service quality, especially the delivery of service quality (see Lovelock and Wirtz, 2004; Zeithaml and Bitner, 2000). In addition there are several excellent books, targeted on managers that integrate these three approaches (Berry, 1995, 1997; Heskett et al., 1997; Schneider and Bowen, 1995). All of the books focus on the delivery of service quality; by this we mean that the focus has been more on the delivery of a service than on the attributes of the "core" service itself (e.g., the food at a restaurant, the clothing in a retail store, the safety of the rides at a theme park, and so forth). In addition, much of the services management literature has focused on consumer services rather than professional services such as law, medicine, or even higher education (for an exception see Maister, 1997). Below, we briefly highlight the major contributions from the three disciplines as they relate to HRM in service firms.

Marketing contributions

Marketing scientists have been the most active in pursuing the world of services, followed by operations management scholars and, last, HRM researchers. From marketing we have learned that service delivery and goods production, in the extreme, anchor opposite ends of several continua (see Zeithaml and Bitner, 2000; Schneider and Bowen, 1995): (1) relative intangibility, (2) relative customer participation in production, and (3) relative simultaneity of production and consumption. In brief, services tend to: (1) be less tangible (think of attending a Disney theme park as an extreme example where the service is purely the intangible experience), (2) more frequently involve the customer as a co-producer (think of going to the bank and using your ATM card), and (3) be more likely to be produced and consumed simultaneously (think of going to a concert or a restaurant).

210

In contrast, goods are more tangible (think of a computer or a car), require less active participation in their production (we do not produce our car or our computer), and less simultaneously produced and consumed (your car may have been made 6 months ago in a far away place). The implications of these characteristics of services for HRM have received very little formal attention (for exceptions see Bowen and Schneider, 1988; Lengnick-Hall, 1996; Mills *et al.*, 1983).

In addition to the conceptual work accomplished in understanding service quality, marketing scholars have also been at the forefront of the design of measures for the assessment of customer perceptions of service quality (Parasuraman *et al.*, 1994), studying issues surrounding service recovery (Tax and Brown, 2000), and understanding the nature of the customer–firm relationship (Patterson and Ward, 2000). These and other topics are well covered in Swartz and Iacobucci (2000). But not everyone agrees that services and goods are distinguishable and/or that the distinctions we draw are useful.

However, in an important paper, Bowen and Ford (2002) reviewed the literature to see if there were differences in the *management* of manufacturing and service organizations. That is, they proposed that if the kinds of continua for describing manufacturing and services enumerated earlier do exist then they should be reflected in the ways service organizations, compared to manufacturing organizations, function and are managed. In a very comprehensive review they showed that, among other things, the three continua noted earlier produce real differences in the ways organizations function and are managed. For example, they showed that because in service there is simultaneity in production and consumption: (1) the setting in which these occur is an important part of the total experience (Bitner, 1992), (2) employees are required to manage the customers they serve (Rafaeli, 1989), and (3) employees who are hired should have attributes that will promote customer satisfaction (Frei and McDaniel, 1998). Perhaps most centrally from an HRM vantage point, Bowen and Ford note that the emotional labor (Hochschild, 1983) required of employees in service production and delivery is a qualitative difference with important management implications for selection, training, and performance and stress management. Winsted (2000) for example, found that customers of service organizations expect employees to be civil and congenial as well as competent and that service providers who are proficient in all three are skilled at managing their emotions. She goes on to note that different kinds of service jobs require the management of different emotions; think funeral director versus Playboy bunny. It is the requirement of having to appropriately manage emotions that creates challenges for employees, and those challenges produce the stress that also requires management (Pugh, 2002; Tansik, 1990).

The Bowen and Ford (2002) paper is important because of the attention they pay to the management implications of the differences between manufacturing and service production, including implications for the training (how to manage customers) and selection (the personal attributes required) of employees, as just noted. In addition, their review concerns itself also with the implications for the service production process itself, the domain of operations management.

211

Operations management contributions

From operations management, a major insight into the world of service production and delivery has been the idea that the presence of the customer makes the world of service production different from the world of goods production (Chase, 1981; Kellogg and Chase, 1995). In the production of goods, standardization, or the elimination of variability in production, is a given, or at least a goal to be achieved. In contrast, in the world of services, variability is something that must be managed since it cannot usually be eliminated, especially in the world of consumer services (Fitzimmons and Fitzimmons, 1994). The variability in service production is attributed to the different kinds of demands different customers make of service providers, thus yielding the very variability that the world of goods production works at eliminating; in the world of service production, the goal is to manage it (McLaughlin, 1996). Sometimes called the "customer contact model" (Chase, 1981), the implications of the variability customers introduce into service operations has received quite a lot of attention (Chase et al., 1998). The implications for HRM of the presence of the customer and the variability in demand this presence may introduce have not received much attention at all, something we will discuss in later sections.

OM scholars have also been at the forefront in understanding: (1) the importance of demand and capacity tradeoffs (Chase et al., 1998), (2) the implications of waiting time in customer satisfaction (Taylor and Fullerton, 2000), and (3) the relationship between service processes and revenues (Schmenner, 1995). Indeed, this last issue has produced interesting models for calculating the likely payoffs in revenues associated with given proposed investments in improving service quality (Rust et al., 1995). From an HRM standpoint, this last point in particular deserves attention: what is the payoff in revenues for investments in such HRM practices as selection, training, and stress management (Schneider and White, 2004)? The models and methods for such utility analyses (Boudreau, 1991) exist but their application to the world of HRM investments in service organizations has been sparse.

HRM contributions

Perhaps the major contribution HRM has made to understanding service quality and service delivery has been through a focus on those who deliver service. Thus, while marketing has focused on the customer and the attributes of service, and operations management has focused on delivery processes, HRM has logically focused on the human service deliverer. The major work accomplished in this arena is associated with Schneider and his colleagues (Schneider et al., 1980; Schneider and Bowen, 1985; Schneider et al., 1998; see Schneider and White, 2004, for a review) who have shown that employee experiences of the service climate in which they work significantly predict customer satisfaction. They and others have shown this "linkage effect" (Wiley, 1996) to be robust across industries as diverse as banks, insurance companies, supermarkets, automobile financing offices, retail, hotels, and restaurants (Heskett et al., 1997; Schneider et al., 2000).

In this long-term program of research, the facets of organizational life that constitute a service climate for employees have been fairly well documented: a leadership focus on goals and planning for service, recognition and rewards for service excellence, internal support

212

from others on whom service deliverers depend, adequate tools and equipment to deliver service quality, competent co-workers, and a sense that the service that is delivered is of the highest quality (Lytle *et al.*, 1998; Schneider *et al.*, 1998; Schneider and White, 2004). This being true, the HRM implications are important for all those things in which HRM is involved: leadership, motivation, selection and training, and in general the creation of a climate that promotes effectiveness in service delivery (Schneider and Bowen, 1995).

Indeed, more specifically with regard to HRM practices in service settings, research suggests the following as "high performance" work practices for service companies (Wright *et al.*, 2003): (a) for *selection and staffing*, the use of structured interviews, promotion opportunities for qualified employees, and formal selection tests; (b) for *training*, at least 15 hours of formal training per year per employee; (c) for *performance management*, the use of formal performance evaluations, merit-based pay raises, and opportunities to earn bonuses for individual performance; and (d) in terms of worker *participation*, inclusion of employees in participation processes such as quality improvement and problem solving groups, and the provision of fair complaint/grievance processes (Wright *et al.*, 2003). In their study involving a food service company within the US, Wright and his colleagues found that business units that employed these "high performance" work practices were characterized by higher employee commitment and higher organizational performance in terms of both service quality and profits. It may be usefully concluded, then, that there is a set of HRM practices and a set of general management practices focused on service quality that link fairly directly to customer satisfaction.

However, there is also some evidence that the very same set of HRM practices may be differentially associated with customer satisfaction depending on the management goals to which employees attribute HRM practices. More specifically, Nishii (2003) found that in departments of a service firm in which employees attributed the goal of HRM practices to service quality (as opposed to other goals such as cost reduction or legal compliance), customers reported higher levels of satisfaction. Her findings suggest that not only is it advantageous for service firms to adopt specific service quality-focused HRM practices, as stated earlier, but they should also engage in communication practices that lead their employees to accurately perceive that the firm's HRM practices are designed with the explicit goal of service quality in mind.

While these kinds of linkage results appear to be robust across setting and industries (Wiley and Brooks, 2000), these findings have yet to yield significant research programs in the way of contingency models or frameworks that explore service climate antecedents and consequences that would further aid our understanding of the complex management issues confronting service organizations. On the issue of boundary conditions, for example, Gittell (2002) proposed that the stronger the relationships among service providers in interdependent and time-constrained service delivery roles, the more satisfied customers would be. She tested this proposal in a hospital setting with data from care providers and patients and found that provider–provider relationships positively influenced provider–patient relationships that, in turn, positively related to patient satisfaction. Schneider *et al.* (2002) hypothesized that the stronger the climate in which employees work the stronger the relationship would be between employee reports and customer satisfaction. On a sample of bank branch employees and customers they showed that when there is a strong climate (employees agree more

213

rather than less on the climate), customers report higher levels of satisfaction and there is less variability in those customer reports. In a conceptual piece that has received considerable attention, Bowen and Lawler (1992) presented the argument that employee empowerment may be useful in the service sector but particularly when the service to be delivered offers increased opportunities for discretion on the part of employees, is a more customized service, and employees have higher skill sets. Hartline and Ferrell (1996) found mixed support for these ideas with empowerment producing some positive (self-efficacy) and some negative (role conflict) consequences; obviously more research is needed.

In the arena of service climate antecedents and consequences, there has also begun to emerge beginnings of potentially useful research programs. For example, Hartline and Ferrell (1996) proposed and found that manager emphasis on service quality has long-term (indirect) consequences for customer satisfaction—what the leader does is not immediately reflected in what the customer experiences. Schneider et al. (2003) have revealed similar findings and, in addition, they showed that service climate is mediated by service provider citizenship behavior in its relationship to customer satisfaction. In a neat twist on the findings with regard to citizenship behavior, Hui et al. (2001) showed in a field quasi experiment of bank branches that in branches where good citizens are trained to be service quality leaders, those branches will have higher levels of customer satisfaction. Finally, Schneider et al. (1998) and Rogg et al. (2001) have shown that the HRM practices of small businesses (bank branches for Schneider et al. and auto dealerships for Rogg et al.) are mediated by climate in their relationship to customer satisfaction.

Within the general field of HRM itself, however, the implications of being in a service business have not received much attention. Some will argue with this statement, noting that HRM has become far more strategic in the past ten years than it was earlier. While this statement is true, strategic human resources management (SHRM) has focused more on the contributions of HRM to overall organizational goals (organizational performance) than it has on the implications of specific strategic initiatives of a firm for how HRM should be carried out. For example, while there has been some attention to speculating about the specific HRM tactics associated with Porter's (1980) generic organizational strategies (Wright and Snell, 1991), there has been little attempt to link specific service strategies with the HRM practices that would facilitate goal accomplishment. In fact, SHRM has developed with a focus on internal capabilities (the resource-based view of the firm; Wright et al., 2001) and not on the external demands on the firm (i.e., in the form of customers) nor on the kind of industry in which the firm operates. By this we mean that SHRM seems to focus more on attempting to identify and unleash the generic internal human capabilities of the firm than on identifying the specific strategic goals of the firm in its industry and the implications of those goals and the industry for the development and implementation of HRM tactics.

Our impression is that the key to understanding the strategic value of HRM for service business performance is to identify contingencies—boundary conditions—that specify the nature or form of the relationships between HRM practices and organizational outcomes like customer satisfaction. For example, following from operations management one might ask the question about the HRM implications of the firm being a high customer contact service business. Earlier we noted that Bowen and Ford (2002) have worked through some of these implications, but their work stands in relative isolation. Following Bowen and Ford's lead, one kind of thinking and research might concern the linkage of climate to customer satisfaction as a function of the degree of customer contact that characterizes firms. Dietz *et al.* (2003) conducted a study that is the closest we have found to this issue. They found, in a study of 160 bank branches, that frequency of customer contact moderates the relationship between climate and customer satisfaction. In their study they operationalized customer contact in terms of customer reports of the frequency with which they visited the branch, and found that the relationship between climate and customer satisfaction was significantly stronger in branches that were characterized as high contact branches. A similar logic to the Dietz *et al.* approach might be used to conceptualize the way intangibility might function as a moderator of this relationship; in other words, that service climate is more important for customer satisfaction under pure service (intangible) conditions. Of course, involving the customer in production has implications not only for HRM or employees but for the HRM of customers, too, especially with regard to training (Bowen *et al.*, 2000).

Following from the marketing logic, Schneider (1994) has conceptualized SHRM in service businesses to be a function of the market segmentation of the firm in terms of their strategic emphasis. In his view, service firms can segment their market in ways that define three major strategies: tender loving care (TLC), and/or speed, and/or customization. In the TLC environment a focus is on pleasing the customer through personal attention and relationship considerations; speed focuses on quickness and responsiveness; and, customization focuses on the quality of the service (both the core service and delivery) as tailored to individual customer needs and expectations. Schneider argues that the more the HRM tactics of a firm promote (through leadership, training, selection, reward systems, performance appraisal) accomplishment of the service strategy the more successful the firm will be in terms of customer satisfaction. Chung (1996) has found some support for this hypothesis, and Batt (2000) has also shown similar findings. Batt proposed that firms can segment their markets but that they must do that segmentation in ways that match the skills of employees and the HRM system that shapes the relationship between employees and customers. She studied 350 call centers and showed that as the relationship between callers and service representatives was strategically closer and more important, the more likely it was for the organizations to use high involvement work practices.

Lovelock (2000) has been a leading proponent of this kind of cross-discipline thinking to define strategy in service organizations. He has summarized his perspective by noting the cross-implications for each of marketing, OM, and HRM imperatives. For example, he notes that marketing sets the goal and the market, and then OM must design tactics to meet customer expectations for cost, schedule, and quality, and also continually reduce costs and improve productivity, while HRM must hire, train, and pay employees in ways that achieve both operational effectiveness and customer satisfaction. The implications for the one on the other are neither well understood nor well studied.

Summary

In a few pages we have tried to provide the reader with a "feel" for services management, especially the role of HRM in services management. But a unique feature of services management is the growing awareness of the dependencies across the various subdisciplines of services management. Of special interest to us was the role of OM and marketing to help begin to define some of the contingencies for HRM practice, i.e., to define the fact that HRM is not generically good or bad, but that it depends. It depends on a number of boundary conditions, particularly the level of intangibility of the service, customer partic- ipation in production, and simultaneity in production and consumption, as well as market segmentation and variability in customer demands.

This last boundary condition—variability in customer demands—is a boundary condi- tion that is posing a more significant challenge to service firms in this era of increased globalization and demographic diversity, and about which the editors have asked that we extend our discussion of the world of HRM in services. The reader will see that we can begin to conceptualize such implications by appeal to concepts not only from the imme- diate world of HRM practices but principles from other disciplines relevant to service as well. Our approach here will be to borrow concepts from cross-cultural psychology and from the organizational diversity literature to extend the range of ideas that begin to yield some potentially new and interesting insights into service issues in an international and diverse world.

REINVENTING HRM IN SERVICES: CONTINGENCIES POSED BY INTERNATIONALIZATION

Given the emphasis we have placed on boundary conditions in understanding HRM and service, it is important to recognize that not all services are the same and thus services are not similarly affected by cultural context. The extent to which globalization affects services depends on the processes involved in creating and delivering the service (Lovelock, 1999). There are a variety of types of international services, ranging from services that require contact between service providers and customers (theme parks, retail), to those that do not (e.g., communication services delivered via radio, television or satellite; Clark and Rajaratnam, 1999). Of particular interest in the current paper are high contact intangible services, as they are both produced for and delivered to customers face-to-face. The ques- tion we pose is whether a service firm operating in one country can manage its foreign subsidiaries in ways that mirror the parent country's management style, and still deliver quality service. As we will show, the answer is typically "no," although the extent to which a firm's HRM practices need to be adapted to foreign cultural contexts will depend on the degree of cultural distance between the parent and foreign countries.

The extent to which a firm's HRM practices are adapted to foreign cultural contexts will also depend on its stage of international growth (Dowling et al., 1999). In the early ethno- centric stage of development, companies offer their products/services only in the domestic market. As overseas demand for the products/services increases, firms tend to begin to export them without altering them for foreign consumption. However, as foreign markets become a more important or substantial contributor to business success and companies enter the multi-domestic phase of development, they establish foreign subsidiaries and start becom- ing more sensitive to cultural differences. In the beginning, companies may focus on trans- planting the ways of headquarters within their foreign locations and may wrongly assume the transferability of HRM practices without recognizing that their HRM practices reflect assumptions and values from the home culture. With time, companies recognize that there may be different, but equally or more effective, ways to manage the foreign subsidiaries and they no longer expect foreign subsidiaries to adopt the ways of headquarters. Thus, HRM activities become adapted to each country's cultural requirements. Ultimately, as companies establish worldwide businesses and become transnational, they begin striving for some consistency in their ways of managing employees worldwide in order to satisfy pressures for coordination, efficiency, and/or internal equity.

Indeed, there has been some discussion around the potential benefits of developing global HRM practices that are consistent around the world. However, much like our earlier claim that the market segment for which a firm's services are tailored influences the HRM practices that will be effective—and that therefore there is no one-size-fits-all solution to HRM in services—we contend that there is no such thing as a one-size-fits-all global solution to international HRM for service companies. At most it might be possible to establish worldwide goals for HRM, but the means through which those HRM objectives are achieved in practice will largely depend on the cultural context of each subsidiary—again always with the understanding that the closeness of the subsidiary to the parent culture is an important boundary condition.

In highlighting aspects of services management that are particularly Western-specific, we focus our discussion on the management and boundary tiers of service firms (Schneider and Bowen, 1995) as they represent the clearest implications for HRM. With regard to the management tier, we discuss previous research which suggests that the effectiveness of the HRM practices introduced by management can be culturally contingent. As for the boundary tier, where employees meet customers, we focus our discussion on the nature of job design, particularly with regard to issues involving employee empowerment and autonomy as a means of delivering quality service (Bowen and Lawler, 1992), as well as the potential negative influence of role conflict and ambiguity (Bowen and Ford, 2002; Hartline and Ferrell, 1996; Weatherly and Tansik, 1993). The third tier of service organizations according to Schneider and Bowen (1995) is the customer tier. It is relevant to our discussion in so far as differential customer demands for services across cultures necessitate concomitant differences in the HRM strategies required to satisfy them. Our primary goal is to illustrate the ways in which the science of services management may be laden with Western assumptions that may not be appropriate in other cultural contexts and, in doing so, highlight potential areas for future research.

Management tier

Although little attention has been paid to the influence of globalization on HRM in the services area, research on international HRM, more generally, has expanded within the last decade (e.g. Erez and Earley, 1993; Earley and Erez, 1997; Hofstede, 2001; House et al., 2004). This research has illustrated that the content and effectiveness of HRM practices tend to vary across cultures. This implies that the HRM practices which have been identified as best practices for services management within the Western literature may not necessarily be as effective in other cultural contexts, although the extent to which this is true will depend on both the foreign cultural context and the specific HR practices of interest.

Most likely, the overarching notion that service firms will be most effective in motivating their employees to serve customers well by serving the employees themselves well, is a universally sound guiding principle. However, the HR practices that are associated with high employee capability and commitment will likely vary. As noted earlier, within the US, research has identified HRM (Wright et al., 2003) and management (Schneider et al., 1998) practices focused on service quality that appear to be robustly related to customer satisfaction. The question naturally is whether and to what extent these management and HRM practices would be consistent with local norms in other cultural contexts, and/or be similarly associated with enhanced employee commitment and performance in other cultural contexts. Before reviewing some research which suggests that the answer to both of these questions may often be "no," it is important to briefly describe the major dimensions of cultural variation.

Based on the pioneering work of Hofstede (1991), there are five dimensions of cultural variation that have received the most research attention. They include: (1) *individualism-collectivism*, which differentiates between cultures in which an individual's personal attributes and uniqueness are central to identity, and those in which an individual's relationships with and obligations to others are the focus of identity, respectively (Gelfand et al., 2004a); (2) *power distance*, which describes the extent to which ascribed hierarchy and social status are accepted and expected in society (Carl et al., 2004); (3) *uncertainty avoidance*, which refers to the degree to which individuals in a culture experience stress and anxiety in the face of uncertainty and therefore engage in efforts to enhance predictability within their environments (De Luque et al., 2004); (4) *masculinity/femininity*, which refers to the extent to which the dominant values in society are masculine (e.g., assertiveness, acquisition of money and things) versus feminine (e.g., nurturing, caring for others), and there is inequality between the sexes (Emrich et al., 2004); and (5) *future or long-term orientation*, which describes the extent to which people in a culture live and plan for the future as opposed to the present (Ashkanasy et al., 2004).

Returning now to the question of whether HRM "best practices" might be culture-specific or universal, we maintain that service-related HRM practices are often not generalizable across cultures because: (1) the bases for human cognition, emotion, and motivation are culturally dependent and thus the HRM practices required to effectively guide and motivate employee behavior will necessarily also be culturally dependent (Aycan et al., 1999); and (2) customer expectations and perceptions of service quality can differ across cultures and, therefore, the HRM practices required to elicit the differential boundary employee behaviors required for delivering quality service will also differ. With regard to customer expectations, ample research within the marketing literature has established that there is no such thing as a culture-general service for contact-based services that require a high degree of contact between boundary employees and customers (e.g., Kim and Jin, 2002; Lee and Ulgado, 1997; Mattila, 1999). The degree of cultural customization that is necessary will increase as a function of the cultural distance between the home and local cultures, the amount of contact required, the complexity of the service involved, and the degree of certainty regarding the service outcome (Riddle, 1992).

The degree of cultural distance between the home and local cultures is important because the relative importance of service quality dimensions is dependent on customers' values and beliefs—which are intricately related to customers' cultural backgrounds. Thus, customers from different cultures can be expected to hold different expectations for the same service (e.g., Donthu and Yoo, 1998) and/or attach different weights to different service quality criteria (Furrer et al., 2000; Mattila, 1999). As a result, they form different perceptions of service quality in the face of the same service stimuli. Recognizing these cultural differences is the first step in defining, and being able to provide, service quality (Akan, 1995); it provides useful information to service companies in terms of how they should design their HRM practices and direct their employees in different cultural settings (Furrer et al., 2000; Riddle, 1992). As they stand, US-based service management philosophies may only be effective in cultures that share similar cultural characteristics (i.e., are individualistic, low in power distance and uncertainty avoidance, and moderate in masculinity and future orientation). Otherwise, the types of employee behaviors that US-based management practices elicit, such as employee discretion and friendliness, may be a reason for failure in cultural contexts that value, instead, standardized and formal employee behavior.

However, even if the service expectations of customers were the same across cultures—and research suggests that they often are not—differential HRM practices would often be necessary to satisfy those customer expectations because of cultural differences in human cognition, emotion, motivation, and behavior (Erez and Earley, 1993). To be more specific, in what follows, we take several HRM management practices and discuss research that attests to their culture-bound nature in an effort to show that national culture is an important boundary condition for HRM in service.

Selection

Recent research involving firms from 20 countries showed that the cultural dimension of uncertainty avoidance accounts for considerable variance in selection practices (Ryan et al., 1999). Ryan and her colleagues (1999) found that firms in countries that are high in uncertainty avoidance tend to use more selection tests (number and frequency), conduct structured interviews, and audit selection processes to ensure that they are working as planned.

Although recent research suggests that the US is only moderately high on uncertainty avoidance (House et al., 2004), the selection practices that Ryan and her colleagues found (1999) to be associated with higher uncertainty avoidance are consistent with the selection "best practices" that tend to be adopted in the US (e.g., Wright et al., 2003). These selection practices reflect the American belief that selection tests are critical for predicting future performance and making fair employment decisions, and that hiring decisions should be based on rational calculations of compatibility between an applicant and a specific job (Ramamoorthy and Carroll, 1998). However, in some cultural contexts such as Italy, France, Sweden, and Portugal, selection tests are avoided because their use in selection is perceived as an invasion of privacy and/or as a barrier to the holistic representation of oneself (Gelfand et al., in press; Shackleton and Newell, 1991; Sparrow and Hiltrop, 1994). Some tests, such as personality tests, may need to be adapted before use in other cultural contexts. For example, personality tests may need to be contextualized before use in collectivistic cultures since people's personality traits are context-dependent, rather than context-independent and generalizable across situations as they are, perhaps, more likely to be in individualistic cultures (Markus and Kitayama, 1991).

Indeed, the very idea that one's job-related KSAs (knowledge, skills, and abilities) should form the basis of employment decisions is more consistent with individualistic ideals than it is of collectivistic ideals. In individualistic cultures, where people are independent of others and behavior is based on one's internal traits, a measure of people's internal KSAs may be an appropriate and valid predictor of future job performance (Gelfand et al., 2004a). However, in collectivistic cultures where group membership is the central aspect of one's identity and behavior is based on one's social obligations to and relationships with others, one's social background, duties, and obligations are central in employment decisions (Ramamoorthy and Carroll, 1998). In Japan, selection decisions are based on shared university affiliation, as the belief is that people who are part of a shared social network are more likely to "fit in" and be loyal to the organization (Wasti, 2003a, 2003b; Yoshimura and Anderson, 1997). Similarly, staffing decisions in other Confucian countries, which are high in collectivism and power distance, tend to be based more on one's ascribed status and socio-political connections than individual merit and credentials (Wong and Slater, 2002; Gelfand et al., in press). Firms also tend to prefer internal recruitment and promotions to external recruitment in order to reward employees for their loyalty to the firm. In addition, they also prefer to hire generalists rather than specialists; thus, specific job descriptions do not play a part in the selection process (Begin, 1997). The preference for hiring generalists may also account for the use of interpersonal selection criteria rather than individual, KSA-related criteria. In sum, in some cultural contexts, US service firms may face local pressures to adapt their selection practices to fit local cultural beliefs.

Training

When it comes to training, it is hard to deny that investments in employee training are likely to be perceived as "high performance" practices across cultural contexts, although compared to many other countries such as Japan and Germany, American companies offer considerably less formal training to their employees (Begin, 1997). A relative lack of investment in employee training may be related to the US emphasis on external numerical flexibility, or the ability to hire and fire employees at will in order to respond to fluctuations in the marketplace, for if companies do not offer employment security there is little in the way of ensuring that their investments in employee development won't be lost when employees leave the company (Begin, 1997). It may also be true that US companies, operating in an individualistic culture, place more emphasis on individual striving and individual initiative to discover the knowledge and develop the skills required for job performance. Yet, to be competitive in other contexts, US firms may need to offer more training and in different formats such as group-based training or apprenticeship programs.

More notable cultural differences may have to do with the content and delivery of training rather than its duration. As for content, there is some research to suggest that self-focused training has a larger impact on trainee self-efficacy and performance than group-focused training in individualistic cultures, but that the opposite is true for individuals in collectivistic cultures (Earley, 1994). While the focus of training is likely to be job-specific and skills-based in individualistic and low uncertainty avoidance contexts, training will likely focus more heavily on organizational rules and policies in high uncertainty avoidance contexts in order to enhance predictability, and on building collective organizational identity in collectivistic cultures (De Luque et al., 2004; Gelfand et al., 2004a; Gelfand et al., under review).

In terms of delivery, there are some differences between high and low power distance cultures. In high power distance cultures, it is important for the instructor to be a rather imposing person with an impressive list of credentials in order to be perceived as credible (Filipczak, 1997). In addition, high-level managers are preferred over external consultants as trainers, and participative and casual training formats tend to be less effective than highly formal and structured ones (Filipczak, 1997). Finally, in highly masculine cultures, trainees may respond more positively to a male instructor than to a female instructor (Filipczak, 1997).

Performance management

With regard to performance management, the largest cultural differences may arise as a function of individualism-collectivism. Within Western contexts, performance management practices tend to focus on the individual employee, with pay and incentive systems being tied to individual performance (e.g., Wright et al., 2003). However, in collectivistic cultures, it is much more common for performance management to be focused on the group rather than the individual. For example, Earley (1993) found that while the performance of individuals in individualistic cultures is higher when they work alone rather than when they work in a group, the opposite was true for individuals in collectivistic cultures. Thus, formal appraisal systems that are focused on individual performance, coupled with individual-focused reward systems, tend not to be used as much in collectivistic contexts (Ramamoorthy and Carroll, 1998; Triandis and Bhawuk, 1997). Furthermore, promotions decisions in collectivistic, high power distance contexts tend to be based more on seniority than on merit (Ramamoorthy and Carroll, 1998). Imported HR practices that strive to promote employees based on merit regardless of seniority can be met with great opposition in Confucian cultures in which elders would lose face when placed under the supervision of more junior individuals; similarly, those in junior positions might feel that they lack credibility to be in the more senior position (Harrison et al., 2000).

More fundamentally, the very notion of "effective" performance is culture-bound. In individualistic cultures such as the US, evaluation criteria are objective, quantifiable, and observable, and they focus primarily on employee productivity (Jackson and Schuler, 2003). In contrast, performance evaluation in collectivistic cultures focuses more on social and relational criteria such as awareness of duties and obligations, willingness to work hard for the group, ability to maintain harmonious relationships, and conformity (Gelfand et al., in press; Gelfand et al., 2004a). While US laws protect employees from being evaluated on their character traits rather than what they do, in many Asian firms employees are judged on their integrity, loyalty, and morality. In other words, performance appraisal can, at times, be at odds with the cultural emphasis that is placed on character appraisal (Gelfand et al., 2004a).

221

Individualism-collectivism is not the only cultural dimension with implications for the way that "effective" performance is defined. The masculine emphasis on being assertive, achievement-oriented, and proactive that is common in the US, for example, may be less appropriate in feminine cultures.

As for methods of evaluation, 360-degree evaluation methods, which are popular in low power distance and individualistic cultures such as the US, tend not to be as effective in high power distance or collectivistic cultures. To begin with, it is inappropriate for subordinates to evaluate their superiors in high power distance cultures, as it undermines the supervisors' authority (Gregersen *et al.*, 1996). In collectivistic cultures, 360-degree evaluation is ineffective because individuals are likely to provide team members with consistently high evaluations as a result of both in-group bias and a desire to maintain group harmony (Bjorkman and Lu, 1999). Individuals tend to also be inaccurate (and reluctant) judges of their own behavior because of tendencies toward self-effacement biases (Markus and Kitayama, 1991). Finally, there is also a tendency to avoid performance appraisals so as not to damage social face and harmony. Rather, there is a tendency in collectivistic cultures to be indirect in nature, as individuals strive to maintain harmony and social face; thus, feedback is usually delivered in indirect, subtle, and non-confrontational ways, thereby making formalized face-to-face feedback sessions unlikely and ineffective (Fletcher and Perry, 2001).

Other methods of performance appraisal, such as management by objectives (MBO) may be similarly less appropriate in other contexts. MBO practices assume that employees have control over their environment and can achieve goals, performance can be objectively measured, and that managers and their subordinates can engage in open dialogue about objectives. Yet, the idea of mutually established objectives can be ineffective in high power distance contexts such as France in which managers feel they have little control over the goals they are asked to achieve, and two-way dialogues with the boss seem untenable (Schneider and Barsoux, 2003). In sum, multinational service companies have to caution against relying on the same performance criteria and methods for performance appraisals that are used in the parent country.

Empowerment/participation

Worker participation practices may also need to be adapted in order to be culturally appropriate in other contexts. In high power distance cultures, for example, managers adopt a more authoritative role with their subordinates than is true in low power distance cultures such as the US. As a result, empowerment practices aimed at shifting responsibility from the manager to the subordinate can undermine the credibility of managers in high PD cultures, who are expected to have all the answers and make decisions on behalf of their subordinates (Mendonca and Kanungo, 1996). In order to be effective, empowerment efforts likely have to be combined with increased feedback from supervisors in order to be effective, as supervisory feedback is a more critical ingredient for effective performance in high, as compared to low, power distance cultures (Earley and Stubblebine, 1989). More extensive supervisory feedback is also important for the performance of individuals in high uncertainty avoidance cultures, who rely on such feedback to reduce risk and uncertainty

(Earley and Stubblebine, 1989). In fact, the constant need for enhancing predictability in high uncertainty avoidance cultures suggests that efforts to increase employee autonomy and formalized annual performance reviews (as compared to constant informal feedback) may both be unrealistic and ineffective methods of managing performance in such cultures.

Leadership

In addition to the challenges associated with these traditional HRM practices, there are also important HRM implications with regard to the role of leadership and rewards (for service excellence) in the creation of a service climate that promotes the delivery of service quality (Schneider and Bowen, 1995). First, with regard to leadership, substantial research has documented the culturally contingent nature of leadership. In the most comprehensive study on the topic, project GLOBE researchers across 62 countries found that while there are some leadership behaviors and traits that are universally associated with in-/effective leadership, there are also numerous leadership characteristics that are considered effective in some cultures but ineffective in others (House et al., 2004). For example, participative leadership behaviors are associated with effective leadership in cultures such as the US which are low in uncertainty avoidance and power distance, but not in cultures such as Japan that are high in uncertainty avoidance and power distance. In addition, risk-taking behaviors and concern for, and involvement in, the private lives of subordinates are not universally valued as contributing to outstanding leadership (Den Hartog et al., 1999). A review of many other such examples is beyond the scope of this chapter; it suffices to say that the types of leadership behaviors that are necessary to create and sustain a positive climate for service and motivate employees toward delivering quality service may also be culturally contingent and therefore worthy of future research.

Rewards

As for rewards, Schneider and his colleagues (Schneider and Bowen, 1995; Schneider et al., 1998) have recognized the important role that rewards and recognition for service excellence play in building a climate for service and ensuring the delivery of service quality. Because rewards and recognition for superior performance can come in many forms, and cultural values are associated with the motivating effects that particular rewards have on individuals (Gomez-Mejia and Welbourne, 1991), service firms should be attentive to the HRM implications of such differences. For example, in individualistic cultures such as the US, rewards that recognize individual accomplishment are highly motivating, whether they are monetary or non-monetary. In contrast, in collectivistic cultures like Japan, individual awards can cause disharmony among group members, and thus rewards that satisfy needs for affiliation are more motivating (Erez, 1994). In support of this idea, Money and Graham (1999) found that many of the rewards that are used to recognize star performers in the US (e.g., money, fancy vacations, expensive material objects) are not equally effective in Japan, where group-focused rewards such as offers to take an entire sales team bowling or out to dinner are more motivating. For Japanese salespeople, reinforcements to their sense of shared goals and values with their group members can be more valuable than monetary rewards, the reverse of which was found for American salespeople.

Summary

In sum, the research reviewed above suggests that in order to be maximally effective abroad, service firms would benefit from adapting the content of their "high performance" work practices to the local culture in which they wish to operate. In reality, some HRM practices may be more likely to be adapted to fit local norms than others. Research by Rosenzweig and Nohria (1994) suggests that the degree to which a subsidiary is dependent on local inputs is associated with union representation, is culturally distant from the parent country of the firm, and is positively associated with the extent to which a subsidiary's HRM practices are adapted to resemble local HRM practices. In addition, they found that practices that are mandated by local laws, are highly visible, affect a large number of locals, or entail a high degree of interaction with locals, face stronger pressures to conform to local HRM practices, while practices that are most likely to raise concerns of internal equity within the company at large (e.g., executive compensation) tend to resemble parent practices (Rosenzweig and Nohria, 1994). Thus, the HR practices that affect boundary workers, particularly the more salient practices that govern the structure of boundary workers' jobs, are especially susceptible to pressures to conform to local norms, particularly in countries typified by strong cultural distance from the parent country. We turn next to a discussion of how cultural context may be related to the structure of boundary workers' jobs.

It is clear from what we have presented that the HRM practices of firms operating in different cultures will require at least adaptation to the culture if they are to be effective. Here, the concept of segmentation may again be useful. That is, Chung (1996) showed that HRM practices adapted to the service segment yielded higher levels of customer satisfaction within the segment; it follows that HRM practices adapted to national cultural norms and values will also likely be more effective. Thus, culture may usefully be thought of as a macro-level boundary condition for HRM in service firms.

The boundary tier

As discussed above, one of the main means through which organizations deliver quality service is by creating a climate in which employees are encouraged to work towards satisfying customers. The idea here is that by providing employees with adequate direction through management practices that emphasize service quality, employee discretion to respond to customers in positive ways can be optimized. So, when managers focus their efforts on service quality, and employees are rewarded for delivering quality to customers and are served well internally by others and company resources, then a focus on satisfying customers is legitimated. Under such conditions, service quality can further be enhanced when employees are given the power to make decisions in favor of meeting customer needs and expectations (Bowen and Ford, 2002; Bowen and Lawler, 1992; Schneider and Bowen, 1995).

The potential usefulness of this kind of service climate that empowers boundary workers to try to satisfy customers is predicated on the assumption that such psychological conditions enhance employee capability—that is, that employees feel better about themselves and their jobs, and feel that management is simultaneously looking after their needs when they are empowered (Heskett *et al.*, 1997). The idea that employee empowerment can lead to positive outcomes is not unique to the service context, as evidenced by the widespread acceptance of the job characteristics model (cf., Griffin and McMahan, 1994) according to which "enriched jobs" (characterized by greater autonomy, variety, task identity and significance, and performance feedback) are associated with positive work outcomes and employee satisfaction. However, employee empowerment and autonomy may be particularly important in the world of intangibles and high customer contact, where the split-second decisions and behaviors of boundary employees directly influence the quality of the service that is delivered. This is not to say that employee empowerment is *the* key to customer satisfaction; it is *a* key that works well within the Western context when it is combined with a management focus on service, appropriate tools and equipment, quality internal service, and a positive overall climate for service.

We focus on the empowerment of boundary employees in this section for the aforementioned reasons and also because this aspect of the boundary tier may have some of the largest cross-cultural implications because it is predicated on the Western assumption that the psychological conditions that are created by employee empowerment are intrinsically motivating for boundary employees. However, in non-Anglo samples, job enrichment is not always associated with increased motivation (Adigun and Stephenson, 1992; Huang and Van de Vliert, 2003) and therefore is not a central HRM practice (Aycan *et al.*, 2000). Instead, extrinsic job factors (Huang and Van de Vliert, 2003) and group-focused job enrichment (Erez, 1994) are more motivating. In collectivistic cultures, increased choice and autonomy are not associated with higher intrinsic motivation; instead, individuals tend to be more intrinsically motivated when choices are made for them by trusted authority figures and in-group members (Iyengar and Lepper, 1999).

Further, because empowerment practices involve the sharing of authority, they are also less acceptable in high power distance cultures in which inequalities in authority and power are not only common but expected. Thus, when leaders relinquish authority to their subordinates, their employees report having less favorable perceptions of their leaders and being less satisfied (Robert *et al.*, 2000). In the eyes of the subordinates, leaders are expected to take charge and be in total control, to give orders, and to know what is best. When leaders take actions that contradict these assumptions, they can be discredited in the eyes of their subordinates, leading to dissatisfaction on the part of those subordinates. Moreover, in order for empowerment to be effective, leaders must believe that their employees can act independently of their leadership—something that, again, runs counter to the values and assumptions that are held in high power distance cultures. Thus, US service firms aiming to implement their empowerment practices in high power distance cultures should proceed with caution. They might be more successful if they slowly increase the empowerment of their employees and have leaders actively engage in mentoring/coaching roles to their employees (Mendonca and Kanungo, 1996).

In addition, the level of employee discretion that is associated with employee empowerment may be a source of anxiety rather than satisfaction or fulfillment in cultures that are high in uncertainty avoidance, in comparison to the beneficial effects of employee discretion in low uncertainty avoidance cultures such as the US. In the US, increased autonomy, along with increased socio-emotional consideration from supervisors and feedback, but particularly autonomy, has been found to help reduce role ambiguity. Finding ways to reduce this role ambiguity—which is always implicit for workers in boundary roles due to the attempt to meet both organizational and customer needs—is of natural interest because the more ambiguity employees experience, the less satisfied their customers are likely to be (Weatherly and Tansik, 1993). However, increased autonomy may not always help employees to cope with ambiguity. In particular, increased autonomy will likely exacerbate the role ambiguity that is experienced by service employees in high uncertainty avoidance cultures, who are likely to prefer their jobs to be highly structured and governed by explicit rules instead. Thus, in high uncertainty avoidance cultures, service organizations may best rely on well-defined organizational policies and extensive employee training directed at learning those policies, in order to guide the behavior of employees rather than rely on increased autonomy (Kelley, 1993).

Indirect support of this notion is provided in the work of Smith and his colleagues (Smith et al., 1996), who found that managers in the UK and the US tend to rely most heavily on their own experience and skills to make decisions and respond to ambiguous situations, while their more uncertainty avoidant counterparts in China are more likely to turn to rules and procedures. Indeed, scholars have suggested that organizations in high uncertainty avoidance cultures tend to be more formalized in general, with a greater number of written policies and rules, decision-making procedures, and employee manuals (Rodrigues and Kaplan, 1998). Thus, increasing the autonomy of service workers' jobs as a means of reducing role ambiguity may be more effective in cultures such as the UK and US than in high uncertainty avoidance cultures such as those found in East Asia.

Customer perceptions regarding the appropriateness of boundary workers' discretion may also vary across cultures. Hsieh and Hsieh (2001), for example, found that job standardization, or the extent to which service employees follow standard operating procedures to perform their jobs, is positively associated with customer perceptions of service quality in Taiwan, which is high on uncertainty avoidance. These customer preferences are likely to extend to the arena of service recovery, in which customers in high uncertainty avoidance cultures are likely to prefer service recovery efforts that are driven by clearly defined procedures rather than by the discretion of the particular service provider who delivers the service.

Summary

The main point of this section is that the basic assumption that autonomy/empowerment is desirable must be reconsidered in some cultural contexts, and that empowerment practices should be adopted under a contingency approach—not only according to the type of service that is being delivered but also according to the cultural background of the service providers. Next we turn our attention to the HRM implications of increased demographic diversity within the US service market.

REINVENTING HRM IN SERVICES: CONTINGENCIES POSED BY INCREASED DIVERSITY

In some ways, service firms in diverse domestic markets face similar challenges to firms serving international markets, with regard to the need to serve multiple market segments each with its own set of expectations and values. The more diverse a population, the more diverse are the values on which individuals evaluate service experiences. Since customers are more satisfied when they experience services that are congruent with their values (Dominguez and Gelfand, 2001), this means that service firms have to be prepared to either tailor their services to specific customer segments or implement HRM practices that enable them to serve diverse customer markets simultaneously. Because the latter represents more of a departure from traditional modes of managing service firms—and probably also an increasing reality for US service firms—we focus on it here.

There are a number of HRM responses that can help service firms to serve diverse customers more effectively. To begin with, there is research that points to the benefits of building a workforce that is demographically similar to a firm's customer base, thereby suggesting the importance of staffing policies. Smith (1998), for example, found that employee–customer similarity in work attitudes, gender, and life stage is positively associated with the quality of employee–customer relationships. In addition, there is some support for the notion that when employees match their customers in terms of gender and ethnicity, service firms are able to empathize with customer needs more quickly and tailor their services more appropriately than service firms without comparable representations of women and ethnic minorities (Weidenfeller, 1992). In other words, firms with workforces that mirror their customer base appear to be better able to anticipate the needs and expectations of their customers and therefore provide superior service.

Kale and Barnes (1992) draw from social psychological theory to suggest that the reason why employee–customer similarity is beneficial is because it enhances the effectiveness and outcomes of dyadic communication. When the characteristics of the customer match those of the service provider, both parties to the interaction are more likely to agree on the preferred content and style of the interaction. In addition, in cases involving customers of diverse ethnic backgrounds, shared language can obviously play a large role in facilitating communication and effective interaction between the service employee and customer (Cooper and Niles-Jolly, 1994).

For these reasons, a beneficial practice for enhancing customer satisfaction among diverse customers is to institute practices that ensure that women, older workers, and people of color (among other underrepresented groups) are represented in the employee sales force. Service firms might even structure their service delivery systems in ways that allow customers to select a service provider who is similar to them in terms of cultural values or with whom they otherwise feel most comfortable (Riddle, 1992). In addition, organizations will likely benefit from hiring employees with flexible or highly adaptable personalities who possess cultural sensitivity and awareness—characteristics that may overlap with the "perceiving" dimension of the Myers-Briggs Type Indicator (Kale and Barnes, 1992). A "perceiver" may be better able to serve diverse customers because he or she will try hard to observe and understand the perspective of the customer and adapt his/her behavior

227 ■

accordingly. There is good evidence that personality measures that focus on "service orientation" have considerable predictive validity (Frei and McDaniel, 1998). What is not known is the degree to which they may have differential validity as a function of: (a) the ethnicity of the boundary worker; (b) the ethnicity of the customers; and/or (c) the fit or match of worker and customer.

In addition to selecting people who are most appropriate for the job, service firms will benefit from investing time and money to first understand the expectations and attitudes of their diverse customers (Smith, 1998), and second, to translate that knowledge to service delivery tactics through employee training. For example, as described by Cooper and Niles-Jolly (1994), a Midwestern bank found success when they used a three-step approach to improving the quality of services that they delivered to elderly customers: (1) educate employees about elderly populations (e.g., about lifestyle factors and subgroups of the elderly, how to effectively communicate with the elderly, how to change the servicescape to serve elderly customers better); (2) test employees on their learning; and (3) reward employees for applying their learning. Similar approaches can be taken to train employees about how to interact effectively with other population groups as well, such as training employees on how to overcome barriers to effective cross-sex relationships (Smith, 1998), or training them on how to greet, solicit, assist, and show appreciation to customers from various cultural backgrounds (Cooper and Niles-Jolly, 1994). Finally, firms will also benefit from implementing internal information sharing networks to help employees share the knowledge that they accumulate with regard to responding effectively to diverse markets.

The aforementioned HRM practices are all customer-oriented; they are designed explicitly with the external customer in mind. However, practices aimed at valuing diverse external customers will only be as effective as the value that is placed on treating diverse internal customers (i.e., employees) fairly. Many scholars have convincingly argued that merely increasing the representation of minority workers within a firm's workforce is not enough. In order to reap the potential benefits of a diverse workforce (i.e., enhanced ability to respond to diverse customers, increased innovation), the diverse employees must be included in the fabric of the organization. Put differently, firms must also have positive climates for diversity or inclusion in which all employees, regardless of background, are able and willing to reach their full potential and contribute to the organization's success (Cox, 1994).

Thus, a climate for diversity or inclusion may be best thought of as a foundational requirement for building a climate for service in firms that serve demographically diverse customers. A number of related conceptualizations of climate for diversity/inclusion have surfaced, all with a common focus on shared employee perceptions regarding the policies, practices, and procedures that implicitly and explicitly communicate the extent to which fostering and maintaining diversity and eliminating discrimination is a priority in the organization (Gelfand et al., 2004b). In practice, when an organization has a positive climate for diversity, all employees are integrated into the fabric of the organization and are motivated and supported to attain their full potential unhindered by their group identities. In the case of service firms, the assumption is that boundary employees in organizations with positive climates for diversity will feel more valued and motivated to serve their diverse customers well when compared to employees in organizations with negative climates for diversity.

228

In sum, for service firms that are serving diverse customers, there is a need not only to have a diverse workforce that mirrors the composition of the customer base, but also to develop a climate in which those diverse employees feel included and valued. Indeed, there is recent research that suggests that the "value in diversity hypothesis," according to which diversity can be beneficial for organizations when effectively managed (Cox et al., 1991), may only hold true in cases where the diverse employees feel included in and valued by the organization. More specifically, Nishii and her colleagues (Nishii et al., 2004) found that racial diversity is positively associated with profits in a service organization, but only in departments in which the racial minorities feel included in the department leader's "in-group" (as measured by their perceptions of the LMX, or leader-member exchange, relationships that they share with their department managers). The beneficial effects of employee tenure on departmental customer satisfaction and profits were similarly more pronounced for departments in which more employees felt that they were part of their leader's in-group.

A number of HRM practices have been identified by researchers as being important for building such inclusive climates. They include: (1) intervention by top management/pressure to direct reports to foster diversity; (2) targeted recruitment of employees at all levels; (3) diverse representation at all levels of the organization, including senior management levels; (4) EEO monitoring and the appointment of diversity specialist positions; (5) inclusion of diversity in performance evaluation goals and ratings, and the removal of bias in the evaluation process itself; (6) inclusion of diversity in promotion decisions and criteria as well as upward development programs for all employees; (7) inclusion of diversity in management succession planning; (8) diversity training programs; (9) networks and support groups; (10) work and family policies and flexible cafeteria style benefits programs; and (11) internal advocacy groups (Cox, 1994; Gelfand et al., 2004b; Morrison, 1992, 1993). However, there is no research to date that explicitly links the adoption of these diversity practices to enhanced organizational performance. We believe that the relationship between these diversity HRM practices and customer satisfaction will be particularly strong for high-contact services that involve diverse customers and, as such, this constitutes an important area for future research among service scholars.

CONCLUSION: TOWARD A CONTINGENT HRM

We have shown here that HRM is not HRM; HRM has boundary conditions. The editors asked us to suggest what HRM might look like with internationalization and domestic diversity as foci and we have presented the beginnings of a discussion on those topics. What is interesting is that, by asking us to focus on the world of *service*, the editors implicitly provided us with a macro level boundary condition, that being manufacturing versus service.

In the introduction to the chapter we identified three continua along which service production and manufacturing might differ: tangibility, customer participation in production, and simultaneous production and consumption (sometimes called inseparability; Zeithaml and Bitner, 2000). These then were shown to have potential influence on HRM practices in organizations (Bowen and Ford, 2002); a second level of contingencies. The third contingency we introduced concerned the degree of customer contact service deliverers have with customers (Chase, 1981) and the fourth concerned the specific market segment on which the service business was focused (Schneider, 1994).

Thus, even prior to exploring national cultural issues and domestic diversity issues as contingencies in understanding the HRM practices likely to be effective in a business, there was a host of other boundary conditions to which attention had to be paid. Indeed, the detailed discussion of national cultural facets and the implications of them for management, boundary workers, and customer service delivery revealed just how complex service delivery as a function of HRM practices can be.

Our academic message is a simple one: extensive theory and research are required for us to understand HRM effectiveness in business and we hope that identification of some of the boundary conditions requiring attention specifically for service businesses will facilitate such efforts. Our message for practitioners is equally simple: use our listing of boundary conditions as a check-list for maximizing the possibility that HRM practices will fit the situation (tangibility, customer contact, market segment, nature of the domestic customer, and national culture) and be effective in the real world of business.

REFERENCES

Adigun, I.O. and Stephenson, G.M. (1992) Sources of job motivation and satisfaction among British and Nigerian employees. *The Journal of Social Psychology*, 132(3), 369–376.

Akan, P. (1995) Dimensions of service quality: A study in Instanbul. *Managing Service Quality*, 5(6), 39–43.

Ashkanasy, N., Gupta, V., Mayfield, M., and Trevor-Roberts, E. (2004) Future Orientation. In R. J. House, P.J. Hanges, M. Javidan, P.W. Dorfman, and V. Gupta (eds) *Culture, Leadership, and Organizations: The GLOBE Study of 62 Cultures*. Thousand Oaks, CA: Sage Publications.

Athanassiou, N. and Nigh, D. (2000) Internationalization, tacit knowledge, and the top management teams of MNCs. *Journal of International Business Studies*, 31(3), 471–487.

Aycan, Z., Kanungo, R.N., and Sinha, J.B.P. (1999) Organizational culture and human resource management practices: The Model of Culture Fit. *Journal of Cross-Cultural Psychology*, 30(4), 501–526.

Aycan, Z., Kanungo, R.N., Mendonca, M., Yu, K., Deller, J., Stahl, G., and Kurshid, A. (2000) Impact of culture on human resource management practices: A 10-country comparison. *Applied Psychology: An International Review*, 49(1), 192–221.

Batt, R. (2000) Strategic segmentation in front-line services: Matching customers, employees and human resource systems. *International Journal of Human Resource Management*, 11, 540–561.

Begin, J.P. (1997) *Dynamic Human Resource Systems: Cross-National Comparisons*. New York: Walter de Gruyter & Co.

Berry, L.L. (1995) *On Great Service: A Framework for Action*. New York: Free Press.

Berry, L.L. (1997) *Discovering the Soul of Service: The Nine Drivers of Sustainable Business Success*. New York: Free Press.

Bitner, M.J. (1992) Servicescapes: The impact of physical surroundings on customers and employees. *Journal of Marketing*, 56, 57–71.

Bjorkman, I. and Lu, Y. (1999) A corporate perspective on the management of human resources in China. *Journal of World Business*, 34(1), 16–25.

Boudreau, J.W. (1991) Utility analysis for decisions in human resources management. In M.D. Dunnette and L.M. Hough (eds) *Handbook of Industrial and Organizational Psychology*, 2nd edn, vol. 2. Palo Alto, CA: Consulting Psychologists Press, pp. 621–745.

Bowen, D.E. and Lawler, E.E. III (1992) The empowerment of service workers: What, why, how, and when. *Sloan Management Review*, 33, 31–39.

Bowen, D.E. and Schneider, B. (1988) Services marketing and management: Implications for organizational behavior. In B.M. Staw and L.L. Cummings (eds) *Research in Organizational Behavior*, vol. 10. Greenwich, CT: JAI, pp. 43–80.

Bowen, D.E., Schneider, B., and Kim, S.S. (2000) Shaping service cultures through strategic human resources management. In T.A. Swartz and D. Iacobucci (eds) *Handbook of Services Marketing and Management*. Thousand Oaks, CA: Sage Publications, pp. 43–80.

Bowen, J. and Ford, R.C. (2002) Managing service organizations: Does having a "thing" make a difference? *Journal of Management*, 28, 447–469.

Brockner, J., Ackerman, G., Greenberg, J., Gelfand, M.J., Francesco, A.M., Chen, Z.X., Leung, K., Bierbrauer, G., Gomez, C., Kirkman, B.L., and Shapiro, D. (2001) Culture and procedural justice: The influence of power distance on reactions to voice. *Journal of Experimental Social Psychology*, 37, 300–315.

Carl, D., Gupta, V., and Javidan, M. (2004) Power distance. In R.J. House, P.J. Hanges, M. Javidan, P.W. Dorfman, and V. Gupta (eds) *Culture, Leadership, and Organizations: The GLOBE Study of 62 Cultures*. Thousand Oaks, CA: Sage Publications.

Chase, R.B. (1981) The customer contact approach to services: Theoretical bases and practical extensions. *Operations Research*, 4, 698–706.

Chase, R.B., Aquilano, N.J., and Jacobs, F.R. (1998) *Production and Operations Management: Manufacturing and Services*, 8th edn. San Francisco, CA: Irwin/McGraw-Hill.

Chung, B.G. (1996) Focusing HRM Strategies Towards Service Market Segments: A Three-Factor Model. Unpublished doctoral dissertation, University of Maryland.

Clark, T. and Rajaratnam, D. (1999) International services: Perspectives at century's end. *Journal of Services Marketing*, 13(4/5), 298–310.

Cooper, C. and Niles-Jolly, K. (1994) Diversity, customer service, and organizational effectiveness. Paper presented at the 9th annual conference for the Society for Industrial and Organizational Psychology, Nashville, TN.

Cox, T. (1994) Cultural diversity in organizations: Theory, research and practice. San Francisco, CA, CA: Berrett-Koehler Publishers, Inc.

Cox, T.H., Lobel, S.A., and McLeod, P.L. (1991) Effects of ethnic group cultural differences on cooperative and competitive behavior in a group task. *Academy of Management Journal*, 34, 827–847.

Day, S. (2003) Restaurant hiring may lead the way to wider job gains. *The New York Times*, December 10, 2003, p. 1.

De Luque, M.S., Javidan, M., and Aditya, R.N. (2004) Uncertainty Avoidance. In R.J. House, P.J. Hanges, M. Javidan, P.W. Dorfman, and V. Gupta (eds) *Culture, Leadership, and Organizations: The GLOBE Study of 62 Cultures*. Thousand Oaks, CA: Sage Publications.

Den Hartog, D.N., House, R.J., Hangs, P.J., Ruiz-Quintanilla, S.A., and Dorfman, P.W. (1999) Culture specific and cross-culturally generalizable implicit leadership theories: Are attributes of charismatic/transformational leadership universally endorsed? *Leadership Quarterly*, 10(2), 219–256.

Dicken, P. (1998) *Global Shift: Transforming the World Economy*. New York: Guildford Press.

Dietz, J., Pugh, S.D., and Wiley, J.W. (2003) When climate matters: Customer segments and the importance/unimportance of service climates. Unpublished manuscript, Ivey School of Business, University of Western Ontario.

Dominguez, A.L. and Gelfand, M.J. (2001) The importance of values and context in understanding customer reactions to service encounters. In B. Chung (Chair), *Understanding the Sources of Heterogeneity in Service Encounters*, Symposium presented at the 16th annual conference of the Society for Industrial and Organizational Psychology, Chicago.

Donthu, N. and Yoo, B. (1998) Cultural influences on service quality expectations. *Journal of Service Research*, 1(2), 178–186.

Dowling, P.J., Welch, D.E., and Schuler, R.S. (1999) *International Human Resource Management: Managing People in a Multinational Context*, 3rd edn. Mason, OH: South-Western College Publishing.

Earley, P.C. (1993) East meets west meets mideast: Further explorations of collectivistic and individualistic work groups. *Academy of Management Journal*, 36(2), 319–348.

Earley, P.C. (1994) Self or group? Cultural effects of training on self-efficacy and performance. *Administrative Science Quarterly*, 39, 89–117.

Earley, P.C. and Erez, M. (1997) *New Perspectives on International/Organizational Psychology*. San Francisco, CA, CA: The New Lexington Press.

Earley, P.C. and Stubblebine, P. (1989) Intercultural assessment of performance feedback. *Group & Organization Management*, 14(2), 161–181.

Emrich, C.G., Denmark, F.L., and Den Hartog (2004) Cross-cultural differences in gender egalitarianism: Implications for societies, organizations, and leaders. In R. J. House, P.J. Hanges, M. Javidan, P.W. Dorfman, and V. Gupta (eds) *Culture, Leadership, and Organizations: The GLOBE Study of 62 Cultures*. Thousand Oaks, CA: Sage Publications.

Erez, M. (1994) Toward a model of cross-cultural industrial and organizational psychology. In H.C. Triandis, M.D. Dunnette, and L.M. Hough (eds) *Handbook of Industrial-Organizational Psychology*, 2nd edn, vol. 4. Palo Alto, CA: Consulting Psychologists Press, Inc, pp. 559–607.

Erez, M. and Earley, P.C. (1993) *Culture, Self-Identity, and Work*. London: Oxford.

Filipczak, B. (1997) Distance learning across cultures. *Training*, 34(1), 40–48.

Fitzimmons, J.A. and Fitzimmons, M.J. (1994) *Service Management for Competitive Advantage*. New York: McGraw-Hill.

Fletcher, C. and Perry, E. (2001) Performance appraisal and feedback: A consideration of national culture and a review of contemporary and future trends. In N. Anderson, D. Ones, H. Sinangil, and C. Viswesvaran (eds), *International Handbook of Industrial, Work and Organizational Psychology*. Beverly Hills, CA: Sage Publications.

Frei, R.L. and McDaniel, M.A. (1998) Validity of customer service measures of personnel selection: A review of criterion and construct evidence. *Human Performance*, 11, 1–27.

Furrer, O., Shaw-Ching Liu, B., and Sudharshan, D. (2000) The relationships between culture and service quality perceptions: Basis for cross-cultural market segmentation and resource allocation. *Journal of Service Research*, 2(4), 355–371.

Gelfand, M.J., Bhawuk, D.P.S., Nishii, L.H., and Bechtold, D. (2004a) Individualism and collectivism. In R.J. House, P.J. Hanges, M. Javidan, P.W. Dorfman, and V. Gupta (eds) *Culture, Leadership, and Organizations: The GLOBE Study of 62 Cultures*. Thousand Oaks, CA: Sage Publications.

Gelfand, M.J., Erez, M., and Aycan, Z. (forthcoming) *Frontiers in Cross-Cultural Organizational Behavior*. Thousand Oaks, CA: Sage Publications.

Gelfand, M.J., Nishii, L.H., Raver, J.L., and Lim, B.C. (under review) Cultural tightness-looseness: Multilevel perspectives and implications for organizations. Manuscript under review.

Gelfand, M.J., Nishii, L.J., Raver, J.L., and Schneider, B. (2004b) Discrimination in organizations: An organizational-level systems perspective. In R.L. Dipboye and A. Colella (eds) *Discrimination at Work: Psychological and Organizational Bases* (A SIOP Frontiers series book). Mahwah, NJ: Lawrence Erlbaum Associates, Inc.

Gittell, J.H. (2002) Relationships between service providers and their impact on customers. *Journal of Service Research*, 4, 299–311.

Gomez-Mejia, L.R. and Welbourne, T. (1991) Compensation strategies in a global context. *Human Resource Planning*, 14(1), 29–41.

Gregersen, H.B., Hite, J.M., and Black, J.S. (1996) Expatriate performance appraisal in U.S. multinational firms. *Journal of International Business Studies*, 27(4), 711–738.

Griffin, R.W. and McMahan, G.C. (1994) Motivation through job design. In J. Greenberg (ed.) *Organizational Behavior: The State of the Science*. Hillsdale, NJ: Erlbaum, pp. 23–43).

Harrison, G.L., McKinnon, J.L., Wu, A., and Chow, C.W. (2000) Cultural influences on adaptation to fluid workgroups and teams. *Journal of International Business Studies*, 31(3), 489–505.

Hartline, M.D. and Ferrell, O.C. (1996) The management of customer contact service employees: An empirical investigation. *Journal of Marketing*, 60, 52–70.

Heskett, J.L., Sasser, W.E. Jr., and Schlesinger, L.A. (1997) *The Service-Profit Chain*. New York: Free Press.

Hochschild, A.R. (1983) *The Managed Heart: Commercialization of Human Feelings*. Berkeley: University of California Press.

Hofstede, G. (1991) *Cultures and Organizations: Software of the Mind*. Berkshire: McGraw-Hill.

Hofstede, G. (2001) *Culture's Consequences: Comparing Values, Behavior, Institutions, and Organizations Across Nations*. Thousand Oaks, CA: Sage Publications, pp. 209–278.

House, R.J., Hanges, P.J., Javidan, M., Dorfman, P.W., and Gupta, V. (eds) (2004) *Culture, Leadership, and Organizations: The GLOBE Study of 62 Cultures*. Thousand Oaks, CA: Sage Publications.

Hsieh, Y.M. and Hsieh, A.T. (2001) Enhancement of service quality with job standardization. *The Service Industries Journal*, 21(3), 147–166.

Huang, X. and Van de Vliert, E. (2003) Where intrinsic job satisfaction fails to work: National moderators of intrinsic motivation. *Journal of Organizational Behavior*, 24, 159–179.

Hui, C., Lam, S.S.K., and Schaubroeck, J. (2001) Can good citizens lead the way in providing quality service? A field quasi-experiment. *Academy of Management Journal*, 44, 988–995.

Iyengar, S.S. and Lepper, M.R. (1999) Rethinking the value of choice: A cultural perspective on intrinsic motivation. *Journal of Personality and Social Psychology*, 76(3), 349–366.

Jackson, S.E. and Schuler, R.S. (2003) *Managing Human Resources Through Strategic Partnerships, 8th edn.* Mason, OH: South-Western.

Kale, S.H. and Barnes, J.W. (1992) Understanding the domain of cross-national buyer-seller interactions. *Journal of International Business Studies,* 23(1), 101–132.

Kelley, S.W. (1993) Discretion and the service employee. *Journal of Retailing,* 69, 104–126.

Kellogg, D.L. and Chase, R.B. (1995) Constructing an empirically derived measure for customer contact. *Management Science,* 41, 1734–1749.

Kim, S. and Jin, B. (2002) Validating the retail service quality scale for US and Korean customers of discount stores: An exploratory study. *Journal of Services Marketing,* 16(3), 223–237.

Knight, G. (1999) International services marketing: review of research, 1980–1998. *Journal of Services Marketing,* 13, 347–360.

Lee, M. and Ulgado, F.M. (1997) Consumer evaluations of fast-food services: A cross-national comparison. *The Journal of Services Marketing,* 11(1), 39–52.

Lengnick-Hall, C.A. (1996) Customer contributions to quality: A different view of the customer-oriented firm. *Academy of Management Review,* 21, 791–824.

Liu, B.S., Furrer, O., and Sudharshan, D. (2001) The relationships between culture and behavioral intentions toward services. *Journal of Service Research,* 4(2), 118–129.

Lovelock, C.H. (1999) Developing marketing strategies for transnational service operations. *Journal of Services Marketing,* 13(4/5), 278–289.

Lovelock, C.H. (2000) Functional integration in services: Understanding the links between marketing, operations, and human resources. In T.A. Swartz and D. Iacobucci (eds) *Handbook of Services Marketing and Management.* Thousand Oaks, CA: Sage Publications, pp. 421–438.

Lovelock, C. and Wirtz, J. (2004) *Services Marketing: People, Technology, Strategy,* 5th edn. Upper Saddle River, NJ: Pearson/Prentice-Hall.

Lytle, R.S., Hom, P.W., and Mokwa, M.P. (1998) SERV*OR: A managerial measure of organizational service-orientation. *Journal of Retailing,* 74, 455–489.

McCahill, R.J. and Moyer, B.C. (2001) Gross domestic product by industry for 1999–2001. *Survey of Current Business,* 82 (November 2002), 23–41.

McLaughlin, C.P. (1996) Why variation reduction is not everything: A new paradigm for service operations. *International Journal of Service Industry Management,* 7, 17–30.

Maister, D.H. (1997) *True Professionalism.* New York: Free Press.

Malhotra, N.K., Ulgado, F.M., Agarwal, J., and Baalbaki, I.B. (1994) International services marketing: A comparative evaluation of the dimensions of service quality between developed and developing countries. *International Marketing Review,* 11(2), 5–15.

Marchese, M.C. (2001) Matching management practices to national culture in India, Mexico, Poland, and the US. *Academy of Management Executive,* 15(2), 130–132.

Markus, H.R. and Kitayama, S. (1991) Culture and the self: Implications for cognition, emotion, and motivation. *Psychological Review,* 98, 224–253.

Mattila, A.S. (1999) The role of culture in the service evaluation process. *Journal of Service Research,* 1(3), 250–261.

Mendonca, M. and Kanungo, R.N. (1996) Impact of culture on performance management in developing countries. *International Journal of Manpower,* 17(4/5), 65.

Mills, P.K., Chase, R.B., and Margulies, N. (1983) Motivating the client/employee system as a service production strategy. *Academy of Management Review*, 8, 301–310.

Money, R.B. and Graham, J.L. (1999) Salesperson performance, pay, and job satisfaction: Tests of a model using data collected from the United States and Japan. *Journal of International Business Studies*, 30(1), 149–172.

Moorman, R.H. and Blakely, G.L. (1995) Individualism-collectivism as an individual difference predictor of organizational citizenship behavior. *Journal of Organizational Behavior*, 16(2), 127–142.

Morrison, A.M. (1992) *New Leaders: Guidelines on Leadership Diversity in America*. San Francisco, CA: Jossey-Bass, Inc.

Morrison, A.M. (1993) Leading diversity. *Training and Development*, April, 39–43.

Moynihan, L.M., Gardner, T.M., and Wright, P.M. (2002) High performance HR practices and customer satisfaction: Employee process mechanisms. *Center for Advanced Human Resource Studies Working Paper Series*, Working paper #02–09.

Niles-Jolly, K. and Cooper, C. (1994) Diversity, customer service, and organizational effectiveness. Paper presented at the Society for Industrial and Organizational Psychology, Nashville, TN.

Nishii, L.H. (2003) The psychology of Strategic Human Resource Management: The effect of employee attributions for HR practices on unit commitment, satisfaction, organizational citizenship behaviors, and customer satisfaction. Unpublished dissertation, University of Maryland, College Park.

Nishii, L.J., Mayer, D.M., Goldstein, H.W., and Dotan, O. (2004) Diversity and bottom-line performance: The moderating role of leader-member exchanges. Paper presented at the 19th annual conference for the Society for Industrial and Organizational Psychology, Chicago, IL.

Palich, L.E. and Gomez-Mejia, L.R. (1999) A theory of global strategy and firm efficiencies: Considering the effects of cultural diversity. *Journal of Management*, 25(4), 587–606.

Parasuraman, A., Zeithaml, V.A., and Berry, L.L. (1994) Alternative scales for measuring service quality: A comparative assessment based on psychometric and diagnostic criteria. *Journal of Retailing*, 70, 201–230.

Patterson, P.G. and Ward, T. (2000) Relationship marketing and management. In T.A. Swartz and D. Iacobucci (eds) *Handbook of Services Marketing and Management*. Thousand Oaks, CA: Sage Publications, pp. 317–342.

Porter, M.E. (1980) *Competitive Strategy*. New York: Free Press.

Pugh, S.D. (2002) Service with a smile: Emotional contagion in the service encounter. *Academy of Management Journal*, 44, 1018–1027.

Pullman, M.E., Verma, R., and Goodale, J.C. (2001) Service design and operating strategy formulation in multicultural markets. *Journal of Operations Management*, 19, 239–254.

Rafaeli, A. (1989) When cashiers meet customers: An analysis of the role of supermarket cashiers. *Academy of Management Journal*, 32, 245–273.

Ramamoorthy, N. and Carroll, S.J. (1998) Individualism/collectivism orientations and reactions toward alternative human resource management practices. *Human Relations*, 51(5), 571–588.

Redman, T. and Mathews, B.P. (1998) Service quality and human resource management: A review and research agenda. *Personnel Review*, 27(1), 57–77.

Riddle, D.I. (1992) Leveraging cultural factors in international service delivery. *Advances in Services Marketing and Management*, vol. 1, 297–322.

235

Robert, C., Probst, T.M., Martocchio, J.J., Drasgow, F., and Lawler, J.J. (2000) Empowerment and continuous improvement in the United States, Mexico, Poland, and India: Predicting fit on the basis of the dimensions of power distance and individualism. *Journal of Applied Psychology*, 85(5), 643–658.

Rodrigues, C.A. and Kaplan, E. (1998) The country's uncertainty avoidance measure as a predictor of the degree of formalization applied by organization in it: Propositions for the European Union Countries. *Management Research News*, 21(10), 34–45.

Rogg, K.L., Schmidt, D.B., Shull, C., and Schmitt, N. (2001) Human resources practices, organizational climate, and customer satisfaction. *Journal of Management*, 27, 431–449.

Rosenzweig, P.M. and Nohria, N. (1994) Influences on human resource management practices in multinational corporations. *Journal of International Business Studies*, 25(2), 229–251.

Rust, R.T., Zahorik, A.J., and Keiningham, T.L. (1995) Return on quality (ROQ): Making service quality financially accountable. *Journal of Marketing*, 59, 58–70.

Ryan, A.M., McFarland, L., Baron, H., and Page, R. (1999) An international look at selection practices: Nation and culture as explanations for variability in practice. *Personnel Psychology*, 52, 359–391.

Schmenner, R.W. (1995) *Service Operations Management*. Englewood Cliffs, NJ: Prentice-Hall.

Schneider, B. (1994) HRM – A service perspective: Towards a customer-focused HRM. *International Journal of Service Industry Management*, 5, 64–76.

Schneider, B. and Bowen, D.E. (1985) Employee and customer perceptions of service in banks: Replication and extension. *Journal of Applied Psychology*, 70(3), 423–433.

Schneider, B. and Bowen, D.E. (1995) *Winning the Service Game*. Boston, MA: Harvard Business School Press.

Schneider, B. and White, S.S. (2004) *Service Quality: Research Perspectives*. Thousand Oaks, CA: Sage Publications.

Schneider, S.C. and Barsoux, J.L. (2003) *Managing Across Cultures*. Essex: Prentice Hall.

Schneider, B., Parkington, J.P., and Buxton, V.M. (1980) Employee and customer perceptions of service in banks. *Administrative Sciences Quarterly*, 25, 252–267.

Schneider, B., Salvaggio, A.N., and Subirats, M. (2002) Climate strength: A new direction for climate research. *Journal of Applied Psychology*, 87, 220–229.

Schneider, B., White, S.S., and Paul, M.C. (1998) Linking service climate and customer perceptions of service quality in banks: Test of a causal model. *Journal of Applied Psychology*, 83, 150–163.

Schneider, B., Bowen, D.E., Ehrhart, M.G., and Holcombe, K.M. (2000) The climate for service: Evolution of a construct. In N.M. Ashkanasy, C.P.M. Wilderom, and M.F. Peterson (eds) *Handbook of Organizational Culture and Climate*. Thousand Oaks, CA: Sage Publications, pp. 21–36.

Schneider, B., Ehrhart, M.G., Mayer, D.M., and Saltz, J.L. (2003) Toward a multi-faceted mediated model of organizational–customer relationships in service settings. Unpublished manuscript, Department of Psychology, University of Maryland.

Shackleton, V. and Newell, S. (1991) Management selection: A comparative survey of methods used in top British and French companies. *Journal of Occupational Psychology*, 64(1), 23–36.

Smith, J.B. (1998) Buyer-seller relationships: Similarity, relationship management, and quality. *Psychology and Marketing*, 15(1), 3–21.

Smith, P.B., Peterson, M.F., and Wang, Z.M. (1996) The manager as mediator of alternative meanings: A pilot study from China, the USA, and UK. *Journal of International Business Studies*, 27(1), 115–137.

Sparrow, P. and Hiltrop, J.M. (1994) *European Human Resource Management in Transition*. Hertfordshire: Prentice Hall.

Swartz, T.A. and Iacobucci, D. (eds) (2000) *Handbook of Services Marketing and Management*. Thousand Oaks, CA: Sage Publications.

Tansik, D.A. (1990) Managing human resources issues for high contact service personnel. In D.E. Bowen, R.B. Chase, T.G. Cummings, and Associates (eds) *Service Management Effectiveness*. San Francisco, CA: Jossey-Bass.

Tax, S.S. and Brown, S.W. (2000) Service recovery: Research insights and practices. In T.A. Swartz and D. Iacobucci (eds) *Handbook of Services Marketing and Management*. Thousand Oaks, CA: Sage Publications, pp. 271–286.

Taylor, S. and Fullerton, G. (2000) Waiting for service: Perceptions management of the wait experience. In T.A. Swartz and D. Iacobucci (eds) *Handbook of services marketing and management* (pp. 147–170). Thousand Oaks, CA: Sage.

Triandis, H.C. and Bhawuk, D.P.S. (1997) Culture theory and the meaning of relatedness. In M. Erez and P.C. Earley (eds), *New Perspectives on International Industrial/Organizational Psychology*. San Francisco, CA: The New Lexington Press/Jossey-Bass, pp. 13–52.

Wasti, S.A. (2003a) The influence of cultural values on antecedents of organizational commitment: An individual-level analysis. *Applied Psychology: An International Review*, 52(4), 533–554.

Wasti, S.A. (2003b) Organizational commitment, turnover intentions and the influence of cultural values. *Journal of Occupational and Organizational Psychology*, 76, 303–321.

Weatherly, K.A. and Tansik, D.A. (1993) Managing multiple demands: A role-theory examination of behaviors of customer contact service workers. In T.A. Swartz, D.E. Bowen, and S.W. Brown (eds), *Advances in Services Marketing and Management*, vol. 2. Greenwich, CT: JAI Press, pp. 279–300.

Weidenfeller, N. (1992) Celebrating diversity. *Public Utilities Fortnightly*, 129, 20–22.

Wiley, J.W. (1996) Linking survey results to customer satisfaction and business performance. In A.I. Kraut (ed.) *Organizational Surveys: Tools for Assessment and Change*. San Francisco, CA: Jossey-Bass, pp. 330–359.

Wiley, J.W. and Brooks, S.M. (2000) The high performance organizational climate: How workers describe top performing units. In N.M. Ashkanasy, C.P.M. Wilderom, and M.F. Peterson (eds) *Handbook of Organizational Culture and Climate*. Thousand Oaks, CA: Sage Publications, pp. 177–192.

Winsted, K.R. (1997) The service experience in two cultures: A behavioral perspective. *Journal of Retailing*, 73(3), 337–360.

Winsted, K.F. (2000) Patient satisfaction with medical encounters: A cross-cultural perspective. *International Journal of Service Industry Management*, 11(5), 399–421.

Wong, A.L.Y. and Slater, J.R. (2002) Executive development in China: is there any in a Western sense? *International Journal of Human Resource Management*, 13(2), 338–360.

Wright, P.M. and Snell, S.A. (1991) Toward an integrative view of strategic human resource management. *Human Resource Management Review*, 1, 203–225.

Wright, P.M., Dunford, B.B., and Snell, S.A. (2001) Human resources and the resource based view of the firm. *Journal of Management*, 27, 701–721.

Wright, P.M., Gardner, T.M., and Moynihan, L.M. (2003) The impact of HR practices on the performance of business units. *Human Resource Management Journal*, 13(3), 21–36.

Yoshimura, N. and Anderson, P. (1997) *Inside the Kaisha: Demystifying Japanese Business Behavior.* Boston, MA: Harvard Business School Press.

Zeithaml, V.A. and Bitner, M.J. (2000) *Services Marketing,* 2nd edn. New York: McGraw-Hill.

Chapter 13

Integrated speed and flexibility
Delivering customer solutions

Jay Galbraith

Over the past decade, companies have learned how to create organizations that rapidly develop new offerings and get them to market.[1] They have perfected techniques like "rapid prototyping" and the process for "follow the sun" development. Some companies have created organizations that are both fast and flexible. They break up into many small units, each of which can quickly turn on a dime. But today companies like investment banks and computer manufacturers are facing the challenge to be fast, flexible and integrated. Creating organizations that can deliver all three requirements is today's state of the art organizational design problem.

This challenge to companies like those in the computer industry arises when they attempt to deliver customer solutions. They are finding that some of their customers prefer to buy combinations of products and services rather than stand-alone products. They prefer solutions when a vendor can integrate the products and services more effectively than the customer can. For the vendor the challenge is to integrate the organizational units that provide the stand-alone services and products in a time frame that is desired by the customer. In this just-in-time world that desired time is becoming shorter and shorter. Then, when the vendor has accomplished this rapid integration for one customer and solution, another customer will want a different solution requiring a different combination of products and services. The vendor in the solutions business must, therefore, have an organization that can combine and recombine the products and services from different units to create different solutions in fast time frames. This chapter describes what companies like Sun Microsystems, Nokia and IBM are doing to create organizations that are simultaneously fast, flexible and yet integrated.

These cases are selected from 14 case studies conducted over the last three years. The selected cases represent the extreme situation and the extreme challenge from which we can learn the most and then apply those lessons to less extreme situations. The chapter starts with a model of organization which will be used to describe the practices that the companies have evolved. Then, the different types of solutions will be defined so that the extreme cases can be understood. The next sections will describe the organizational structures, processes and human resources practices that are being employed. The focus will be on the companies' ability to assemble and disassemble teams rapidly to capture solution opportunities and to execute the solutions projects when the capture is successful. The selected companies have evolved processes for just-in-time staffing and structures to provide flexible resources for projects. Finally, generalizations will be drawn for creating fast, flexible and integrated organizations.

STRATEGY AND ORGANIZATION MODEL

A model for linking different strategies to different organizations is shown in Figure 13.1 below.[2] It depicts an organization as consisting of four dimensions. The first is the structure, which determines the location of decision-making power. Second are the information and decision-making processes. Third is the reward system that influences the motivation of people to perform and address organizational goals. And the fourth category of the model is the people dimension, which focuses on the human resources policies. These influence the employees' mindsets and skill sets.

The message of the Star Model is that these dimensions must be consistent with strategy and consistent among themselves. Our purpose here is to identify the different solutions strategies and the different combinations of organizational dimensions that characterize the fast and flexible organization that will integrate and deliver these solutions. In the next section we will define what the different types of solutions are that present the speed, flexibility and integration challenge.

SOLUTIONS STRATEGY

Different solutions strategies will result in different challenges for the fast, flexible and integrated company. There are four dimensions of solutions strategy that appear to make a difference to the organization. These dimensions are the type of solution, the scale and scope of solutions, the degree of integration of products constituting a solution, and the percentage of total revenue deriving from solutions. The scale and scope and the integration dimensions are the ones that challenge the fast and flexible organization.

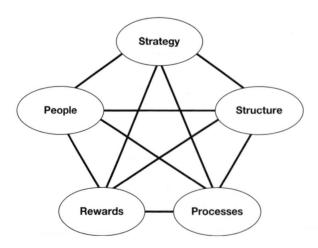

Figure 13.1 The Star Model

Types of solutions

There are two main types of solutions, horizontal and vertical. Horizontal solutions are generic and apply across customer categories. For example, Sun Microsystems creates and delivers a human resources portal solution. This portal can be used for the human resources function across all industries. IBM, on the other hand, delivers industry-specific solutions as well. For example, e-Agency is a solution to put the agency network of an insurance company on the internet. These industry-specific solutions are referred to as vertical solutions. Clearly, the vertical solutions require a more customer-centric organizational unit than do the horizontal solutions.

Scale and scope

The strategic factor having the greatest organizational impact is the scale and scope of the solution. Scale and scope refers to the number of products and the number of different kinds of products that are combined into a solution. For example, a small scale and scope solution would be a local area network for a work group. A dozen desktop computers, a shared printer and disk storage could all be linked by an Ethernet cable and form a network. A larger scale and scope solution would be computer-aided design (CAD) system for an engineering department of several hundred engineers. This CAD solution would require desktops, servers, storage units, CAD software, database software, network software, installation and maintenance services. It may also require financing. This CAD solution comprises many more products and many different kinds of products, like software and services as well as the hardware products. At the extreme end of scale and scope, Mitsubishi Trading Company could order state of the art trading floors for 10,000 traders at six worldwide sites. This solution requires hardware, software, and services for computers, telecom, financing and training. Large turnkey projects such as these are an extreme challenge to the fast and flexible organization, and require a highly integrated approach.

Integration

A third dimension is the degree of integration between the components that comprise a solution. Integration varies from a loose assortment of products to a highly integrated combination. In between are combinations that use modular architectures. Little integration is needed between products supplied by agriculture firms to farmers. The firms try to bundle seeds, herbicides, insecticides and consulting. However, the farmer can easily buy each as a stand-alone product from a different supplier. An example of larger scale but also limited integration can be found at ServiceMaster. They try to provide as many simple services as possible. They provide one-stop shopping for security, catering, janitorial, parking lot management, landscaping, building maintenance and many other similar services. But each is a relatively independent service that could be provided by an independent service company. A more integrated offering is the set of solutions from computer companies. Figure 13.2 shows what Sun Microsystems calls "the Integrated Stack". The stack shows hardware on the bottom, software in the middle and services on the top.

241

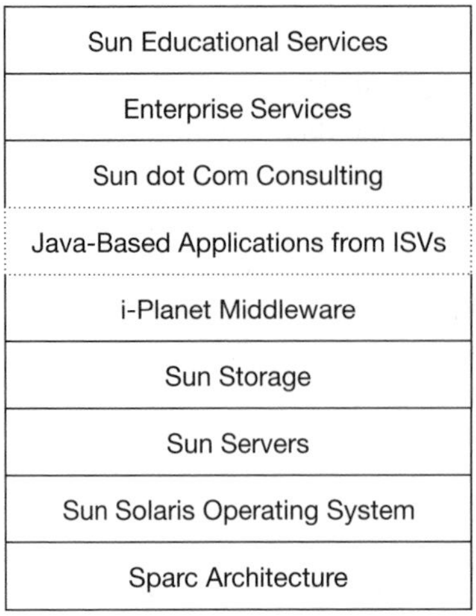

Sun Educational Services
Enterprise Services
Sun dot Com Consulting
Java-Based Applications from ISVs
i-Planet Middleware
Sun Storage
Sun Servers
Sun Solaris Operating System
Sparc Architecture

Figure 13.2 *Sun's integrated stack*

All components have to operate in an integrated manner. But thanks to standards like the Java programming language, components using Java can be substituted for other components. For example, a customer could choose BEA's middleware and substitute it for Sun's i-Planet middleware. So components in the information technology industry must be able to operate with other components. By following standards they give the customer the choice of mixing and matching different components.

At the extreme are integral solutions in which the components are unique but are designed specifically to work together. A simple integral solution would be an anti-lock braking system (ABS) for an auto manufacturer. Each ABS is unique to an automobile model. Johnson Controls is a more complex example. The company designs and manufactures interiors for Toyota, Chrysler and other automobile OEMs. Each Toyota model has a unique interior comprised of unique parts. These parts cannot be used on a Chrysler interior. The significance of the integration dimension for the organization is the coordination required. The organization reflects the solution. The more interdependent the components, the more interdependent the organizational units responsible for those components and the larger the challenge to rapidly mobilize them.

The combination of scale and scope with integration determines the coordination requirements and the organizational features to provide the coordination. Figure 13.3 shows this combination and some different solutions strategies that have been discussed.

Figure 13.3 shows that scale and scope and integration increase as the solutions move from the southwest to the northeast corner. The consequence is that the coordination requirements increase in the same manner. We will focus on the solutions in the north and east portions of the chart as indicated by the shading.

Revenues

The last strategic dimension is the percentage of total revenues that comes from solutions. If, like Motorola, solutions contribute 10 percent or less, the firm can simply add a

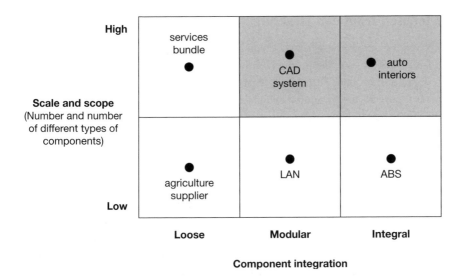

Figure 13.3 *Coordination requirements of different solutions strategies*

solutions unit whose task is to integrate the firm's products into solutions. When the percentage gets higher, like at IBM, the company has sufficient volume to specialize the solutions units that serve different customer segments. Instead of one solutions unit, IBM has about 12 units, each specializing in a customer segment.

Summary

A solutions provider desiring to respond quickly to customer opportunities faces greater challenges as its strategy increases in:

1   the scale and scope of the solution provided;
2   the degree of integration of the components comprising the solution.

Scale and scope increase the number of organizational units that must be integrated quickly. Integration relates to the coordination effort needed to accomplish the integration.

STRUCTURES

The companies in our study transformed themselves into solutions providers by changing three structural areas: they formed a single sales organization focused on customers and opportunities; they created a unit responsible for developing solutions; and they increased the flexibility of human talent. These companies had previously been organized by business units or product lines. The business units typically remained and continued to develop and manufacture their product lines. All of the companies continued to supply stand-alone products to those customers that desired them. In addition, they integrated products and services into solutions for those customers who preferred solutions.

Customer-focused front end structure

The solutions vendors typically organized around customer opportunities.[3] They created single sales forces by combining the product sales people into customer-focused units. These units were organized around customers, customer segments and/or geography. Sun Microsystems is typical of the computer manufacturers in its organization, shown in Figure 13.4. In July 2000, Sun combined its separate product sales forces into its Global Sales Organization.

The structure continues to evolve but it consists of four main units, two of which will be explained here. Most customers are handled through a geographic sales organization which they call Time Zones. Others are handled through channel partners like Value Added Resellers (VARs), Independent Software Vendors (ISVs), Systems Integrators (SIs) and others. But somewhere around 20 large, global customers are handled individually in a customer unit. IBM, which is ten times the size of Sun, focuses on 1,000 global customers and organizes the accounts into industry segments like Financial Services, Manufacturing, etc. And, finally, there is a Solutions unit that focuses primarily on horizontal solutions. IBM locates its horizontal solutions unit in Global Services. These customer and solutions units have the primary responsibility for speed, flexibility and integration.

The rest of the structure consists of the product lines for services, hardware and software. Each group is further subdivided into individual products like education services

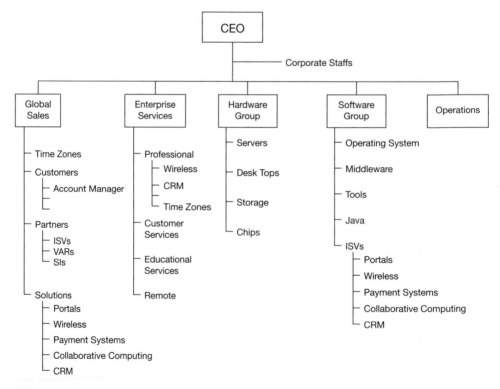

Figure 13.4 Sun Microsystems organization structure (c.2001)

and desktops. The operations group is the manufacturing assembly operations that are increasingly outsourced.

Global account management

The largest and most profitable accounts, like Nokia and eBay, get a dedicated team to serve them. The team structure is shown in Figure 13.5. The team is a re-creation of the company in microcosm. Each product line is represented on the team.

The team is to deliver all of the company's capabilities to the customer. They are to mobilize and integrate Sun's total offerings on behalf of the customer.

The team articulates a customer strategy and prepares a customer plan by product line, geography and solution. The sales people are the links to the product lines. The planning process builds the relationship with the product lines and educates everyone about the high priority customers. The plan also identifies investments to be made to win big solutions contracts. These opportunities, like a wireless application for a customer's sales force and field personnel, could be a $250 million global project and take three years of preparation and investment to win. Solutions are a patient money game. But the time allows the team to prepare all the product lines to act when the request for proposal is finally issued.

The key roles in this unit are the Global Account Manager (GAM), the Project Manager (PM) and the solutions sales person. The GAM is not just a sales person, however. Most GAMs are general managers for the accounts that amount to about $100 million per year. Growing and finding these general managers is a challenge and often limits how fast a company can transition to solutions. The other key role is the Project Manager. This person and the GAM marshal the resources from across the company to respond quickly to capture opportunities. The PM manages the proposal effort and the implementation when a proposal is won. Growing and finding these people is another human resources challenge. PMs who can manage the $250 million project mentioned above in 85 countries are rare. The other role is the solutions sales person who joins the team when a large solution opportunity is

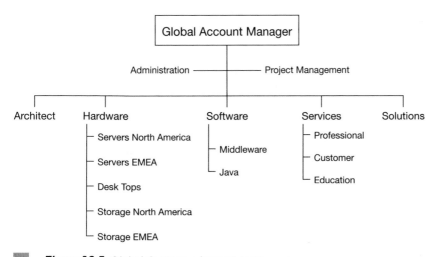

Figure 13.5 Global Customer Account team

anticipated. So a wireless person would join for a time when the wireless opportunity is alive. Then a portal solutions person may join when portals become an opportunity. These people are part of the solutions unit and move from opportunity to opportunity.

Solutions unit

The solutions unit is to develop and implement those solutions that the company has chosen to offer. The solutions vendor typically chooses to offer solutions at which it is superior and which can be replicated across multiple customers. The large companies cannot make money by offering solutions on a one-off basis. Sun has chosen about eight areas in which they offer replicable horizontal solutions like portals, wireless, payment systems, collaborative computing (computer aided design or CAD), electronic markets and customer relationship management (CRM). Each solution is a combination of products from Sun's hardware, software and services units, as well as software from ISVs like Oracle and Peoplesoft along with consulting, systems integration and outsourcing from firms like EDS and Accenture. The solutions unit is to select the best products from inside and outside of the company to combine into a solution.

The solutions unit shown in Figure 13.4 has a department for each chosen solution area. There is a champion for the solution who heads the department and a team of six to ten

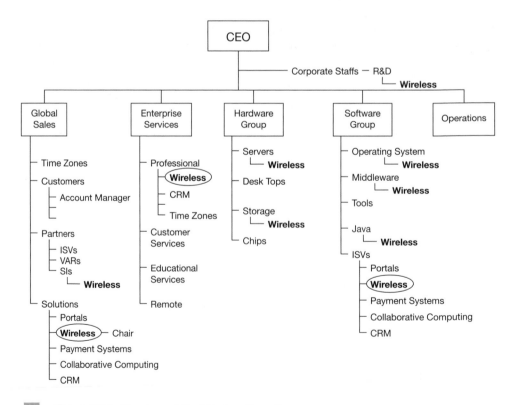

Figure 13.6 *Structure of the Wireless Council*

people. These teams consist of eight- to ten-year company veterans who have a combination of marketing, engineering and sales backgrounds. One or two may come from outside the company to provide unique expertise. In each Time Zone there are salespeople who assist account teams in the capture of solutions opportunities, as shown in Figure 13.5. Each solution has about 15 to 20 people in the field for this purpose.

Each solution team has a Solutions Council that connects to the product lines or business units. Figure 13.6 shows the product lines that contribute a representative to the Wireless Council.

These product lines have offerings that make up the solution. Some products, like servers in hardware, may require some modifications to make the solution perform better. Figure 13.7 shows the Payment Systems Council. These include systems sold to an oil company that wants to set up smart card pay stations at gasoline pumps connected to the internet. Each solution involves different product lines in the offering. The council system is intended to allow Sun to configure whatever products and capabilities it needs in order to form a solution. It does not create a separate business unit for a solution. It uses councils to configure and reconfigure the company's capabilities into solutions that customers value.

Each product line also needs to create flexible resource units that can provide talent to swing into action when an opportunity arises.

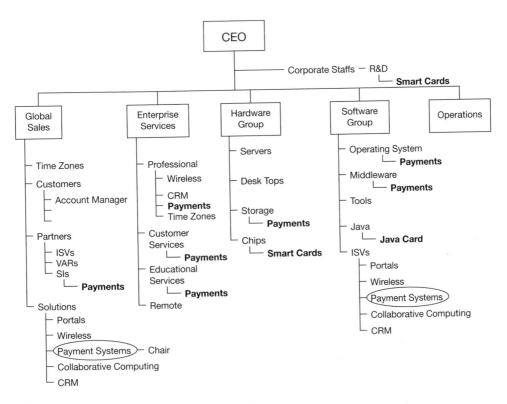

Figure 13.7 Structure of the Payment Systems Council

Flexible resource units

The solutions vendors all created talent pools, both internally and externally, that could be tapped and organized quickly into capture teams or execution teams (see Figure 13.8). They also found ways to leverage the talent and design the work to match the scarcest skills. And finally, they developed processes for allocating talent to the top priority opportunities. The talent allocation will be discussed in the section on processes (see pp. 251–256).

Talent pools

Each vendor created pools of talent that could be used flexibly and quickly in responding to customer opportunities. One pool that all of them created was a professional services unit. These units were staffed with mostly outsiders who were consultants in the solutions area and systems integration specialists. These professional services units were run like consulting firms. The talent moved from project to project. Each person had to be billable. The GAMs all had budgets and would buy time from these people for customer calls, workshops, conferences, project execution and proposal preparation. The computer companies typically hired a partner from a consulting firm and gave them the responsibility to build the unit.

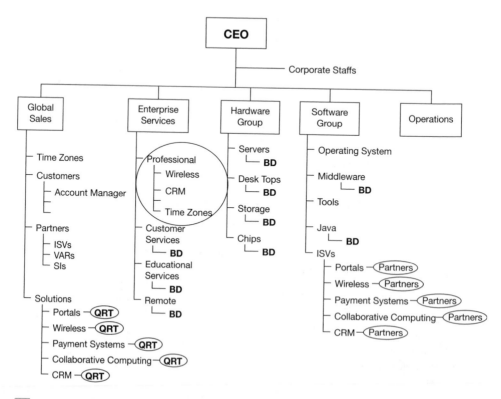

Figure 13.8 Flexible resource units

Another practice was the creation of quick response teams in the solutions units. These were professionals who were trained in the skills to support the solutions. At Sun the 15–20 people in the field were available for staffing capture teams in their solution's area. At IBM several hundred people were available for regional and even global assignments to capture and execute wireless solutions. IBM's size gives it the opportunity to create these specialized quick or rapid response units.

At Sun the product lines all had business development units and growth goals to encourage them to respond to solutions opportunities. These units were staffed with marketing and engineering types who could be dispatched quickly and work on a capture team for four weeks and then return to another opportunity. For some large projects and for top priority customers engineers and architects in the business units may be pulled off current work to capture opportunities. If these big opportunities can be anticipated to some degree, these people can be selected in advance and participate in the preparation of customer and solution plans. Then when the opportunity materializes, they can take their place on the capture team and be ready to run. This reserve capacity works best when there is some lead time to prepare the people. The reserves can then create a plan for filling in for themselves when they are called. In these ways flexible talent pools, both full time and reserve, are available for real time staffing of opportunities.

Leveraging talent

The computer companies, investment banks and consulting firms all tried to leverage talent on a regional and global basis.[4] Sometimes leverage was achieved by changing organizational structure, sometimes by structuring the work and skills, and sometimes by moving work to the talent.

In the early 1990s almost all consulting firms, investment banks and computer companies were organized by country. As a result, talent was locked up in country silos and the firms were unable to respond quickly enough on cross-border opportunities. By the late 1990s, these same firms had eliminated country profit centers and had moved to global accounts, as shown in Figure 13.5, and organized talent by regions, such as Europe Middle East Africa (EMEA). Both IBM and Accenture reorganized after they lost opportunities to EDS, which had a global customer and regional talent structure. IBM and Accenture simply could not move fast enough on cross-border opportunities, so customers subsequently awarded the contracts to EDS, who could. Today, global customer and regional talent structures are the rule for professional services companies and the services units of other companies.

All firms providing solutions faced the challenge of leveraging specialist skills that were in short supply. In the late 1990s, Hewlett-Packard put together an e-commerce strategy for Europe. However, they could implement only a fraction of it. In Europe, H-P had only ten people who were qualified to install secure transactions over the internet. And even though every bank in Europe wanted to implement an e-commerce program, no bank would sign a contract until they saw that one of the ten experts was going to work on their project. The consulting firms were limited first by scarce SAP-skilled programmers, then by XML programmers. When solutions providers take on large scale and scope solutions, there is a high likelihood of encountering a scarce skill that limits the opportunities that the companies can pursue.

249

The firms in the study responded to the scarcity of talent in a number of ways. Most tried to increase the talent available. They ramped up their training of internal people, launched recruiting drives and searched for outsourcing partners (to be described next). In the short run they leveraged their existing talent by designing key roles for them and by adopting human resource practices to retain them. The talent in the limiting skill was usually ranked from critical to normal and placed in two or three categories. The people in the critical category were then given their choice of projects. They were also paid at market rates, which were higher than normal company salary rates. These critical thought leaders would also float across projects and get in early on a project. Their early entry would usually lead to key guiding design decisions. Then they would move to the next project and normal talent could move in as the need for critical skills fell. These same people would be used in review boards to re-enter the project at key checkpoints. The early entry and re-entry at checkpoints allowed the scarce critical talent to be leveraged and to provide coaching to develop the normal talent.

Another way to leverage talent was to move work to where the talent exists. One way is to employ "follow the sun" development processes used by most software developers to reduce development time. Another example can be found in engineering and construction (E&C) firms like Fluor-Daniel. These turnkey project performers allocate their design and management work for maximum leverage. In one case an E&C firm was building a refinery in a developing country. The firm put the project management into its Calgary office. An experienced project manager was located there principally because the Canadian government provides funds at attractive rates when projects are located in Canada. The critical catalytic cracking design was assigned to the Irvine, California office where the center of excellence was located. Mechanical and civil work went to the Houston office where capacity was available. Then, when the critical top 40 percent of the design work was completed, the remainder of the work was sent via satellite to the Philippines where it was finished at more cost effective rates. The Filipino engineers, many of whom had been trained in the US, completed the 15,000 isometric drawings to guide the refinery construction. Each of these allocations leveraged the E&C company's skill base. As CAD systems develop on the internet, knowledge work can be moved to where the best talent exists.

So the electronic movement of work takes its place with work and organizational restructuring, all of which enable fast, flexible solutions firms to leverage talent.

Partners

The solutions providers always went outside for partners for talent. The large scope solutions always exceed the talent repertoire of even the largest firms, like IBM. These partners are also a source of talent pools and scarce talent when responding to customer opportunities. The skilled solutions firm invests a lot of time recruiting, certifying, and building relationships with its partners. Sun is a good example of a sophisticated partnering firm.

The solutions unit at Sun is one hub around which the company's capabilities are gathered for the customer. A second hub is the ISV unit in the Software Group. The ISV unit identifies and recruits independent software vendors (ISVs) which can be gathered into the company's solutions. This unit has an identical structure to the solutions unit. There are the same departments for Wireless, Payment Systems, etc. The Wireless department identifies the top application software vendors for the wireless solutions that Sun chooses to offer. It works with these ISVs to get their software to run well on Sun computers. Another hub is the Systems Integrator (SI) unit in the Channel Partners group. Like the ISV unit, they identify the best SIs to be partners for solutions. Some are best for wireless in Financial Services applications, others for wireless in manufacturing applications. Some are best in Europe and others are strong in Japan. The solutions planning process, driven by the solutions unit, is the forum in which partner selections are finally reached.

The selected partners then go through a process of certification. That is, a team from Sun audits the partner and certifies its capability to meet Sun's solution criteria and talent availability. The partner may then use the certification in its own advertising. Sun holds annual conferences for its partners where all participants in a solution can meet and discuss current practice and future developments. One of the issues the partners discuss is their common process for developing solutions. Then, when a solution opportunity arises, the partners can focus on *what* to do, having already agreed upon *how* to do it.

Sun works hard to develop a partner community. They select partners based on complementary competencies and on common values. The partners they select agree on non-compete areas and open systems standards. The conferences, common web sites, joint advertising, joint display booths at trade shows, common processes and common values all are important features in creating a community of partners, which Sun sees as an advantage. In addition, Sun pays commissions to the sales forces of community companies that make sales and generate leads for other community companies. And every year the CEO of Sun has "Summit Meetings" with the CEOs of Sun's major partners. In these ways, Sun builds and maintains a community of partners whose resources can be marshaled quickly to pursue solutions opportunities.

In summary, the case study firms moved to become integrated, fast and flexible by creating customer-focused units to address the customer opportunities and marshal the company's resources to meet them. They selected solutions that were valued by the customer and at which the company could excel. The company's capabilities were organized into councils to better enable the development of solutions and preparation of plans. These councils were staffed with talent from pools that were organized to provide just-in-time staffing to respond to customer opportunities. These pools were both internal and external to the firm. Talent was leveraged across the firm with regional pools, critical talent programs and the electronic movement of knowledge work to where the best talent could be found. The mechanisms making this solutions system work were the management and business processes that were designed to deliver speed, flexibility and integration.

PROCESSES

The solutions provider, like the company organized by business units, employs management processes, such as planning and budgeting, as well as business processes, such as new product development and supply chain management. But the solutions provider has some additional processes and modifications to the standard ones. In the planning process, the solutions provider has customer and solutions strategies and plans, as well as a reconciliation process with business unit plans. Solutions providers use a product portfolio planning process in addition to the new product development process. And finally, there is the opportunity management process. In this process there are key decisions of staffing the capture and executing teams and pricing the products and services comprising the solution. These processes are the primary vehicles through which management achieves the integration and the speed to deliver solutions to customers.

Strategic planning

The strategic planning process lays the foundation on which the solutions provider can then move with speed and flexibility. In this sense, planning is, indeed, preparing to move opportunistically.[5] Even in these fast moving companies, activities are not 100 percent sense and respond. They plan when they can and respond when they cannot plan. They use planning to reconcile product and customer plans, develop solutions policies and arrive at priorities for customers.

The strategic planning process is to achieve the integration dimension. Like the business unit firm, the solutions provider prepares strategies and plans for product lines. But the solutions provider also prepares customer and solutions strategies and plans. These plans then need to be reconciled in order to achieve goal alignment prior to taking action. All of the firms used some type of spreadsheet as shown in Figure 13.9. For example, they would compare plans for server capacity and resolve differences so that product and customer goals were the same.

These discussions would also raise issues about solutions prices and product prices in a solution. The discussions would lay the ground work for the solutions pricing policy. Another issue might be whether a product line could opt out of a solution if it did not like

Customer/Solution Units

		A	B	C	D
	1	Revenues Profits Growth etc.			
Product Units	2				
	3				
	4				

Figure 13.9 *Spreadsheet to reconcile solution and product plans*

the price given to its product. And if it could opt out, could the solutions unit use a competitor's product in its place. All of these are contentious issues. The function of the planning process is to raise, debate and resolve these issues prior to responding to opportunities. Planning allows the company to go on maneuvers before using live ammunition.

The other outcome of the planning process is customer priorities. A company cannot respond immediately and totally to every customer opportunity. So the solutions providers place priorities on customers based on profitability, ability to learn, or future profitability. They will respond to the top priority customers in a manner that is fast and integrated. The critical talent will be assigned to these customers' opportunities. Planning is the forum for the debates around which customers are top priority customers.

Product portfolio planning

Each product unit develops its own products but each unit's products must work together with the products of other units to provide a solution. The strategy dimension of component integration is important in determining how much effort must go into planning the entire portfolio so that the products will work together. For example, if Nokia is going to offer Third Generation equipment[6] it must have switches and transmission products, software, consulting practices, customer service contracts as well as handsets that all work together using 3G technology. The product units cannot independently develop their own product lines without a dialogue. A strong top management team is required to guide the portfolio planning process. The Nokia software product business may want to challenge Microsoft. However, Nokia will also need a totally integrated product line in order to provide customer solutions. Through the portfolio planning process, the software and other product groups have to develop a strategy that advances their product line as well as integrates the products into solutions offerings.

Many companies move to modular architectures and adopt industry standards. These practices loosen the integration of products required to form a solution. Business units can opt in and out more easily. Customers may want to choose which products make up a solution. Competitors' products meeting industry standards can then be substituted. The product portfolio process is the forum for deciding on standards and modular architectures.

Opportunity management process

The structuring and planning described above create a platform on which the solutions provider can then sense and respond.[7] When opportunities materialize, they are not always like the plan, at the anticipated price, and usually the exact timing is different. The company must then match resources to opportunities in real time. This matching is the key management process in achieving speed, flexibility and integration. There are two aspects to this real time response to opportunities. One is pricing and the other, on which we will focus, is the assembly and disassembly of capture teams and execution teams.

The pricing decision was one of the issues debated in the strategic planning process. The output was a solutions price, and prices for all products and services comprising the solution. More important was the pricing policy and opt in–opt out policy. But the real price is always different and the likelihood of disputes is high. The disputes slow the response to the customer opportunity. In order to move quickly, Sun put the pricing decision with the GAM and the customer unit. The P+L responsibility rests with the Global Sales Organization. The product lines are product development oriented cost centers. At IBM, the final pricing decision rests with the Finance unit. They decide quickly so that everyone focuses on the opportunity and the customer.

The other challenging aspect is the real time staffing of teams to capture solutions opportunities and execute the projects when opportunities are won. The best case scenario is the one where the planning works. The GAM gets out ahead and learns that an automobile OEM is going to buy a collaborative computing (CAD) solution in 18 months. The account PM gathers a team based on the solutions unit's recommendations from the business development units of the product lines, from the chosen ISVs and from the SIs. They put together a preliminary plan as part of the annual planning process. Then, when the customer issues its request for proposal, the team is reactivated and a more detailed and current proposal is created. A few months later the contract is awarded and the execution team swings into action led by the account PM. A few opportunities follow this optimistic scenario. More likely, they follow the realistic scenario.

Most of the time the actual opportunity is different than anticipated, is later than planned, and the original team is busy on other projects. Some opportunities come out of the blue because of an acquisition or are postponed because of a revenue shortfall. There is often a surprise limiting skill area. Under these circumstances, the GAM, the PM and the customer priorities come into play. The PM goes to the scheduling unit for professional services, to the company yellow pages and web sites, and to the other flexible resource units. The resource units allocate available people to the opportunity. For high priority customers and large opportunities, the resource units may reassign the top people to the new opportunity and replace them with others who are available. When disagreements arise, the GAM may go to his or her network to persuade resource units to make their top talent available. Some staffing issues may find their way to higher levels in the hierarchy for resolution. All of the firms started with this informal process. But some thought there was a better way.

Some firms think that the best way to staff the attractive opportunities is to have an explicit process for allocating talent. They want to conduct real time, or just-in-time, staffing from a total company perspective. The informal process described above may take too long, there may be a large number of disputes about the limiting talent specialty and this may result in suboptimal allocations. They want the matching of talent to opportunities to match the priorities and needs of the business rather than powerbase of the GAMs.

There were different processes chosen by a number of the firms, but they were all flexible as to when a decision-making group would be convened. IBM had the most regular process. The European Leadership Team (ELT) would meet weekly but the frequency could be increased to twice a week if the number of decisions required increased. The ELT would consist of the head of Europe and all of his direct reports. In addition to other issues, the ELT would match talent to opportunities for large solutions. This process allowed real time staffing on a regional basis.

The EDS process was conducted on a global basis. The top team, led by the CEO, would monitor and discuss the top ten opportunities in the world. When one was activated, the team would choose and dispatch the talent to the capture team location. The effectiveness of this process caused Accenture to reorganize. The Managing Partner of Spain informed Accenture's head of Europe of an opportunity in which Banco Santander was going to outsource its global information technology operations. Accenture agreed to put together a capture team to bid on the opportunity. The very next day the Spanish Managing Partner called the head of Europe to tell him that, overnight, 50 professionals from EDS had arrived in Madrid and were working on the proposal as they were speaking. The head of Europe was shocked. He had just begun negotiating with the country heads to free up talent to work on the Spanish opportunity. He figured it would take him another week to staff the team. Even then he could not be sure that the best talent was working on the opportunity. Banco Santander was impressed and EDS won the contract. A little later Accenture reorganized into customer industry groups and regional, not country, talent pools with a regional allocation process.

The challenge of implementing regional and global talent allocation processes is in accessing all the information needed to get a good match between the opportunities and the talent. The decision-making group needs to know the set of opportunities available, the scope of work at the projects for these customers and the nature of the talent available. It is the information about the talent that is particularly challenging. Most management teams are experienced at allocating money from a total company perspective. But talent involves three issues that make allocating it on a company-wide basis difficult. For starters, a dollar equals a dollar. But a software programmer does not equal a software programmer. It is believed that a good programmer can be ten times more productive than a mediocre one. So the decision-makers need to know the individuals, but there may be hundreds or more people in the talent pool. Second, dollars do not care if they are spent on R&D or advertising. But people care very much where the project is located and whether it is challenging or not. The top-down assignment of critically skilled people to projects that they do not like will cause them to leave and join a competitor. So the decision-makers need to know the work preferences of the critical people. And finally, dollars do not care with which dollars they are combined to fund an initiative. For people, the co-workers are important. Again, the decision-makers need to know something about the chemistry between key team members. These factors are all important to the effective functioning of opportunity teams.

Some firms try to capture as much of this information as possible. Some of it can be captured in formal information databases to create a company "yellow pages" for talent that can be accessed by decision-makers. But much of it cannot be captured. So in order to bring all the data to the table, some consulting firms increase the number of people at the decision-making meeting. Ernst and Young (E&Y) Consulting would convene a regional task force for one or two days if needed to match talent to their opportunities. Like other consulting firms, E&Y used scheduling managers at all of its large offices. For most projects the account managers, project managers and scheduling managers can arrive at acceptable staffing plans for projects. But in the late 1990s there was a shortage of programmers who knew the SAP application language. Then E&Y, at the initiation of the scheduling managers, would convene a task force when shortages developed. They would gather people who knew the customers, the projects and the talent specialties. They would even include some of the key specialists in the meeting. These people could choose assignments or have a voice in the assignments that they felt were attractive. The task force could involve 30 to 45 people in matching resources to opportunities. But, in this manner, the firm was able to get a total perspective on the set of opportunities, the business priorities, the nature of the projects and the needs and desires of the talented people. (E&Y even experimented with a spot market for an SAP programmer for a week.)

These real time talent allocation processes are the current challenge for fast, flexible and integrated firms. It is difficult to get a total company perspective and also know the details of preferences of talented people and the chemistry of combinations of them. Yet, this information is exactly what's needed to satisfy important customers and to motivate and retain the talent that services those customers. The consulting firms and investment banks are probably the most advanced in this area. The solutions providers need to advance their management teams to this level. The management teams are used to deciding global issues on a periodic, not real time, basis. They have learned to discuss talented people in assessing promotion needs of the company and development needs of the top 150. But matching talent to the top opportunities is a new challenge for them.

Summary

The fast, flexible and integrated company is one that has aligned its organization and strategy to attain these three attributes. While all companies are struggling with the challenge to become simultaneously fast, flexible and integrated, the solutions providers are a good source of lessons in how to do it. The most advanced firms are those offering solutions that have many different kinds of components, and are integrating those components into valuable packages for the customer.

This strategy is matched with a structure that consists of business units plus new units for customers, solutions and flexible resources. There is usually a team connecting all units that form a solution. In addition to the usual management processes, there are modifications like reconciling business, customer and solutions strategies and additions like a product

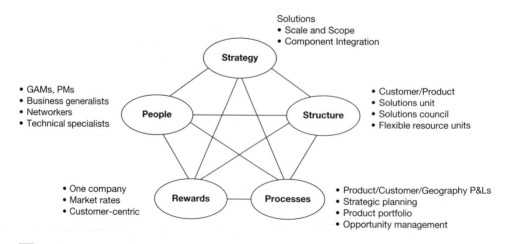

Figure 13.10 *Solutions Star Model*

portfolio plan and an opportunity management system. The key element in this latter process is the real time matching of talent to opportunities. The reward systems are those that emphasize one company and customer metrics like retention and customer share. The human resource issues are the challenges of finding Global Account Managers and Project Managers, and creating and maintaining flexible talent pools. These units consist of people who like change and variety and operating in consulting firm environments. Collectively, these policies combine to support the speed, flexibility and integration required to deliver solutions to customers who want them.

NOTES

1 See G. Stalk and T. M. Hout, *Competing Against Time* (New York: The Free Press, 1990).

2 See Jay R. Galbraith, *Designing Organizations*, revised edition (San Francisco, CA: Jossey-Bass, 2002).

3 See Russell Eisenstat *et al.*, "Beyond the Business Unit," *McKinsey Quarterly*, no. 1 (2001).

4 See Jay R. Galbraith, *Designing the Global Corporation* (San Francisco, CA: Jossey-Bass, 2000).

5 See J. B. Quinn, *Strategies for Change* (Homewood, IL: Richard D. Irwin, 1980).

6 Third Generation (3G) is a wireless technology that will permit handsets to connect to the internet and to various company databases.

7 See S. P. Bradley and R. L. Nolan, eds, *Sense and Respond* (Boston, MA: Harvard Business School Press, 1998).

Chapter 14

HRM and innovation

Ralph Katz and William M. James

The field of management practices has witnessed a constant parade of fads and shifts over the last number of decades. Over this period, for example, we've experienced dramatic shifts in the focus of industrial R&D-based strategies. The 1980s and early 1990s were characterized by an almost obsessive focus on quality programs and continuous improvement, the direct result of the successful Japanese quality and product proliferation movement as they gained rapid market share in many industries, including consumer electronics, semiconductors, and the automobile industry. The Asian industrial juggernaut turned out incrementally improved products at reduced cycle times that gave pause to any industrial firm that wanted to view itself as an innovation leader. HRM was quickly asked to develop the policies, practices, and education/training that would support these fast-cycle time kinds of product initiatives.

This trend gave way to the re-engineering era, the product of the early 1990s' economic downturn. Re-engineering became synonymous with downsizing and with it came a real decline in most industrys' R&D efforts. HRM was now asked to shift its focus to helping the organization function in a more lean, productive, and efficient manner. This phase evolved into the "irrational exuberance" of the late 1990s in which R&D expenditures grew to focus on organizational growth through radical or breakthrough innovations. All too many CEOs were constantly being heard making bold announcements to analysts that their organizations would "double in size over the next four to five years through new technical breakthroughs." After issuing such kinds of unsubstantiated predictions, the CEOs quickly turned to their R&D V.P.s and said: "Can you do it?" The R&D V.P.s, who were now stuck with these demands, would in turn ask their HRM V.P.s to develop the policies, practices, and education/training that would yield these still unknown but requisite creative breakthroughs.

The effect of these trends has been a dramatic transition from bottom-line financial improvements to top-line growth and, with it, the need to concentrate more broadly about managing increasingly significant innovative advances. The "dot.com" revolution rose and fell precipitously during the last few years and with it came a rebirth of the technology "rainmaker" or, in the vernacular, the "knowledge athlete." These technical gurus and specialists became revered as the backbone and spirit of new technology enterprises whose goal was to replace older, less innovative companies or create entirely new businesses. The successful commercialization of new technologies, such as biotechnology, IT, telecom, and e-commerce, has made heroes of many of these new technologists. At the same time, many research studies have now convincingly demonstrated a very consistent pattern of results with respect to the management of innovation. In almost every industry studied, a set of leading firms, when faced with a period of discontinuous change, failed to maintain its industry's market leadership in a new technological era. This pathological trend, described by many as the *tyranny of success*, in which winners often become losers—in which firms lose their innovative edge—revealed that the very factors that led to a firm's success also played a significant role in its demise. The leadership, vision, strategic focus, valued competencies, structures, policies, rewards, and corporate culture that were all so critical in building the company's growth and competitive advantage during one period can become its Achilles heel as technological and market conditions change over time.

Continuous improvement, followed by downsizing, then radical innovation and, finally, the "dot.com" boom is an almost schizophrenic series of changes in the brief period of a little more than a decade. At the organization's operating level, managers should have been asking whether their human resource policies and practices were robust enough to keep pace with these shifts in strategic emphasis. It is our strong belief through our combined years of research, consulting, and practical experiences, that HRM practices need to be firmly grounded in a few basic concepts to weather that broad range of business environments that will continue to occur in order to provide the foundation for good personnel practices that will support the necessary innovative efforts.

DUALISM AND CONFLICTING ORGANIZATIONAL PRESSURES

It is first important to recognize that patterns of success followed by failure—of innovation followed by inertia and complacency—are not deterministic. They do not have to happen! Success need not be paralyzing. To overcome this tendency, especially in today's rapidly changing world, the HRM function has to recognize and deal more than ever before with the conflicting challenges of *dualism*, that is, it has to function efficiently today while innovating effectively for the future. Not only must the organization be concerned with the financial success and market penetration of its current mix of products and services, but it must simultaneously focus on its long-term capabilities to develop and incorporate what will emerge as the most customer-valued technical advancements into future offerings in a very quick, timely, and responsive manner. A corporation today, no matter how it is structured and organized, must find ways to internalize and manage both sets of concerns simultaneously. In essence, HRM must help build internally those contradictory and inconsistent structures, competencies, and cultures that not only foster more efficient and reliable processes but that will also encourage the kinds of experiments and explorations needed to re-create the future even though such innovative activities are all too often seen by those running the organization as a waste of or threat to its current priorities, practices, and basis of success.

But even getting an agreement on a common definition of innovation demonstrates the challenge that underlies this work. Innovation activities have generally been classified as either radical or incremental, continuous or discontinuous, competence-enhancing or competence-destroying, and most recently as sustaining or disruptive (see Utterback, 1994; Tushman and O'Reilly, 1997; Katz, 2003; and Christensen, 1997 for more details on these innovation models). Much research on these classifications had focused on which type of innovating activity is the most important and effective for enhancing organizational success. But most astute managers and leaders understand the necessity for both and the need to identify and somehow manage the issues associated with these apparent contradictory innovation approaches. The simple point is that HRM function must realize that organizations need to have split personalities to simultaneously manage both approaches, and do it well. A singular strong cohesive organizational culture can easily undermine this need for multiplicity—this ability to create ambidextrous organizations that concurrently work and commercialize the different kinds of innovation streams (Tushman and O'Reilly, 1997).

While it is easy to say that organizations should internalize both sets of concerns in order to transform themselves into the future, it is a very difficult thing to do. Witness, for example, the experiences of Procter and Gamble (P&G) over the past few years. In the beginning, the analysts claimed that P&G was doing a very good job at managing its existing businesses but unfortunately was not growing the company fast enough through the commercialization of new brands or new product categories. P&G then impressively introduced a number of very successful new products (Swiffer, Whitestrips, Thermacare, and Febreze—just to name a few) that were collectively bringing in considerably more than a billion dollars in added revenue per year. The analysts, however, switched gears again acknowledging P&G's new product initiatives but criticizing them for taking their eye off its existing brands and losing important market share to very aggressive competitors. It is not particularly surprising that these same analysts wanted P&G to de-emphasize its new venture strategies and investments in order to concentrate on protecting and strengthening its major bedrock brands. The pendulum just seemed to keep on swinging.

The unfortunate reality is that there is usually much disagreement within a company operating in a very pressured and competitive marketplace as to how to carry out dualism rather than the back and forth pendulum. Amid the demands of everyday requirements, decision makers representing different parts of the organization rarely agree on the relative merits of allocating resources and management attention among the range of competing projects and technical activities; that is, those that directly benefit the organization's more salient and immediate needs versus those that will fuel long-term growth sometime in the future. Consider the reactions of individuals representing different functions of the organization to a very simple question like: "What is heaven to you from a product line point of view?" Managers in a manufacturing setting would typically respond that in their "heaven," there would be only *one* product with no design changes. This would help enable them to build the most reliable processes for rapid and high output volume that hopefully would be defect free. Marketing managers, on the other hand, would have a diametrically opposite point of view. In their "heaven," there would be unlimited product variations so that they could customize and personalize their products and services as rapidly as possible to each and every individual customer. This would enable them to be close to their consumers to gain as much market share as possible. R&D personnel would give yet a third response. From their point of view, "heaven" would be characterized by their ability to work on the most exciting, state-of-the-art, technical breakthroughs to eventually deliver superior, value-added products to either established or new markets. And naturally this could be more easily achieved if there were essentially no monetary budgets or time deadlines. This "heavenly" description, however, would scare the daylights out of the finance (e.g., the controller) function who see their "heaven" as one with strong monetary, budget, and schedule controls so that they could both predict and report accurate information in as timely a fashion as possible. This would help minimize uncertainty and yield the strong financial controls necessary to sustain growth, profitability, and overall market value.

None of these individual points of view in and of themselves are wrong; in fact, they are all necessary. The organization needs manufacturing and operations to continuously work towards greater efficiencies and lower costs especially as product lines become more mature, customers expect better values, and competition becomes much more grounded in relative costs. In a sense, customers no longer want just better products, they now want them better and cheaper. At the same time, the organization doesn't need just people in marketing—it needs people who know the markets. The marketing people have to know their customers and consumers and the changes that are taking place in the many different environments so that appropriate products can be successfully developed, distributed, and sold to meet customer and user needs.

But, unfortunately, not all needs are easily identifiable or articulated. Consumers cannot readily visualize new products or new benefits beyond a logical extrapolation of their current experiences. While they can tell you about their explicit uses and experiences with current products and services, they can't easily tell you what might be technologically feasible. The R&D function, therefore, must not only work with marketing and manufacturing on improving existing product line features and services, it should also strive to develop the future products and services that meet unarticulated or tacit needs based on relevant enabling technological developments and capabilities that are occurring on a global basis. Finance, on the other hand, needs to ensure that the organization will remain fiscally responsible and sound and that the new products, services, acquisitions, strategic initiatives, etc. are not "out of control." At the same time, it must work not just to *control* R&D, marketing, and manufacturing but also to support and work with these functions over time to determine the combined functional strategies that will enable the company to make money from new R&D, engineering, and market-based initiatives.

The critical factor, for example, that allowed Xerox to become so successful in commercializing its new copying machines was not the photostatic technological breakthrough per se. After all, *Business Week*'s evaluation of Xerox's new product when it was first introduced was very pessimistic. In its September 19, 1959 evaluation, *Business Week* concluded:

> Office copying is a field where Haloid (Xerox) will find plenty of competition. Most of the 30 or so copying machine manufacturers are already in it with a variety of products and services including such strong competition as 3M (thermofax) and Kodak (verifax).

What fooled the experts and permitted the ultimate success of Xerox was the *financial* leasing strategy that allowed customers to primarily pay only for the copies they made rather than having to make a huge capital outlay to purchase very expensive machines. Amazingly enough, businesses and consumers never believed they would ever need to make a lot of copies. But once the machines were installed and available, users soon uncovered all kinds of "new" needs and uses and, as we all know today, the amount of copies being made has probably grown exponentially over time despite the constant "paperless office" predictions. Many similar examples can be found in the joint functional implementation strategies of many other successful breakthrough products. The implication for the HRM function is not getting the functional areas to think alike, to be similar, or to be harmonious (at least one major company actually titled their HRM V.P. the "V.P. of Harmony"). The trick is to have them maintain and use these differences as they work together to come up with, and more importantly, execute a business strategy. Functional areas do not have to be "team players;" they should be "people playing and working together as a team." Much too frequently this approach runs amok in the execution of HRM policies and practices, including its feedback, and reward systems, where there is, in fact, great pressure to "harmonize HRM systems" to a "one-size fits all" approach. All this despite the desire to create and maintain organization sub-cultures that recognize the differing needs of the ambidextrous organization.

HRM AND THE AMBIDEXTROUS ORGANIZATION

In most organizations, HRM concentrates on the functioning aspects of the organization. It develops policies and practices that primarily support the on-going operations, including job descriptions, performance appraisals, reward, and recognition systems, and educational/training programs. Given this emphasis, the HRM function in most organizations has failed to gain strong credibility within the innovating community. All too often, R&D mistrusts HRM, viewing it as too soft, irrelevant, and unrealistic. To overcome this barrier, HRM needs to understand some subtle but important differences between professional individuals working on future innovative areas (e.g., R&D) and those professionals working on existing product lines and services (e.g., the other functional areas).

At the center of this controversy is one irrefutable but poorly understood concept. Professionals working on cutting edge technologies and new-to-world products must have a high tolerance for uncertainty, the operating definition of which is, "those things that you don't and can't know . . . but wish that you did." This is importantly different than the "risk management" approaches commonly used in the continuous improvement innovations. Risk is the probability or odds of achieving a loss and the inherent financial implications if you do. This difference is extremely important in the implementation of effective HRM policies and practices, which may unwittingly create greater uncertainty. For example, seemingly insignificant changes in employee benefits and plans, performance evaluations and reward systems that are in any way vague will be interpreted as heaping even more uncertainty on those professionals whose daily life is already a sea of project uncertainties. The response to even a marginal increase in uncertainty can become an irrational response, often even an "off the chart" response, to what was intended to be a simple, minor change in some HRM system.

Motivation

At the heart of most of HRM concerns lies the broad area of motivation. But what exactly is the secret to having motivated employees? While there's no shortage of specific models and frameworks, it is generally recognized that a person's true commitment and/or intrinsic motivation comes from the intrinsic nature of the work he or she is asked to do. Put simply, people in general, and technical professionals in particular, like to do *neat* things—"to boldly go where no man has gone before." If technical employees believe their work is challenging and innovative, provides the opportunity for recognition, growth and advancement, and gives them the freedom for independent action, they will strive to meet the demands of their job, independent of its degree of difficulty. While extrinsic factors, such as salary, benefits, status, security, and working conditions are also important, decades of research studies convincingly show that they do not instill the kind of commitment and excitement needed in a creative work environment where employees are expected to stretch their thinking, push their ideas, and persevere to find solutions to tough, unyielding problems. The degree of motivational potential of any specific job is dramatically influenced by how the person views the job assignment on which he or she is working at a given point in time, including how tasks, information, reward, and decision-making processes are organized, structured, and managed. Even in situations of high pressure and unrealistic demands, R&D professionals report that their work was truly motivational simply because they really felt they were having *fun* while doing it. In some sense, then, highly motivating work assignments should be similar to the activities individuals choose to do for fun on their own.

To pursue this analogy, let's assume that many professionals enjoy playing golf or even like to go bowling. Let us further suggest that one of the underlying reasons people like to golf or bowl is that it's a use of their own skills and abilities, performing their activities by themselves based on their own individual styles and competencies. They can set their own target scores and strive to achieve those scores at their own pace without holding others back or being dependent on someone else's capabilities. Notice, however, that most university settings are structured in ways that ask students to take courses, prepare homework, solve problems, complete exams, and get final grades as individuals. This *individualism*, however, can become problematic in organizational settings when the professional is now required to work interdependently on a project with others who may not be as technically creative or as capable as him or herself. It is one thing to work with or be on a team with someone who is at least as talented and as motivated as oneself. It is much more difficult and, at times even exasperating, to work with someone who is less capable or less motivated. Since technical competence and creativity are rarely uniformly distributed among project team members, HRM education and training programs need to address the issues of how to work and interact with others on either end of this distribution. If not, the R&D professional and/or function is likely to end up working separately rather than interdependently which, in turn, leads to the uncooperative organizational silos and communication barriers that characterize far too many cross-functional relationships. Of course, such frustrations can also occur in bowling or golfing if one does not develop the patience and sensitivity for having fun with individuals or teammates who cannot play as well, or who are much less talented, or who play at a much slower or more methodical pace.

Most likely, technical employees also like to bowl or play golf because they have a complete understanding of what the *whole* game is from beginning to end. They see themselves playing an active and genuine role during the game because their contributions are valued and respected. As a result, they feel they are significant and somewhat equal players or colleagues within the overall team effort. Status and positional differences are minimal since all scores count. No employee would be excited to play, on the other hand, if one was told that his or her score did not count—or that one's score was going to be canceled or shelved—or if everyone else's scores were seen as more pivotal or were weighted more highly.

Even though the goals and objectives of the games are clear, bowlers and golfers are given a lot of autonomy within which to play. They are free to develop their own individual style, movement, and pace within the rules and constraints of the game. They also know exactly how well they are performing while playing. Feedback is quick and unequivocal—and they know how they're doing compared with others in the game. But again, no one would like to bowl or golf if the alleys or fairways were draped so one couldn't see the pins or greens, or if one was told to come back in six months for a performance appraisal. Nor would anyone enjoy the game if a boss stood by with constant suggestions such as: "Move to your left, watch the red line, keep your grip steady, your arm straight." And finally, who would want to play if, as soon as one achieved a terrific score, the CEO ended up congratulating the boss rather than the player? It is doubtful that anyone would truly find bowling or golfing *fun* under these kinds of conditions. If work is to be viewed in the same vein as having fun, then the job's tasks should have some of the same characteristics as golfing and bowling. But what are these task characteristics that create such high levels of intrinsic work motivation? Referring to the motivation framework put forth by Hackman and Oldham (1980), Figure 14.1 shows that people are more motivated when they feel their jobs require them to use a wide variety of skills and abilities. All too often, professionals who work in well-defined positions become dissatisfied and unexcited when narrowly structured tasks allow them to use only a small portion of their overall competencies and educational training. Or, perhaps even more disillusioning, their assigned tasks might involve only existing, older, or more mundane technologies rather than the newer and more state-of-the-art ones that are being developed within their disciplines. The evidence accumulated from many previous research studies seems to indicate that the broader the range of skills and abilities tapped early in a person's career, the more likely it is that the person will remain to become a more effective and successful contributing member of the organization in the future. The key is not how many different projects or tasks individuals are asked to perform, but whether they are able to develop the cumulative knowledge, perspective, and credibility essential for continued success within the organization's particular setting and culture.

In his seminal study of professionals in technical organizations, for example, Pelz (1988) discovered that scientists and engineers were judged most effective when they devoted their time across the range of activities within the research, development, and technical service continuum rather than concentrating in only one of these domains. Young professionals not only have to solidify their technical reputations by focusing activities and accomplishments in a major project and/or technical area, they must also have enough diversity and exposure

Dimensions of task characteristics	Definitions
Skill variety	The degree to which the job requires the use of different skills, abilities, and talents
Task identity	The degree to which the person feels that he or she is part of the whole job or project activity from beginning to end
Task significance	The degree to which the job is considered important by, and has impact on the lives of, others
Autonomy	The degree to which the job provides freedom, independence, and discretion in how the work is carried out
Feedback	The degree to which the person is provided with clear and direct information about the effectiveness of his or her performance

Figure 14.1 *A framework for work motivation*

Source: adapted from Hackman and Oldham, 1980

in their task challenges and networks to take the kinds of initiatives and come up with the kinds of ideas that will enable them to become the organization's future high flyers and star performers (McCall, 1998; Kelley, 1998).

But getting one's technical career off to a good start is not a foregone conclusion. Dalton and Thompson's (1993) work indicated that the establishment of a "professional identity" is the critical first step in a successful technical career. It usually involved landing a challenging first assignment and demonstrating technical competency. It evolves to gaining independence from the need for daily supervision and focusing on an area of expertise in which the new hire becomes the company, or even a world, expert, albeit in a very narrow and specific area. At this stage aspiring professionals are independent and sought after for their expertise. They've become a member of the "technical club" that enables informal exchange of information and networking that's necessary for greater competence development.

Interestingly enough, it is not just the technical aspects of the work that are important. Of the many job experiences investigated in our own organizational and research panel studies of technical professionals' early career years, the ones that seem the most predictive for achieving promotions to higher managerial positions within an organization are the opportunities to work at jobs that help familiarize them with the ways in which the organization deals with business and financial information. Most likely, these fiscally related experiences and activities provided these individuals more opportunities of developing into, and of being seen as, broader contributors. They were perceived as more capable of putting together the kinds of *business* plans and strategies that make those managing the organization's existing operations and finances more comfortable—at least in terms of focus, scope, and language—rather than the more one-sided, narrow *technical* arguments that are all too often put forward by those who come to be viewed as individual contributors, specialists, or just one-dimensional thinkers. It is extremely important for technical managers to learn how to frame or "couch" their ideas and efforts into the kinds of business screens and financial terminology that are specifically used by those in power to run and evaluate the organization's day-to-day pressures and alternative interests. Even *Fortune Magazine*'s most admired CEO, General Electric's Jack Welch, points out in his recent autobiography that as a Ph.D. chemical engineer, he was sufficiently "green" in the intricacies of finance that he asked his staff to prepare a book translating all of GE's financial jargon into layman's terms so he could be more conversant with the people in the businesses (Welch, 2001).

Two other analogous and important characteristics of work in Figure 14.1 are *task identity* and *task significance*. HRM needs to constantly remind managers that work assignments are more fun and motivating when people are given a complete picture of the project and feel as if they are *real* members of the project team. And it is through the kinds of communications, involvements, and reward systems (or lack thereof) that take place that employees build perceptions of these task dimensions. Consider, for example, the experience of a project team of about 25 engineers from one of our research studies. These 25 professionals had worked feverishly and had struggled together for several years to accomplish the kind of technical breakthrough that would truly distinguish their product line from the competition's products. What really mattered to this research team after all these years of effort was not pay raises, promotions, or managerial praise and recognition. What they valued was the opportunity to present their "breakthrough" as a team at their profession's annual international conference in order to impress their colleagues and sort of "stick it" to their competitors (the company was even going to aggressively and publicly promote this breakthrough to enhance the product's market attractiveness). Rather than rewarding this team to enhance its motivational commitment for future accomplishments, the organization routinely replied to the team's request by logically explaining that traditional HRM practices and procedures *only* allowed for one or two members of a project to present results at a conference (even though the company would be spending hundreds of millions of dollars to build its future business around this breakthrough). You can, of course, predict how this perfunctory response affected the future enthusiasm of this team's technical staff to want to continue to work on this product, a team whose members had literally put their lives "on hold" to meet incredibly aggressive deadlines. Their dimensions of task identity and significance plummeted virtually overnight. While money, title, and praise may be very visible on report cards, they are not always the most valued incentives—what really drives most technical innovators is excitement in their work, pride in their accomplishments, and the ability to receive recognition from those colleagues whom they value.

A fourth task characteristic in Figure 14.1 that's key for inducing higher levels of motivation is autonomy—the degree of freedom a person has in carrying out work requirements. As autonomy increases, individuals tend to become more reliant on their own efforts, initiatives, and decisions. They begin to feel more personal responsibility and are willing to accept more personal accountability for the outcomes of their work. In helping to design motivating work environments, HRM must ensure that organizations do not confuse the distinction between *strategic* autonomy and *operational* autonomy—between *what* has to be done in terms of goals, expectations, direction, and constraints versus *how* one chooses to accomplish the goals. Many managers, unfortunately, combine or even reverse these two aspects of autonomy. Rather than clarifying expectations and establishing clear parameters that would encourage people to make decisions and take initiatives within well-defined boundaries, organizations often give too much free reign with aphorisms such as, "Take risk" or "Don't be afraid to fail." Then, as they get increasingly nervous, organizations try to control and micromanage the work, imposing all kinds of unanticipated constraints and changes. In interviews of several former Bell Lab employees, for example, we heard stories of how Bell Lab's management would often give initial research assignments to young technical professionals with well-intentioned but rather unclear mandates such as, "Go be creative" or "Go think great thoughts." Many of these young professionals would then go off on their own trying desperately to be creative. Many would eventually emerge months or even years later with some wonderful new thoughts or ideas only to discover that Bell Lab managers were not really interested in pursuing something in that particular area, something that risky, or something that required that much money or time, etc. Managers need to be trained to "empower" the other way around. They need to clarify expectations and conditions as much as possible and then give people the freedom to function within those definitions and constraints.

To sustain motivation, individuals also need to see the results of their work. Achievement provides a continuous source of personal and peer recognition that drives productive behavior. Providing a climate for motivation involves creating opportunities for both individuals as well as the teams in which they participate to experience success. This comes from setting stretching goals that encourage risk taking, thereby providing opportunities for overachievement. In doing so there is a sense of personal value that motivates the individuals and ties their success to the goals of the organization. If professionals cannot determine whether they are performing well or poorly, they have no basis for trying to improve. The remaining but important motivating task characteristic in Figure 14.1, therefore, is *feedback*—the degree to which individuals receive clear information and unambiguous evaluations of their performance. Although technologists often feel that as professionals they are excellent judges of their own roles and performances, they still have a need to calibrate their activities and career progress against the expectations of others. They especially want to know how others, whom they respect and whose opinions they value, judge their abilities, efforts, contributions, and success.

As technical and business managers gain more experience, they eventually learn one of the most important tenants of motivation. It is easier to destroy morale than to create excitement. Michael Badawy (2003) captured it well: "the typical manager confuses motivation with manipulation. The challenge is to create the conditions conducive to meeting the corporate goals of productivity and profitability as well as the technical professional's needs for satisfaction and motivation." Only by closely examining how jobs are structured and organized along Hackman and Oldham's five dimensions of task characteristics can managers hope to foster the kind of settings in which professionals might find themselves having fun as they do their work. Furthermore, the combined research, consulting, and managerial experiences we've had in professional type settings seems to show that feedback is the most deficient task characteristic. It also seems to be the one around which technologists complained the most. There are probably at least three reasons for this. First, in most creative-type settings where one is often trying to do something that has never been done before, it is very hard to define or measure exactly what good work is. Trying to explain what constitutes "good code," for example, is very difficult to do ahead of time—only after one sees it can one really say whether or not the code was "neat" or cleverly done. Also, one may not be able to determine for quite some time whether a new idea is truly creative or stupid. Or to say it another way, the most creative idea and the most stupid idea often look the same at the early stages; and one may not know for quite some time whether the idea was brilliant or just plain foolish.

The literature is replete with innumerable stories of how some of the most important innovations were initially viewed as foolish and dumb. In fact, when we conducted an internal retrospective study of P&G's breakthrough-type products some years ago, we discovered that almost none of them at their early stages of development and testing would have passed the normal marketing, manufacturing, and financial evaluation screens that were being used by the organization to identify potential "winners." A second reason for feed-back being low is simply that most managers and supervisory leaders in technical settings are not particularly comfortable or well trained at giving constructive feedback. And third, most technical professionals are not particularly good at receiving feedback, especially feedback that may not be totally positive. It is not uncommon to discover that many of the most creative individuals have never received feedback or been given anything but uniform praise in the past. This can make the transmission of what was intended as "constructive" interaction into a troublesome and unpleasant exchange.

While R&D professionals may complain the most about the inadequate communication, information, and feedback they get surrounding job performance and career opportunities, it is not the most powerful task dimension for establishing a high level of work motivation. The most critical dimension by far for elevating motivation is task significance. Professionals become more excited and energized when they feel they are working on something important—something that clearly makes a difference within the business unit and is not considered trivial or low priority. Interestingly enough, even though task significance seems to be the dominant task characteristic for influencing motivation and performance, the dimension that often surfaces from survey responses is autonomy. HRM, however, needs to be careful in interpreting self-report surveys. It is easy for technical professionals to say they want a lot of autonomy; it does not necessarily mean they will thrive under autonomy. And autonomy decoupled from a sense of significance can lead to very dissatisfying and unpleasant work experiences.

Multidimensional task dimensions

As previously described, one can easily examine any job for its motivational potential by trying to determine whether it is relatively strong or weak with respect to each of these five task characteristics. One of the problems of managing and motivating professionals in RD&E (Research, Development, and Engineering) type environments, however, is that there are at least two alternative ways of looking at each of these task characteristics (see Figure 14.2).

Hackman and Oldham's previous motivational framework, for example, talked about skill variety. Organizations hire professional employees because they need them—they want to use their skills, knowledge, and abilities. The individual's prior education, training, and work experiences are all strongly considered in the organization's decision to hire new personnel and in its distribution of critical work and project assignments among its present employees. On the other hand, from the professionals' points of view, they not only want to be used, they also want to grow. They want to learn—to extend their skills, knowledge, and abilities. That's the professional norm! For professionals working in organizations, what makes a job or project especially enticing is the belief that they will learn a great deal as they carry out their task activities and complete their assignments. Put simply, they not only want to utilize what they already know, they also want to keep up to date, incorporating relevant leading-edge thinking and advances from their disciplines and areas of expertise into their project's requirements and specifications. In a rapidly changing environment, keeping up with the latest knowledge is essential for sustained success and some techies are manic about keeping abreast of the latest developments.

While executives and professionals would readily agree that *both* skill utilization and extension are crucial elements of any job environment, the HRM needs to deal with the reality that there are major differences in how these two groups, the organization at large and the professional work force, rank order the relative priorities of skill utilization and extension. Such priority differences are usually not a problem when there are lots of

Task dimensions	Organizational orientation	Professional orientation
Skill variety	To utilize one's skills and abilities	To learn and develop new skills and abilities
Task identity	To become a contributing member of the organization	To become a contributing member of the profession
Task significance	To work on projects that are important to the organization	To work on projects that are exciting within the profession
Autonomy	Strategic clarity	Operational autonomy
Feedback	Subjective data and information processes	Objective data and information proceses

Figure 14.2 Multidimensional framework for work motivation

resources, lots of good times. It can become de-motivating and counterproductive if disagreements and conflicts materialize and are left unresolved, especially when the organization undergoes periods of stress. Without active leadership intervention, stress will tend to exacerbate these priority differences. HRM's tuition reimbursement programs are often one of the first things to go when the organization feels monetarily constrained. R&D professionals have often complained during our research interviews that HRM won't fund their taking technical courses because the technology is not yet being used in their products. Yet, the technologists can't use the technologies until they take courses to learn it—the proverbial catch 22. In such cases, the R&D professional becomes frustrated, disenchanted, leaves, or interestingly enough decides to enroll in an MBA program.

In a similar vein, organizations and knowledge workers can view the dimensions of task identity and task significance in very different ways. Is the professional employee a member of the organization or a member of the profession? In essence, they have one head but two hats. Are they software or hardware engineers at IBM, for example, or are they IBM employees doing software or hardware engineering? Most managers would contend that professionals who work for them should perceive themselves first as organizational contributors and second as members of their profession. The opposite, however, is often the way in which many professionals prioritize their orientations, scientists and Ph.Ds in particular (Allen and Katz, 1992). A similar pattern often occurs with respect to task significance. Is it more important to work on projects that are important to the organization or on technical issues that are exciting to the profession? Is it more important to try to incorporate the most sophisticated technological developments and features or to focus on technological advances and features that fit within infrastructure of use, that are manufacturable, reliable, cost effective, etc. Once again, many professionals might prefer to work on breakthrough solutions for problems defined as important by their fields. Organizations, on the other hand, would prefer they concentrate on coming up with technical advances that are "good enough"—advances that solve customer problems and can be quickly turned into products, services, or intellectual properties that eventually make money (Steele, 1988).

Many professionals see themselves as having studied and internalized a body of knowledge and a code of conduct that supersedes the companies they work for. At the same time, however, they want to influence (but not necessarily lead or make) decisions that determine the projects on which they'll work and on how their expertise will be used and applied. These individual contributors often have strong beliefs and personalities and are more motivated when *pulled* rather than *pushed*. They want to know *why* something is asked of them and they want to mull over ideas, information, assignments, and strategies and then have the opportunities to challenge any with which they're uncomfortable or disagree. These professionals respond best to leaders who have an empathetic understanding of their technical problem solving worlds and who make their lives easier by: (1) respecting their expertise; (2) supporting them in their technical efforts; (3) providing them with the best available tools, equipment, and information; and (4) protecting them from nonproductive hierarchical demands and inflexible bureaucratic constraints.

As previously discussed, there are also two kinds of autonomy: strategic and operational. If organizations want to enrich jobs and motivate employees through empowerment, that is, giving them the freedom to function independently and make decisions based on their own careful, professional judgments, then business managers need to establish as much strategic focus and clarity as possible and then let their technical personnel function autonomously within these clearly defined goals and boundary conditions. In developing new products and services, project teams are constantly making critical decisions and trade-offs. And the clearer the organizational leadership is about its expectations and constraints, its proverbial "lines in the sand," the easier it is to empower the teams and project groups effectively. Managers and leaders have to be careful not to do it the other way around, confusing people with unclear directives and support while simultaneously maintaining rigid control over the means by which they have asked their people to do things differently, i.e., to be creative and innovative.

And, of course, there are two kinds of feedback: *subjective* and *objective*. While both kinds of information are important and have to be integrated in some way during any organiza-tional decision-making process, when objective data conflicts with a manager's subjective gut, i.e., his or her more intuitive analysis and understanding, the subjective elements are more likely to dominate. But remember, technical professionals come from, perhaps, the most objective environments in the world, namely educational and university type institu-tions. When students take courses, they are told what to read, when to read, and even how long it should take them to read and study distributed materials. They are told which models and formulas to memorize and when tested, they are given all information they need to solve carefully crafted technical problems. There is, moreover, a single correct solution to each of the test's problems, and individual answers are separately scored to give each student his or her own objective piece of feedback, called a grade. Finally, if the person takes and passes any prescribed sequence of required courses and electives, he or she will graduate in a pre-defined and expected time frame. All of this programmed structure fits nicely with the educational culture and philosophy propagated within technical professions—cultures in which analyses and decisions that are based on logical thinking, clear discussions, and reliable, unambiguous data are highly valued.

In the real world of work, however, the opposite sets of conditions typically apply. Technical professionals soon discover that problems are not well defined or self-contained but are intertwined with all sorts of organizational politics and behavioral-type issues. Nor are they given all of the formulas, tools, and information needed to come up with appropriate solutions. In fact, they usually have to figure out what it is they need, where to get it, what may or may not be valid information, who they can or should believe, and what is and is not acceptable. Some problems may not even be solvable. Promotions and rewards, moreover, are not guaranteed. And unlike the university, feedback is no longer based on objective grading from test answers evaluated by professors who have more tech-nical expertise than the students. Feedback is now based on the subjective perceptions of one's supervisor or manager who may actually have less technical knowledge and under-standing about the tasks and problems on which the individual has worked. In short, the critical skill for performing effectively in the university is *solving* problems that have been carefully structured and communicated. The real skill in the world of work, however, is being able to *formulate* (or get *formulated*) comprehensive definitions of what are often incom-plete or ill-defined problems, especially in arenas strongly influenced by subjective interpretations, preconceived judgments, and personal emotions and commitments.

HRM needs to understand that it should try to "solve" the differences highlighted in Figure 14.2. It needs to constantly make sure that its practices, policies, and procedures are flexible enough to deal with both dimensions of the professional's job setting. Without recognizing these differences up front, the HRM function is more likely helping the organization to destroy morale and excitement rather than to create it. While the former is easy to do, the latter is the much more difficult and, in fact, it is the latter that is the real challenge for the organization and its HRM function. Many researchers and experienced managers, in addition, have also observed that "fat, happy rats never run mazes" (Manners *et al.*, 1988). Stress, tension, differences are not necessarily all bad, in fact, they *are* needed for creativity and change. The most critical question for the HRM function is whether it focuses towards helping the organization turn these differences into *positive energy* or *creative tension* (Pelz, 1988) or whether it allows the priority differences to lead to further cynicism and dissatisfaction. And it is the success of the organization long term that will be influenced by the answer to this question.

REFERENCES

Allen, T. and R. Katz (1992) Age, Education and the Technical Ladder. *IEEE Transactions on Engineering Management*, 39, 237–245.

Badawy, M. (2003) Why Managers Fail. In R. Katz (ed.), *The Human Side of Managing Technological Innovation*. New York: Oxford University Press, pp. 86–93.

Christensen, C. (1997) *The Innovator's Dilemma*. Boston, MA: Harvard Business School Press.

Dalton, G. W. and P. H. Thompson (1993) *Novations: Strategies for Career Management*. Provo, UT: Novations Group Press.

Hackman, J. R. and G. R. Oldham (1980) *Work Redesign*. Reading, MA: Addison-Wesley.

Katz, R. (2003) *The Human Side of Managing Technological Innovation, 2nd edn*. New York: Oxford University Press.

Kelley, R. E. (1998) *How To Be A Star Performer*. New York: Random House.

Manners, G., J. Steger, and T. Zimmerer (1988) Motivating Your R&D Staff. In R. Katz (ed.), *Managing Professionals in Innovative Organizations*. New York: Oxford University Press, pp. 19–26.

McCall, M. W. (1998) *High Flyers: Developing the Next Generation of Leaders*. Cambridge, MA: Harvard Business School Press.

Pelz, D. C. (1988) *Engineers and Scientists in Organizations*. New York: John Wiley.

Steele, L. (1988) Managers' Misconceptions about Technology. In R. Katz (ed.), *Managing Professionals in Innovative Organizations*. New York: Oxford University Press, pp. 280–287.

Tushman, M. and C. O'Reilly (1997) *Winning Through Innovation*. Cambridge, MA: Harvard Business School Press.

Utterback, J. (1994) *Mastering the Dynamics of Innovation*. Cambridge, MA: Harvard Business School Press.

Welch, J. (2001) *Jack: Straight From the Gut*. New York: Warner Books.

Index